THE SOCIAL CRISIS OF
OUR TIME

The Library of Conservative Thought
Russell Kirk, Series Editor

THE SOCIAL CRISIS OF OUR TIME

Wilhelm Roepke

*With New Introduction by William F. Campbell
and a foreword by Russell Kirk*

Transaction Publishers
New Brunswick (U.S.A.) and London (U.K.)

Library of Congress Catalog Number: 91-21962
ISBN: 1-56000-580-7
Printed in the United States of America

Library of Congress Cataloging-in-Publication Data

Röpke, Wilhelm, 1899-1966.
    [Gesellschaftskrisis der Gegenwart. English]
    The social crisis of our time/Wilhelm Roepke; with a
foreword by Russell Kirk and a new introduction by William F.
Campbell.
        p.   cm. – (The Library of conservative thought)
    Translation of: Die Gesellschaftskrisis der Gegenwart.
    Includes bibliographical references and index.
    ISBN: 1-56000-580-7
    1. Economic policy. I. Title II. Series.
    HD84.R62   1991
    338.9'001–dc20   91–21962
                                                              CIP

CONTENTS

PART ONE: INTERPRETATION AND INVENTORY

CONTENTS

PART TWO: ACTION

FOREWORD

MINDFUL OF Edmund Burke's denunciation of "sophisters, economists, and calculators," I have regarded with some suspicion many practitioners of the Dismal Science—even though I have myself written a textbook in economics for high school students. In general, I have found economists a blinkered breed, worshipping the false god Efficiency.*

But from this impeachment I exempt Wilhelm Roepke, who was an eminent economist, but also something more. It was Roepke's advice, carried out by his disciple Ludwig Erhardt, that produced Germany's economic recovery after World War II. Yet, beyond technical economic doctrine and practice, Roepke was a social thinker of unusual penetration.

He was no apologist for an abstract "capitalism." Indeed his influence extended to some curious quarters.

----

* The more imaginative economists of the past four decades have been aware of this failing among men of their discipline. Take W.A. Orton, in *The Economic Role of the State*: "Let us therefore praise the great god Efficiency. All he demands is that we make straight his path through the desert and purge the opposition. . . . We arrive at 'justice' without mercy, 'liberation' without liberty, 'victory' without peace, 'efficiency' without effort, 'power' without potency—because the means we collectively employ lie on a plane so different from that of the ends—we humanly desire that, the more they succeed, the more they fail."

He discovered, for instance, an interesting Italian disciple. Professor Roepke was invited to Florence to have a medal or some other distinction conferred upon him. Upon arriving at the railway station, he found an escort of mounted carabinieri awaiting him. Escorted soon to the Palazzo Vechio, he was received there by a throng of all the rank and fashion and officialdom and intelligentsia of Firenze, greeting him with high ceremony. This crowd parted abruptly to make way for some personage of importance, who hurried straight up to Roepke. The man approaching him was seemingly effeminate, fantastically dressed in unusual colors, fat, gesticulating. This person seized Roepke's hands to kiss them ardently. "Maestro! Maestro!" he ejaculated; then, bowing low, he retired backward into the assemblage.

Roepke had been astonished at the splendor and cordiality of this gathering in his honor; he was yet more surprised at the adulation of this conspicuous person. "Who is that gentleman?" he inquired of an official host.

"Why, don't you know him, Professor Roepke? He is your disciple, the man who invited you here and arranged this ceremony. He is the chief of the Communist party of Florence."

Italian Communists sometimes have differed from their comrades elsewhere in Europe; already, at the time of Roepke's visit to Florence, they were endeavoring to appear bourgeois. Their Firenze chairman appears to have perceived in Roepke an economist fruitful in means, however much he might differ with him in ends. But Roepke and I agreed in ends as well.

He and I met at two gatherings of the Mont Pélerin Society, and once at his house in Geneva, and elsewhere; we corresponded fairly frequently during the fifties, and I suggested to him what became the title of one of his books published in America, *A Humane Economy*.

He was all energy. When skiing, he disdained chair lifts and funiculars; having whizzed down, he would clamber up a peak on shank's mare. Man is made for action, not for ease. Roepke's intellectual action, expressed in his several books, was a resolute endeavor to humanize the industrial order, and to undo the mischief worked by Nazis and by Communists.

His humane imagination is suggested by an incident he once related to me. During the Second World War, the city of Geneva had allocated garden plots, along the line of the vanished city walls, to citizens wishing to grow their own vegetables in a time of food shortage. This use of public land turned out to be popular; the city continued the allocation of plots after the war.

Roepke heartily approved of this undertaking, which both enabled people to obtain independently part of their own sustenance and offered the satisfaction of healthy achievement outside factory walls. Utilitarians thought otherwise.

When Ludwig von Mises, disciple of Jeremy Bentham, came to visit Roepke at Geneva, Roepke took him to inspect those garden plots.

Mises shook his head sadly: "A very inefficient way of producing foodstuffs!"

"But perhaps a very efficient way of producing human happiness," Roepke told him.

Roepke seemed to have read everything in the field of social thought. He was familiar, for instance, with the political writings of Calhoun and of Fenimore Cooper–of which most American university graduates are thoroughly ignorant. He knew history and poetry, ethics and religion. He was lively in conversation, a good companion outdoors or indoors. Edmund Burke, despite his general commination of economists and his uneasiness with Adam Smith, would have relished Roepke's company.

His major book *The Social Crisis of Our Time* was his analysis of the menace that Roepke called "the cult of the colossal." Social equilibrium had been overthrown in the twentieth century, Roepke wrote; he did not hesitate to propose remedies. Of all social evils in this age–produced by moral decay, by consolidation, by the worship of bigness–the worst was proletarization, he declared. Capitalism may have created the modern proletariat, but socialism was enlarging that class to include the whole of humanity. Salvation lay in a third choice:

> Socialism, collectivism, and their political and cultural appendages are, after all, only the last consequence of our yesterday; they are the last convulsions of the nineteenth century, and only in them do we reach the lowest point of a century-old development along the wrong road; these are the hopeless final stages toward which we drift unless we act. . . . The new path is precisely the one that will lead us out of the dilemma of "capitalism" and collectivism. It consists of the economic humanism of the "Third Way."

Roepke's Third Way was not gas-and-water socialism or consumer cooperatives or a managed economy. Instead it was economic activity humanized by being related to moral and intellectual ends, humanized by being reduced to human scale. Roepke proposed to abolish the proletariat, not by reducing everyone to proletarian status–the method of socialism–but by restoring property, function, and dignity to the mass of folk. He believed in government from local institutions upward, not in government by a centralized bureaucratic elite; he believed, too, in economic organization from the bottom up. He hoped for a society with reverence, manners, stability, and secure personal rights; he saw that if we do not restore such a society, presently we will have no civilized society at all. The work of the French Revolution must be undone, not to reinstate a rule of force, but instead to venerate again just order, coherence, authority, and hierarchy, established by prescription and consent. Society cannot be organized "in accordance with rational postulates while disregarding the need for genuine communities, for a vertical structure."

The same infatuation with rationalism that terribly damages communal existence also produces an unquestioning confidence in the competitive market economy and leads to a heartless individualism "which in the end has proved to be a menace to society and has so discredited a fundamentally sound idea as to further the rise of the far more dangerous collectivism." In such a world, where old landmarks have been swept away, old loyalties ridiculed, and human beings reduced to economic atoms, "men finally grasp at everything that is offered to them, and here they may easily and understandably suffer the same fate as the frogs in the fable who asked for a king and got a crane."

In his chapter "The Splendor and Misery of Capitalism," Roepke examined succinctly the maladies of the twentieth-century economy, observing that the same economic disharmonies become chronic under socialism; then he turned to the second part of his book, "Action":

> Socialism–helped by the uprooted proletarian existence of large numbers of the working class and made palatable for them by just as rootless intellectuals, who will have to bear the responsibility for them–is less concerned with the interests of these masses than with the interests of these intellectuals, who may indeed see their desire for an abundant choice of positions of power fulfilled by the socialist state.

Roepke relished the rule of persons of this class even less than he did the domination of monopolists and corporate managers. His object was to restore liberty to men by promoting economic independence. The best type of peasants, artisans, small

traders, small and medium-sized businessmen, members of the
free professions and trusty officials and servants of the commu-
nity-these were the objects of his solicitude, for among them old
human nature still had its healthiest roots; and yet throughout
most of the world they were being ground between "capitalistic"
specialization and "socialistic" consolidation. They need not
vanish from society; they may constitute once more the masters
of society; for Switzerland "refutes by its mere existence any
cynical doubt regarding the possibility of realizing our program."

Loathing doctrinaire rationalism, Roepke was careful not to
propound an arbitrary scheme of alteration and renovation. Yet
his suggestions for deproletarizing were forthright. Family
farms, farmers' cooperatives for marketing, encouragement of
artisans and small traders, the technical and administrative possibilities of industrial decentralization, the diminution of the average size of factories, control of competition and restraint of
monopolies, the graduate substitution for the "old-style welfare
policy" of an intelligent trend toward self-sufficiency–none of
these projects was novel, but they were urged by an economist
possessing both wide reputation and frank common sense.
Roepke saw no insuperable difficulties. To cushion society
against fluctuations of the business cycle, for instance, the better
remedy was not increased centralization–a dubious palliative–
but instead the stimulating of workers to get a part of their sustenance from outside the immediate domain of financial disturbance.

Humanizing of economic structure, *à la taille de l'homme* in
the phrase of Ramuz, was the kernel of Roepke's proposals. They
were not detailed; they were not buttressed by statistical tables;
but they were cheering. Roepke reminded his auditors and readers that the art of politics has an ethical foundation and that the
purpose of industry is personal security.

Often the Swiss have been accused of lacking imagination.
Then what should be said of social imagination in Russia, or in
Britain, or in the United States? Roepke spoke of the human
condition, but Moscow, London, and Washington were obsessed
by the gross national product.

Dr. William Campbell's thorough and lucid introduction to
The Social Crisis of Our Time, with an appended bibliography,
may persuade a good many thoughtful Americans to look further
into the writings of this cheerful and manly social thinker.

Russell Kirk

INTRODUCTION TO THE
TRANSACTION EDITION

WILHELM ROEPKE (1899-1966) was awarded the Willibald Pirckheimer Medal in 1962. The place was Nuremberg, Germany. The citation included the statement: "The measure of the economy is man. The measure of man is his relationship to God."

Nuremberg was a microcosm of the German Problem which so preoccupied Roepke throughout his entire career. Nuremberg at its best was the city of Christian humanism as exemplified in Albrecht Dürer, Hans Sachs, Pachelbel, and Willibald Pirckheimer. But Nuremberg was not always at its best. For the past century it played a more sinister role.

The spiritual inflation of German romanticism in the nineteenth century culminating in Richard Wagner's *Die Meistersinger* set the stage for Nuremberg in the twentieth century. Hitler's Nuremberg rallies in the twentieth century carried further the Triumph of the Will. Nuremberg then went through the hell of Hitler, intense Allied bombing, and the retribution of the Nuremberg trials. The world was turned upside down in more ways than one.

Roepke sturdily opposed all totalitarian and Nazi perversions from the beginning. It was fitting for him as a philosopher of reason, moderation, and proportion to receive the Pirckheimer medal in the city of Nuremberg. The world was turned rightside up.

Two years earlier Roepke had received a Hugo Grotius medal in Munich. This was further evidence of his abiding Christian humanism. Although a Protestant, Roepke was a Protestant in the tradition of Hugo Grotius that flowed from the Erasmian tradition. As a Christian humanist in the best sense of the word, he was very sympathetic to Catholic traditions. In particular, he labored at the reasoned application of the traditional Catholic principle of the subsidiarity more than any other economist in this century.

Economists are prone to pride themselves on being concerned with the long run. The man on the street thinks short run; journalists are hit-and-run. The uniqueness of Roepke among economists is precisely the fact that eternity and the good of the human soul are the foundations of his social science. Both he and Keynes believed that in the long run we are all dead, but the implications for the two thinkers were entirely different.

Yet Roepke like all the rest of us lived in the world of historical flux. In the world of events, Roepke lived and learned. He just seemed to learn more than others. In fact, he was on the right side of almost every controversial series of historical events in which he participated.

He fought Hitler and the brown-shirted totalitarians at great loss to his own personal advancement and comfort. He fought the red totalitarians in the Soviet Union and communist bloc countries in the 1930s, long before it was acceptable; it is still not "fashionable." He told the West of the gulags and the Ukrainian peasants in the 1930s; he also had no illusions of the great economic progress of the Soviet Union. But of course nobody paid any attention to him.

He also warned us after World War II of the dangers of the EEC and the unresolved tensions in that organization which have brought us to the bright cheery hopes for 1992. The same doubts that he aired in the 1950s and the 1960s are with us still. The unresolved tensions and problems leave the future of the EC still in doubt.

To understand the full complexity of this man, let me weave together his European odyssey and see it as a unified rejection of ideological thinking. We shall also see that his thought provides the pattern for a complete American conservatism. The importance of Roepke for Americans is that he combines the best of the strands of American conservative thought into one harmonious whole. "Fusionism" is alive and well in the thought of Wilhelm Roepke.

Furthermore, precisely because of his European inheritance he links the American conservative tradition to its European roots. To put it paradoxically, the American conservative philosophy may be parochial, but we are not parochial.

World War I to the Great Depression

Roepke pointed out that the birth of his ideas stemmed from the international crisis that created the conditions for World War I. But he learned that the international crisis is only a manifestation of the deeper social crisis of our times. Those who start with the international level usually end up with the superficial nostrums of disarmament and world economic conferences, debt revisions, amending the Statute of the League of Nations, central bank cooperation, projects for economic unions, and so on. This litany of nostrums sounds all too familiar. Roepke was always suspicious of the call to a "new age" and would probably be skeptical of a "new world order."

Not only does "charity begin at home," so also the sources of chaos begin at home. Peace in the world ultimately depends on peace in the human heart; love of neighbour begins with respect for one's self.

As a result of the trauma of World War I and his experience in the trenches, the idealism of socialism made an initial appeal to him. He rejected socialism only as the result of learning and bitter personal experiences following World War I. Out of this ferment, Roepke and the Ordo Liberals crafted their "third way" or "economic humanism."

The word "capitalism" was never one of Roepke's favorites. He always preferred the phrase, "the market economy," when he wished to refer to a positive ideal.

He had learned to reject "capitalism" in the trenches. By capitalism Roepke did not simply mean an ahistorical free market order. Capitalism was for him a particular historical and cultural complex. It is true that Roepke tends to equate capitalism with anarchistic laissez-faire or the debased forms of the interventionist regulatory state where the special interests call the shots.

To replace the laissez-faire liberalism of the nineteenth century (the "night-watchman state"), Roepke argued for a neoliberalism or Ordo liberalism, in which the state would play a positive though limited role in maintaining the social framework of the free market–those social, political, and economic arrangements which work in tandem with competition to preserve a "free, happy, prosperous, just, and well-ordered society."

It is in the spirit of *ceteris paribus* that Roepke supports free markets. Other things being equal the business principle of voluntary exchange should be honored. But this did not freeze Roepke into a theoretical position of libertarianism.

The distinction that Roepke makes between conformable and nonconformable interventions is an important part of all his thinking. Nonconformable interventions are the kind that paralyze the price system from working. Rent controls and price ceilings will lead to continual governmental intervention that will attempt to clean up the mess caused by the government intervention in the first place. Conformable interventions are not always wise but they do not paralyze the nerve centers of the price mechanism.

Roepke, along with Ruestow and Luigi Einaudi, emphasized more than other members in the Ordo group the importance of the "Third Way"—which emphasized the importance of restoring small property ownership. In a European context, this meant sympathy for peasant agriculture, independent craftsmen, and small merchants.

There has been a great deal of confusion on the concept of the "Third Way." It is not what economists would call a "mixed economy" or a soft socialism in contrast to the hardness of collectivism and laissez-faire. In essence it is an attempt to socially nurture the ethic and spirit of the bourgeois.

The "Third Way" clearly had much in common with the Southern Agrarians in the U.S. and the English Distributist movement of Chesterton and Belloc. The latter were explicitly acknowledged by Roepke. Roepke fondly used agrarian analogies like the concept of the "aerated society" stressed by French philosopher and farmer Gustave Thibon.

In *The Solution to the German Problem* (1946), Roepke argues that the centralization and concentration of power that took place under Bismarck destroyed the roots of German culture. The result was a moral and intellectual vacuum that he called the "German dust bowl." Roepke's "Third Way" program was intended to promote social decongestion and deproletarization. "We must decentralize, put down roots again, extract men out of the mass and allow them to live in forms of life and work appropriate to them."

The Southern agrarian tradition stressed that functions and responsibilities be lodged in the person and the family first, the broad range of community and voluntary organizations second, and the state last. Roepke did not attack state functions with libertarian zeal, but instead tried to construct institutions appropriate to the human person.

But here is the essence of the approach of Roepke. He is the philosopher of the normal. He does not take the extreme case or what may be demanded by temporary expediency as the basis for setting up legal and economic systems. Nor does he take one simple principle that is usually correct and strain all of social reality through it. Voluntary exchange is generally a good thing but it is not the only thing in the social universe.

To the doctrinaire advocates of laissez-faire Roepke would write in *A Humane Economy* that "the market economy is not everything. It must find its place in a higher order of things which is not ruled by supply and demand, free prices, and competition. It must be firmly contained in an all-embracing order of society in which the imperfections and harshness of economic freedom are corrected by law and in which man is not denied conditions of life appropriate to his nature."

The Great Depression and Keynesianism

Roepke never proceeded from an ideological commitment to a laissez-faire, do-nothing position. During the Great Depression Roepke wanted a "bold" and "confidence-inspiring" conservatism. In fact, to counteract what he described as the "secondary deflation," he promoted expansionist, Keynesian-type policies of increased government spending.

Roepke, like the early Chicago School, did not deny that the Great Depression was a circulatory phenomenon demanding radical medicine in the form of stimulation of total demand: "Had Keynes stopped there, he would have done no more than the rest of us, who at that time advised a policy beginning with the 'spending' end." Instead Keynes took the exception, the emergency which demanded expediency, and made a "General Theory" which turned the micro-world upside down. The message "took" because the macro-formulation was redolent of "economic engineering with a proliferation of mathematical equations" and at the same time could turn the bourgeois world upside down; *pour épater* the freshman undergraduate.

Roepke in fact in his work during the thirties espoused what later came to be called "functional finance," built on the ideas of Keynes that advocated deficits in depressions and surpluses in inflationary period, and a "balanced budget" over the entire cycle if not in any given year.

One of the members of the Mont Pelerin Society even went so far as to sigh in relief at the fact that economists today do not read the Roepke of the *Crises and Cycles*. They would find too much Keynesian-type policy. Roepke himself later recanted in *The Humane Economy* his earlier views. He said that he had to take his share of the blame for "functional finance." He no longer believed in it on prudential grounds. His argument is the same which today is offered by the public choice movement: the politicians cannot be relied on to use their surpluses in inflationary periods to decrease demand when there are votes to be had.

Even if Keynesian theory could be turned into a neutral technique that can be applied to the problems of inflation as well as deflation, it has its dangers. These lie in "the damnably unmathematical circumstance that one cannot talk Parliament and public opinion into saving and economical management, by exceptionally praising them as virtues, if all the rest of the time they are reviled as folly and sin, not to speak of modern mass democracy's built-in obstacles."

In addition to a technical critique of Keynesianism, Roepke also understood the antibourgeois nature of Keynes's thought. He saw that it was fundamentally an attack upon the moral foundations of the bourgeois order that depend upon prudence, savings, and responsibility. His great skepticism toward the welfare state also reflected these same moral concerns.

Roepke in Turkey and Switzerland

Roepke's outspoken attacks on the Hitler regime resulted in his being one of the first professors to leave Germany. The Nazi brain drain gave us the leavening agents of Mises, Hayek, and Eric Voegelin as well as numerous democratic socialists and more pernicious intellectual fads. In many ways it is a shame that Roepke did not settle in the United States instead of Turkey, where he taught until 1937. In that year he joined the graduate Institute of International Studies in Geneva, Switzerland.

In 1940 Roepke decided to stay in tense, uncertain Switzerland when he could have come to the United States. It is doubtful, however, that he would have had any more impact on the mainstream of the economics profession than Mises and Hayek. It is only in recent years that they have received their due. Roepke is still to receive his due.

Undoubtedly his stay in Switzerland was an important formative influence on his social thought. If Roepke could be accused of having a Utopia, Switzerland would have been the only country to qualify. Switzerland was nonfeudal, democratic, small-scale, and bourgeois.

Wilhelm Roepke is the philosopher of the bourgeoisie. But he is not the philosopher of a craven bourgeoisie who wishes peace at any price. He is not the philosopher of those who wish conflict avoidance as the highest good. He is not the philosopher of bourgeois consumerism and materialism. His is the tough bourgeoisie of the Swiss.

Roepke never wished to "épater le bourgeois" (astonish the old fogeys) as most progressive intellectuals do. Instead he wished to call the bourgeois to its highest capacities. Never far from his mind was the possibility and necessity of a natural aristocracy in the sense that John Adams and Thomas Jefferson might have agreed upon.

Roepke attacked Benedetto Croce for his aloofness to the free market, even though he recognized Croce for his great contributions to letters. In one brief passage Roepke sums it all up: "When we characterize a system like this as a middle-class order in the widest sense of the term, this is the fundament on which the ethos of economy must rest. This system sets out to promote not only independence and a sense of responsibility in the individual but also the civic sense which links him to the whole and limits his appetite. In this field, moral authority of that thin layer of *nobilitas naturalis*, readily accepted by their fellow-citizens, proves to be indispensable–a layer to which a handful of them aspire by virtue of an exemplary life of self-denial and hard work, rigorous integrity and fine example as they ascend to a position above the classes, interests, passions, hatreds, and follies, thus embodying the moral sense of the nation and culminating in such supreme figures as *Fridtjof Nansen* or *Albert Schweitzer.*"

The role of the bourgeoisie in history was an important one. One of my favorite passages from Roepke is the following: "There are enough millenaries of recorded history behind us to teach us in the most unequivocal manner that whenever in their dark course of the light of freedom, progress and humanity shines it was a period when a sufficient number of people had private property to enable them to throw off their economic dependence on the feudal lord, or–even worse perhaps–the state. Those periods of emancipation and enlightenment would have been impossible without the existence of a large bourgeoisie in that noble but now almost forgotten sense which brings it into a more than philosophical relationships with the term 'civilization.' It lies with us whether or not one of the longest and most brilliant of these periods shall now come to an end like all its predecessors."

There is a Jeffersonian radicalism in Roepke which denies that an aristocracy comes into the world booted and spurred, ready to ride mankind.

Post-World War II and the German Economic Miracle

Roepke also attacked another fossil of the Keynesian episode coming out of the Great Depression, Hansen's idea of the "mature economy" where investment opportunities have dried up, population is declining, and the only alternative is massive government spending to offset this declining economic situation. Both Roepke and Luigi Einaudi had to battle with these kinds of forecasts and economic policies after World War II.

Wilhelm Roepke maintained a steady vigilance against what he called the "glum philosophy" that was the secret of all collectivist regimes. He was steadfastly opposed to forced savings as he saw it attempted in post-World War II Europe; "austerity" reminded him of the moral equivalent for war problem. It would work under war or siege conditions but not for a well-functioning economy.

The hostility to luxury goods that surfaced after World War II was a return to the heroic spirit of mercantilism that stressed manufacturers. He criticized the politicians who give "their speeches the dignified accents of unworldly asceticism and patriotic concern."

Roepke accepted the usual economic considerations that condemned this discouragement of luxurious imports and encouragement of manufactured exports on the basis that they would lead to a misallocation of precious resources. But in addition his final criteria was more supply-sided than anything else. If you did not allow consumers to buy the luxury goods, they would buy leisure and work less.

Roepke's most important historical impact came in the postwar reconstruction after World War II. His arguments concerning the foundations of a good society and the policies necessary for reconstruction and economic reform gained great influence with many European leaders including Chancellors Adenauer and Ludwig Erhard. In fact, Roepke, along with his friend Alexander Ruestow and the other Europeans in the German Ordo school of liberalism, were the thinkers behind the postwar German economic "miracle." Similar movements in Italy and France were led by his friends Luigi Einaudi and Jacques Rueff.

The dedication of the Germans to free markets, competition, monetary and fiscal stability, and the social market economy are in large part the result of Roepke and his colleagues. He never thought of it as an "economic miracle" but simply the result of freeing incentives in a stable economic order.

Wilhelm Roepke and Ideological Thinking

Roepke is as important in the battle of ideas as he was in the battle of policies. He often quoted Georg C. Lichtenberg, "When it is a mistake to be moderate in condemning, indifference becomes a crime." Roepke could never be accused of being indifferent.

He clearly understood that the enemy was "leftism" and not just simply totalitarian variants. In a talk to the Mont Pelerin society Roepke referred to the recent Italian *apertura a sinistra* ("the opening to the left") and the related *sinistrismo* ("leftism"). Roepke clearly understood that the germs of totalitarianism are nurtured and spread in the climate of leftism.

Progressive economic and social policies are best considered not in isolation, but in the context of the underlying ideas and hopes for human nature. Wilhelm Roepke often referred to the "optimism" of progressivism, which he described as the fundamental malady of the twentieth century. Fascism and Communism were simply extremist variants of the same ideal. Fundamentally the optimism is a theological concept akin to Pelagianism.

Even more important than the ideologies themselves were the conditions of the theoretical social sciences that spawned them in the first place. Roepke was a steady opponent of the scientism which he saw issuing from both the right and the left.

Roepke would have wholeheartedly agreed with the great German physicist Hermann von Helmholtz, who in 1852 criticized the pseudophysics of Goethe on the grounds that Goethe's devotion to ideal beauty and culture led him to disregard the quantitative aspects of physical reality. One experiences the drama out front without paying any attention to the backstage reality of ropes, wires, and pulleys. He concluded his talk with the warning, "We cannot triumph over the machinery of matter by ignoring it; we can triumph over it only by subordinating it to the aims of our moral intelligence. We must familiarize ourselves with its levers and pulleys, fatal though it be to poetic contemplation, in order to be able to govern them after our own will, and therein lies the complete justification of physical investigation, and its vast importance for the advance of human civilization."

One can easily imagine a modern mathematical economist or econometrician making the same defense of his highly quantitative tools. All they want to do is to lay bare the network of real connections, the correct model of the machine which will allow us to govern social reality after our own will.

Roepke's genius is to follow neither Goethe nor Helmholtz. He would agree with Goethe that the experiences of men are closer to the drama and the quest for beauty than the brute reality of inanimate nature. But he did not succumb to the idealistic temptation of taking for real only that which was beautiful.

He would agree with Helmholtz that idealism in whatever form—moralism, aestheticism, and eroticism—must be "subordinated to the aims of our moral intelligence."

Let us take as an example the treatment of a particular area of economics given over to scientistic formulations, the area of production. I well remember at one time sitting in on a graduate course in microeconomic theory to brush up on the more technical aspects. We started with several weeks of beautiful, consistent mathematical models of consumer behavior and utility maximization. Constrained optimization was the order of the day. No actual commodities and no actual persons were allowed to rear their ugly heads—only the "jth" commodity and the "ith" person. Very, very scientific and rigorous, and as we got to the end of it and proceeded to production and supply, the professor was notably relieved.

He was relieved because we had finally got to something that was not subjective. We had finally arrived at something to which the language of mathematical functions, inputs, and outputs was truly applicable. Production functions deal with the measurable and not such fuzzy concepts as unobservable subjective utility.

But there are mistakes of all kinds here. First of all "opportunity cost" is just as subjective and unobservable as utility. It is, in fact, the same thing. Furthermore, producers still have to be understood as maximizing utility rather than simply maximizing profits that are one element in their utility function.

Wilhelm Roepke would also simply add that there is an ethics to the production function and to the understanding of the firm which modern economics neglects to its disadvantage.

In the theory of the firm, Roepke started the disentangling process in one of the most important and most neglected articles of his entire career. The Invisible Factors of production shares some of the fundamental insights of Leibenstein's x-efficiency but deepens it into the moral and spiritual realms. The problem is essentially one of leadership and rhetoric properly conceived. Leadership of whatever sorts and varieties requires paying attention to the moral and ethical dimensions. This is true in the organization of the firm, advertising, business ethics, as well as in politics. An employer had duties to his workers in his capacity as a patron.

Roepke was ever distrustful of Taylorism, scientific management, and scientistic approaches to the production process. These had swept Europe and the Soviet Union during the 1920s an era when American cultural (as opposed to our countercultural exports such as bluejeans and rock music) swept Europe. Commodities yes, culture no!

Roepke persistently fought the scientistic components in economic thought, whether they issued from the left, the kind which Professor Hayek has so brilliantly dissected, or from those followers of the classical liberal tradition who believe that they can rise above moral values with a value-free technique or process appropriate to all aspects of human order. Sometimes this technique is the free market, Pareto-optimality, negative definitions of liberty, or public choice mechanisms based on voluntary consent.

The basis for liberal scientism is precisely the relativism which issues from the fact-value distinction that Roepke vigorously attacked. Economists unfortunately have perennially confused the fact-value distinction with the positive-normative distinction, which is a useful admonition to men to distinguish between the way the world is and the way they would like it to be. No one has a quarrel with the latter distinction. But the fact-value distinction is much stronger and asserts that there is no basis in truth for moral judgements.

The sin of indifference is to take the category of the indifferent things and extend it to all moral goods. The replacement of reason by sentiment is the step which Roepke refused to take. Here is the basis for the claim that he had a conservative economics and not simply a liberal economics.

Roepke closed one of his speeches to the Mont Pelerin Society with the plea, "Never also has it been more necessary to give a moral example: of courage; of standing firm on first principles; of having a sure sense of the right order of values; of remembering that to be a man standing for the value and the patrimony of our civilization is infinitely more than to be a scientist to whom we may apply the famous saying of Rabelais, 'Knowledge without insight means only the destruction of the spirit.'"

Whether the academy and scholarship since that time have heeded this admonition is doubtful. But the need for the strong medicine is greater than ever.

Conclusion

In essence *The Social Crisis of Our Times* is a book that needs to be savored. A classic is a book which needs to be read and reread; its meaning cannot be extracted with one reading. As one experiences life and ideas, one can go back to an old text and discover fresh meanings and interpretations to which one was not properly attuned the first time through.

Let me give as an example, a passage which I had missed in my previous readings. In this passage Roepke provides a very balanced view of what we would today call environmentalism. In one paragraph he states a conservative position which does not fall into worship of nature or worship of laissez-faire institutions: "The decline of indigenous rural life is usually accompanied by a tendency to polarize men's relationships to nature, on the one hand, and on the other, national parks, camping and nudism, whilst the happy medium—peasantry and small towns—is vanishing. It is part of the picture of this disease that the urbanized remoteness of Western man from nature leads to the extreme of a city-bred, fashionable and condescending cult of the peasant, which bears the stamp of high-brow artificiality and which the genuine peasant cannot but find embarrassing."

On the same level of realistic analysis his analysis of the degeneration of the family to a consumers' cooperative or an entertainment cooperative is at the expense of "the natural sphere of the woman, the proper environment for raising children and indeed the parent cell of the community."

The quality of thought that Roepke brings to bear again and again is a realistic analysis of functions that any civil society has to provide. The moral and spiritual needs of mankind are not just treated as a taste or a preference to be provided for by the efficiency of a free market.

It could be argued here that Roepke was aware of a much more significant type of "constitutional economics" than the misuse of the current positive-normative distinction would permit. He recognized that the "constitution" of a country includes its manners, mores, and customs, as well as its laws written in statutes or even constitutions. If self-interest is relied on to promote the market, then it becomes difficult to defend the market against the self-interest of groups and rent-seekers. People can occasionally learn their lessons only too well.

The great dangers which he constantly and determinedly fought are the same as today: special interest groups (monopolies, heavy industry, and big landowners), pressure groups, movements toward protectionism, autarchy, political radicalism, and nihilism.

If man is measured by his relation to God, then the *Mene Tekel* of the Old Testament reminds us that human beings have been weighed in the balances and found wanting. Roepke had no illusions about the inherent goodness of human nature.

There was no sunny optimism in Roepke; but neither was there despairing pessimism. Man is obligated to create a culture, polity, and economy where decency, comfort, and piety can go hand in hand. "The measure of the economy is man. The measure of man is his relationship to God."

William F. Campbell

APPENDIX I

Brief Reader's Guide to the Works of Roepke

In the realm of ideas many of Roepke's books and articles have been translated into English. There are many works of Roepke that are accessible to the general reader as well as the scholar. The book being reprinted here is part of a trilogy. The first volume, being reprinted here from the English/American edition of 1950, was originally published in German in 1942. *Civitas Humana* was first published in 1944 in German and the English translation in 1948. Finally *International Order and Economic Integration* appeared in German in 1945 and was not translated into English until 1959.

A book that makes a wonderful companion volume to Hayek's *Road to Serfdom* is Roepke's *The Solution of the German Problem*, which appeared in 1946. The title sounds as if the book might be dated, but it is full of reflections on German and European history, language, and literature.

Among the many other English translations of both books and articles by Roepke, *A Humane Economy* (1960) has been one of the more influential and easily accessible. It is this book with which most American conservatives are familiar. The Intercollegiate Studies Institute has widely circulated this book among college students. Another collection of essays *Against The Tide* (1969) has also been widely circulated but never played the part that *Humane Economy* did, because of its more miscellaneous character.

One final work should be mentioned in even a brief survey. *Economics of the Free Society* (1963) is a translation of Roepke's textbook which first appeared in 1937 and was continually revised over his lifetime. An excellent introduction to the basic concepts of economics, it allows the student of economic principles to sink his teeth into something worthwhile; the graphical analysis which is missing could easily be supplied by the instructor. Paired with *Humane Economy*, one could use these volumes to teach economic principles with an appreciation for the benefits of the market place, but without setting it up as an idol.

It should be mentioned that a Roepke bibliography found in the German tribute to Roepke *In Memoriam* (Marburg, 1968) numbers over 800 items and is still not complete. Unfortunately, there are many items in numerous languages which have not been translated. A bibliography of the articles and books translated into English is provided as an appendix to this introduction.

Work about Roepke is even harder to find than his own works. More recently, the Ordo liberals presented their views in an extremely useful English translation of *Standard Texts on the Social Market Economy* (Gustav Fischer: New York, 1982). This collection of works by Roepke and other Ordo liberals was edited by contemporary German followers of Roepke, including Christian Watrin, Hans Willgerodt, Wolfgang Stutzel, and Karl Hohmann. This volume has gone almost entirely unnoticed and unreviewed.

The most recent treatment is two volumes edited in 1989 by Alan Peacock and Hans Willgerodt, *German Neo-Liberals and the Social Market Economy* and *Germany's Social Market Economy: Origins and Evolution*. The one volume provides a comprehensive history and analysis of the Social Market Economy and the other is a collection of readings.

APPENDIX II

The Works of Wilhelm Roepke in English

An almost complete bibliography can be found in the German tribute, *In Memoriam* (Marburg, 1968). Items not included in that bibliography are noted with a star (*) in this bibliography. It should be noted that Roepke's bibliography extend to well over 800 items, many of which have not been translated into English. Not all editions of every book are listed.

Books and Independent Pamphlets

What's Wrong with the World? Philadelpia: Dorrance & Co., 1932.

German Commercial Policy. London: Longmans, Green and Co., 1934.

Crises and Cycles. Glasgow: William Hodge & Co. Ltd., 1936.

*International Economic Disintegration.*Glasgow: William Hodge & Co., 1942, subsequent reprintings.

The German Question. London: George Allen & Unwin Ltd., 1946. Includes an Introduction by Professor F.A. Hayek. An American edition, *The Solution of the German Problem* by G.P. Putnam's Sons, New York, 1947, appeared with no introduction by F.A. Hayek, and other changes.

Civitas Humana. Glasgow: William Hodge & Co., 1948. Subsequent reprintings.

The Social Crisis of Our Time. Chicago: University of Chicago Press, 1950.

The Problem of Economic Order. Cairo, 1951. Reprinted in *Two Essays by Wilhelm Roepke: The Problem of Economic Order, and Welfare, Freedom and Inflation.* Ed. Johannes Overbeek. Lanham, Md: University Press of America, 1987.

The Economics of Full Employment. New York, 1952. Reprinted in *The Critics of Keynesian Economics.* Ed. Henry Hazlitt. Princeton: D. Van Nostrand Co., 1960, pp. 362-85.

Welfare, Freedom and Inflation. London: Pall Mall Press Ltd., 1957, pp. 13-70. With an introductory essay by Graham Hutton, "Unfreedom and Inflation," pp. 386-90, in the Conservative Book Club, *Omnibus Volume 4.* New Rochelle: Conservative Book Club, n.d., pp. 391-438. Also published by the University of Alabama Press, 1964 with Freeman foreword and Hutton essay. Also reprinted in *Two Essays by Wilhelm Roepke: The Problem of Economic Order,* and *Welfare, Freedom and Inflation.* Ed. Johannes Overbeek. Lanham, Md: University Press of America, 1987.

International Order and Economic Integration. Dordrecht-Holland: D. Reidel, 1959.

A Humane Economy: The Social Framework of the Free Market. Chicago: Henry Regnery Company, 1960.

Economics of the Free Society. Chicago: Henry Regnery Company, 1963.

Against the Tide. Foreword by Gottfried Dietze.   Chicago: Henry Regnery Company, 1969.

Articles

"Trends in German Business Cycle Policy." *Economic Journal* (September 1933): 427-41.

"Fascist Economics." *Economica* (February 1935): 85-100.

"Socialism, Planning and the Business Cycle." *The Journal of Political Economy* (June 1936): 318-38.

"Industrial Germany," book review of H. Levy. *Economica* (February 1936): 84-89.

"Explanatory Note on the Review of Roepke's *Crises and Cycle.*" *American Economic Review* (March 1937).

"International Economics in a Changing World." In *The World Crisis* (London: 1938), 275-92.

"Totalitarian Prosperity: Where Does it End?" *Harper's Magazine* (July 1939).

"The Industrialization of Agrarian Countries." *Revue de la Faculte des Sciences Economiques de l'Université d'Istanbul* (1940 or 1941?).

"A Value Judgement on Value Judgments." *Revue de la Faculte des Sciences Economiques d'Istanbul* (1942): 1-19.

"The German Dust-Bowl." *The Review of Politics* (October 1946).

"Free Trade and the German Problem." *The Free Trader* (January/February 1947).

"New Germans must shape the New Germany." *New York Times Magazine,* (13 October 1946).

"Economic Disease in Germany." *Time and Tide* (1-8 February 1947).

"German Economy in State of Pernicious Anemia." *The Commercial and Financial Chronicle* 27 February 1947).

"Repressed Inflation." *Kyklos* 1, 3 (1947).

"A Workable Plan for Germany." *Plain Talk* (June 1947).

"Liberalism and Christianity." *Commonweal* (18 July 1947).

"Liberalism and Christianity." *Modern Age* (Fall 1957).

"Repressed Inflation-Economic Cancer of Europe." *The Commercial and Financial Chronicle* (4 September 1947).

"Decentralization in Germany." *Time and Tide* (24 and 31 May 1947).

"Anglo-American Agreement on Germany." *Time and Tide* (June 1947).

"The Key to the Marshall Plan." *Time and Tide* (6-13 September 1947).

"Germany after the London Conference." *Time and Tide* (3-10 January 1948).

"Western Germany: Portent of Europe's Economic Future." *The Commercial and Financial Chronicle* (29 April 1948).

"Socialism in Europe Today." *The Commercial and Financial Chronicle* (7 July 1949).

"The Iron Curtain of Money." *The Commercial and Financial Chronicle* (7 July 1949).

"Crusade Against Luxuries." *Time and Tide* (16 October 1948).

"Socialism and European Union." *Time and Tide* (11 December 1948).

"The Iron Curtain of Money." *Time and Tide* (16 July 1949).

"The Proletarianized Society." *Time and Tide* (1-8 October 1949).

"Barriers to Immigration." In *Twentieth Century Economic Thought*. New York 1949, 607-645.

'The Fight for Economic Sanity in Europe." *The Commercial and Financial Chronicle* (16 March 1950).

"Germany: The Political Climate." *Time and Tide* (1 April 1950).

"Germany: The Economic Problem." *Time and Tide* (8 April 1950).

"The Economic Integration of Europe." *Measure*, (1950).

"Inflation: Threat to Freedom." The Freeman (9 April 1951).

*Contribution to *Democracy in a World of Tensions*. Ed. Richard McKeon. Chicago: University of Chicago Press, 1951, 361-62.

"Toward a New 'Liberal' Conservatism." Microfilm in Library of Congress, 1557n, translation from two essays in *Mass und Mitte*. Zurich, 1950.

"European Economic Integration." *Time and Tide*. (2-9 June 1951).

"The Malady of Progressivism." *The Freeman* (30 July 1951): 687-91.

"Alternative to Serfdom." *American Mercury* (July 1952): 31-49.

"The Treatment of Diseased Balances of the Payments." *The Journal of Finance and Credits* (1/2/August 1953): 8-11.

"How to Integrate Europe?" *The Freeman* (18 May 1953).

"Economic 'Miracle' in Germany." *The Freeman* (24 August 1953).

"Free Economy and Social Order." *The Freeman* (11 January 1954).

"Diagnosis of our Time." *Social Order* (April 1954): 147-52.

"Social Presuppositions of the Market Economy." *The Owl* (January 1954).

"Economic Order and International Law." *Recueil des Cours de l'Academie du Droit International a la Haye* (1955): 202-73.

"Economic Welfare in a Free Society." *National Policy for Economic Welfare at Home and Abroad*. Columbia University Bicentennial Conference Series. (Garden City, N.Y. 1955), 344-49. Reprinted in *Freedom First* (Autumn 1955): 5-7.

'The Place of Economics among the Sciences." *On Freedom and Free Enterprise: Essays in Honor of Ludwig von Mises* (New York: 1956): 111-27.

"Inflation–Hot and Cold." *National Review* (18 January 1956).

"A European Looks at American Intellectuals." *National Review* (10 November 1956).

"Liberalism and Christianity." *Modern Age* (1957).

"Front Lines Old and New in Economic Policy." *Confluence* (1958).

"Political Enthusiasm and Economic Sense: Some Comments on European Economic Integration." *Modern Age* (1958).

"Europoean Free Trade–The Great Divide." *The Banker* (September 1958).

"Germany: Over-Full Employment." *National Review* (2 March 1957).

"The Welfare State through the World." *The Commercial and Financial Chronicle* (25 September 1958).

"The Economic Necessity of Freedom." *Modern Age* (1959/3).

"The Free West." *Freedom and Serfdom.* Ed. Albert Hunold. Dordrecht: Reidel, 1961, 59-82.

"The Moral Necessity of Economic Freedom." *Christian Economics* (29 December 1959). Reprinted by the Intercollegiate Society of Individualists.

"Moralism–Right and Wrong." *Christian Economics* (12 December 1961).

"A Protestant View of 'Mater et Magistra'." *Social Order* (April 1962): 162-72.

"Will West Germany's Free Enterprise System Survive?" *The Commercial and Financial Chronicle* (14 June 1962).

*"The Intellectual Collapse of European Socialism." *New Individualist Review* 1, 4 (Winter 1962): 35-36, translated by Ralph Raico.

*"Where We Must Stand." *National Review* (13 March 1962).

"Keynes Revisited." *National Review* (1963).

"Washington's Economics–A German Scholar sees Nation moving into Fiscal Socialism." *The Wall Street Journal* (1 April 1963).

"A World without a World Monetary Order." South African Institute of International Affairs, Johannesburg, 1963, 1-16.

"European Prosperity and its Lessons." *South African Journal of Economics* 3 (1964).

*"Education in Economic Liberty." In *What Is Conservatism?* Ed. Frank Meyer. New York: Holt, Rinehart and Winston, 1964, 78-87.

"European Economic Integration and its Problems." *Modern Age* (Summer 1964).

"The Place of the Nation." *Modern Age* (Spring 1966).

PREFACE TO THE ENGLISH LANGUAGE EDITION

I FEEL particularly pleased and honored that, thanks to the initiative of the publishers, an American/English edition of this book will now be available. I want to acknowledge how much I feel obliged to them. At the same time, I wish to express my warmest thanks to Mr. and Mrs. Peter Schiffer Jacobsohn to whose intelligence and devotion I owe a translation which, in my long but sad experience, is an altogether rare achievement and which I appreciate all the more highly as I can well imagine how difficult it must have been. I have checked every word, and I am glad to say that the English text not only is an exact rendering of my ideas but also a singularly successful effort in recording the undercurrents of the language.

The present edition is based on the fifth edition of the Swiss original (1948), with only slight alterations made for the American and British readers. It should be borne in mind that this book was written in the later part of 1941 at the time when Hitler was at the very height of his triumph, and in the solitude of the Swiss Alps which were then a small island within a continent swamped by tyranny. When, on this island, we were never sure whether the next morning would still see us free, the author felt impelled to make a desperate effort in spiritual orientation. He does not want to speak immodestly of himself, but as a sober statement of an interesting fact he might go as far as to say that the echo of this book throughout Europe has been as gratifying as it has been unexpected. Because of its scholarly appearance—which at times has been deliberately stressed in order to deceive the censors in the different countries—its dangerous character was discovered too late for smothering the spreading influence of the hundreds and thousands of copies smuggled into the "Fortress of Europe." The author is proud to have hoodwinked even the clever Dr. Goebbels for some time.

Only little efforts have been made to change the original in the course of the several editions which have become necessary since that time. It was thought that this was a case where it is preferable to preserve the original text instead of rewriting it so as to create the impression as if the ideas had been born yesterday and not in 1940-41. This could be done all the more light-heartedly as the author is able to refer to other books embodying his subsequent ideas: *Civitas Humana* (third edition, 1950, English translation published by W. Hodge & Co., London), *Internationale Ordnung* (1945, French translation, published by Les Editions du Cheval Ailé, Geneva, 1947), *The German Question* (London, 1946), *Die Lehre von der Wirtschaft* (fifth edition, Erlenbach-Zürich, 1949, French edition published by the Librairie de Médicis, Paris), *Die Krise des Kollektivismus* (Erlenbach-Zürich, 1947, French and other translations).

WILHELM RÖPKE.

GENEVA, *September,* 1949.

PREFACE TO THE SWISS EDITION

THIS book is the result of the reflections of an economist on the sickness of our civilization and on the manner of its cure. These subjects have been in his mind for years and have gradually reached fruition, benefitting from a continual exchange of ideas with friends and sympathizers whom he can hardly thank enough for their help and interest. However, to write a voluminous book around these thoughts always seemed to him so bold an undertaking that he continued to postpone it with the excuse that he had not yet found the final solution to many problems nor had his research covering so many fields of knowledge been completed. However, there comes a time when such an excuse is no longer adequate and simply serves to cloak diffidence in facing the public. But the reproach of inactivity finally tipped the scales.

Yet the author would not have decided to write this book if he had not become more and more convinced that the world's mental confusion had reached such a pitch that even a modest and inadequate attempt at orientation would meet with appreciation and serve a useful purpose. Millions are in the position of people who, buried by an avalanche, have lost their bearings completely and know no longer whether they are standing on their feet or on their heads; in abject terror they dig their way ever deeper into the snow. It may therefore be assumed that every honest endeavor to help them will meet with understanding.

There is nothing pontifical about this offer of guidance. It purports nothing more than that as many as possible should be spared the years of mental struggle and the diverse errors through which the author himself had to pass before he attained to the degree of understanding which he believes himself to possess today. If he has now made one last effort in order to propagate his findings to the best of his ability, this still amounts to nothing more than the expression of the thoughts of a man who also needed orientation, but had to struggle for it alone. He simply wishes others to fare better.

Naturally, we have to ask the reader to co-operate: he must show good will and share the author's zeal for unsparing truth and clarity. The ideas in this book form a closely knit whole and must be considered in that light regardless of whether this or that group interest is involved in a welcome or unwelcome manner. The book would have failed in its purpose had it become a quarry from which everyone could take whatever struck his fancy, throwing the remainder impatiently or contemptuously aside. Apart from that, we must in such cases take comfort from what during the fatal crisis of the ancient world, fifteen hundred years ago, Boethius described as the task of the philosopher: *pessimis displicere*.

WILHELM RÖPKE.

GENEVA, *November,* 1941.

INTRODUCTION TO THE ORIGINAL EDITION

THE GREAT INTERREGNUM—
SPIRITUAL COLLECTIVIZATION—THE THIRD WAY

On the steps of the scaffold the hapless Louis XVI is supposed to have said: "I have seen all this coming for the past ten years. How was it possible that I never wanted to believe it?" There are but few people in the world today who would not wholeheartedly say the same of themselves; there are, in fact, none except those who saw nothing of the sort coming because they lived blindly from day to day, and those who not only saw the disaster approaching but also disdained to silence their own pessimism with cheap words of comfort. Sooner or later, however, they were bound to be seized by the feeling that the ground was rocking under their feet and thus all became ready for the question which had since long occupied the thoughts of those whose soul or body had first been affected by the convulsions of our civilization: what uncanny disease has invaded our world and what exactly has been happening in those countries which have already succumbed to it?

As nothing happens without sufficient cause it must surely be possible to find an interpretation and explanation for this catastrophe, offering sounder reasons than just coincidence, stupidity and malevolence. As the vast dimensions of the rupture became increasingly evident and one could no longer avoid the impression that the fissures reached deep down into the foundations, it appeared necessary and natural to detach oneself from the ever changing vicissitudes of the moment and to consider oneself more consciously the heir of an age-old civilization which now seemed more and more openly jeopardized. Becoming accustomed to seeing ourselves in perspective against the majestic background of history we have learned to turn our thoughts to ultimate values, origins and "constants," and to ask ourselves: Where do we stand? Whence do we come? Whither are we drifting? What are we? What is, and even more, what should be our goal?

In this manner a growing number of people have learned to view this world of ours, so sadly out of joint, from a viewpoint which lets the incidentals recede behind the essential, the variables behind the constants, the ephemeral behind the permanent, the fluctuating behind the durable, the fleeting moment behind the era; and our own unimportant personality behind the responsibility which we bear towards society, towards the heritage of the past and the promises of the future. We are experiencing the despair

A

of one who has gone astray, and to be told the way is almost more important to us than to be given bread.

Just as the space surrounding us has shrunk and we are constantly aware of the earth as a whole, as something familiar and intimately affecting us, the historical distances, too, have been foreshortened in our minds, so that the distant past seems to reach forward into the present and more than ever before do we consider ourselves the last member of a continuous chain. "The Burden of Three Thousand Years" (Goethe) has become an integral part of the life of every thinking person today. We are continually looking back on the various stages of our civilization, Miletus, Jerusalem, Athens, Rome, Florence, Paris, London or Weimar; we thrill to the dramatic spectacle of the ship of progress threatening to founder on so many rocks and yet, by a veritable miracle, always regaining its course, and anxiously we ask whether this miracle will be repeated today, or whether the inevitable end is now approaching for the development which began with the Ionians during one of the greatest moments of world history. On the other hand, we can now recognize more clearly the cross roads in the course of history where the wrong path was taken which finally led us to the present. To the same extent to which we are consciously re-living the passage of our own civilization through the ages, we gain a clearer understanding of the general possibilities and prerequisites for human civilization and society by studying the experience of other civilizations and the remotest origins of mankind that prehistoric research, ethnology, and anthropology are gradually revealing to us. What we learn here tends to strengthen in us a feeling which divides us as much from the nineteenth century, drunk with progress, as it links us with the eighteenth which is constantly growing in our estimation, a feeling, namely, that we represent by no means the dizzy summit of a steady development; that the unique mechanical and quantitative achievements of a technical civilization do not disembarrass us of the eternal problems of an ordered society and an existence compatible with human dignity; that these achievements complicate rather than facilitate the solution of these problems; that other civilizations have come nearer to the answer than we, and that throughout the centuries and civilizations the range of human potentialities has remained surprisingly small notwithstanding radio and motion pictures. The sun which shone on Homer is still smiling on us, and all the essentials around which life revolves have remained equally unchanged—food and love, work and leisure, religion, nature and art. Children still have to be born and raised, and we may surely be permitted to presume that other times, without radio and motion pictures, have done better than we in this respect.

The shock would hardly have been so great if it had merely been a question of a slow and gradual decline. Ours has, however, this in common with most historical crises, and even with an ordinary economic crisis, that we have suffered a headlong downfall from heights never reached before and considered completely safe. The saying, "It is only a step from the Capitol to the Tarpeian Rock" also applies in history. It is first of all true in a narrower and more familiar sense in that the outbreak of the economic and political catastrophe at the end of 1929 had been preceded by a period during which the postwar hangover had been effectively displaced by exceptional world-wide recovery and an excess of optimism. But the maxim is also true in a much wider sense if we consider this crisis as a general crisis of civilization beginning in August 1914, and then look back on the preceding hundred years. We shall then realize with astonishment that this unique period between 1814 and 1914 was predominently a century of peace and at the same time the century of liberal capitalism, and this century, whose spirit of progress, order, stability, and increasing prosperity is unequalled in history, is succeeded by a period of disruption which in turn surpasses most of its historical predecessors. Truly a sudden descent from the proud pinnacle on which the nineteenth century—despite the predictions of a few far-sighted prophets—had felt so secure! An understanding of our times is therefore impossible unless we first gain a reasonably accurate picture of what exactly took place beneath the deceptive cloak of peace and progress in the period between Waterloo and Sarajevo. Unless we choose to look upon the World War and all its consequences up to the present as an utterly stupid historical coincidence, there can be no doubt that it was the result of conditions created in the period immediately preceding it, and during the final quarter of the last century the atmosphere had indeed become more and more stifling. But how, we may well ask, was it possible that the calamitous conditions for a world crisis would arise in such a period of order, peace, freedom, and general prosperity?

These are the questions that are besetting all of us and to which we are the more anxious to find an answer since we know that it will not only provide the key to understanding the present, but will also help to open the gate to a better future. Here, as everywhere else, no treatment is likely to succeed without proper diagnosis, and even the very understandable impatience of those who expect from us an immediate and detailed plan of action cannot change our fundamental conviction. And yet we cannot, alas, hope to find an easy and simple answer. On the contrary, it is likely to be so exceedingly complicated that we must not be surprised at the ensuing general perplexity, but must rather rejoice if we seem to be making any progress at all in our quest for a solution. In fact, all simple explanations are bound to fail and we are no less suspicious of those whose diagnosis consists of monotonously repeating the same formula than of those whose therapeutics are based on a single patent medicine. For a decade we have now been observing the best intellects of all countries at work producing an interpretative literature which is gradually assuming immense proportions, and it is most encouraging to see that this analysis has led to a progressive ripening of our ideas.

In the course of this process former contrasts are being gradually smoothed out, and a regrouping of old fronts and a growing unification on a new wide front can be observed, a front uniting all people of good will and foresight who are disregarding differences which have become unimportant. Now that we are searching for ultimate truths, we are glad to discover a continually surprising similarity in our findings which in itself proves the correctness of one of the most important of these findings, namely, that there are fundamental truths on which all men are agreed and that there are courses of action corresponding to them which are therefore, so to speak, "natural." When not abandoning themselves to the ecstasy of mass intoxication, people know after all very well what is healthy and what is unhealthy, what is strong and what decadent, what is just and what unjust, what is legitimate and what against the law, what is in keeping with the nature of man and what is not. If they do not know it yet they will sooner or later discover it, when they have awakened and become mature.

And men also remember—to quote Lichtenberg, one of the wise and loveable figures of the eighteenth century—that one has to believe in certain ultimate values because it would be absurd not to believe in them. I know, at any rate, of no other explanation for the exceedingly comforting and cheering experience that as soon as one has found the right word and has given clear expression to the general feeling, one meets a measure of consent which is an ever recurrent surprise, and discovers the existence of a great invisible community of people who feel and think the same, a community of men of good will which extends across all classes, strata and group interests. And we also have to learn again, in case we have forgotten it under the influence of the radically wrong sociological doctrine of the nineteenth century, that men's actions are not exclusively, and not even predominantly, determined by their class interests, but at least as much by general and fundamental emotions and concepts of value which unite them beyond all barriers of class and group interests and without which society and state could, in fact, not exist, and to which one need only appeal to evoke an echo: they are a simple sense of justice, a desire for peace, order and unity; a love of the native soil; a feeling of affinity with the national cultural and historical traditions, readiness for sacrifice, helpfulness, chivalry and fairness. It is to this we point when we are asked how on earth we expect any group interests to support us if we propagate a plan of action which seems to be so contrary to all interests that it is bound to incense now the industrial monopolies, now the trade unions, now this association and now that. In fact we can pay back in like coin by saying that this question seems to spring from a form of sociology which is not only narrow-minded but has been strikingly refuted by the experiences of the most recent days. He who continues to dispute this, has simply not grasped the main secret of Fascist and National Socialist success; but that we surely should have learned from them in the meantime!

*

An exhaustive diagnosis of the world crisis and a thorough presentation of the appropriate therapy would require a voluminous and systematic book. For many years it has been my intention to write such a book, but it seems to me as if the execution of such an undertaking deserves more time than the urgency of a preliminary clarification and orientation permits. Not only does a really thorough treatment of the subject require extremely extensive preparations which in view of the ramifications of the problems often exceed the strength and competence of an individual whose training has been confined to a special field, but also probably every one of us has the feeling that he is still in the midst of an unfinished process of clarification in which new outlooks and insights are continually gained, however firmly the fundamentals may be laid. Thus the time for the final accounting has not yet come, and the best we can do at the moment is to give a sort of interim accounting, which is what in fact we are attempting here. Although we hope that the following chapters will speak for themselves and that the attentive reader will be able to recognize the underlying cohesion of the opinions which make up the whole, it may yet be helpful to do more and describe, as well as can briefly be done, the scheme in which the ideas comprising this book are arranged.

We adhere to the natural division into diagnosis and therapy, interpretation and action. And starting with the first, we arrange the pathological aberrations of our occidental society in two large groups according to their causes and their symptoms: The spiritual and ethical group, and the political, social and economic (sociological) group. We must, of course, always bear in mind that both spheres of the crisis—the spiritual-ethical as well as the sociological—pervade and influence each other most profoundly, because society, its many components and manifestations notwithstanding, always forms a whole in which everything is integrated and interdependent.

To fathom the spiritual-ethical aspect of the world crisis means to assign to our epoch its proper place in the history of thought. How is it to be distinguished from the preceding epochs and how did it evolve from them? To find the answer to this question is obviously exceedingly difficult because the true nature of a period can be fully appraised only once it has passed. Can one seriously imagine Lorenzo de Medici one day stopping Botticelli in the streets of Florence and confiding to him his discovery that they were now living in the Renaissance, or imagine that Leibnitz was privately concerned about the period of the Baroque?

The true historical quintessence of the great periods in the history of thought and culture does in fact not emerge clearly until afterwards, and thus we, too, can today no more than guess under what label we and our time are going to be known in history. But the mere fact that we seem able to venture such a guess proves that at heart we have already detached ourselves from our time and are about to overcome it. At present, it seems entirely possible to us that our age may one day be considered a "spiritual interregnum" (it may even be called that), the "terrible, the kingless" age of a spiritual and moral vacuum which was brought about by the dissolution and disintegration of all traditional values and norms, by the drain of one whole century on the cultural reserves. The old conceptions have been worn out or devaluated, everything has become soft and flabby, what used to be absolute has become relative, the firm fundament of norms, principles and faith has been undermined and is rotting away, scepticism and the "bogy of ideologies" (H. Plessner) are corroding everything, and the "warm, uncanny breath of the foehn," which Nietzsche sensed, has done its work. "Nous vivons du parfum d'un vase vide," Renan had said. However, at the moment we can perceive only a very faint outline of what is destined to replenish this vacuum. That is why the "makeshift," the bumptious pseudo-authority of self-appointed leaders, why nihilism, pure activism and dynamism striving to drown the meaninglessness of our time, why lack of principles has become as much a characteristic of our age as mankind's hunger for the definite, the stable and absolute, a hunger as comforting and touching as it is conducive to the most dangerous aberrations and perversions.

There is unanimous agreement that we are faced with an unequalled moral and intellectual decadence, a spiritual chaos, a general "abandon des certitudes essentielles" (Henri Massis), a boundless relativism (which, with involuntary humor, calls itself positivism), and only the times of the later sophists such as Gorgias or Thrasymachus, who derive the concept of right purely from utility, provide us with a historical parallel. We are also comparatively clear concerning the process which has led to this result:

it is apparently a cultural retreat where each sacrifice has entailed others, a continual watering down, a squandering of our inheritance, a living on our substance, a process which was bound to end in bankruptcy. That substance was essentially the spiritual and moral capital which pagan antiquity and Christianity have handed down to us as their joint heritage.

The Christian element, however, which predominated in this heritage has, since the beginning of modern times, been subjected to a continuous process of secularization until finally the power of faith, which had at first consciously and then unconsciously nourished the secularized concept of progress, rationalism, liberty and humanity, began to flag, thus becoming responsible for the withering of those very concepts, since no alternative sources of faith and certainty had been provided. Regarding this interpretation, too, there is general agreement today, although it would still have to be established in detail whether the drain on the reserves has not been greater in some countries than in others, and has only reached a really catastrophic point in those countries where society has already completely disintegrated. The conclusions to be drawn from this will vary according to the attitude of each observer towards Christianity, but everything duly considered, the differences of really responsible opinion on this cannot be so very great. Can we seriously agree with Nietzsche's extremist view that the time has come "when we have to pay for having been Christians for two thousand years," that it is the Christian religion itself which is to blame for not being able to hold men enthralled for thousands of years and that it is consequently responsible for the vacuum which it has finally left behind? This strange application of the maxim that "not the murderer but the murdered is to blame" must needs turn out to be a mere mental radicalism, which cannot alter the very real fact that the Christian religion is one of the strongest formative forces of our civilization, which cannot, in fact, be imagined without it. This realization seems to us to insure that minimum of affirmation of Christianity which our cultural responsibility demands. But on the other hand, there can be no question of artificially "replanting Christianity for the sake of good conduct" (Jacob Burckhardt), and this illuminates the full gravity of the present task, of which both theologians and anti-theologians tend to make light.

We can, however, skirt a discussion of these questions on this— in any case unsuitable—occasion with a clear conscience, the more so as we must yet considerably broaden our interpretation of the process of disintegration and dissolution. Along with the slackening of the powers of faith and conviction, whatever their origin may be, people have also lost a certain natural sureness of instinct and the feeling for what is due to man to such a degree that their relationship to the most elementary things—work and leisure, nature, time and death, the other sex, children and the succession of generations, youth and old age, the natural enjoyment of life, the incomprehensible and the supernatural, property, war and peace, intellect, emotion and the community—has been most seriously disturbed. Men, having to a great extent lost the use of their innate sense of proportion, thus stagger from one extreme to the other, now trying out this, now that, now following this fashionable belief, now that, responding now to this external attraction, now to the other, but listening least of all to the voice of their own heart. It is particularly characteristic of the general loss of a natural sense of direction—a loss which is jeopardizing the wisdom gained through countless centuries—that the age of immaturity, of restless experiment, of youth, has in our time become the object of the most preposterous overestimation.

This process of intellectual and moral disintegration can be observed in all spheres of civilization and is thus impressing its stamp on every aspect of Western society. The arbitrariness and vagueness of viewpoints and the accompanying outcrop of virtuosi and aesthetes, the general loss of style, the lack of respect for language, the consequent decay of the art of writing and vital expression, "the expulsion of man from art" (which even such a clear-sighted critic of our civilization as Ortega y Gasset saw fit to praise), the increasing emotionalizing, not to say sexualizing of music since the end of the so-called classic period—all of this is pervaded by a *haut gout* noticeable even by those who are by no means used only to simple fare. The effects of this process of disintegration have, however, been particularly striking and disastrous in the case of science, for, influenced by inward instability it has increasingly become a prey to the misunderstanding that all opinions whatsoever and all decisions based on concepts of value are incompatible with the dignity of science and must needs comprise subjective arbitrariness—commonly known as "ideology." The effects of this relativism and agnosticism in science were bound to be all the more dangerous since it thus eliminated itself as the leading authority just at a time when the Church had already lost most of its authority. In this way a vacuum arose which was rightly felt to be unsupportable and which was finally filled by a form of pseudo-science and political pseudo-theology, a political theology of the state which in turn in many countries forcefully transformed science into a political institution; and it was precisely the spiritually rootless scientist who was the least able to oppose this development. Thus Rabelais' witticism: "science sans conscience n'est que ruine de l'âme," has once more proved true, not only to the spiritual detriment of the scientists, which need not perhaps cause us concern, but above all to the detriment of our civilization.

However, here as elsewhere the worst is already over and a re-orientation has been going on for some time. In science as in other cultural spheres a vanguard—perhaps small as yet and by no means very certain of itself—has long passed the nadir of decadence but as always in these cases the new spiritual development is taking place quietly and far from the noise of the great stage of the world where the last act of the old drama is still being played out. However, in accordance with the law of "historical interference" (of which we shall speak in more detail later on), the majority of the public today is still subject to the influence of that tired refusal to take sides and that vagueness parading in aesthetic verbiage, which until recently dominated science and literature. This influence—coupled with sociological symptoms of decadence— explains the oppressive phenomenon of a decadent bourgeoisie which, in its view of history, abandons itself to the cult of historic pseudo-greatness and is prepared to kow-tow before power and success, since it has lost all belief in values higher than those of its own security and comforts and in its cowardice has become stupid. It is idle to deny the existence of such a decadent liberal-bourgeois world, and presumably the time has passed when one risked being misunderstood if one considered Fascism's or Communism's criticism of this world justified. In the meantime we have witnessed many countries falling victim to this weakness, and the names of the statesmen personifying it are as yet unforgotten.

*

Whether or not one considers the degenerative symptoms in the spiritual and moral domain decisive, it is indisputable that they are extremely important, that they will probably show us the way to the origin of the world crisis and that in certain countries they actually point to the explanation of the breakdown. They deserve first place in our diagnosis, especially when we are dealing with countries where the sciences of a purely socio-economic kind have not been striking enough to explain the breakdown—predominantly middle class and farming countries with a balanced property distribution where spiritual collectivization had made less progress than in other countries. In fact, one would not have thought some of these countries as far gone as they later turned out to be, had it not been a case of spiritual rather than socio-economic disease, a "désordre mental" as Henri Massis recently called it. Only thus, it seems, can we fully explain the emergence here and there of a plutocratic leader caste which was prepared to capitulate both at home and abroad—"quanto quis servitio promptior" (Tacitus, *Annals* I 2).

Generally speaking, it is, however, true to say that as the crisis of Western society is total its causes are also extensive and intricate. Reference to the spiritual and moral crisis is therefore an inadequate explanation which must be supplemented by analysing the socio-logical symptoms of degeneration because both form an interactive entity. This must also be borne in mind when we turn to the actual sociological (i.e. the political, social and economic) appearance of the disease.

The disease which has been holding Western society in an ever firmer grip for more than a hundred years is characterized by a process of social decomposition and agglomeration for which the term "collectivization" has been coined, a process with which large circles have become acquainted—in a manner admittedly still in need of some corrections—through Ortega y Gasset's book, *The Revolt of the Masses*. A healthy society, firmly resting on its own foundation, possesses a genuine "structure" with many intermediate stages; it exhibits a necessarily "hierarchical" composition (i.e. determined by the social importance of certain functions, services and leadership qualities), where each individual has the good fortune of knowing his position. Whereas such a society is based on the grouping functions of genuine communities filled with the spirit of human fellowship (such as the neighbourhood, the family, the parish, the Church, the occupation), society has during the last hundred years moved further and further away from such an ideal and has disintegrated into a mass of abstract individuals who are solitary and isolated as human beings, but packed tightly like termites in their role of social functionaries. The inhabitants of a large apart-ment house are complete strangers to each other and meet perhaps for the first time in the air raid shelter, but on the other hand, they have the closest anonymous relations with the totality of their fellow men, relations of an external and mechanical kind, as buyers and sellers, as members of crowds jostling each other, as voters, as radio listeners and visitors to the motion pictures, sharing the same acoustic or optic impressions with millions of others, as tax payers, as recipients of pensions and public assistance, as members of health insurance societies and this or that centrally organized association. The place of a genuine integration created by genuine communities, which requires the ties of proximity, natural roots and the warmth of direct human relationships, has been taken by a pseudo-integration, created by the market, competition, central organization, by "tenementing," by ballot papers, police, laws, mass production, mass amusements, mass emotions and mass education, a pseudo-integration which reaches its climax in the collectivist state. The more tightly individuals are packed together and the greater their dependence on each other, the greater is their inner isolation and loneliness, and there is a direct connection between the grinding down of society into the sand-heap of myriads of individuals and its conglobation into unorganized, structureless and amorphous mass formations, which provide a luxuriant breeding ground for the mass instincts and mass emotions which are responsible for the befuddled and hysterical instability of present day society.

Pseudo-integration of mass society goes hand in hand with pseudo-leadership, i.e. in the political, cultural and social spheres leading positions are occupied by men who cannot legitimately claim authentic spiritual leadership because, not having attained detachment from the one-level mass society around them, they are really part of it both as regards their knowledge and their emotional reactions, and they owe their leadership positions merely to the masterly interpretation and handling of these reactions. Through them mass man—*homo insipiens gregarius*—himself takes over the reins, mass man as Ortega y Gasset describes him: with his shallow popular culture, his entirely baseless and obtrusive presumption, his dogmatic self-importance, his lack of judgment and his spiritual and moral herd life. A century of misinterpreted democratization of learning as well as of predominantly intellectual training has, in conjunction with the crumbling of the hierarchical structure of society, resulted in a product all of whose features are ultimately traceable to a lack of reverence, that reverence which—in the sense of that grand passage in *Wilhelm Meisters Wanderjahre* (Book II, chapter 1)—is perhaps the most fundamental element of every civilization. It is Cicero's *verecundia, sine qua nihil rectum esse potest, nihil honestum* (*De officiis*, I, 41). When Leibniz was writing not more than a few hundred people in Europe rightly claimed to understand him, whilst the worthy denizens of Hanover knew him only as *"oler Loevenix"* (old "doubting Thomas"); and although the feudal structure of the Germany of those days, based as it was on exploitation and domination, is open to the strongest criticism, the intellectual hierarchy which we have described was doubtlessly sound. Today, assuming the existence of sufficient interest, Leibnitz' monadism would be popularized in lectures, books and evening classes, on the radio and on the screen, &c., until everyone had understood the residue of platitudes and was repeating them ad infinitum—or worse, mass man, spoiled by such successive popularization and arrogating to himself the high office of cultural arbiter, would forbid Leibnitz to write such nonsense.

This lack of respect deserves to be placed in an even wider frame of reference, which may be illustrated as follows. The human body possesses a complicated and variegated system of reflexes, which have to function to ensure life's normal flow and protect it from all kinds of dangers. If a foreign body enters the eyes, they begin to water, if it enters through the mouth it is thrown up by the pharynx, the skin disposes of it by suppurating, and in the intestines unwholesome matter is removed by peristalsis. Society, viewed as a whole, presents a very similar picture. It too, must have at its command prompt and infallible reflexes, which vouch for and, at the same time, reflect the health of the social organism, and which, if they become weak, irregular or fail altogether, indicate a pathological condition. They are reflexes of approval and disapproval, which show us that society is guided by inviolable concepts of value. These reflexes should always begin to function easily and promptly as soon as we step beyond the wide field of what is permissible and what can be left to the judgment of the individual, as soon, in fact, as we enter the border zone where a joke ceases to be a joke. When such a point has been reached every sign of vacillation and irresolution, of uncertainty and paralysis is an emphatic warning that something has seriously gone wrong within the social organism. In a case like this we speak of a moral crisis, a crisis in legal conceptions, or a crisis in taste, but in the last resort we always mean the same thing, and when we diagnose this condition as moral, political or aesthetic nihilism we want to indicate that society is in a condition which corresponds to paralysis in the human body.

All value reflexes of society, both positive and negative, can finally be traced back to two main reflexes: one of them, reverence, we know already, the other is unqualified indignation. To have these two reflexes at one's command is to possess a scale of values where the valuable is as securely fixed at the top as the worthless is at the bottom. Society, knowing instinctively when to doff its hat, must know with equal certainty when to put it on indignantly without wasting another word. When it is no longer sure of the right moment for either, when opinion on ultimate values is beginning to waver, it is time to sound the alarm. The reflexes have stopped to function and we are faced with the morbid degeneration of all norms and values, without which no society can exist for any length of time. With reverence declining at one end of the scale, unqualified and uncompromising indignation automatically dwindles at the other. A society is indeed in a bad way if its patellary reflexes no longer react instantaneously to the bludgeon blows of broken laws and arbitrary power, of inhumanity, intolerance, cruelty and mercilessness and if that apathy sets in which is the harbinger of the coming breakdown. The deepest low, however, is reached when indignation, which countenances no excuse, is replaced by whitewashing, by morbid interest, by appeals for "understanding," by the argument that the end justifies the means, by cynical rationalizations and snobbish flirtations with the abnormal. Here Lichtenberg's words are well applied: where moderation is a fault, indifference becomes a crime.

All this, we feel, is the least that must be said even in an introductory survey of the process of collectivization in order to prevent it from being obscured by wide-spread misconceptions. However, it might be just as well to add here that one would be mistaken to let a wholly misplaced social pride allow one to associate the term "masses" with low income groups and small property holders. We are, on the contrary, faced with a sociological process of degeneration which takes place quite independently of the size of income and has indeed affected least of all those groups, such as peasants and artisans, who though by no means well-to-do, are comparatively speaking most securely anchored in fixed conditions. There are enough mass men at the top of the income pyramid and social snobbery is precisely one of their characteristics.

What then are the sociological conditions which favour collectivization?

It will perhaps help to clarify matters if we divide the sociological factors which further collectivization—the spiritual and moral factors no longer concern us here—into three groups: into the demographic, the technological and the political, social and institutional components. Let us then find out what this means and start with the demographic component, which will probably require least explanation.

It is obvious that the tremendous and unparallelled increase in population which took place during the last hundred years—caused by a "historical interference," namely the concurrence of the "new," i.e. a low, death rate, with the "old," i.e. a high, birth rate, whose effects continued to be felt for a considerable time—flooded the earth with a "mass" in the rough arithmetical sense of the word which was bound to stamp its mass character on our whole civilization. It is this aspect of the population problem which is more important than all the arguments advanced in this dispute by economists, statisticians and social hygienists: the flooding of the West by countless millions of newcomers created an economic, social and cultural tension which hardly any society would have been able to withstand without losing its structure and degenerating into a mass society. The increase was too overwhelming and came about too suddenly to be assimilated without a break in continuity and the dissolution of the social and cultural tradition. Today, more than one example has taught us that a nation can beget a barbaric invasion from its own midst:

δεινοὶ πλῆθος τ'ανάριθμοι

("Fearful, countless myriads"—Aeschylus, *The Persians*).

Even if no other forces had been at work, this unparallelled spring tide of humanity would have forced upon mankind that colossal and over-complicated apparatus for catering for the masses, that orgy of technology and organization, mammoth industries, infinite division of labor, bloated big cities and industrial areas, the speed and instability of economic life, that materialist and rationalist life without tradition, mass production, mass entertainment, centralization, organization, world-wide interdependence, garish profusion, the constant shuttling of men and goods, the undermining of everything permanent and rooted, the subjugation of the whole globe by a mechanical, positivist civilization.

Under the impact of all this and by a process which may be called "proletarization," if that term is given a sufficiently wide meaning, a considerable part of the world's population has been pushed into a sociological and anthropological position which is characterized by economic and social dependence, a rootless, tenemented life, where men are strangers to nature and overwhelmed by the dreariness of work. We are faced with a development where the demographic component coupled with the technological and politico-socio-institutional components has exerted its disastrous influence to the full. It is not only the increase in population but also today's machine technology, the manner of its application, the forms shortsightedly favored in factory organization, and finally also certain political and social measures taken by the state, which are responsible for proletarization having become the fate of the masses, a fate which threatens the life of our society more than anything else and condemns millions to an existence which prevents the positive development of their faculties either as human beings or as citizens. Their misfortune is no longer thin wage envelopes or excessive working hours; this stage has long been passed in the leading countries—which are, precisely, those which are most threatened by spiritual collectivization—and it is the peasant and artisan, the opposite of the proletarian, who is usually worst off with regard to the material aspects of life. No, what characterizes proletarization is its psycho-physiological side: the devitalizing effect of the proletarian-industrial way of life and work, which cannot be improved upon either by higher wages or by bigger cinemas; the dependence and insecurity which rule out ownership as well as long-term incomes; the regimentation of labor which has to be performed anonymously and under the invisible overseer's whip of the machine giants, under constant discipline and as part of an oppressive totality, thus largely losing all meaning and dignity; a form of existence estranged from nature and an organic community life, unsuited to man's constitution and depriving him of the natural and social integration he needs. In brief, this is a mode of life, work and habitation which in the physiological sense is unsatisfactory to the highest degree, and which has never existed before to this extent.

Proletarization does not necessarily always exhibit all the characteristics we have enumerated; rather, we find it in many stages of development and it has affected different population groups and different countries in varying degrees, and a few have even been left untouched to a remarkable extent. However, a country will always have to be considered far gone on the road of proletarization when giant enterprises and concentrations of property have made a large part of the population dependent, urbanized cogs in the industrial-commercial hierarchy, recipients of wages and salaries, thus bringing about that socio-economic collectivization with which we are now acquainted. Let us also not forget that every time an independent livelihood is destroyed, this process is accelerated and that socialism of whatever kind merely marks its climax, and this in a twofold sense: it is nurtured by this process and at the same time it carries the process to its final conclusion. This holds good to such an extent that the term proletarism can be substituted for socialism, and that term has, moreover, the advantage of demonstrating how much socialism is essentially only the extremist continuation of a development which has already progressed far under a degenerated capitalist system.

Into this over-all picture of spiritual collectivization, proletarization, mechanization and centralization all those details have to be fitted which are known to everyone and which again and again remind us of the total disease, though it is not always possible to say with certainty to what extent they are causes, consequences or merely symptoms. The most serious of them is perhaps the disintegration of the family, a concomitant of the general pathological development and particularly striking proof of how deeply it is affecting the basis of a healthy human existence and of a well-integrated society. It has, in fact, created economic and social conditions under which the family—which is the natural sphere of the woman, the proper environment for raising children and indeed the parent cell of the community—must needs wither and finally degenerate into a mere common address, with the reservation that the contract can be terminated by divorce at any time. Apart from the as yet unaffected peasant and artisan classes and apart from those instances where the allotment movement, the revival of peasant industries and related endeavors have been initiated as remedial correctives, the family has been degraded to a mere consumers co-operative—at best, an entertainment co-operative—often enough without children or, if there are any, without the possibility of bestowing on them more than a summary education. If those are right who maintain that in large circles of the bourgeoisie home education can hardly be said to exist any longer, and if we remember that, on the other hand, the public authorities—quite contrary to Pestalozzi's teaching—are more and more monopolizing all forms of education and schooling and thereby influencing man's development in an increasingly one-sided manner, and if we realize that one, viz. the female, half of society, is threatened by this trend in the fulfilment of its vital functions and thus becomes its real victim, we can, without exaggeration, describe the decline of the family as one of the gravest symptoms of the disease of our time. But we must not forget that mere exhortations and lamentations are as cheap as they are vain until we concentrate our efforts on changing those sociological conditions under which the family plainly cannot flourish.

We gain a scarcely less melancholy impression when we consider another aspect of spiritual collectivization and proletarization: the desolation of rural community life, the decline of the village in favor of the city, and the urbanization and commercialization of the open country itself. Nobody who has attentively followed the development in certain countries can fail to note what is happening —the decrease in number and influence of the intellectual elite of the countryside, the decay of communal life in the village, the degradation of the country to the position of an urban green belt in both an economic and cultural sense, the increasing destruction of rural cultural life, &c. We notice this above all in France, the United States and England, to a certain extent also in Germany, whilst Switzerland's healthy singularity finds perhaps its most telling expression in the fact that there we see hardly any traces of such a process of decay but, on the contrary, find that the country-side has almost completely retained its specific mental and socio-logical importance, and the lament so often heard, for example, in France, "Le médecin de campagne, c'est fini," would cause some surprise in Switzerland. Those who, unlike the author, have not experienced this process of decay at first hand will perhaps find in Louis Bromfield's novel, The Farm, its best, most powerful and moving portrayal. Here we may add that the decline of indigenous rural life is usually accompanied by a tendency to polarize men's relationship to nature: instead of the balanced interplay between it and civilization, we have extreme urbanization, completely estranged from nature, on the one hand, and on the other, national parks, camping and nudism, whilst the happy medium—peasantry and small towns—is vanishing. It is part of the picture of this disease that the urbanized remoteness of Western man from nature leads to the extreme of a city-bred, fashionable and condescending cult of the peasant, which bears the stamp of high-brow artificiality and which the genuine peasant cannot but find embarrassing. "Rien n'empêche tant d'être naturel que l'envie de le paroître" (La Rochefoucauld).

*

It is impossible for us at this point to describe, with any claim to adequacy, the sociological symptoms of disintegration as we meet them in the form of spiritual collectivization and its related processes. However, as the most essential factors have been mentioned, we can now turn to the symptoms of the disease in the narrower sphere of the political and economic systems of the various nations and thus round off our over-all diagnosis.

It is so universally obvious that the spiritual-moral and the sociological crises combined have engendered an extremely serious crisis in the Western political system, that only a few words need be added here. On the one hand, symptoms of disintegration and decay—known as the crisis of democracy—have been receiving attention in the democratic countries for more than a generation and increasingly so after the First World War; on the other hand, a new form of government known as collectivist (totalitarian) has been gaining ground since the Russian Revolution of 1917 and its imprint on our time has been so great that there has already been talk of an "era of tyranny."

The crisis of democracy consists in the dogmatic failure to understand the limitations inherent in the democratic and liberal principle, the resulting spiritual collectivization, the arrogance of vested interests, the fanaticism of minorities. It consists in the general leveling down which accompanies spiritual collectivization and leads to "plebeianism," the decreasing understanding of the requisites of a well constructed democratic state and of the sacrifices which have to be made for it, the disintegrating effects of the crisis of the economic system as well as of the policies of economic intervention and planning. All these and a few other factors have rendered the functioning of democratic institutions increasingly more difficult, have led to the dissolution of the authority, impartiality and unity of the state and to a weakening of the political will, which in certain well known cases and situations have developed into an actual volitional paralysis internally and externally, and has given free play to various destructive forces. At the same time growing centralization and bureaucracy have mechanized the state at the expense of an organic vertical structure based on federalism or communal self-government, and have thus repeated in the narrower sphere of constitutional and administrative problems the levelling process of spiritual collectivization characterizing society as a whole.

We may today count on general understanding if we point out that that highly disturbing and revolutionary form of government, the collectivist (totalitarian) state, can be comprehended as essentially arising from the crisis of democracy, but beyond that also from the spiritual and sociological crisis. If we wish to be at home in the world of today and not become a prey to grave misunderstandings, we must keep two things firmly in mind which in reality are only two aspects of one and the same fact. On the one

hand today's diseased democracy harbors the germs of the collectivist system, which we define fairly correctly if we call it an
authoritarian and collectivist mass state (plethocracy); the crisis stage
of democracy can thus up to a point be termed "pre-collectivist."
But, on the other hand, it also follows that it would be totally
wrong to see in the collectivist system the solution of democracy's
crisis; it is rather the last and most serious result of the crisis, the
climax of the disease which it has introduced into modern mass
society. It would simply amount to an error of 180 degrees to seek
recovery in this quarter.

And finally, as regards the causes, symptoms and consequences
of the total crisis in the sphere of the economic system of the
European-American world, commonly called "capitalism," we can
be very brief here, too—not so much because in this field concepts
can be assumed to be universally clear, but because this subject will
be dealt with in great detail in the following chapters. To complete our outline it must for the moment suffice to know that the
crisis of the economic system reflects in a particularly striking
manner directly affecting everybody, the general spiritual-moral and
sociological crisis from which it mainly derives. It would, however, be quite wrong to be reassured by this statement and to
indulge in the delusion that the economic system is only the innocent
victim of destructive forces operating outside it. That is certainly
not the case. It would rather be true to say that the crisis of
capitalism possesses features largely its own so that it is more likely
to be cause than result of the total crisis, if it is indeed at all possible
to distinguish cause and effect in the latter. In other words: the
economic system itself contains sufficient flaws, contradictions and
degenerative features which would have led to a serious crisis of its
own even without the repercussions caused by the total crisis. We
need only recall what has been said above regarding the causes of
spiritual collectivization in order to realize the responsibility a
misdirected capitalism bears for the sickness of our society.

It can certainly not be over-emphasized that ten years ago (1931)
our economic system would not have collapsed in so thorough a
fashion if it had not been for the non-economic convulsions which
have been shaking the world since 1914 and under the burden of
which another economic system would probably have suffered a
really irrevocable breakdown at a much earlier date. Yet there can
scarcely be any doubt that sooner or later man would have revolted
against an economic system which, however sound its fundamental
principles, invites a large degree of criticism owing to the way in
which in many countries it has unfortunately been allowed to
develop: its instability; its lack of social justice; the growing opportunities for monopolistic enrichment and the blackmailing policies
of special interest; the faulty functioning of many individual

markets; proletarization, commercialization and concentration of power, excesses of speculation and destruction of capital; the insensate and unnatural way of life imposed on men against which they finally rebel, driven by a vague feeling of discontent and lured by nebulous goals.

*

Just as the crisis of democracy leads to totalitarianism, the rebellion against the Western economic system has resulted in the anti-capitalist movement and its many more or less radical variants, among them socialism and collectivism. But as the former, far from overcoming the crisis of democracy, only serves to bring the sickness of the body politic to a head, socialism too, as the expression of anti-capitalist mass rebellion, is nothing but a reaction imperiling everything. It simply follows certain aberrations to their logical conclusion, and it is certainly therefore not the salvation it pretends to be. This juxtaposition of totalitarianism and socialism is more than a mere comparison; the two tendencies are, on the contrary, so closely interrelated that, as can be proved in detail, they are, in the last analysis, one. Both—the one in the political and cultural, the other in the economic and social field—complete the total crisis of society; both provide anything but a solution: rather, they mark the outermost point which we can reach in wandering away from the answer to the problem.

We certainly do not pass this judgment on socialism because we delight in the provocation and still less because we are out of sympathy with the motives of many socialists, or because we lack understanding of the historical factors which have forced mass rebellion against the malformations of our economic system down the road of socialism. We would also add that only those are really entitled to pass such a judgment who not merely do not gloss over these malformations but deduce from them the necessity for vigorous and intelligent countermeasures which, although definitely anti-socialist, are at least as radical as the socialist proposals. We naturally consider it beneath our dignity to answer those who would counter our objective attitude by unchivalrously suspecting our own motives.

If we consider the term "socialism" in the sense it has acquired in the course of history and in which we should continue to use it, that is, a totally planned economy which eliminates markets, competition, and private initiative, it would really seem time to describe it, especially in the interest of those sections of the population which are clamoring for it, purely and simply as what it is, an aberration, a routine mental habit of people whom we understand very well, and to whom, in certain circumstances, we may feel very close. In this way we justify all the more our attempt to reason with them.

It is time to say quite frankly and bluntly that it is an error to think that relentless criticism of the drawbacks of our economic and social system must necessarily lead to socialism and that, vice versa, every opponent of socialism must necessarily be a malevolent reactionary or a hypocritical apologist and appeaser. We are not concerned with the reasons others have for their opposition: we ourselves base our arguments on grounds which in the end we expect to convince anyone who lives *for* socialism (although it may not convince all those who live *by* it). There are definite reasons, based on the vagaries of history, why radical critics of the short-comings of our economic system should all have chosen socialism as a rallying point, and next to the role which certain intellectuals such as Karl Marx have played, blindness and intellectual barren-ness of non-socialists are among the major causes. But that is really no reason for perpetuating this state of affairs into eternity; on the contrary, we have travelled sufficiently far down this blind alley to know it for what it is. If, in spite of turning away from it, one wishes to retain the term "socialism," it may be argued that what matters is the content and not the name; however, even such a suggestion would be fraught with risk at a time when every-thing depends on exact thinking, precise concepts and clear-cut decisions, and it can only lead to growing confusion and want of orientation. Accurate concepts and frank language are not the least important requisites for transcending an era among whose chief characteristics are deep seated insincerity and an invidious camou-flage of words.

It is also true that the vague and thoughtless use of terms such as "planned economy" and "socialism," so common today, is respons-ible for considerable confusion. These pretentious words are more and more frequently being used in instances when much more harmless problems, in fact obvious necessities, are involved, about which nobody has so far made any great to-do, such as the drawing up of plans for urban developments, the expansion of co-operatives or standardization of agricultural products. In all these cases such big words should be avoided since they are compromised in no small degree by having been assigned to something quite specific, namely the conscious direction of the economy by a bureaucracy instead of the market and price mechanism. This generous use of the terms "planned economy" and "socialism" recalls the touch-ing figures of the old socialists of the so-called revisionist persuasion, who were quite willing to accept municipal burials or milk dis-tribution in lieu of the indefinitely postponed onset of the "big crash" and the "expropriation of the expropriators." In such a case it is really nothing but pious self-deception to continue calling oneself a socialist. We should rather insist on using the term "socialism" in its original trenchant and clear-cut sense and then have the courage to say that we have thoroughly finished with it and that what we want is at least as far removed from socialism as from the old brand of liberalism. Now, when everything depends on clarity and decisiveness, the word is still far too much encumbered by a confused jumble of bitter feelings and proletarian romanticism.

When it comes to discussing the proper therapy, socialism can serve us as an example for all the various abberations that are completely unable to lead to a cure of the symptoms which the diagnosis of the general crisis of society has disclosed. The course that is likely to result in success will follow from our description of the disease. However, if we remember how extremely comprehensive and complex we found that crisis to be, how it touches upon every aspect of cultural life, it will be understood why we are so adverse to presenting—with the disagreeable self-assurance of a man who has settled everything long ago and now refuses to listen to any further objections—an exact and detailed recovery plan and to advertising it cheerfully as promising a prompt and infallible cure. What matters at the moment is that, firstly, the diagnosis should be clear and convincing, as otherwise all action will be nothing but amateurish vivisection practiced on the tortured body of society, and that secondly, it should indicate to us the general direction which each individual operation must follow. Only when unanimity of opinion has been reached on these points can the details of the various measures be discussed and a task be tackled which is in any case beyond the powers of one person. Apart from this, it should be clear that we are here concerned with a reconstruction job as tedious and trying to our patience as the re-afforestation of a barren tract of land.

While at this point we confine ourselves to a warning against dilettante impatience and for the rest put our trust in the persuasive powers of the subsequent arguments, we still think it appropriate to sketch the general character of the economic policy appearing on the horizon. The time really seems ripe for a new type of economic program which does not fit any of the usual patterns and which, for this very reason, appeals to us.

We are thinking of an economic policy which is in one sense conservative and radical in another, equally definite sense: conservative in insisting on the preservation of continuity in cultural and economic development, making the defense of the basic values and principles of a free personality its highest, immutable aim—radical in its diagnosis of the disintegration of our "liberal" social and economic system, radical in its criticism of the errors of liberal philosophy and practice, radical in its lack of respect for moribund institutions, privileges, ideologies and dogmas, and finally, radical in its unorthodox choice of the means which today seem appropriate for the attainment of the permanent goal of every culture based on the freedom of the individual. The advocates of this program are as aware of the fundamental errors of nineteenth century liberalism as they are opposed to collectivism, however dressed up, and the political-cultural totalitarianism that inevitably goes with it—not only as an impracticable solution but also as one harmful to society.

This vigorous rejection of collectivism shows at the same time that nothing is further from the thoughts of the representatives of our program than the idea of adopting a fundamentally hostile attitude towards liberalism as such. They simply do not cling to that particular form which liberalism assumed both in theory and practice in the course of the nineteenth century and which finally discredited it so hopelessly. They are solely concerned with liberalism in that more general and inviolable sense which has retained its vigor through the ages: liberalism in the sense of an individualist culture, a delicate balance between liberty and constraint, which man needs, and a society delivered from the original sin of violence and exploitation, a non-collectivist, non-feudal and non-mediaeval society. In stressing this they show how deep the gulf is between themselves and that reactionary obscurantism which is so busy today making capital out of the general hangover resulting from the most recent period of history, and which is trying to persuade us to surrender the greatest asset of our epoch: the victory over every form of mediaevalism based on a hierarchy of force.

Precisely in order to preserve this sacrosanct core which today is most gravely threatened by the collapse of historical liberalism, the representatives of liberal revisionism are so relentless in their criticism of what has now broken down, that they have to suffer that dullards reckon them among members of the hostile camp. They believe that this pitiless and unsparing frankness is not only in the best interests of truth but also in the interests of the cause itself. They furthermore have the advantage of not being among those who wring their hands before the deserted altars of liberalism in hopeless despair over the stupidity of others, but are rather in the fortunate position of being able to point to mistakes which have been committed by their side, but can be righted. Since self-improvement notoriously holds more promise than the attempt to better others, the liberal revisionists have chosen a point of vantage which, as matters stand today, is the only one that does not appear hopeless from the start.

It is a program, therefore, which offers battle on two fronts: on the one against collectivism and on the other against that brand of liberalism which developed and influenced most countries during the nineteenth century and which is so much in need of a thorough revision. It goes without saying that such a two-fronted battle requires mental and moral resources of an uncommon order, and that there are phases when resistance seems to flag on one front while all reserves are being rushed to the other. It is also inevitable that as long as this program is still in its growing stages, irritating confusion and misunderstandings will continue to arise and the novelty and singularity of these economic proposals will not be recognized. In fact, we are dealing here neither with a species of historical liberalism nor with mere "interventionism," nor by any means with something even faintly akin to that collectivism which today is making so much headway everywhere. What is really involved, however, is so elusive and so difficult to define that only a voluminous book could do it justice. It follows that any attempt at labeling, however necessary, can for the time being only be provisional. We shall, however, not be far wrong in using such terms as "constructive" or "revisionist" liberalism, "economic humanism" or, as I have suggested myself, the "Third Way." I feel that the last mentioned term has proved reasonably useful since it seems to be neither too comprehensive nor too narrow and above all expresses the main purpose of the new program: the elimination of the sterile alternative between laissez-faire and collectivism. Today a select circle—at present still small, but steadily expanding thanks to the lessons which contemporary history has so effectively, if painfully, taught us—is in various ways and in many countries engaged in a clear, precise and detailed evolution of such a program, whatever its ultimate name.

*

The observation—which finds growing confirmation every day— that the ideas discussed here can count on the approval of a continually increasing circle of contemporaries in every country, encourages us to conclude this survey on a more hopeful note and to modify the pessimism of the statements we have made so far.

Three things we want to emphasize here. First, it must be understood that our pessimism calls for disillusionment as well as for constructive action. It is thus not only opposed, as a matter of course, to all shallow optimism, but also to that decadent and utterly pagan fatalism of those who, tired and resigned, submit to a supposedly inevitable fate, or of those who, secretly rejoicing behind a mask of melancholy philosophy, and assuming the air of sages who have been granted a preview of the designs of providence, hoodwink the mentally indolent with the sham argument of predetermination. We, on the other hand, who do not leave the decision to a mystical destiny but seek it within ourselves, are particularly concerned to show beyond doubt how grave and at the same time how unavoidable it is. At the moment, however, it has not yet been made, and we are still free to choose, if only we have the will and the understanding and if we do not allow ourselves to be paralyzed by an entirely unmanly and baseless fatalism. Only he who is pessimist enough to realize the whole extent of the danger is qualified to take part in averting it—a task where optimists and fatalists are equally useless encumbrances. It is pessimism that makes us foresee that we are doomed by fate unless we do something, but we are in no way compelled to believe in a fate that will overtake us regardless of what we do. And we are citing but an age old truth if we add that hope and fear are always inseparably bound up with each other.

In the second place we base our argument on the observation, cited above, that the spiritual and moral change indispensable to a lasting improvement is taking place before our eyes, a change which includes the resolve to carry through a radical re-orientation aided by a growing awareness of what is likely to be the right way. No one, moreover, can overlook the increasing signs that along with this spiritual and moral transformation a change for the better is also beginning to take place in various fields in the economic and social spheres. Just as the forces for the conquest of the spiritual interregnum are astir everywhere, the resistance to collectivization, proletarization, mechanization and the other sociological defects of our society is gradually growing stronger. Whilst the universal slowing down in the reproduction rate alone sees to it that matters do not get out of hand, there are also signs in some countries that in many respects a right way has been found to combat the spiritual collectivization which is still spreading so terrifyingly in the collectivist countries. The peasantry is coming into its own; the magnetic power of the giant cities is on the wane; legislators, administrators and the judiciary as well as other intelligent leaders are taking the first bold steps in loosening the ubiquitous grip of centralization, in abandoning the worship of the colossal, in resisting monopolization and group egoism, and in creating new and more humane forms of industry; men are fleeing from monotony to variety, from the artificial to the natural, and but for this new World War, we might have been able to register steady progress in these and many other domains. But it is by no means certain whether in the end the devastation and the as yet wholly incalculable consequences of this World War will not be balanced by the probability that this catastrophe, which is reducing life to its basic elements, which is burning down all the deadwood and confronting everyone point blank with the ultimate questions of existence, may prove to be a preceptor, as cruel as it is effective, in the reconstruction of society and the conversion of men.

The prospects of continued favorable development—and this brings us to the third and last point—are all the greater as the process of disintegration has by no means affected all countries, nor, within each country, all groups of the population, to the same degree. On the contrary, in most countries—and, with the exception of what is most corrupt, even in the collectivist states—more or less considerable moral reserves, a spiritual sense of direction and quite influential remnants of an undegenerated and uncollectivized society have been preserved; in a few countries even, disintegration and spiritual collectivization remain confined exclusively to that section of society which until now has merely been allowed to set the fashion. Almost everywhere then, relatively healthy parts of society are in existence which have only to be strengthened and encouraged in order to serve as a basis for effecting what in the more favorable instances may be a surprisingly rapid change in attitude.

However, the most hopeful sign and the one which most strikingly refutes the feeble objections of those who consider our program a Utopian illusion, is that among the intellectually and economically leading nations of the European-American cultural sphere there actually are countries where most of what we think is so urgently needed exists in a more or less perfect form and has demonstrated an almost provocative sturdiness. We know of no country of which this would be truer than that in which this work can be published on this tragic hour of Europe's history (1942). One would indeed be rendering a great disservice to Switzerland if one were to compliment it on its perfection with winning hypocrisy, and it would lose one of the main aspects of its vitality if it were ever to forego its moral fibre and intellectual capacity for constant and relentless self-criticism, and would come to ape the disastrous examples of the big nations. But we believe it to be so robust that it can listen to praise and criticism with equal composure, and therefore we can hold it up to a world striving for guidance, as one of the most shining examples in history of spiritual greatness within physical smallness and as the most vital and convincing refutation of the assertion that the fundamental problems of mass civilization, of democracy and of the moral crisis of the West are insoluble. It is true, Switzerland is an exception in the sense that everything in history that is almost wholly successful is an exception, but not in the sense that it does not encourage general and whole-hearted emulation as something approaching the ideal. As the common enterprise of freedom-loving peasants and burghers, it has offered the world a living example of the harmonious integration of peasant and city culture, and from this synthesis it has drawn the strength to fuse society's conservative and progressive forces, to blend continuity and flexibility, tradition and modernity, reason and faith, technology and humanitarianism, valor and love of peace, order and freedom, community life and individuality, prosperity and

spirituality, into a well-balanced whole. Perhaps only by review-
ing the historical experiences gained through the ages and the
examples of most other countries—and not by concentrating on
every imperfection and mistake—can we fully appreciate that here,
in the heart of Europe, there is a country, alone among its kind,
which, thanks to its strength and its mountains, but thanks also
to a benevolent providence and the configurations of history—*Dei
providentia et confusione hominum*—has been able to grow to full
stature without the destructive admixture of socially poisonous
feudalism and comparatively free from that ancient sin of violence
and exploitation. It may be that only from such a point of vantage
can one gauge the total extent of the tragedy that would befall
us if, amid the deadly threats of the present world crisis, this
country were to lose the inward strength it needs for safeguarding
itself and its unique patrimony. The most essential elements of
that strength, however, are clarity of thought and sureness of
judgment, for not in vain is it said: *Quos perdere vult Deus,
dementat prius*—"whom the gods would destroy they first make
mad."

NOTES TO INTRODUCTION

*Note No. 1 (page 5). The overestimation of self-interest as a sociological
motive:*

It was indeed one of the cardinal sins of the past and typical of the
thoroughly inadequate psychology of the democratic-liberal world, that one
thought mainly in terms of economic interests and the social groupings they
create, and believed that they embody a sociological motivating force so
important that it must be brought into play if anything is to be achieved.
Notwithstanding their otherwise divergent aims Marxism and Liberalism
were in complete agreement on this as on other fundamental points, which
explains their simultaneous downfall. We are here dealing with one of
the many forms of overestimation of the purely economic—"economism," as
we call it—which was so characteristic of the entire nineteenth century. It
was a highly imperfect form of sociology and bound to result in catastrophe
in the field of political tactics, too; its failure has, during the last years,
become particularly apparent in the prognoses—advanced with great self-
assurance—that the totalitarian countries were going to collapse for economic
reasons, prognoses which have consistently turned out to be false. Such a
system of ideas could tempt one to agree with the liberals that a free competitive economy could be sustained by each individual's self-interest; or, with
the Marxists, that the class interests of the masses could be mobilized in
behalf of a new society. These ideas are the basis of the materialist view of
history; they have led to that unrealistic disregard of the daemonic quality
of naked political power and they are also responsible for the fallacious
theory that society's gravest crises—revolutions and wars—should be attributed
to economic causes (the theory of economic imperialism). In short, our own
rationalism was thought to be the hub of the universe. The truth is of

course, that man lives not by bread alone but that, regardless of his economic position, he is also moved by wholly elementary and over-powering passions and emotional complexes, which cut across all strata, classes and group-interests. All this had long been known to conservative political scientists but it was undeniably totalitarian collectivism that first made such ruthless and overwhelmingly successful use of that knowledge for its own purposes. Collectivism has proved that men can be controlled and moved not only by promises but even more by demands on and appeals to their capacity for sacrifice and devotion. It has also shown what tremendous forces can be released by altruism, enthusiasm and the struggle for a supra-personal goal, and the rest of the world has by no means yet drawn all the conclusions and learned all the lessons from this discovery.

Note No. 2 (page 7). Enlightment, liberalism, humanitarianism and democratism seen as the secularization of the Christian heritage:

While formerly these movements were looked upon as secularizing in the sense that they were emancipatory movements directed against Christianity (a classical example is W. E. H. Lecky's *The Rise and Influence of the Spirit of Rationalism in Europe*, London, 1865), we know today that this is only apparently so. In reality important elements of Christian concepts continue to act as strong ferments within these movements, only they do it underground and cut off from their source. Here reference should be made to the particularly thorough and well-informed work of the English Catholic historian Christopher Dawson, *Progress and Religion*. The literature available on this subject has become so extensive that we must limit ourselves to mentioning the important work done by Max Weber (*Gesammelte Aufsätze zur Religions-soziologie*, I, Tübingen, 1920), Ernst Tröltsch (*Die Soziallehren der christlichen Kirchen*, Tübingen, 1923), G. v. Schulze-Gävernitz (*Die geistes-geschichtlichen Grundlagen der anglo-amerikanischen Weltsuprematie*, Archiv für Sozialwissenschaft, vols. 56 and 58, 1926-1927); A. Rüstow (*Das Vervowjen des Wirtschafts liberalismus als religionsgeschichtliches Problem*, Zürich-New York, 1945). Regarding in particular the influence of Calvinism and the Protestant sectarian movement (as opposed to Lutheranism which had quite different effects), it is well-known, since G. Jellinek wrote his pioneer work *Die Erklärung der Menschen- und Bürgerrechte*, 3rd edition, 1919), how close is the connection between Christianity and the basis of political liberalism and humanism. Another book that can now be conveniently consulted on this subject is Fritz Ernst's excellent *Die Sendung des Kleinstaats* (Zürich, 1940, pp. 35-57). For some qualifications see: W. Röpke, *Civitas Humana*, 3rd edition, pp. 192-194. Many useful suggestions and references can also be found in H. Plessner's book *Das Schicksal deutschen Geistes im Ausgang seiner bürgerlichen Epoche* (Zürich, 1935).

Note No. 3 (page 7). The drain on spiritual and moral reserves has been greater in some countries than in others:

One of our most urgent tasks is a thorough investigation of each country's spiritual and moral resources, as well as of the reasons why some have been able to withstand the universally disintegrating effects of mass civilization so much better than others. Considered under this aspect each of the main countries presents a separate problem, first of all Germany (cf., W. Röpke, *The Solution of the German Problem*, New York, 1948); then France (L. Romier, *Explication de notre temps*, Paris, 1925; J. Giraudoux, *Pleins Pouvoirs*, Paris, 1939; Henri Massis, *Les idées restent*, Lyons, 1941); then Italy (Carlo Sforza, *The Real Italians*, New York, 1942); England (Ernest Barker, *National Character and the Factors in its Formation*, London, 1939; Léo Ferrero, *Le secret de l'Angleterre*, Geneva, 1941); and finally the United

States (Eduard Baumgarten, *Die geistigen Grundlagen des amerikanischen Gemeinwesens*, Frankfurt a.M., 1936; B. Fay, *Civilisation Américaine*, Paris, 1939). As summaries: E. Halévy, C. Bouglé and others, *Inventaires. La crise sociale et les idéologies nationales*, Paris, 1936; Hans Zbinden, *Die Moralkrise des Abendlandes*, 2nd edition, Berne, 1941.

Note No. 4 (page 8). The exaggerated cult of youth:

It has been left to our time (the "Century of the Child," as it has been called with involuntary humor), to reverse the natural relationship between the age groups to an almost unprecedented degree, a tendency only parallelled by the equally frantic attempts at transposing the relationship between the sexes. More than anything else, this boundless overestimation of youth and the corresponding devaluation of age, throws a revealing light on the contemporary crisis and the inversion of status and rank, because it is evident that they are most intimately tied up with the dynamic-activist nihilism of values, with discontinuity and the frittering away of the cultural patrimony, with disrespect; spiritual collectivization, &c. Everyone can probably tell from personal experience of the strikingly great proportion of the younger generation which does not know its place in the presence of its elders and assumes a studiously rude manner especially if the latter are deserving of particular respect, or even gratitude. A world that has lost its instinct for these elementary principles must indeed be thoroughly out of joint. The neurosis of youthfulness, however, amounts fundamentally to nothing but a disingenuous self-deception, which is perpetuated against one's better judgment, and which will sooner or later provoke a reaction. This reaction will coincide with the rediscovery of the eternal human values and order of precedence and with a welcome release from the tension·of the empty frenzy of dynamism. Then it will once more be admitted that different things befit youth and age, that "gaudeamus igitur" simply corresponds to a state of alcoholic and erotic intoxication, which may abruptly terminate in suicide—so frequent among adolescents; that the effervescence of feeling and being young is usually coupled with a lack of equilibrium, with vagueness, aimlessness and the inner crises of the young; and that the decrease of physical vitality in old age is commonly balanced by proper adjustment, a knowledge of life's truths and a feeling of happy serenity. I wonder how many would, from their own experience, agree with Edgar Quinet when he says: "Je vous étonnerais, en vous disant que l'âge ou j'ai le plus souffert, celui ou j'ai le plus senti le fardeau de l'existence, le seul où j'ai désiré la mort, a été la jeunesse. . . . Quand la vieillesse est arrivée, je l'ai trouvée incomparablement moins amère que vous me prétendiez. . . . Je m'attendais à une cime glacée, déserte, étroite, noyée dans la brume; j'ai aperçu, au contraire, autour de moi, un vaste horizon qui·ne s'etait encore jamais découvert à mes yeux. Ce n'était plus cette attente désespérée d'une clarté qui me fuyait. Dans ma longue route, j'avais recueilli quelques vérités qui, chaque jour, devenaient plus certaines. Elles étaient pour moi comme le fruit de la vie." (*L'esprit nouveau*, Paris, 1874, pages 309-313). It is also obvious that the "confusion de la volupté et de la mort" (Massis), characteristic of youth, is one of the most important elements of war, because an aggressive war can only be waged with young people.

One would thoroughly misunderstand the foregoing if one took it to mean that age, from its temporal vantage-point, were putting high-spirited youth in its place. On the contrary, this lamentable confusion is, as always, primarily the fault of the older generation, and this is also proved by their frantic attempts either to put themselves on a level with youth or peevishly to defend their position of authority in which at heart no one really believes any longer. It is they, in fact, who were the first to lose all feeling for what is proper for each age group; it is their fault if this break in continuity has taken place; it is they, who have succeeded in creating "the problem of youth," because they no longer know what to do with the young and because they only too often left unsatisfied and unused that natural readiness for self-sacrifice and devotion which is youth's happy privilege, allowing it to be forced into the most dangerous channels. It is very symptomatic that the cult of youth and the disparagement of age was a striking characteristic even of the French Revolution and since then every revolution has invariably been accompanied by paeans to youth. It should also be noted that this absurd revaluation of the age groups is most closely linked to the positivist-scientific myth of progress, according to which the younger generation, being the "more progressive," may, naturally, look down upon the older. Cf. the following more recent publications: A. L. Vischer, *Old Age, its Compensations and Rewards,* London, 1947; J. Ortega y Gasset, *Toward a Philosophy of History,* New York, 1941, pp. 24-40.

Max Picard's beautiful book *Die Flucht vor Gott,* Erlenbach-Zürich, 2nd edition, 1935, should also be consulted for its discussion of the inner restlessness of modern man.

Note No. 5 (page 8). The decadence of positivist science:

Concerning this exceedingly important cause of our world crisis, there still exist too many misconceptions to which even eminent scholars have fallen victim. They are due to the naive assumption that value judgments are unscientific and bound to lead to the justly feared politicalization of science. Science, it is true, was born when the ancient Ionian philosophers, in opposition to oriental theology, established the axiom that science is autonomous, i.e., in its search for truth it is subject only to the conscience of the scholar as the highest court of appeal, and quite independent of the heteronomous authority of secular or clerical bodies. Galilei's "eppur si muove" will for ever remain a wonderful symbol for this, and everything else is a betrayal of science, "trahison des clercs" (J. Benda). However, this autonomy by which science is defined can never mean the abandonment of all premises, as was naively believed at one time. Absence of premises in the sense of complete independence of the scientist from subjective conditions has long been recognized as an illusion or even as an absurdity, since everyone cannot but look through his own eyes, is circumscribed in his perspective by place and time, possesses his own inner experience and certain concepts of value, some of which are general and others more subjective, and all we ask is that he should not deceive himself or others regarding these subjective conditions. But this does not make science heteronomous. I may, e.g., for perfectly legitimate scientific reasons hold peasant agriculture to be essential for the good of society, although I may also be influenced by certain judgments of value and by rudimentary scientific theories, so that my thesis is anything but without premise. It is, however, something entirely different if I am deprived of my professorship in one country because I hold this theory, and in the other, because I attack it. This would automatically put an end to autonomy in science and therefore also to science itself. Exigencies of space do not allow us to prove here how qualitative judgments are in certain cases not only scientifically legitimate but also urgently required (cf. Wilhelm Röpke, *Civitas Humana,* 3rd edition, Erlenbach-Zürich, 1949, pp. 151-161). In his valuable book, *Uber die Rechtsethik des Schweizerischen Zivilgesetzbuches* (Zürich, 1939), August Egger has made out an impressive case against the particularly disastrous effects of positivism in legal science. That it is possible to make objectively valid judgments is also proved by the increasing unanimity of successive centuries regarding the truly immortal works of literature. Today Shakespeare's classic status is as undisputed as is the mediocrity of his playwright contemporaries. There is such a thing as a *consensus saeculorum.*

Note No. 6 (page 9). The treason of the privileged classes—lack of moral backbone:

Present day experience suggests that it might be worth our while to trace the historical role of the corrosive and treasonable influence of a materialistic, spiritually decadent patrician class worried about its possessions and social privileges—an influence called "moderate" by its advocates, though beyond question deplorable—and to assemble the findings in a uniform sociological picture; one might also study in conjunction with this the sociology of an intellectual leadership frightened of losing its material and spiritual position. If we recall the Athenian "appeasers," against whom Demosthenes pitted his oratory, or the intrigues in which the Carthaginian patricians, led by Hanno, indulged against Hannibal, who was prevented from fully exploiting his victories by a clear instance of armament sabotage, or the Prussian Junkers who after 1806 declared that they preferred a defeat like Jena to an agrarian reform—if we go back over these and many other examples, we are amazed by the monotony with which the same situation has repeated itself up to the present day. Contemporary instances of the opposite kind of conduct should, of course, likewise be viewed in juxtaposition with their historical counterparts. Perhaps the most moving and at the present time most inspiring document of this nature is Thucydides' description (*History of the Peloponnesian War,* chapter V) of the conduct of the inhabitants of Melos. The arguments of these undaunted people in their fight against Athenian imperialism have not lost any of their force and freshness even today, and the fact that among them, too, a "fifth column" was at work enhances their actuality.

The history of all conquests proves, moreover, that internal weakness on the part of a subjugated people has always been at least as important as the strength and skill of the victors. That is true of Alexander's conquest of Greece not less than of the triumphal advance of Islam; it is as true of the Ottoman and Napoleonic expansion as of all their historical parallels. Today it may be presumed to be common knowledge among students of history that the invasions of the numerically weak Germans would not have destroyed the Roman Empire if it had not already been rotten to the core.

Note No. 7 (page 10). Spiritual collectivization, lowering of intellectual standards and destruction of the intellectual hierarchy:

This inexhaustible subject can be further illuminated, firstly by a glance at the level of the popular newspapers in most countries and the corresponding low intellectual and moral level of all mass entertainments and mass movements; secondly, by the revealing question of who were in the past and who are today the true popular heroes and celebrities; and thirdly, by reference to the sociology of language.

The symptoms of spiritual collectivization in a people's language deserve indeed much more attention than has been accorded to them so far. It even appears to be a completely unexplored field of research, owing, of course, to the fact that the sociological elucidation of the phenomenon of spiritual collectivization is of very recent date. (A pioneer contribution is probably Weinbender's treatise in volume 8 of the journal "Osteuropa," on the development of language in Soviet Russia, to which Professor A. Debrunner in Berne has kindly drawn my attention.) Of course, the sagacious Nietzsche had anticipated something like this (*Fröhliche Wissenschaft,* Aphorism No. 104). This condition refers not only to the tendency to level off all differences in dialect and to centralize even language, but also to the intellectualizing process, arising from the intellectual ambitions of the half-educated, which is peculiar to spiritual collectivization. The admirable W. H. Riehl (*Die bürgerliche Gesellschaft*, 6th edition, Stuttgart, 1866, p. 334 ff.) described the "rogue," who "found it hard enough to unlearn the live views and blunt and earthy language of the social class in which he had grown up in order to exchange them for alien and well-bred phrases." But: "In the speech and ideas of the peasants there shines the old and hardy natural strength of our language, in the speech of the burgher the richness and variety of its vigorous growth, in the abstract, tidy and fashionably smoothed phrases of the 'educated' elite we meet it in its emasculated senility." No one who has followed the development of the German language during the last century and particularly during the past twenty years can ignore the tell-tale symptoms of spiritual collectivization which become apparent in the continually increasing spread of a dry-as-dust, uniform, pretentious, snooty and semi-educated herd language permeated with stereotyped and artificial neologisms. In it we can sense the mental and social environment of those who speak or write it. (Here I must again thank Professor A. Debrunner for pointing out that similar phenomena—such as pompous phrases corresponding to the German "unter Beweis stellen"—were also known in the Hellenistic era and in Byzantine Greek.) This spiritual collectivization of the language is, however, not only characterized by continuous repudiation of the organic linguistic heritage of peasant and regional origin, and by a progressive substitution of concrete speech forms by dry and abstract forms, but also by a coarsening of the sense of language and a shockingly blunted feeling for the laws of the mother tongue as well as of logic in general. Today not only have we assumed language and speech of the culture-glutted megapolitan mass man, but also we are in a hurry, want to create an impression, want to intimidate, to soft-soap others, and just as the musical hit is supplanting the folk song, the brash and ephemeral slang of the cities is displacing dialects.

Note No. 8 (page 10). The sociological phenomenon of spiritual collectivization:

We are well aware that what we have said in this chapter is in need of further elucidation and definition. But at this point we must be content with listing the following more important works among the very extensive literature on this subject: L. Romier, *Explication de notre temps*, Paris, 1925; Ortega y Gasset, *The Revolt of the Masses*; Karl Jaspers, *Die geistige Situation der Zeit*, Leipzig, 1932; Walter Lippmann, *An Inquiry into the Principles of the Good Society*, Boston, 1937, London, 1938; La foule, 4e semaine internationale de synthèse, Paris, 1934; N. Berdiajew, *The Fate of Man in the Modern World*, London, 1935; K. Heiden, *Europäisches Schicksal*, Amsterdam, 1937; J. Huizinga, *In the Shadow of Tomorrow*, London, 1936; C. Dawson, *Progress and Religion*, C.-F. Ramuz, *Questions*, Paris, 1936; Kurt Baschwitz, *Du und die Masse*, Amsterdam, 1937. Louis Bromfield's autobiographical novel, *The Farm*, also deserves mention here as it surpasses many sociological treatises in insight. A valuable pointer that spiritual collectivization meets with far greater obstacles in small countries, is to be found in Fritz Ernst's book *Die Sendung des Kleinstaats*, Zürich, 1940. For the rest see my own book *Civitas Humana, supra,* and English edition, London, 1948.

Note No. 9 (page 14). Population increase and spiritual collectivization:

That the invasion of our civilization by the "masses," similar to a landslide burying cultivated land, is in the first place and in an almost tangible manner the result of the colossal increase in population, should be self-evident. In whatever direction we trace the course of spiritual collectivization, we come up against this vexatious relationship. It is obvious how much the increase in population is responsible for the changes in the economic and social structure, which in the form of proletarization, mechanization, urbanization, mammoth industries, &c., have destroyed the structure of our society. But even the spiritual and moral crisis, the "interregnum," cannot be understood if we fail to appreciate that the population increase has made continuity in cultural traditions as well as cultural assimilation of the coming generations more and more difficult (cf., e.g., Marcel Dutheil, *La population allemande*, Paris, 1937). These long-term sociological effects of the population increase far surpass in importance all other aspects of the population problem. It is all the more surprising, then, that they, in particular, find so little mention in the literature dealing with this problem, that it is almost impossible to give any references. Apart from the above mentioned books by Ortega y Gasset, Romier and Heiden, we refer to W. Röpke, *Die Lehre von der Wirtschaft*, 5th edition, Erlenbach-Zürich, 1949, pp. 80-94.

Note No. 10 *(page* 16*). The decay of the family:*

An excellent and concise characterization of this very extensive problem, is offered by the American sociologist, F. H. Giddings (*The Principles of Sociology*, 3rd edition, London, 1924, p. 352). He divides the development of the family into three stages. Regarding these he says: "To perpetuate a patrimony and a faith, the religious-proprietary family sacrificed the inclination of individuals. To gratify the amatory preferences of individuals, the romantic family has sacrificed patrimony and tradition; of late, it has even gone to the extremity of sacrificing children. The ethical family sacrifices individual feelings only when they conflict with right reason or moral obligation, but then it sacrifices them without hesitation. It regards a genuine love as the most sacred thing in the world except duty, but duty it places first, and in the list of imperative duties it includes the bearing and right training of children by the vigorous and intelligent portion of the population." Here, too, we find that the solution is found in a "Third Way."

Note No. 11 *(page* 16*). Artificiality as a symptom of spiritual collectivization:*

Our present mode of life has by now become so natural to us that we can hardly imagine it different, let alone realize how exceptional and artificial in its most important respects, is this way of life which mass civilization has forced upon us, as against what has been normal in history. That is true even of such an innocent institution as the vacationing habit of the modern city dweller (the peasant or farmer knows no "vacations"!), "this leisure-ideal of an over-worked century" (Nietzsche, *Morgenröte*, 178). A social history of vacations remains yet to be written, but even without it we know that this succession of an unnatural working life and hardly less unnatural leisure periods is, as a mass phenomenon, a stupendous novelty, to say nothing of the unnatural fact that even during our vacations our conscience is still wrapped up in work, attempting to justify them as an opportunity to "recover" our strength, i.e., using them as mere means to an end, the end being further work. Our forefathers had no exhausting and vitally unsatisfying work to perform and also knew better than we what to do with their free evenings and their Sundays. Their life was a harmonious whole of work and leisure, while we place one after the other. But each one of us knows only too well which is the happier and more normal way of life.

Until recently the city dweller's vacations were a consequence—necessary for reasons of health and a balanced life—of mass living, but just lately collectivization extended its domain to include vacations, too, not by enabling larger sections of the population to enjoy them (which one certainly would not begrudge), but by putting even on vacations the stamp of a mass enterprise: even here the individual is not allowed to find himself. A climax in this development seems to be the installation of ski-lifts, whereby the principle of the conveyor belt has been transferred from the factory to the winter sport resort.

Note No. 12 (*page* 26). *The paradigm of Switzerland:*

In this context the following should be consulted among many others: Fritz Fleiner, *Tradition, Dogma, Entwicklung als aufbauende Kräfte der schweizerischen Demokratie,* Zürich, 1933; Werner Naef, *Die Schweiz im europäischen Umbruch,* Neue Schweizer Rundschau, March, 1941; Emil Duerr, *Urbanität und Bauerntum in der Schweiz,* Die Schweizerische Jahrbuch der Neuen Helvetischen Gesellschaft, 1934, pp. 140-182.

B

PART ONE

INTERPRETATION AND INVENTORY

CHAPTER I

SEED AND HARVEST OF TWO CENTURIES

Nothing is sadder to behold than the inconsequent striving for the Unconditional in this wholly conditional world.
—GOETHE, *Maxims and Reflections.*

The Two Revolutions

THE present world crisis is the result of a spiritual and political development which, originating in the Renaissance, yet growing more pronounced only in the course of the last two centuries—the eighteenth and nineteenth—has finally led to the situation in which we find ourselves today. This fateful period was marked by a plenitude of changes in the intellectual, spiritual and physical world, culminating in two events both of which are equally unique: the political and the economic revolution. All the intellectual currents of modern times converge in them and at the same time they are the fountain head of all our present-day problems. Together they amount to an upheaval more gigantic than any that has occurred within our purview of history. They have created the world as it confronts us today and if we want to solve the problems posed by it we must examine and substantiate our point of view regarding these two revolutions. In doing so, we shall at the same time gain an opportunity of unrolling all the problematic aspects of both these centuries and of realizing at which point the course of events took a fatal turn.

The two revolutions, the political as well as the economic, are, for obvious reasons, very closely interlocked; their common breeding ground is the sociological climate as developed by the modern movement for intellectual emancipation—from the Renaissance via the humanists, the Reformation, rationalism, individualism and liberalism down to the present civilization of the West. Both also have this in common, that the generation of our day tends to judge them from the extremist's point of view, meting out unqualified praise or, and this has become increasingly frequent, equally unmodified criticism. It will be our task to replace this crudely extremist view by a more discerning and analytical attitude and to divide the good from the bad.

Turning our attention first to the political revolution (in its widest sense, that is, not confining ourselves to the actual event of the French Revolution), we shall find that everyone is conversant with the two extremist views on it. The one side embraces spirit and content with unquestioning fervor; it readily brands any qualification and criticism as "reactionary" and is inclined to see in the counter movement which has been apparent for a considerable time, nothing but malice and stupidity. In its eyes the Ancien Régime, to say nothing of the Middle Ages, is as manifestly black as what succeeds them is radiantly white. On the other hand, its extreme opponents, who today hold the field, adhere with equally dogmatic fervour to the view that the political revolution produced nothing but ruin and—this is important—that this was its inevitable outcome, since its essence is damnable apostasy and ruination. While the first faction is turning a deaf ear to all criticism of the political revolution, the latter is equally deaf to any reference to the great things which the revolution set out to achieve with such sublime enthusiasm and which, to a not inconsiderable degree, it did achieve. What was black there, appears here as white, and not a few are already talking with a sigh of relief of the "new middle ages" which are reportedly about to replace our dissolute times.

We refuse point blank to limit our choice to these two extremes, the doctrinaire radicals and the equally fervent doctrinaires of reaction, and in our search for a third point of view we shall concern ourselves first and foremost with discovering the role of this political revolution in the context of world history. There can only be one answer: the Western political revolution of the last two centuries—in which the French Revolution played the most radical and dramatic part—represented, by unfurling the flag of democracy and liberalism, the most comprehensive and gigantic, the most deliberate and enduring attempt so far undertaken by mankind to stamp out the ever-recurring original sin of force and oppression in all their social, political, spiritual and economic manifestations—that original sin which, as we know, was brought thousands of years ago by the first highly developed civilizations and organized states into the peaceful world of the primitive and undifferentiated cultures and which has constituted what we term feudalism, absolutism, imperialism, monopolism, exploitation, the class state, war and lastly "mediævalism." During this immeasurable time magnificent attacks, whose repercussions can still be felt today, have repeatedly been mounted against the absolute state in an attempt to deliver man from the political and spiritual fetters fastened on him: first and foremost by the Ionic Greeks whose exciting genius laid amid remarkable circumstances the foundations for everything we call European civilization. Again and again "Middle Ages" have given birth to a "Renaissance" and a "Modern Age," and without these we could not conceive even of those elements of culture which the reactionary is as loath to miss as anyone else—the absence of which would, in fact, lead to his intellectual insolvency. Thus it is sheer intellectual mulishness as well as inexcusable ignorance, to divest the political revolution of

the laurels of a freedom movement the like of which the world
had not witnessed until then, a movement directed towards a goal
which all right thinking and enlightened men have pursued in
every age with equal vigour and to deny which would be tanta-
mount to the fatuous denial of the elementary fact of our humanity.

It is only natural that the cruel disappointments of the political
revolution loom larger in the eyes of people, many of whom have
personal experience of them, than the intolerable yoke cast off by
our ancestors. Perhaps it is not altogether surprising that there are
a number of people—by now possibly again on the decrease—whose
sensibilities have been so blunted by these disappointments as to
make them deaf to the noble pathos of the immortal lines which
Schiller in the ripe wisdom of his years puts into Stauffacher's
mouth:

> When the oppress'd looks round in vain for justice
> When his sore burden may no more be borne
> With fearless hand he reaches up to Heaven
> And thence brings down his everlasting rights
> Which there abide, inalienably his,
> And indestructible as are the stars.

All the more, then, must we insist on rekindling the memory of
that pre-revolutionary era with its abuse of power, its arbitrariness
and oppression, its exploitation and humiliation of the masses held
in subjection by State, Nobility and Patriciate: that time of the
enslavement of the peasantry in large parts of Europe and its exter-
mination in England, of the cruel suppression of every free and
daring thought, of the enthrallment of the middle classes in the
small German states, of class justice and class taxation and the most
brazen-faced enrichment, of the trading and ill-usage of soldiers
and the harsh laws of war, of the negro slave trade and the inhuman
cruelties of colonization overseas. In order to prompt our dulled
imagination, we add that in the eighteenth century with all its
vigorous intellectual ferment a Margrave of Ansbach could still
display his marksmanship to his mistress by shooting a tiler from
the castle tower for the sheer fun of it and then most graciously
hand his widow a florin; a Duke of Mecklenburg could command
the Privy Councillor von Wolfrath to be put to death in order to
make his widow the ducal mistress; and a Prince of Nassau-Siegen
was able to deal with a peasant in the same fashion just to prove
that it was within his power; and in Swabia a lawyer could be
beheaded because he had quoted Voltaire in a tavern.

No, we shall certainly not let our disappointment over the fruits
of the political revolution be used to persuade us that those were
better times, times of an idyllic patriarchalism, and thus allow our
sense of what is due to man to be confused. All our lost illusions
notwithstanding we shall persist in bluntly describing such efforts as

reactionary obscurantism and we shall do this all the more emphatically as otherwise our criticism of the political revolution might induce the dull-witted to suspect the self-same attitude in us. Although we may find that it is precisely the avowed counter-revolutionary literature that contains valuable criticism and although we should freely make use of it, we nevertheless know what to think of its unblushing attempts to make palatable the downright evil aspects of dominion and power. When studying this literature in its entirety—starting with J. de Maistre and Karl Ludwig von Haller down to the present—even the most sceptical should know where to draw the line, and though Shakespeare himself in *Coriolanus* poetically glorifies the principle of feudal power, we should still be on our guard.

It was Louis de Bonald, one of those eminent counter-revolutionaries of the French Restoration, who said among many other wise things that "depuis l'évangile jusqu'au Contrat Social ce sont les livres qui ont fait les révolutions," that literature is the expression of the society of today and creates that of tomorrow and that ideas are the true masters of this world. We subscribe to every word of this view, but would add that the mind is the ultimate and indispensable basis not only of revolutions, but also of the tyrannies which they bring down. Since they cannot rely on naked force alone, they require for their existence an uncritically accepted system of ideas (an "ideology") which, extending subjugation to the soul, turns the oppressed into the willing subjects and accessories of their rulers. "La servitude abaisse les hommes jusqu'à s'en faire aimer" (Vauvenargues), and not until it has achieved this—this "servitude volontaire" with which already in the sixteenth century La Boétie concerns himself in a treatise bearing this title and relevant even today—has it brought about the deepest degradation of man and at the same time, its own security. Since, however, concept and practice of tyranny are diametrically opposed to the workings of the sane mind, every ideology of force must make a strong point of confusing minds. Every liberation must in consequence begin with that of the mind and in the process make use of the critical faculties and, accordingly, tyrannies are right in seeing in the free exercise of the mind their worst and, in the long run, invincible foe. Hence the alliance of every emancipatory movement with rationalism, which becomes also an alliance—for obvious reasons particularly pronounced in the liberation movements of modern times—with the shortcomings of rationalism gone astray. These were the final cause of the failure of the political revolution which we shall have to study in more detail later on. It is these aberrations of a rationalism inestimable in itself which must be held in equal measure responsible for the ultimate débâcle of the political as well as the economic revolution.

The world would not be in its present hopeless state, nor would this book ever have been written if the errors of rationalism—more fatal than all misguided passions—had not caused all the great and promising beginnings of the eighteenth century to end in a gigantic catastrophe of which we can still feel the effects: the French Revolution. This monumental and glorious century gave us music which promises to remain for thousands of years what the Parthenon is to us in architecture, it gave us Lessing, Goethe, Schiller, Herder, Montesquieu, Vico, and Kant, and in the domain of politics it produced a piece of work so mature and enduring as the American Constitution—yet in 1789 it ended in a tragedy which marked the beginning of a world crisis lasting until this day; and it is this date which for many has sullied the memory of the eighteenth century to an extent that blinds them to its true greatness and its yet unfulfilled promises.

How then are we to assess the French Revolution and its vast and incalculable consequences? It is precisely this question on which popular opinion has for too long been highly confused and divided in a manner which has muddled all our political thinking and it seems that we are only now able to see somewhat more clearly. For an entire century two views remained sharply opposed to each other, one lauding the event as liberation, the other condemning it as disintegration. Only in our day has this conflict been settled by the more profound realization that the French Revolution itself was a dichotomous event exhibiting that ambivalence characteristic of so much that is problematic. It is precisely this which constitutes the tragedy whose repercussions we can still feel. The revolution was at one and the same time liberation and disintegration and a malevolent fate would have it that it could not be the one without the other, that, indeed, political liberalism was unable even to recognize this innate defect. It was not only a stirring drama enacted on the great stage of the world, fit to enthrall the romantically inclined; it was also an emancipation movement in the face of whose superlative élan at first only the most hardboiled reactionaries managed to keep their heads. As such it has created the Europe which today has to get ready for the last stand because it is saddled with such an evil heritage. It has turned France itself into a land of peasants and bourgeois and it has cast its seeds over every country that calls itself European. The "ideas of 1789" have created the life-giving air which all of us—including the most envenomed of counter-revolutionaries—still breathe. All this is true, and yet the revolution was a catastrophe. Let us see in what sense.

To begin with, it cannot be stressed too strongly in the face of all revolutionary romanticism that every revolution is a real misfortune. It is a cataclysmal crisis of society whose eventual outcome is never certain and whose highly pathological character is discernible even in its outward forms. It is a potentially fatal paralysis of society; it is anarchy, dissolution of order, destruction, it is the primeval battle of passions and instincts, and nothing is clearer proof of this than the fact that if not stayed in time (a vain attempt was made to stay the French Revolution), it tends to cast up the dregs of the people and subjects men to the temporary rule of notorious neurotics. No amount of hero-worship and romanticising can alter this, not even in the case of the French Revolution which is particularly conducive to such attitudes.

But it is when we look at its works that the French Revolution seems especially catastrophic. The pre-revolutionary period (the Middle Ages and the Ancien Régime, which strikes us as a degenerated form of the Middle Ages), had been no less ambivalent than the French Revolution. While we must firmly keep in mind the mediaeval character of sovereignty in those times, we should not forget that it was a society with a real structure in which men appear to be hierarchically integrated and embedded in a true community, and if we look at the crowning glory of the Middle Ages, the period of the culture of the cities, it would seem to us as if it was in many ways a promising and exemplary era. Yet it was destroyed in the major part of Europe—particularly in Germany and France, though hardly at all in Switzerland—by a new victory of the power principle in the form of feudalism and absolutism. But even the Ancien Régime thus created had at least enjoyed the advantage of a life embedded in a united and organic society. It was the tragedy of the French Revolution that, afflicted by the sociological blindness of rationalism of which we shall treat later, it confused the evil in force with order, coherence, authority and hierarchy and was not capable of differentiating between aristocracy and the true élite, the "aristes"; that it believed that in abolishing the hierarchy of exploiters which at that point appeared as something intolerable to men, it had to do away with every kind of hierarchy; that it forgot that no society can exist without a hierarchy, i.e., without a vertical and horizontal structure; and that a social and economic system relying solely on freedom for its orderly existence, will succumb to disintegration and eventually to despotism, which in the last analysis is but organized anarchy. One might say that there was too much of Rousseau and Voltaire and too little of Montesquieu. The social hierarchy against which the Revolution rose was bad because it had largely degenerated into what was essentially an exploiters' hierarchy, but the revolutionaries were unable to distinguish between this historical form of a hierarchy and hierarchy as such, which is the indispensable ingredient in the establishment of any society. They did not know that there is such a thing as a functional hierarchy, that in fact such a hierarchy

is essential if society is to survive. The positive aspect of the Ancien
Régime, that is, the genuine structure of society, was destroyed,
and its negative aspect, i.e., the despotism of the state was maintained in an even more pronounced form. Order, internal
coherence, rules and norms, continuity, authority and hierarchy—
all these smacked of damnable reaction, but only because the forms
which these indispensable elements of order had assumed in the
eighteenth century were at the same time those of force and had
thus become unbearable. Here the critics of the revolution (the
Maistres, Bonalds, Burkes, Saint-Simons and all the others) had an
easy task, and the same lack of discrimination prompted them, in
good faith or bad, to commit the opposite mistake of presenting the
essential need for a functional hierarchy as the need for a feudal
and absolutist hierarchy of exploitation: an attempt to smuggle
back the old privileges in the name of sociology. It remains true,
nonetheless, that, produced by rationalist delusion, the very revolution which among other things transformed France into a country
of peasants, has become at the same time the source of that breakdown of society which we call spiritual collectivization as well as
the prelude of that process of disintegration whose epilogue is mass
civilization, nihilism and collectivism. And now we are faced
with the question of whether we shall at last succeed where they
failed: in the creation of "Eukosmia," the "City of Man," the
synthesis of freedom and order.

This revolution produced disintegration and spiritual collectivization which in their turn brought forth Napoleon—and of the effects
of his deeds we have not seen the last yet: among them Bismarck
and the seed he sowed. The evil's family tree is plainly manifest
and least of all must we be deceived by the person of Napoleon
which is so near to the heart of every romantic. We must not
allow our sound judgment to be confounded by the shameful
difference of standards between then and now, nor by the indisputable stature of Napoleon himself, nor by the liberal side of his
mission which he had taken over from the Janus-faced revolution
and which makes him such an ambiguous personality himself, nor
by any other consideration. We will have nothing to do with the
romantic Napoleon cult (the number of whose adherents has
presumably dwindled of late), and at best we look at Napoleon as
one of those "terribles simplificateurs" as J. Burckhardt called them,
who, like whirlwinds clearing the forests of dead wood, leave yet
nothing but ruin in their wake. The fact that he was at the same
time a man of great intellectual stature makes him all the more
dangerous, in that it renders the task of discovering his true nature
and of correctly fixing his place in history so enormously difficult
as to make even a man like Goethe spend some time over it. That
he was so remarkably successful in posing as the titan who was

hindered alone by the shortsighted powers of reaction in the fulfil ment of his mission of finally uniting and pacifying Europe, merely proves his ability as propagandist and the obtuseness of his dupes. Genghis Khan, too, had he been able to write, could have embellished his memoirs with a similar interpretation of his activities in Asia. Despite all evidence to the contrary, the sum of Napoleon's achievement is conquest and destruction of law and order, global chaos and usurpation, the consequences of which still weigh heavily on us today.

The great experiment of the French Revolution had indeed to come to a tragic end. In 1941 we can hardly be accused of exaggeration if we say that the world of 1789 has finally broken down and since the ideas of that year have spread across the entire globe, all countries are victims of that collapse to the extent to which they have followed the French example. However, the intellectual confusion implicit in this must be vigorously combatted. For it cannot be stated emphatically enough that the French Revolution presents nothing more than a special case, that, indeed, only the dishonest or ignorant can place the ideas of democracy and liberalism on a level with those of 1789. The only acceptable excuse for this view is the fact that the outstanding role played by France in the history of the European intellect constantly tempts us to look upon it as a model in the political field also and to ignore the almost overwhelming political and social problems of that country, which are possibly exceeded only by those of Germany. On no account must we forget that the pathological character of the French Revolution is matched by that of French absolutism and feudalism which it succeeded, and that for centuries French society had been in a state which could not but lead to this end the moment the appropriate intellectual ferment of the French enlightenment was added.

It is little short of tragic that a country which in the course of its own history had never been able to master the problem of establishing a tolerably healthy society and which is laboring at this task up to this day, could become the acknowledged model in the domain of politics. It has thereby compromised democratism and liberalism in a manner crying out for correction. All we have to do here is simply to point to the examples of healthy democracy for which we claim, in legal language, the right of exclusion from the bankrupt's estate of 1789; first of all, Switzerland, then the Nordic and Anglo-Saxon democracies, all of which are preserving their vitality because they represent an entirely different, older and far more organic branch of democracy and liberalism. On the other hand, these countries appear to be debilitated to the precise extent to which the errors of 1789 have caused them to lose faith in their traditions. The mere existence of these democracies stultifies any attempt to label democratism and liberalism the invention of 1789 and to obscure their true ancestry. They owe their origin not to the rationalist sophistries of philosophers and lawyers, but to peasants and commoners who fought for liberty since the early Middle Ages, resisting—like the unhappy Stedingers—the deadly encroachments of feudalism and absolutism and building up their state from base to top on a co-operative basis. The beginnings of Swiss democracy are marked by the co-operatives of the valleys and the communities of the Alpine peasants, and American democracy commences with the town meetings which eventually grew into the Union. The spirit of liberty stemming from these roots was cast by the Reformed Church into the forms of those human and civil rights which ultimately found their way from the democracies of New England to France.

The annals of democratism and liberalism contain dates which indeed surpass in importance the milestone of 1789: the Swiss Charter of Federation of 1291, the Magna Charta of 1215, the Swedish Common Law of Magnus Erikson (about 1350), the Petition of Rights of 1628, the Mayflower Compact of 1620, the Dutch Federation of 1579, the Declaration of Rights of 1688, the American Declaration of Independence of 1776, the American Constitution of 1788, as well as its famous amendments, the so-called Bill of Rights; and the Swiss Constitution of 1848 and 1874. But it is precisely the characteristic quality of these vigorous, organically integrated democracies that these dates represent nothing but the stages of a gradual growth and that nearly all these events took place without any of the drama of history. There is no trace of the operatic stage management, the new flags, the "new era" and the new calendar, but in their place we find that steadfastness and rooted strength which only slow and natural growth can produce. These original democracies are thus endowed with heightened powers of resistance in the present world crisis which is leaving its mark also on them.

*

The political revolution of the West which we have surveyed up to this point, may be termed a bourgeois revolution in as far as it could never have developed such breadth and momentum—however decisive the stimulus of the liberation struggle of a peasantry oppressed by feudalism—if it had not been able to draw support from the ever more powerful class of the commercial-industrial burgesses, i.e., the bourgeoisie. Since, however, this class is the product of that economic development which finally culminated in the economic revolution of the eighteenth and nineteenth centuries "Capitalism," it is a truism to say that the economic revolution has given a tremendous impetus to the political revolution. Yet the opposite is no less true, viz., that the political was godfather to the economic revolution, since it was the former which first created the conditions for the unhampered development of technology, for the division of labor and commercial interchange.   Only thus can we explain the late advent of the machine age, for the modern spirit had already demonstrated from the Renaissance down its bent and particular genius for the solution of technical problems. Born engineers there had been in abundance, but the restrictive guild constitutions of the Middle Ages and the Ancien Régime forced them to express their art in the by-ways of economic life, those devoted to the manufacture of fanciful toys and articles of worship, of fountains and magic clocks of matchless perfection, of musical instruments of almost inexhaustible diversity and of many other things—with the significant exception of mining whose special character had at an early date turned it into a field of technical experimentation free from guild regulations, up to the first installation of a steam engine and the first railway in an English mine. The early flowering of the watch and clock making industry is part of the same chapter as is the manufacture of astronomical and scientific precision instruments which in the nineteenth century still provided in many localities the basis for the development of the machine industry.

The accumulation through many centuries of unexploitable technical ideas accounts for the violent and in part destructive suddenness with which in the later part of the eighteenth and then in full force in the nineteenth century that economic revolution took place whose most striking feature is the employment of machinery. While the political revolution is unique merely in its intensity and boldness, the economic revolution leaves us altogether without precedents. That we have mechanized production, passed beyond the limits of organic nature, utilized steam power won from coal and the power generated by the internal combustion engine and by electricity —and witnessed in consequence the colossal increase in population, the technological revolution in communications and agriculture, the development of scientific chemistry, the economic interlocking of the entire globe and finally the conquest of the air—all this is so unquestionably unique as to divide us from all preceding millenia by an unbridgeable gulf.   Little wonder then that, facing the economic revolution helpless and without previous experience, we allowed it to follow a course which we know today to have been disastrous and which we are belatedly doing our best to right. And in the unconcern with which our forefathers entrusted their fate to the economic revolution and in the illusions by which they allowed themselves to be guided, we recognize the rationalist-scientific blindness in the face of the eternal laws of life, society and man, which we have already met with in the realm of politics.

It would be fatuous to deny the extraordinary progress towards an easier life and the increase in the material welfare of the masses which we owe to the economic revolution, and since this has irrevocably led to a tremendous rise in population, nobody can seriously wish to put the clock back to the previous stage of development. But this we may be permitted to say: today we are aware of the high price that had to be paid for it and that we will continue to have to pay, and we are by no means still certain that the price is not too high. We distrust the optimistic assertion that technology and the machine are completely innocent of all this and that the blame rests squarely on man alone who is using them in the wrong way and will just have to learn the right one. We know that there are limits to mechanization both of men and work, to the emancipation from nature and the division of labor, limits which cannot be overstepped without grievously impairing man's happiness and the soundness of the social fabric: in the end even ill-treated nature retaliates, e.g., against mechanized agriculture, with a continued deterioration of the soil. The problem of the machine—which happens to be something else than just a highly developed tool—is not merely one of its use, but also one of the machine itself, which, following its own laws and imposing them on man, extracts its tribute from him. To indulge in any illusions about this fact and to evade its conclusions would be feeble self-deception. These conclusions are two in number: we must first of all be prepared to consider seriously at which point the price for the increase in productivity is no longer balanced by its material advantages, and from that point forego further use of the machine; but even before we reach this stage we must, secondly, spare no efforts to discover new ways in the use of machines and the organization of industrial plants which will minimize their imperfections.

We have stressed the full gravity inherent in the problem of the machine, the division of labor and the rapid growth of population in order to combat the view that the universal disappointment amid which the economic as well as the political revolution has ended in our days, is alone or even in greater part due to the character of the political-social economic structure created by liberal-bourgeois society. The intrinsic danger of this view is revealed by the fact that it has played a decisive role in every collectivist revolution after the Russian Revolution of 1917. It is, however, precisely these revolutions which have confirmed the expectation that the replacement of the liberal economy by the collectivist one does not only leave those problems of production techniques, unsolved which are not tied up with the economic system, but that it intensifies them to an unheard of degree. The collectivist cure which not only retains the "capitalist" production technique, but carries mechanization to its utmost limits, can only aggravate the evil until it becomes no longer bearable. We may state this with all the greater emphasis as we make no secret of our opinion that—however firmly we should adhere to all the essentials of the liberal-bourgeois economic system—the economic liberalism of the last two centuries has disastrously gone astray in a manner fully paralleling the mistakes of political liberalism and ultimately stemming from the same source.

The Aberrations of Rationalism and Liberalism

Rationalism too, together with its offspring—political and economic liberalism—belongs to that class of things which should not be praised or condemned wholesale, but should be delimited and then confined to their proper sphere. If rationalism is so discredited today that even the word itself carries a disparaging note, this, as everyone knows, is obviously not only due to a transitory fashion in thought but chiefly to the fact that it suffered abuse in the past. How and in what respect?

A satisfactory answer must again be prefaced by proper definition. The term "rationalism" has come to mean three things which should be kept strictly separate. Rationalism may, first of all, mean comprehending the world by means of the critical intellect, searching for causes, reasons and motives. It may, secondly, mean that we attribute "rational" motives to the social process, i.e., that we identify the instrument which we use to observe the world with the world itself. Thirdly, rationalism may be understood as the endeavor to represent a particular political measure as the only rational one and to call for it in the name of reason. Today it is beyond dispute that the second type of rationalism is pure fiction and as such actually conducive to the most unadulterated irrationalism; it has found its most dogmatic and intellectually preposterous formulation in Hegel's system, but has also for too long infested political economy in the shape of the always rationally acting *homo oeconomicus*. The problem, therefore, is merely one of justifying and defining rationalism of the first and third types.

It is evident that the aberrations of this kind of rationalism cannot have consisted in a surfeit of intellect, which would amount to an invitation to despise "man's foremost power" and "turn the lamp of our reason so low that we are enveloped by a dim but cosy semi-darkness" (A. Rüstow). That happens to be the opinion of a fashionable movement of superficial irrationalists and anti-intellectuals, but it can certainly not be our view. No, abuse of the intellect in the negative sense of rationalism is only possible if the intellect is taxed beyond its capacity, if its nature, its limits and premises are ignored. That has in fact happened and even today we shall find that whenever we have to reject a mental attitude as rationalist, that particular error has been committed which we are going to describe as the blind infatuation with the Unconditional and Absolute. It is true that in the sphere of pure logic and mathematics reason is free and independent, following its own laws, but the error occurs precisely when this *a priori* method of thinking is applied to the realities of life and society, where the intellect is after all merely the judge who has to consider empirical facts and conditions. In the fields which concern us here, reason simply is not autonomous and unfettered, it does not exist in a vacuum, nor is it entitled to spread its wings, but is obliged to recognize the barriers and conditions set by the circumstances of our existence. Otherwise it becomes a threat to life and will bring about that self-obliterative hair-splitting which. we associate with the word "sophist." As soon as reason frees itself from these limits and peremptorily announces its independence, trouble ensues: such is the case of the ethical sophist who, proud of having used his reason to unmask justice as pure "ideology," arrogantly ignores the most certain thing in the world, man's moral compass, in brief, his conscience; such again is the case of the libertarian fanatic who, postulating absolute freedom, forgets that freedom without constraint will end in the worst kind of bondage; further, there is the apostle of equality who airily dismisses the brutal truth that the essence of life is inequality and variety; the same applies to the socialist who builds his ideal state without taking man's unalterable nature and the anthropologically vital character of property into account; it is likewise true of the liberal, who, desiring to turn competitive economy into a precision machine based entirely on men's rational behavior, forces working and living conditions upon them against which their nature finally rebels; into the same category falls the feminist, demanding complete equality with the male sex while remaining blind to the intriguing circumstance that the sexes were, after all, and not without reason, created different; and finally, there is the pacifist who interdicts war as something irrational, but does not, unfortunately, abolish it since he puts his faith in legal and organizational measures, and neglects the sociological background of wars. Our rationalist is always offending against Pascal's wise axiom: "L'homme n'est ni ange ni bête, et le malheur veut que qui veut faire l'ange fait la bête."

Although the liberating effects of rationalism have been so incalculably vast that European civilization cannot be imagined without it, it is yet undeniable that, viewed as a whole, i.e., seen with all its laudable exceptions and ultimately unsuccessful attempts at betterment, it has turned into the blind alley of the Unconditional and Absolute, thus preventing the great age of enlightenment from reaching full fruition. We lack sufficient space to describe the details of this development which began in the seventeenth century.

Only one thing must be stressed emphatically: the quantitative mode of thought, in terms of mathematics and the other natural sciences, whose chief founder was Descartes, was a decisive cause of the aberrations of rationalism, since this form of thinking necessarily blinds one against the facts and demands of life—life which means quality, structure and form. All the protests of Vico, Herder, the Scottish School, Rousseau, Burke, Hamann, the "Storm and Stress" and the Romantic movement notwithstanding—this development has led Western thought astray along a road which, in the nineteenth century, culminated in the "cult of the colossal," and it is our time that has been privileged to help the concepts of quality, of "function" and of "form" to regain their rightful place once more.

It is, above all, in the sphere of politics that we encounter the infatuation with the Unconditional and Absolute and all its catastrophic consequences, and here we remind the reader that Goethe's words at the head of this chapter were written after the experiences of the July Revolution of 1830. This infatuation is first of all demonstrated by blindness towards the structural laws of society, a blindness which encourages the belief that it is possible to organize society in accordance with rational postulates while disregarding the need for genuine communities, for a vertical structure, for authority and hierarchy. A rationalist republican will no more understand that a monarchy can be a superior form of government where it has really legitimate roots than he will be able to grasp how much federalism, the family or a sense of tradition, really mean to the health of the state. The democratic rationalist labors for democracy in its purest and most absolute form and when he has reached his goal, he is surprised by the distressing results, as were, for example, the creators of the Weimar Republic, the "freest constitution in the world," which finally ended in its complete reversal. One of the chief concomitants of this delusion is the framing of the liberal principle in such an absolute form that its enemies profit by it too, and are, in the name of freedom, given every conceivable opportunity to put an end to liberal democracy— as a French pamphleteer of the nineteenth century, Louis Veuillot, so trenchantly put it: "Quand je suis le plus faible, je vous demande la liberté parce que tel est votre principe; mais quand je suis le plus fort, je vous l'ôte, parce que tel est le mien." It is obvious that this absolute tolerance even towards intolerance, this intransigent dogmatism of the liberals, which gives a free hand to all trouble makers and agitators, thereby condemning itself to death with open eyes, must ultimately reduce "pure democracy" to the defenseless victim of anti-liberalism, to a sort of gambling club whose rules include their non-observance. It will always remain a riddle why it needed such very sad experiences to put an end to this delusion. Today

(1941, in Central Europe) we may say with Tacitus (*Vita Agricolae*, II): "Sicut vetus aetas vidit quid ultimum in libertate esset, ita nos quid in servitute, adempto per inquisitiones et loquendi audiendique commercio." It is entirely in keeping with this degeneration of democratism and liberalism through rationalism, that it was possible to maintain, in all seriousness, that lack of opinion and beliefs form the essence of democracy and liberalism, since otherwise they could not be tolerant. Where such a path can finally lead was demonstrated by a certain leader of the Democratic Party in Germany after the 1918 revolution, who, when asked about the program of his party, gave the priceless answer that it was in accordance with the principles of democracy to leave the program to the will of the people itself.

Not only in internal politics, but also in foreign affairs, rationalism has wrought far reaching destruction. Here we are, among other instances, struck by its inability to recognize the living values of nationhood in those under-currents whose discovery we owe to the romantics and their forerunners (Vico, Montesquieu and Herder). Hence the rationalist's incorrigible addiction to constructting states with the aid of maps and T-squares, his contempt for national differences of language and culture in general, and for the small states in particular, and finally also his inadequate understanding of Europe's national diversity, which already Montesquieu described so fittingly as a nation of nations. But once the rationalist has decided to appropriate the nationality principle he will not rest until he has succeeded in flogging it to death, after he has thoroughly discredited it by misuse.

If we are now to describe the evil influence of rationalism on the development of economic life, we encounter that form of economic liberalism whose aberrations, too, cannot be better characterized than by reference to the infatuation with the Unconditional and Absolute. The automatic regulation of a competitive market was certaintly a great discovery which we, who reject collectivism, would be the last to minimize. The glory of liberalism would indeed be unblemished if it had not also fallen victim to rationalism and thereby increasingly lost sight of the necessary sociological limits and conditions circumscribing a free market. It was seriously believed that a market economy based on competition represented a world of its own, an "order naturel," which had only to be freed from all interference in order to stand on its own feet. As it is miraculously directed by the "invisible hand" mentioned by Adam Smith, which in reality is nothing but the "divine reason" of deistic philosophy, men have only a negative duty towards it, namely, to remove all obstacles from its path—laissez faire, laissez passer. Thus the market economy was endowed with sociological autonomy and the non-economic prerequisites and conditions which must be fulfilled if it is to function properly, were ignored. It is typical of that period of enlightenment that what was in reality a highly fragile artificial product of civilization was held to be a natural growth. One was, therefore, basically inclined to acknowledge no bounds to economic freedom, and to range again into the Unconditional and Absolute, granting only grudgingly, and in moments of weakness, the concessions which stark reality finally demanded. One refused to see that a market economy needs a firm moral, political and institutional framework (a minimum standard of business ethics, a strong state, a sensible "market police," and well weighed laws appropriate to the economic system), if it was not to fail and at the same time destroy society as a whole by permitting the unbridled rule of vested interests. Historical liberalism (particularly the nineteenth century brand), never understood that competition is a dispensation, by no means harmless from a moral and sociological point of view; it has to be kept within bounds and watched if it is not to poison the body politic. One held, on the contrary, that a competitive market economy, based on division of labor, was an excellent moral academy, which, by appealing to their self-interest, encouraged men to be pacific and decent, as well as to practice all the other civic virtues. While we know today—what could always have been known—that competition reduces the moral stamina and therefore requires moral reserves outside the market economy; at that time they were deluded enough to believe that, on the contrary, it increases the moral stock.

On a par with this rationalist exaggeration of the competitive principle, based on the egoism of each individual, was the sociological blindness through which the individual was thought to be an isolated, atomized entity who could as such be made the basis of the economy; all the indispensable cohesive forces of the family and the natural social groups (the neighborhood, the parish, occupation, &c.), were considered irksome fetters. In this way that questionable form of individualism was evolved which in the end has proved to be a menace to society and has so discredited a fundamentally sound idea as to further the rise of the far more dangerous collectivism.

It was for the same reason that economic liberalism, true to its rationalist origin, exhibited a supreme disregard for the organic and anthropological conditions which must limit the development of capitalist industrialism unless a wholly unnatural form of existence is to be forced upon men. This spirit of historical liberalism, so alien to everything vital, is responsible for our monstrous industrial areas and giant cities, and even for that perversion in economic development which condemns millions to a life of frustration and has, above all, turned the proletariat into a problem which goes far beyond material considerations. Although the average liberal of that time never thought of looking upon the social question also (or even in the first place) as a problem of vitality, i.e., as a non-economic, spiritual problem posed by the industrial form of life, it would yet be unjust to accuse him of callous disregard for the material condition of the workers. It would also be wrong to assume that in the face of the general upheaval caused by the Industrial Revolution, of the proletarization of the peasantry in England and large parts of Germany, and of the rapid and vast increases in population, there was an even chance of immediate improvements in social conditions; and as regards the general attitude adopted by the liberals on this point, they silenced their conscience by an optimistic trust in the future. Only when, in the course of time, that trust began to wane, did that bad social conscience arise which in all its disguised forms has become characteristic of latter-day liberalism.

But let it be said that all these are only aberrations—however destructive—of liberalism, which we are anxious to separate from the healthy core: this is borne out by the fact that these errors were also typical, although often in different or diametrically opposed form, of contemporary socialism. In its rationalist infatuation the latter is indeed not a whit better than its opponent, in some respects it is, in fact, far worse. This is particularly true of a mental attitude common to both and springing from the same rationalism which, autocratically creating its own postulates, views the world entirely from the quantitative angle: "economism" we have called this attitude because it judges everything in relation to the economy and in terms of material productivity, making material and economic interests the center of things by deducing everything from them and subordinating everything to them as mere means to an end. Those who have become addicts of economism can probably best be described as those who will shake their heads in uncomprehending disapproval over the foregoing pages, but we fear that there will be as many socialists among them as there will be liberals.

Historical "Interference"

Whenever we look back on the past two centuries we encounter things that confuse us. What is one to think, if on the one hand the eighteenth century is praised as the age of Europe's intellectual giants, and on the other hand a man can be branded as an arch-reactionary by being described as a "man of the eighteenth century"? Or, when Montesquieu, Burlamaqui or Vattel are quoted in confirmation of the high standard of international legal concepts, whilst in reality relations in general were then so much fiercer and more bellicose than in the nineteenth century? How

are we to reconcile the fact that the nineteenth century was a
unique period of progress, peace, liberty and order, whilst at the
same time its intellectual life was notoriously succumbing to increasing coarseness and disintegration and towards the end some of its
products reached startling depths of barbarism? And how does
our own time fit into this sequence? Is it epilogue or new departure, and to what extent is it either?

These are some of the questions to which we must find an
answer. It is likely to be found in a most important set of circumstances which we shall call "historical interference" and define as
follows: history apparently always takes its course in two phases, a
phase of internal, mental incubation and a phase of external,
physical realization, and as there is a great time lag between these
two, the most remarkable and confusing phenomena of interference
result from the coincidence of the realization of an already completed mental process of preparation with the incubation of a period
that is yet to come. A second illustration will serve to make this
clear: the great waves of history reach our shores after the steam-
ship which has caused them has long vanished over the horizon and
even after another ship has passed. Applied to our problem, this
means that we are living today in a period of realization whose
incubation took place in the nineteenth century, whereas the external
physical and socio-political happenings of the nineteenth century
are essentially the fruits of the seed sown in the eighteenth century.
Liberalism, humanity, freedom, order, rational control of the
instincts, balance, peace and progress and the other attributes of the
nineteenth century appear in this light to be largely the fulfilment
of the intellectual and moral theories of the eighteenth century, the
cultural heritage on which the nineteenth century lived without
replenishing it because the output of new ideas followed quite
different and coarser patterns. The nineteenth century reaped what
the eighteenth had sown, including the fame which should by
rights have gone to the sower. From this it would appear that one
must not only be careful in the choice of one's parents but also
in the choice of the century preceding one's own. And we, at any
rate, living in the present are in the unhappy position of having to
reap what prominent thinkers began to sow a hundred years ago,
just at a time when the seeds of the eighteenth century—including
the weeds which we already know—were about to shoot up. In
fact, at that time, around the 1830's and 1840's, we notice the first
signs of that general intellectual disintegration, that living on
cultural reserves, which has presented us with the "great spiritual
interregnum" of our day. Yet we must find comfort and encouragement in the thought that the external events of the present are part
of a "realization phase" of a past and closed period, while the
incubation of the future has quietly been taking place for many

years along quite different lines and is influenced moreover by the weight and form of our participation in it.

All this can afford us much enlightenment. It explains why the interpretation of different periods and their prominent men in their multifarious aspects is so difficult. We are beginning to understand what an outstanding part ideas play in historical development, the strange illusions men harbor concerning the place which they happen to occupy in history and the no less curious illusions of certain revolutionaries regarding the epochal novelty of their régime, which, far from being the first phase of a new era, is often only the last ripple of a declining one. It also shows the ambiguity of concepts such as "eighteenth century" or "nineteenth century" and demonstrates the necessity of always adding whether one means the ripening content of ideas or the external development; in the eighteenth century, for instance, the latter compared unfavourably and in the nineteenth favorably with the former. But, above all, these considerations show us what ominous things must have been germinating in that period of spiritual incubation a hundred years ago in order to result in the terrible explosion of our days. About a century ago there occurred, in fact, throughout Europe a break in the development of ideas which found perhaps its most striking demonstration in Germany, a break whose long term effects have been determining factors in today's catastrophe. The lives of many leading men could serve as illustration of this rupture, but it is perhaps advisable to select only one whose story brings out particularly well the nuances of this transitional period in political thought. For this purpose we have chosen that mercurial and ambitious Swabian, the well-known economist Friedrich List, the foremost economic writer and propagandist in the Germany of that time and a fervent patriot to boot, whose main work appeared exactly a hundred years ago in 1841, characteristically entitled *The National System of Political Economy*.

The history of economic theory generally rewards Friedrich List with such good marks that it is difficult to ascribe an even faintly sinister role to him. In any case he was far from being a sinister person and his adroitness and vitality, his rich fund of experience and ideas, and his sincerity have never been questioned. It is, however, more difficult to do justice to his achievements in the field of economics, at least in the few words which are appropriate at this point. He is probably best known for his attempt to breach the free trade doctrine of the classical economists and to prove the usefulness of tariffs for the protection of infant industries in agrarian countries. His claim to have thereby given expression to a conclusive, and since then generally and in principle accepted—though by no means original—idea, remains uncontested and has made of him a kind of national saint in all agrarian countries adopting industrialization. However, if List had imagined that competition between the gradually growing industries would in the end automatically render tariffs for the protection of infant industries ineffective and thus remove it, he was greatly mistaken because events followed a vastly different and completely unforeseen course, chiefly in Germany but hardly less so in the United States: it was precisely the industrial protective tariffs which proved to be highly conducive to the formation of trusts, thus becoming "tariffs for the protection of trusts." When in 1879 Germany changed over to the system of protective tariffs and thereby started out on a path which was politically and economically equally disastrous, List was certainly quoted without justification, but it is equally certain that he had a large share in creating an atmosphere favorable to the rule of protectionist interests.

The doctrine of tariffs for the protection of infant industries is based on a general criticism of classical economics and notwithstanding its gross exaggeration and somewhat rough-and-ready character, it has in many respects hit the mark and long since become part of our economic concepts. Who would today deny that the super-rationalism of the classicists which was so typical of their time, coupled with their blind refusal to view their liberal doctrine as being sociologically and historically conditioned, was in urgent need of adjustment? Who would deny that they had dogmatically simplified and stated in absolute terms things which would sooner or later call for refinement? On all these counts List has his merits, however much we have learned to be sparing in our praise of him.

On closer examination it would even seem as if List—and in this he was typical of the period in the history of thought which had just begun then—in one important respect fell below even the classicists' primitive level of sociological understanding, notwithstanding all the adulation which the historical-romanticist school of economics has lavished upon him on account of his supposed profundity. He saw clearly enough that classical economic science had gone astray in conceiving competitive economy as autonomous, thus adopting that thoroughly erroneous view which we have already discussed. Jointly with others, List attacked this disastrous belief in the sociological autonomy of competitive economy; a belief which was the cardinal error of the laissez-faire philosophers and finally discredited liberalism, so seriously that we find it difficult to salvage its permanent values. He himself, however, committed an even more serious error by endowing industrial competition with the miraculous ability of creating the necessary non-economic framework without our co-operation, merely by virtue of its integrating and morally educative powers. "Evolution" (that magic formula of the nineteenth century), "social laws," "industrial civilization," "social utility," making usefulness automatically identical with justice and ethics, men's fervent devotion to the business of increasing their material wealth—all this became a substitute for what in the eighteenth century had still been accepted (perhaps too much as a matter of course) as the axiomatic basis of a world order. This order owed its ennobling powers not to cotton manufacture, but to a higher authority, an increasingly colorless personal God, and to a concept of "Nature" or "Culture" synonymous with him. A last trace of this eighteenth century deism is to be found in List's ideas but it is almost entirely smothered by the pseudo-religion of the nineteenth century: the religion of evolution (i.e., of aimless progress, which had nothing of the eighteenth century's deeply ethical appeal to what is good in man, but proceeded entirely in accordance with scientific or intellectual "laws" in the manner of Hegel's determinism), the religion of scientific positivism, of biologism, naturalism, and finally "economism," which believes economic considerations to be the driving force in history. When "The National System" was published both Darwin and Marx were becoming known, Saint-Simonism was at its height, Cobden—"the inspired bagman of a Calico Millenium" (Ruskin)—and Bright had forged the spirit of industrial and commercial England, that strange mixture of utilitarianism and idealism, and a few years later Guizot was to admonish the French: "enrichissez-vous." In the same year, 1841, Balzac, pitilessly depicting the society which had followed Guizot's advice, caustically called his series of novels "La comédie humaine." There was still a whole decade to go before we encounter the recklessness of the German materialism of a Moleschott and Büchner, but the robust belief in material strength which pervaded the whole nineteenth century, was already making itself felt and in this respect the difference between List and Marx is only a matter of degree. As if to supply the final proof of our diagnosis even language began to become crude at that time in its vehemence, pathos, drastic expression, and that even grammar itself suffered we have no less a witness than Schopenhauer ("Ueber die Schriftstellerei und Stil"). Ten years previously Stendhal had in his great novels glorified morally blind force.

In fact, if "The National System" were as undated as a papyrus, thousands of years hence philologists should still be able to determine its publication date—not only to the century but to the decade —from its contents and tenor. But even today it can be said that List, however much he may fundamentally have had in common with Cobden's Manchester theories, was, on one decisive point, much worse than his opponent whom he maligned so violently: whereas the former was sufficiently honest and upstanding to follow the doctrine of the competitive economy to its logical conclusion and left it to shoulder its own risks, List opened the back door to state support. While heaping abuse on the free traders, he undertook to give an ethical and philosophical veneer to the insatiable appetite of the vested interests by his theory of protective tariffs. Enrichissez-vous—but not only as Guizot had said "par le travail, par l'épargne et la probité" but also through the good offices of the state. The damage which List caused with this can hardly be estimated: it is the first and therefore still timid beginning of a form of "pluralism," i.e., the rule of interest groups, which sapped the strength of state and competitive economy alike; it started its triumphal march through Germany with the introduction of the Bismarck tariff in 1879 and characteristically spread to at least the same extent in List's second home, the United States, whilst Cobden's country, free trading England, largely succeeded in fending it off. List shared most of the faults of the Manchester school's liberalism and replaced its advantage with a further fault, by being the first to demonstrate how to combine, with an entirely untroubled conscience, the glorification of private enterprise and an "economistic" Weltanschauung on the one hand with the solicitation of state aid on the other, how to run with the hares and hunt with the hounds. It was a form of economism which was no longer even liberal and thus became the forerunner of that national liberalism with which everyone acquainted with Bismarck's Germany is familiar.

The picture which we have drawn of this unhappy and divided man might easily appear distorted unless we add at once that standing at the intersection of two epochs he is a perfect illustration of the "interferences" which we mentioned above and for this reason alone he is of interest to us in this discussion. He resembles many of his contemporaries, particularly the historian Ranke, in that he, while sowing new seed, still carries within him a good deal of the cultural heritage of the eighteenth and the beginning of the nineteenth century, a humanist education, idealism, and an international outlook. On the one hand he corrects the rationalist cosmopolitan attitude of the age of enlightenment by reminding us—as did Montesquieu, Vico, Herder, Moeser and the romanticists—that between the individual and mankind the nation is an essential intermediate stage in the structure of society, but on the other hand, and in spite of many discordant notes, he was by no means a mere nationalist. "The National System" bears the motto "Et la patrie et l'humanité" and many sonorous passages of the work are in accord with this sentiment. That is particularly true of the fine spirit in which he tries to do justice to England, the actual target of his attacks. However honest List may have been in his views, it is apparent from the context that he thought he had to speak to his time in this manner in order not to cause offense and yet he was still sufficiently rooted in such concepts to be able to express them fluently and with conviction.

However, let us not forget the twilight in which this man makes his appearance and which makes him interesting to us: an epoch ended in him and he stands at the beginning of a new one which seems to be drawing to a close only in our time. "This happens to be the peculiar weakness which resulted from List's intellectually ambiguous position: when the nationalist industrial states closed their frontiers with tariffs for the protection of their infant industries, a period of tariff and trade wars was inaugurated which was bound to lead to the gradual extinction of the fundamental ideal of humanity, and once the nations were awakened by being taught to be 'industry minded,' forces were set free whose course no man could predict. Whether List loved the ideal of universal brotherhood only as an abstraction or whether there still lived within him the strong tradition of the classisists, will therefore remain debatable, but 'lasting peace' and 'world-wide free trade' could never be reached along the lines he recommended." (Fr. Schnabel). There can be no doubt that these humane ideas must be credited to a "Zeitgeist" still extant then. But what is new and peculiar in List and others like him is to have actively participated in breaking up these cultural reserves, to have initiated a new and more robust period of acquisitiveness, of a realistic sense of life, of lusty participation in political and economic affairs, of a glorification of power and of "the cult of political unity and national expansion" (Jacob Burckhardt). He stood at that turning-point of history which is innocently symbolized by the son of the composer of the "Freischütz" becoming a railway engineer. Men were forsaking the things of the spirit and turning to externals: both the classic and the romantic periods were coming to an end, the "Biedermeier," too, was drawing to its close, the Germany of Richter, Schwind, Kügelgen, Schubert, Jean Paul, whose tradition was continued by Stifter, Mörike and Raabe has little connection with the Germany that followed List's lead, unless as an object of infinite contempt; everything gentle, tranquil and serene is gradually drowned in noise and bustle, symptoms which prophets like Jacob Burckhardt, as we see from his letters, recognized as ill omens. "Ce qui s'annonce en Allemagne," Edgar Quinet wrote in 1831 in the "Revue des Deux Mondes," "c'est la ruine de l'intelligence . . . cette impuissance des consciences, ce vide moral, cette décadence de la véritable intelligence en Europe." Indeed, no one who compares the Germany of the first part of the nineteenth century with that of the second part, can escape the disheartening impression that this country, more than any other, became a victim of the general intellectual and moral disintegration, and gradually lost its soul, but now we are in a position to trace this melancholy development to its first beginnings—the break took place about a hundred years ago and List played a prominent part in it. But we should not forget that List and everything new that he represented also meant a break in that unique period of Prussian pre-1848 liberalism, which was characterized by the Humboldts and that liberal class of public servants, trained in the humanities (among whom we count Schön, Motz, Maassen, Kunth, Beuth, Nebenius and Delbrück), whose last representatives lived into Bismarck's era and to whom Adam Smith and Kant were more familiar than Hegel. It was a far cry from the Prussia of that time to the Prussia of Treitschke and his even worse successors. But Treitschke's subsequent trumpet blasts repeated in essence what List had sounded in the softer key with which a new era usually begins. Whilst the second half of both the eighteenth and the nineteenth century represents a distinct turning point in the history of thought, it is characteristic of the difference between them that in the eighteenth century it was a turn for the better. The second half of the eighteenth century was a time of purification, readjustment and reflection, of which the German classicists, the Scottish philosophers, Adam Smith and Edmund Burke, and, in a sense, even Rousseau are typical; the second half of the nineteenth century, however, was a period of progressive vulgarity, gloom and disintegration.

If there is any one thing which typifies the latter part of the nineteenth century in a manner which carries its disastrous consequences over into our day, it is that "cult of political unity and national expansion" with which we are going to deal more fully in the following section. It is nothing but the familiar urge for super-organization and centralization and the habit of attaching absolute value to it, while regarding any attempt to question it as heresy, treason or malicious perversity. In the eyes of this cult it is despicable and a sign of reactionary and romantic stupidity to be moderate in one's wants, to stress the necessity for an integrated and varied social structure and to demand as much independence and autonomy as possible for the sub-sections which constitute the larger units (federalism) both in political and economic respects. This megalolatry is the common ideological breeding ground of modern nationalism, imperialism, socialism, monopoly capitalism and statism. We know, to be sure, how much the French Revolution and the Napoleonic era—both continuing, as Tocqueville and Taine point out, the tradition of Richelieu and French absolutism— are responsible for this ideology and its efficacy. However, it must be stressed that during the nineteenth century hardly anyone promoted it more effectively in Germany than Friedrich List, not because he was particularly fanatical but because he was one of its first and most able propagandists. We can better appreciate the novelty of this doctrine of the colossal at that time if we recall the very different spirit of the eighteenth century. Then Matthias Claudius could say that nothing can be truly great if it is not also good, whereas now everything that is considered great is consequently good. We find that in the late nineteenth century it is Adalbert Stifter (in his preface to *Bunte Steine,* 1853) and Jacob Burckhardt (particularly in the famous passage in his *Force and Freedom,* where he discusses the mission of the small state), who still echo with clearness and dignity the noble spirit of the eighteenth century which Claudius represented. The doubts which people like Wilhelm von Humboldt or the Göttingen historian, Heeren, had expressed at the beginning of the nineteenth century regarding the possibility of a unified German state, must indeed have appeared strange at the end of the century!

In List's time and largely owing to his influence, all this is considered out of date and contemptible. Standardization, uniformity, organization (extolled above all by Saint-Simon, the father of planned economy) and centralization are rapidly becoming the ideals of the century and the smaller units in both the economic and political realm are treated with that contempt with which we ourselves have been inculcated. In this respect there is no difference between List, Marx and, later, Treitschke, to say nothing of the non-plus-ultra of Ernst Jünger in our time. List would probably be greatly surprised if he were to learn that we are today seriously beginning to doubt the sublimity of the colossal and are once more learning to appreciate the wisdom of Claudius and Burckhardt. He was an imperialist—of the harmless kind which, in a way, was still in keeping with the humane Zeitgeist—and a whole continent took its cue from him. His sweeping schemes of empire as well as his undisguised contempt for the parochialism of Switzerland and Holland fit well into this pattern. However, here we must submit a plea of mitigating circumstances because the smallness with which List had become familiar had generally been synonymous with pettiness and meanness. He both remembered and saw all his life before him that miserable world of German absolutist and feudal parochialism which in the course of centuries had broken the German burgher's back, and that gallery of "Serenissimi" whose brutality and stupidity could really hardly be matched. Compared with these even Frederick the Great could appear as the virtuous and fascinating hero into which legend has formed him, a legend whose hardiness in the face of the manifest historical facts can only be explained in this way. And finally we must allow that List was writing under the depressing feeling that he belonged to a nation whose history had again and again for a thousand years been cheated of its fruits in spite of the promise of many fresh starts. If we thus partially exonerate him, we must conclude our study of this man with the disturbing realization that the fatality of his work and time is part of the tragedy of German history, which is at the same time Europe's tragedy.

The Cult of the Colossal

C'est sortir de l'humanité que de sortir du milieu: la grandeur de l'âme humaine consiste à savoir s'y tenir.

—Pascal, *Pensées*, I, 9, 17.

Let us return once more to the theme "eighteenth and nine-teenth century." After having surveyed the whole field from a biographical point of view, so to speak, we are now making a new start in order to do justice to the question of the "secular spirit." We shall begin by giving a few fundamental explanations of this concept itself.

Although the secular spirit is an indispensable concept in any history of thought and although everyone realizes that its inclusion is warranted, it is quite clear to us that it has to be handled with care. To start with, it is plain that a century in our calendar is a period invented by men for reasons of expediency, which will only by chance coincide to some extent with the great phases in the history of thought. In spite of the reverent emotions stirred in the human breast by "a century's grave end," we know that it is an event which owes its origin, just as every new year's night, to man's arbitrary division of time. It would really be asking too much to expect the great periods in the history of thought to last more or less exactly a hundred years, and even more, to correspond with the century in the calendar. In this sense, then, the "eighteenth century" or the "nineteenth century" is a very rough concept, which we must not overtax. On the contrary, in using them we must always bear in mind that what we understand by the eighteenth or the nineteenth century cuts in most instances right across our calendar and that these vague temporal divisions cover very significant changes within each century of the history of thought.

Secondly, the historical centuries (which we must distinguish from the calendar centuries) are arranged in the complicated manner which we studied in the preceding paragraphs dealing with "historical interference." And thirdly, we have to apply the same caution to the concept of the secular spirit as we rightly adopt now when dealing with the concept of the national spirit (or national character). Just as the members of the same nation, at least for a certain period, usually betray more or less similar patterns of think-ing and feeling—acquired by whatever process—so every period has in the same way been marked by a certain kinship between mental and emotional patterns extending across all national boundaries, by what, in fact, we call the style of the time or the secular spirit, which permeates the most trivial questions of taste and fashion. By this we do not want to say more than that individual thinking and feeling includes a collective component (be it determined by time or space), and by this formulation we dissociate ourselves decisively from the hopeless determinism which completely subjects the individual to his spatial and temporal surroundings. Indeed, we do not assert more than what the simplest experience forbids us to deny, namely, that since everyone is part of the community, his thinking and feeling display, among others, also a collective component. Only in this sense, and fully aware of the dangers inherent in every kind of typification and generalization, may we talk of a national character and finally also of a secular spirit.

Secular spirit and national character have also in common the fact that their structure can be clearly recognized only from a distance. Just as one can express an opinion on the national character of one's own country only if one looks as it from the outside, that is, compares it with the character of another nation, the secular spirit can, in the same way, assume shape in our minds only when we have already overcome it. That is what is happening to us today when we look back on the nineteenth century and see it as a chapter which is as good as closed, as something that is lying behind us. Although it extends very tangibly into our own time and is only now producing its ultimate political consequences, it requires no sixth sense to realize that the nineteenth century, intellectually speaking, belongs to the past and that everything that still remains of it represents a grand finale. If we still doubted it, the growing clarity with which the intellectual elite of all countries recognizes the outlines of the nineteenth century as a definite chapter in the history of thought, would convince us. Last and most infallible affirmation is the fact that, like every century, the nineteenth century, too, is, politically speaking, drawing its final conclusions, which have been predetermined by long mental preparation. Thus it is only now making its rather sensational exit from the stage. What we saw timidly started in the intellectual sphere in the 1840's is today coming to an end in the political field accompanied by wild convulsions. It is of no consequence that many, unable to appreciate what is going on, curiously enough look upon today's political *epi*logue to an old century as the *pro*logue of a new one. They do not know that there is always a great distance between concrete realization and mental preparation and that while politics today noisily thrash the sheaves of the nineteenth century, the soil has already been planted with new seeds.

All this will become clearer now that we shall endeavour to define more exactly an element of the spirit of the last century with which we are already acquainted, and to study in it the changes which the style of the times has undergone. We call this element the cult of the colossal, and believe that we are thereby expressing the quintessence of our present reaction towards the nineteenth century. It is a trait which, when correctly interpreted, shows the most diverse temporal tendencies in a surprising interrelationship and, at the same time, places this century in sharp contrast to the eighteenth.

It is this difference between it and the eighteenth century which makes us understand the full significance of the nineteenth century cult of the colossal—in the last section we called it megalolatry—and facilitates our interpretation. It is evident that we can talk of the eighteenth century less than of any other without running every risk of generalization and without treating some aspects, which others may deem typical elements, as mere under-currents. We are well aware of the fact that it is particularly the eighteenth century that is full of contradictions and displays, side by side with warm-hearted humanity, the most shocking nihilism and cynicism. In spite of this we believe we are justified in stating that the eighteenth century—which, as we saw, extended, in the intellectual sense, far into the nineteenth—was one of humanitarianism, not only in the high-flown sense of the word humanity, but also in the unassuming one of what is befitting man, and of values based on his capabilities; it was, therefore, essentially an era of moderation, of the "human mean," of reverence for the small and scepticism towards sheer size, of aversion to baroque bombast as well as mere quantity, a century of tranquil happiness, of family life, of bucolic idylls, of fervent interest in psychology and pedagogy (the "pedagogic century"), of progress in the sense of confident appeal to and belief in the possibilities open to the free will of the individual, a century of serenity, of an even frivolous enjoyment of life, of love for the intimate, of sociability within a small circle, of comfortable informality which did not preclude dignity and ceremoniousness in their right place, but rather made them particularly impressive. It was a century whose quiet enjoyment of the world is demonstrated by everything it did. It has perhaps received its most beautiful monument in Claude Tillier's *Mon Oncle Benjamin,* although we find in Casanova's Memoirs or Choderlos de Laclos' *Les liaisons dangereuses* its lascivious frills. It is the century whose naturalness is expressed by Maria Theresia radiantly informing the Viennese theatre audience from her box that "her Poldl has just gotten a boy," and the century in which small towns such as Geneva and Weimar, and even mere country estates like Ferney and later Coppet come to be centers of European intellectual life, until during the later course of the nineteenth century the big city assumes leadership and kills the vivacious world of the small towns and the open country. It is a century which cannot be bluffed and impressed by mere massiveness but lives according to a secularized version of the bible word: "For what shall it profit a man if he shall gain the whole world and lose his own soul?"

Certainly nobody wanted to gain the world at that time. The wars of that period are mainly cold-blooded cabinet and status quo wars. Even missionary activities begin to flag, and after Louis XIV energetic imperialism is in abeyance until Napoleon appears on the scene. It is curbed for the last time by the spirit of the eighteenth century in the Vienna Congress, and then, half a century later, it comes to full and permanent fruition. War and armies are somewhat contemptuously relegated to the background; even patriotism, if we recall a few of the biting dicta of Johnson or Lichtenberg, did not rate very high; Vattel and Burlamaqui formulate humane principles of international law which find general approval, and even Talleyrand later adopts Montesquieu's classic maxim: "Le droit des gens est naturellement fondé sur ce principe, que les diverses nations doivent se faire dans la paix le plus de bien, et dans la guerre le moins de mal qu'il est possible." While the mere "always-wanting-more attitude" is considered an abomination and while mere size is by no means valued highly, people concern themselves all the more with the soul and what might harm or profit it, and become so much concerned with the inner man that they finally tend towards sentimentalism and occultism.

The respect for the small and the concern with the soul are the reasons why that century was really fond of children and seems to have established a natural relationship to the child, completely free of any tendency to inculcate precociousness and free of that disastrous confusion of the hierarchy of the age groups. Prompted by the same feeling, it took a warm interest in the innocence of primitive man. Pestalozzi and Rousseau stem manifestly from the same root, only there is a difference, unfortunate for the latter, in that he wants to assign education in its entirety to the schools, while Pestalozzi gives full play to education within the family. Instead of chasing after the phantom of the colossal and of gaining the world, one preferred to live by the famous closing words of Candide: "mais il faut cultiver notre jardin." We can say that it was a century given to gardening, pedagogy, humaneness, a century which took its cue from man, it was introspective, adverse to spectacular ostentatiousness and obtrusive quantity, and because of that it was at the same time a serene, humorous, disputatious and sociable century, full of joie de vivre. It wanted—to paraphrase Lessing's well-known letter on the occasion of the simultaneous death of his wife and child—to have a better time than other centuries, and for that it had to pay dearly. However, we know that it was by no means blameless for the load of its misfortunes. We know that in spite of all its excellent natural talents it failed in certain things,

c

but this knowledge gives us comfort and encouragement because it teaches us how we can do better.

On the other hand, the nineteenth century—which we consider to begin in the 1840's—is the exact opposite of all this and that in a nutshell really is everything that has to be said. The more it shakes off the tenacious influence of the eighteenth century, the more it abandons itself to the intoxication of mere numbers, of brutal strength and restless busyness, sterile excitement and enormous dimensions; it reveres the strong man; accepts mere quantitative size as a sufficient passport; boundlessness, mechanical organization and centralization become the vogue; aimless development, determined by factors outside and above men, the massive, the over-ornate and the elephantine are in fashion; and this mania makes men full of bathos, stilted and ceremonial; makes them deterministic, fatalistic, humorless, fanatical and full of intense seriousness. And finally they adopt a tragic, heroic mien, and feel it their duty to lead an unhappy life.

Every century making its exit seems to rise to a final effort by means of a "second pull" before it expires and is suddenly replaced by the counter-current of the new century; and so the eighteenth century, too, had its Indian Summer lasting into the nineteenth century in the form of the "Biedermeier" period, which "viewed from the standpoint of the brutality of many a modern barbarism was perhaps Europe's last Sunday" (K. Joël). This echo of the eighteenth century suffered the same fate as Philemon and Baucis at the close of *Faust,* whose quiet and modest idyll is brutally sacrificed by the devil's helpmates, Brawlmonger, Havequick and Speedbooty, to the colossal project with which Mephistopheles had inspired a Faust turned engineer—a profound symbolism, which in the last analysis contains everything worth saying on our subject, and which illustrates most aptly the prophetic vision of the ageing Goethe. Exactly one hundred years later, Russian peasants are "liquidated," after the pattern of Philemon and Baucis, in the interests of technological progress and of the Moloch of the collectivist state.

The cult of the colossal means kowtowing before the merely "big"—which is thus adequately legitimized as the better and more valuable—it means contempt for what is outwardly small but inwardly great, it is the cult of power and unity, the predilection for the superlative in all spheres of cultural life, yes, even in language. It is only since Napoleon's time that the adjective "great" or "grand" begins to make its telling appearance in expressions such as "Grand Army," "Grand Dukes," "Great General Staff," "Great Powers," and begins to demand from men the proper respect, and Europe is actually just as much intoxicated as America by expressions such as "unique," "the world's biggest," "the greatest of all times," "unprecedented." To this style of the time correspond, in equal degree, the unexampled increase in population, imperialism, socialism, mamoth industries, monopolism, statism, monumental architecture, technical dynamism, mass armies, the concentration of governmental powers, giant cities, spiritual collectivization, yes, even Wagner's operas. Since the cult of the colossal reduces qualitative greatness to mere quantity, to nothing but numbers, and since quantity can only be topped by ever greater quantity, the intoxication with size will in the end exceed all bounds and will finally lead to absurdities which have to be stopped. Since, moreover, different quantities of different species can only be reduced to a common denominator by means of money in order to render them comparable in the race of outdoing each other, the result is a tendency to measure size by money pure and simple— as, for instance, in the American seaside resort, Atlantic City, where in 1926 I found a gigantic pier simply being christened "Million Dollar Pier." Thus we find very close bonds of kinship between the cult of the colossal and commercialism.

While this time the world was gained, the soul suffered considerable damage in the process. The abrupt change from the concerns of the spirit to material affairs was bound to result in the withering of the soul. By abandoning humanism one lost the capacity for making man the measure of things and thus finally lost every kind of orientation. Life becomes de-humanized and man becomes the plaything of unhuman, pitiless forces. This results in "the abuse of greatness . . . when it disjoins remorse from power" (*Julius Cæsar* II, 1), hence the increasing indifference to all matters of collective ethics, hence scientific positivism and relativism, which represent such a radical departure from the certain sense of values possessed by the eighteenth century. It further leads to a fanatical belief in a mechanical causality even outside the processes of nature; to the love of mathematics (which the eighteenth century, in contrast to the seventeenth, did not favor, at least not during its latter part); to social laws such as Malthus' "law of population," or Lassalle's "immutable law of wages"; to the oriental-baroque flirtation with fate; in brief to determinism which not only is raised anew to a philosophic dogma, but also dominates sociology, be it in the garb of Marx's materialist view of history, be it in that of geographical determinism, as first developed by Ritter and Ratzel and finally raised in geopolitics to a veritable geographic romanticism, or be it finally as biological or even merely zoological determinism, the final degradation that could be reached along that path.

It is rather fascinating to follow this secular spirit in all its varied manifestations and to discover traces of it even where one had hardly expected it. Let us ignore the difficult field of the history of art, and look more closely into the scientific activities of the nineteenth century: it is incontestable that the decidedly ontological, cosmological and objectivist view which the nineteenth century had of the world, in contrast to the anthropological and subjectivist view of the eighteenth century, was bound to engender that scientific attitude which we call "positivism," and it is just as undeniable that it is closely linked to "relativism," the refusal to hold an opinion, the cool and seemingly objective registration of facts. It is also related to that type of scholar so characteristic of the nineteenth century, with his ceremonious gravity, his antiquated outlook, his love of great systems, schools of philosophy and gigantic works of learning, to whom brevity and a pleasing style are signs of shallowness. These qualities had been regarded likewise by the pedantic and stilted seventeenth century, so completely different from the cheerful and loquacious eighteenth century, which loved essays and apercus, and in which even a man like Kant did not consider it beneath his dignity to write *Dreams of a spirit-seer,* to say nothing of the merry pranks of a Lichtenberg. Just as typical is the concomitant difference between the scholar's life in the eighteenth century—sociable, characterized by extensive correspondence, dinners and disputations—and the masterful dogmatism of the scholars of the nineteenth century, each of whom reigned as despot over the circle of his disciples, bitterly opposed to all the other intellectual despots. How symptomatic of the eighteenth century that the aphorisms written by the physicist Lichtenberg for the "Goettinger Pocket Calendar," and Samuel Johnson's table talk, as recorded by his friend Boswell, are still among the reading we most enjoy! Where would we find this later in the nineteenth century?

What nineteenth century science lacked in the final analysis was the courage to be simple and natural, a courage which this neobaroque century of the colossal lacked in every other respect as well, because it had lost the human measure. We must refrain from following this trait through the various branches of science, such as the natural sciences, or history, where the collective concepts were smothering the concept of man, or medicine, which at that time earned for itself the reputation of treating the disease and not the patient, or finally jurisprudence. But we cannot omit mentioning two exceedingly telling traits by which every century in the history of thought usually gives itself away.

The first concerns the estimation in which the great "strong men" of world history are held at a given period: the Cæsars, the imperators, conquerors and tyrants. The value which an era places on Cæsar, Alexander, Cromwell, Richelieu or Napoleon, typifies it as a whole and there is nothing more characteristic of the century of the colossal than that, like the seventeenth century before it, it looks up, awe-stricken, to this type of man and his works. While in the sixteenth century (which, in its turn, is so very similar to the eighteenth), Montaigne had reproached Cæsar most disrespectfully for "l'ordure de sa pestilente ambition," and whereas Montesquieu had bluntly talked of the "crimes de César," and Lichtenberg had even resignedly spoken of the "biggest and fattest oxen that draw the crowds at the cattle fair," the nineteenth century again begins to discourse mysteriously on the "missions" of the conquerors and to build up a veritable cult around the Cæsars. Even Mommsen wrote his Roman History in this spirit, as did Droysen his history of Alexander the Great, while it is one of Jacob Burckhardt's valid titles to fame that he bravely upheld the standards of true historical greatness and at an early date opposed the Napoleon cult which has finally been exploded in our days. Hand in hand with the over-estimation of the successful, we find a corresponding under-estimation of those, who, like Demosthenes, offered unsuccessful resistance to the conquerors. It is a hopeful sign for our own time that it has again brought the yardsticks of the eighteenth century down from the attic and begins to note the negative side of the conquerors and their deeds, that it criticizes the imperators and tyrants—the Alexanders, Cæsars, Richelieus,· Napoleons and others of their kind—and sees their opponents (from Demosthenes and Cato to Talleyrand, Madame de Staël, and Constantin Frantz) in a new light. It is only today that we have reached the point where, following in Gibbon's footsteps, we are once more prepared to add up dispassionately the terrible liabilities of the Roman Empire.

The second point in which the centuries tend to show a characteristic difference is in their relationship to primitive man, to the so-called "savage," and here, too, ideas on "greatness" play a decisive role. Here, too, we find a decisive contrast between the eighteenth and nineteenth century, which the latter quite clearly appreciated. It was in keeping with the humane spirit of the eighteenth century to see in the primitive first of all the human being and to compare him quite impartially with civilized man, and that held good not only for the primitive but also as for all non-European peoples (the Turks, Persians, Chinese), for whom there existed genuine and highly respectful interest. Therefore, Rousseau's glorification of the primordial state must definitely be considered together with the *Persian letters* of Montesquieu, Cooper's Leatherstocking Tales, Bernardin de Saint-Pierre's *Paul et Virginie,* with the enthusiasm for the Turks (of the Genevese painter Liotard, for instance), the Robinson Crusoe type stories and China's deep influence on eighteenth century culture. In the seventeenth century, on the other hand, Hobbes bases his doctrine of the absolutism of the state on the sentence "homo homini lupus" (which in the eighteenth century Shaftesbury quite rightly declares to be an insult to the wolves), and thus, from a negative estimate of man's primordial condition, arrives at the "Leviathan" of the absolutist state; and here, too, the nineteenth century follows in the footsteps of its penultimate predecessor, though in a somewhat different spirit and on different grounds. With an amazing lack of anthropological understanding and on the basis of the evolutionary doctrines peculiar to the nineteenth century, one now delights in picturing primitive man as a roaming beast, on an altogether different level from modern man, particularly since the latter has been broken in by civilization and the state. This attitude is in keeping with the intellectual imperialism which undervalues the constants in the human soul, an imperialism which prompted the nineteenth century to brutal meddling with primitive and foreign cultures and did not let it rest before it had raised them, clothed in calico and top hats, to its own giddy heights; yet withal it did not realize that it acted from its own deep seated inhumanity and soullessness. It is all the more typical that our own time has, as we know, completely reversed its attitude in these matters; not only with the aid of improved ethnological knowledge, but also from a newly awakened interest in man and a deeper psychological understanding, it has rediscovered in the primitive a human being not so very different from the eighteenth century conception; and if one recalls the panegyric intoned by Montaigne in honor of the Red Indians one recognizes in this our kinship to the sixteenth century.

If we now review once more all the many signs which today point to a repudiation of the nineteenth century, and at the same time to a renewal of the interest taken in the best of what the eighteenth had to offer, we are inclined to come to the extraordinary conclusion that in the history of human thought a rhythm of two centuries seems to obtain and that each century takes after its grandfather. We are far from establishing this at once as a social "law," for that would indeed mark us as unregenerate children of the determinist nineteenth century. At most we can venture the comforting assumption that an excess of stupidity will in the end always correct itself and wisdom will be re-established. However this may be, we cannot but acknowledge that these affinities between the spirit of the centuries do exist and that much what today strikes us as new and full of promise, is the better part of the newly discovered heritage of the eighteenth century; and here we may add the hope that we may avoid copying its many disastrous mistakes, errors and blunders.

There is no doubt that the wind has turned and that a new spiritual climate is developing, of which we dare to predict or at least to hope that its main characteristics will not be unlike those of the eighteenth century. In the midst of all the cultural refuse of the nineteenth century with which we are still encumbered our

great hopes and efforts are directed towards the true twentieth
century, which is still before us. Whatever the individual aspects
of that new century may be, one thing seems to be certain: it will
have no room for the cult of the colossal.

Another, perhaps not entirely unjustified expectation arises from
this. In the introduction we spoke of the relationship between the
secular spirit and the national spirit. Now, on closer examination
it appears, strangely enough, that the secular spirit shows a peculiar
affinity to the national spirit of this or that country, that it is "in
character" with a particular country and therefore assigns it a
leading position. We are not going to discuss how far those are
right who associate the nineteenth century with a shift in the
cultural center of gravity from West to East. One may be certain,
however, that the eighteenth century was not only a "siècle des
Anglais" (Voltaire), but that, especially towards its close, it also
found a spiritual center in Switzerland. Whilst in accordance with
"historical interference" the political and social effects of the
eighteenth century did not emerge there, or anywhere else, until
the nineteenth, Switzerland at that time meant more to the West
than it did for many centuries before or after, though in the sixteenth
century too, the Swiss share in European cultural life had been
prodigious. Rousseau, Pestalozzi, Haller, Gessner, Lavater,
Bodmer, Bernoulli, Euler, Vattel, Burlamaqui and many others cast
their seed over Europe, and it occurred to none of them that the
smallness of their country would preclude its individual citizens
from taking part in the great affairs of mankind, a thought which
would indeed have signified that even a small state bowed to the
cult of the colossal. At that time Switzerland exerted a tremendous
attraction on all of Europe's great men; Voltaire settled there permanently, Klopstock and Goethe stayed for a time, and it inspired
Schiller to write the most accomplished of his dramas. Every court
swarmed with Swiss citizens, Berlin as well as St. Petersburg and
Weimar, and from 1750 onwards Swiss scholars were the most
strongly represented among foreign members of the academies of
Paris, London and Berlin. It was Switzerland which at that time
was primarily responsible for awakening an interest in nature and
for the new appreciation of the peasant, which we find expressed
not only in the doctrines of the French physiocrats but also in the
works of the frequently misunderstood Adam Smith. We hope that
we shall be excused from furnishing further proof for an assertion
which is in any case generally known and undisputed. If we may
therefore consider it proven, we arrive at the conclusion that in the
course of the contemporary development of the history of thought,
to which we are also contributing, Switzerland's great hour will
come again if only it remains true to its own spirit.

PART ONE—NOTES TO CHAPTER I

Note No. 1 (page 38). The original sin of force:

Here our text is based on a conception of history which seems to be confirmed by the convergent results of ethnological, historical and sociological research. The author found the as yet unpublished manuscript of a book by his friend Alexander Rüstow (Professor at the University of Istanbul) particularly stimulating. It will be published soon by Eugen Rentsch Verlag, Erlenbach-Zürich. In the meantime he recommends Franz Oppenheimer's *System der Soziologie*, volumes 3 and 4. Chapter 24 of the first volume of *Das Kapital*, by Karl Marx (a chapter which Marxists like to overlook), will also be of interest here, and in addition Werner Sombart's *Moderner Kapitalismus*, volume 1, page 715 ff.

Note No. 2 (page 39). Schiller's "Wilhelm Tell" and the French Revolution:

Schiller's appreciation of the difference between these revolutions is expressed in the beautiful stanzas which accompanied *Wilhelm Tell* when he sent the play to Dalberg in 1804. As they are very little known we quote them below:

> When angry forces 'gainst each other rise,
> And by blind rage the flame of war is stirred;
> When 'mid the virulence of party cries
> The voice of justice is no longer heard;
> When every crime starts rampant to the skies,
> And license at the very shrine will gird,
> Cutting the cable which the state maintains—
> Here is no matter for triumphant strains.
>
> But when a pastoral and simple race,
> Sufficient for itself, with no desires,
> Hurls off the yoke it suffered in disgrace,
> Which in its wrath Humanity admires,
> And in its triumph wears a modest face—
> This is immortal and our song inspires.

Note No. 3 (page 43). The French Revolution and Napoleon:

As regards recent works on this fateful phase in European history, reference should be made to C. Brinon, *A Decade of Revolution,* New York, 1934, Duff Cooper's well-known book on Talleyrand and the research done by Louis Madelin and P. Gaxotte, but above all G. Ferrero, *The Gamble: Bonaparte in Italy,* 1796-97, London, 1939, and G. Ferrero, *Reconstruction of Europe, Talleyrand and the Congress of Vienna,* New York, 1941, should be consulted. The essential points are also covered in a lecture which Jacob Burckhardt gave in 1881, entitled "Napoleon I in the Light of Modern Research." We take this opportunity to stress how much this whole book is based on the theory of history developed by this great historian and humanist. Cf. also: Karl Loewith, *Jacob Burckhardt, Der Mensch inmitten der Geschichte,* Lucerne, 1936; Alfred v. Martin, *Nietzsche und Burckhardt,* Munich, 1941; Alfred v. Martin, *Die Religion in Jacob Burckhardts Leben und Denken,* Munich, 1942. Edmund Burke, in his *Reflections on the Revolution in France* (1790), prophesied with admirable perspicacity and profound reasoning that a Napoleon would finally be the result of the French Revolution.

Note No. 4 (page 43). The fruits of Bismarck's policy:

The following may be said against the Bismarck cult: Bismarck's greatness consisted merely in his alone being able to master a hopelessly confused situation which he himself had created not only in domestic' affairs (the ultimately untenable character of the Reich structure as evolved by him, the fight against the Roman Catholic Church, anti-socialist legislation, suppression of parliamentary functions and the muzzling of the country's foremost personalities), but also in foreign affairs (after the "blood and iron policy" and the annexation of Alsace-Lorraine followed the "armed peace" and the "cauchemar des coalitions"). The mastering of such a situation constituted a trapeze act with self-imposed hazards, but, as bad luck would have it, the conditions remained the same and even grew worse while the artiste finally had to quit. Viewed in this light, Bismarck's "greatness" seems very relative today and the disastrous aspects of his personality, which in its cynicism and nihilism could have no other than a disintegrating and destructive effect, come to the fore, in contrast to those of the really great statesmen of the time such as Gladstone and Cavour. The similarity between Bismarck and Frederick II becomes very obvious for, as no less an authority than O. Hintze (*Historische und politische Aufätze*, I, page 32) remarks, Frederick's state, too, had been reduced to nothing but a machine that could only be directed by a genius. In both cases a break-down was inevitable. Cf. W. Röpke, *The Solution of the German Problem*, New York, 1947.

Note No. 5 (page 45). The steadfast democracies:

De laudibus legum Angliae written by the English Lord Chancellor, Sir John Fortescue, in 1465, is an early testimony to the difference between a native (organic) democratic system and those parts of Europe groaning under the yoke of absolutism and feudalism. The social and economic basis in history of this essential difference which still exists today, is presented in a particularly striking and convenient form in the well-known book by the Belgian historian, Henri Pirenne, *History of Europe from the Invasions to the 16th Century*, London, 1939. Among the German speaking areas which managed to fend off territorial and political absolutism and feudalism were, apart from Switzerland, also the Hanseatic cities, whose "Western" democratic and liberal tendencies have again and again been demonstrated. After all, it was the citizens of Hamburg who could inscribe the words "Libertatem quem peperere maiores digne studeat servare posteritas" on their town hall and it is no mere coincidence that in the 1840's, for example, both Hamburg and Zürich were centers of unfettered publishing activities for the German speaking countries.

In this connection it is important to remember that Burke, the bitter enemy of the French Revolution, defended the American Revolution, and that Schiller stressed the difference between the Swiss struggle for liberty and the French Revolution in the above quoted dedicatory verses. On the same subject we recommend the masterpiece of the late historian and sociologist Guglielmo Ferrero, *Pouvoir, Les génies invisibles de la cité*, New York, 1942.

Note No. 6 (page 47). The Problem of the machine:

The literature on this subject is extensive but not very fertile; the following books should be consulted: O. Veit, *Die Tragik des technischen Zeitalters*, Berlin, 1935; Gina Lombroso-Ferrero, *La rançon du machinisme*, Paris, 1931; G. K. Chesterton, *The Outline of Sanity*; C.-F. Ramuz, *Taille de l'homme*, Paris, 1935; L. Mumford's books (*Technics and Civilization*, 1934; *The Condition of Man*, 1944); F. Muckermann, *Der Mensch im Zeitalter der Jechnik*, Luzern, 1943; D. Brinkmann, *Mensch und Technic*, Bern, 1946.

Note No. 7 (page 48). The rationalist confronted with inconvenient facts:

Joseph de Maistre, that classical representative of the sovereignty principle and of an almost irreligious theology, that fanatical rationalist who might be called "an inverse Voltaire," has proved that abstract rationalism can also be used for developing a recklessly reactionary theory. "Les faits l'irritent ou l'ennuient," Emile Faguet wrote in *Politiques et moralistes du dix-neuvième siècle*, 1re série, Paris. What Thomas Huxley said of Comte also applies to him: Catholicism minus Christianity.

Note No. 8 (page 49). Rationalism and modern thought:

Ortega y Gasset, *Die Aufgabe unserer Zeit*, Stuttgart; A. N. Whitehead, *Science and the Modern World*, New York, 1926; K. v. Neergaard, *Die Aufgabe des 20. Jahrhunderts*, Zürich, 1940; B. Bavink, *Ergebnisse und Probleme der Naturwissenschaften*, 8th edition, Bern, 1945, inform us on present day efforts at re-orientation.

Note No. 9 (page 50). The infatuation with the unconditional and absolute in politics:

An up-to-date book which says all that is necessary on this subject is W. Astrow's *Grenzen der Freiheit in der Demokratie, Zur geistigen Neuorientierung des Liberalismus*, Zürich, 1940.

Note No. 10 (page 56). Tariffs for the protection of trusts:

What has happened in this field has been discussed in some detail by W. Röpke, *German Commercial Policy*, London, 1934, page 24 ff.

Note No. 11 (page 57). History of nineteenth century thought:

Franz Schnabel, *Deutsche Geschichte im neunzehnten Jahrhundert*, volume 3, Freiburg i. Br., 1934; Karl Löwith, *Von Hegel bis Nietzsche*, Zürich, 1941; H. Plessner, *Das Schicksal des deutschen Geistes im Ausgang seiner bügerlichen Epoche*, Zürich, 1935; Emile Faguet, *Politiques et moralistes du dix-neuvième siècle*, Paris; Hans Kohn, *Prophets and Peoples*, New York, 1946; Benedetto Croce, *History of Europe in the 19th Century*, London, 1934.

Note No. 12 (page 58). Friedrich List on England:

It is surely to the credit of a man whose life work was a battle against British supremacy in industry and political economy, if he nevertheless writes: "Let us, however, do justice to this power and to her efforts. The world has not been hindered in its progress, but immensely aided in it by England. Who can tell how far behind the world might yet remain if no England had ever existed? And if it ceased to be, who can judge how far mankind would be thrown back?" (*National System*, page 293). Or: "Napoleon sought by his Continental system to establish a Continental coalition against the predominant naval and commercial power of England; but in order to succeed it was necessary for him, first of all, to take away from the Continental nations the apprehension of being conquered by France. He failed because on their part the fear of his supremacy on land greatly outweighed the disadvantages which they suffered from the naval supremacy" (*ibid*, page 331). Or: "Thus there will always be a nation who will surpass all others by virtue of its superior spiritual and physical resources and if that is to be so, we are firmly convinced that mankind will fare best if that nation is England" (*Zollvereinsblatt*, 1843).

Note No. 13 (page 60). Prussia before Bismarck:

In order to gain a complete picture it is advisable to study also the old-Prussian conservative and Catholic opposition to Bismarck, in particular personalities such as Radowitz and E. L. von Gerlach (Kreuzzeitung), who in the midst of the flush of victory in 1866 and 1871 spoke of "godless and lawless rapacity" and "the great wicked adventurer." "The final success, the tremendous expansion of Prussia's power and, to crown it all, the establishment of national unity covered up all the accusations of lawlessness, violence and lying which had been levelled against Bismarck's policy" (Gerhard Ritter, *Machtstaat und Utopie,* Munich, 1940, page 132). A further illustration of how quickly inner adjustments were made to outward success is the attitude adopted by leading Hanoverians after the annexation of 1866, in particular by R. v. Jhering, the well known jurist. Cf. again: W. Röpke, *The Solution of the German Problem.*

Note No. 14 *(page* 60). *The affinity between socialism and imperialism:*

An impressive example of this is, among others, the fact that during the Boer War most of the British Socialists supported the imperialist party (G. K. Chesterton, *Autobiography,* London, 1937, page 224 ff.).

Note No. 15 *(page* 60). *The influence of French absolutism and of the French Revolution:*

It should not be forgotten that in Germany the Prussian state, which had been highly mechanized and centralized since the time of Frederick William I and Frederick the Great, has played a similar role. As Novalis emphasized in his *Fragmente und Studien* II, (*Schriften,* edited by Kluckhohn, volume 2, page 56), since Frederick William I no state has been ruled more like a factory than Prussia, and it is really true that the Prussian barracks have been the training ground for the German factories. In the case of Prussia it was, of course, particularly disturbing that nobody knew what ultimate purpose this collectivist machinery was to serve, and one could not help suspecting that like Kant's Categorical Imperative it was an end in itself. Here, then, we find germs of later collectivist nihilism.

Nevertheless, it remains true that the centralization of society went nowhere as far as in France under the Ancien Régime, a feature which the Revolution and the Empire inherited and accentuated. It was French absolutism with its policy of centralization and of reducing the nobility to mere courtiers, that from the time of Louis XI and particularly of Richelieu and Louis XIV has led to that complete necrosis of social life outside the capital and that dissolution of every remnant of federal structure in France which to this very day are the unfortunate characteristics of that country. Compare the picture which Hippolyte Taine has drawn in his classic portrayal "L'ancien régime" (*Les origines de la France contemporaine,* volume 1, Paris, 1876) of French society in the eighteenth century, with Eichendorff's description, "Deutsches Adelsleben am Schlusse des achtzehnten Jahrhunderts," or with the description of the life of the English nobility in the eighteenth century by David Cecil in his excellent *The Young Melbourne,* London, 1939. This is also one of the reasons why our description of the pleasant family life and the modest style of living in the eighteenth century does not apply entirely to the nobility in France. For the same reasons we find in France no "gentlemen farmers" who in the eighteenth century evolved a rational system of agriculture in England, Switzerland and Germany, and whose absence explains the terrible decay of French agriculture of that time.

Note No. 16 *(page* 61). *The star witnesses for the small state:*

For further information on Humboldt's and Heeren's views consult Meinecke (*Weltbürgertum und Nationalstaat,* 7th edition, Munich, 1928). Jacob Burckhardt's classic words read as follows: "Small states exist so that there should be one spot on earth where the largest possible number of nationals are citizens in the full sense of the word. . . . For the small state has nothing but real and effective freedom with which completely to balance —ideally speaking—the tremendous advantages, and even the might, of the large nation." We also add the testimony of the American statesman, John C. Calhoun (*A Disquisition on Government*, 1849): "Nothing is more difficult than to equalize the action of government in reference to the various and diversified interests of the community; to aggrandize and enrich one or more interests by oppressing and impoverishing the others. . . . Nor is this the case in some particular communities only. It is so in all, the small and the great, the poor and the rich irrespective of pursuits, productions, or degrees of civilization; with, however, this difference, that the more extensive and populous the country . . . the more difficult it is to equalize the action of government—and the more easy for one portion of the community to pervert its powers to oppress and plunder the other." Cf. Werner Kaegi, *Der Kleinstaat im europäischen Denken, Historische Meditationen*, Zürich, 1942, pp. 251-314.

Note No. 17 (page 64). Eighteenth century joie de vivre:

In order to make yet one more attempt to acquaint the reader with that world, we shall quote what George Sand's grandmother told her granddaughter (see H. Taine, *Les origines de la France contemporaine*, volume 1, L'ancien régime, Paris 1876, page 181): "Est-ce qu'on était jamais vieux en ce temps-là? C'est la Révolution qui a amené la vieillesse dans le monde. Votre grand-père, ma fille, a été beau, élégant, soigné, gracieux, parfumé, enjoué, animable, affectueux et d'une humeur égale, jusqu'à l'heure de sa mort. On savait vivre et mourir alors; on n'avait pas d'infirmités importunes. Si on avait la goutte, on marchait quand même, et sans faire la grimace; on se cachait de souffrir par bonne éducation. On n'avait pas de ces préoccupations d'affaires qui gâtent l'intérieur et rendent l'esprit épais. On savait se ruiner sans qu'il y parût, comme de beaux joueurs qui perdent sans montrer d'inquiétude et de dépit. On se serait fait porter demi-mort à une partie de chasse. On trouvait qu'il valait mieux mourir au bal ou à la comédie, que dans son lit entre quatre cierges et de vilains hommes noirs. On était philosophe; on ne jouait pas l'austérité, on l'avait parfois sans en faire montre. Quand on était sage, c'était par goût et sans faire le pédant ou la prude. On jouissait de la vie, et quand l'heure était venue de la perdre, on ne cherchait pas à dégoûter les autres de vivre. Le dernier adieu de mon mari fut de m'engager à lui survivre longtemps et à me faire une vie heureuse." Like Voltaire one did indeed try "à mépriser la mort en savourant la vie." But here we are faced with the terribly serious and important question whether the attitude which an era adopts towards the reality of death and the way in which it learns that it has to reckon with its certainty throughout the life of each individual, is not of decisive importance to the "Zeitgeist" and whether we are not right in saying that from this point of view the nineteenth century with its affinity to the seventeenth and to the late Middle Ages, revelling in gruesome death dances, is—in contrast to the eighteenth century—particularly characterized by its fear of death. One need only picture Kierkegaard or Heidegger in the eighteenth century! And how unforgettable is that stoic, almost cheerful dignity with which the victims of the guillotine generally accepted their fate!

Note No. 18 (page 65). The anti-imperialism of the eighteenth century:

In this connection we quote Lichtenberg's famous sentence: "It is immaterial whether the sun never sets in a monarch's empire, which was the one time boast of Spain, but it is important what it sees in these states on its course."

Note No. 19 *(page 66).* *The dismal life of the nineteenth century:*

The gloomy Puritan attitude of the nineteenth century (particularly of the Victorian period) finds expression not only in its prudishness and the sombreness of its male attire, but especially in the cult of "work for its own sake." At the close of this strange development we find Ernst Jünger's "Worker," and also the idea that recreation is justified solely because it affords strength for further work. What Burke (*A letter from Mr. Burke to a Member of the National Assembly &c.,* 1791) had to say to the working maniacs of the French Revolution, sweating in their enthusiasm, is significant: "They who always labour can have no true judgment. You never give yourselves time to cool."

Henceforward everything becomes a duty, including education which with dogged seriousness one now considers an obligation to oneself, while completely ignorant of the necessarily free and serene character of all genuine culture. This, too, is an example of the perversion of value and purpose so typical of the civilization of the nineteenth century.

For further reference concerning work and education in the nineteenth century, cf. Karl Löwith, *Von Hegel bis Nietzsche,* pp. 357-397.

Note No. 20 *(page 68).* *The difficult subject of the history of art:*

It is obvious that there is hardly a better mirror of the "Zeitgeist" than the art of a period, and we borrowed the term "secular style" from the domain of the history of art. There can, moreover, be no doubt that all the fields of art provide evidence of the tendency towards the materialist and inhuman glorification of the purely quantitative and the outwardly "great," which we have termed the "cult of the colossal." But we have to make two very important reservations here:

1. A precise definition of true greatness is even more necessary in this case than elsewhere; mere bulk and vulgarity must be distinguished from what is really great and outstanding, and what is only outwardly slight and small, from what is merely pretty and stunted. The author would feel very misunderstood if he were supposed to condemn the sublime, the mighty, the grave and the solemn alongside with the colossal. Far from it, for, on the contrary, he believes that universal and undifferentiating emotionalization and exaltation will lead from the sublime to the ridiculous, to inner emptiness and dishonesty, to desecration, debasement and a blurring of our scales of value. There is a genuine and a false grandeur, there is a genuine and a false solemnity, if it is genuine it lifts us above our everyday cares and cheers us as does Mozart's music, if it is false it depresses us and fills us with dismal gravity; the intrinsic quality and fitness of what is eminent and solemn vouch for its genuineness. The works of Michelangelo and Rubens speak of true greatness and not mere bloated vulgarity, and no one will compare the sublime grandeur of the Parthenon, of the Hagia Sophia or of St. Peter's with the hippopotamic monstrosities of stone heaps erected by Nero and his fellow dictators of all ages, with the Voelkerschlacht-Memorial at Leipzig, the Paris Opera, or with the horrible neo-renaissance of the nineteenth century secular buildings. Titian's "Charles V after the Battle of Mühlberg" emanates true greatness and strength, while Makart and battle-field painters such as Anton v. Werner manufactured inane, photographic daubs. (Concerning the question of grandeur in architecture and the general problems of modern building connected with it, the excellent essays of Peter Meyer in the journal, *Das Werk, Schweizer Monatsschrift für Architektur, Freie Kunst, Angewandte Kunst,* April, 1938, July and September, 1940,

and April, 1941, should be consulted; and we would also remind the reader of the wonderful chapter "Ceci tuera cela" in Victor Hugo's *Notre Dame de Paris.*)

2. A particular aesthetic difficulty seems to me to lie in the fact that the various art forms differ so completely in their sociological character and thus express the influence of the general "Zeitgeist" in different degrees. Whereas architecture is by nature entirely social and therefore gives direct expression to the peculiarities of a period in the history of thought and society, this applies only with considerable reservations to painting which is so much more individualized, and explains why side by side with the disastrous nineteenth century architecture we find achievements in the field of painting which on the average far outdistance those of the eighteenth century. While Europe's cities were being disfigured, Cézanne was vigorously painting away for thirty years without paying any attention to the "Zeitgeist" which was so unfavourable to him. That would not have been possible for an architect, nor, to a lesser degree, for a sculptor or a composer. Nevertheless, it is, of course, true that impressionism in painting was dependent on the materialist "Zeitgeist" and related to the contemporary naturalism in literature; the friendship between Cézanne and Zola has, therefore, a deeper meaning. But here it must be remembered that "style" in painting is only one side of the art and can be influenced by the times, whereas the other side, ability itself—Cézanne's magic treatment of color, for instance—is something great for all time. However, I would say that painting has been infected by the nineteenth and twentieth century adoration of the colossal in two directions: (a) quite clearly in that form of painting which aiming at external mass reactions, is nothing but painted vulgarity and inhumanity; (b) fundamentally in the compulsive abjuration of feeling which has been taking place since the advent of impressionism, in the conscious distortion and debasement of form (in the deformed torsos painted by the expressionists, for instance, whose predecessor at the turn of the seventeenth century was the now so characteristically overrated El Greco), and finally in the increasing abandonment of man and his understanding as standard and compass, i.e., that "banishment of man from art," which in an unguarded moment Ortega y Gasset (*La Deshumanisación del Arte*) even praised. The last point explains the strange and disquieting fact that modern painting (and also modern music which must be considered in the same way) produces works which are so far above the heads of the people. It appears to me that we have here a complete parallel with the positivist and relativist development of modern science, i.e., the abandonment of human values. "Science pour la science," corresponds to "art pour l'art." A similar interpretation of the frightful disease of modern art may now be found in the important book by Hans Sedlmayr, *Verlust der Mitte,* Salzburg, 1948.

There is one last important point: the cult of the colossal also lacks all appreciation of historical continuity, all sense of harmony and reverence for what has been created. Just as Nero was suspected, perhaps with some justification, of burning Rome in order to erect his showy edifices, the nineteenth century, too, is almost unsurpassed in its destruction of the venerable architectural monuments of the past and of the age-old civilization of the open country, and it is symptomatic that today we find a ruthless building mania wherever the political and intellectual ideas of the nineteenth century have their last fling. On the question of how to explain the decay of architecture in the nineteenth century, see now: A. Rüstow, *Die Geistesgeschichtlischesoziologischen ursachen des verfalls der Abendländischen Baukunst im* 19. *Jahrhundert,* "Archiv für Philosophie" (Istanbul), 1937, vol. II, No. 1.

If we turn to music, we meet the cult of the colossal in the general development which led from Purcell, Handel, Bach, Haydn and Mozart to the compositions of the nineteenth and twentieth century, where everything is brought into play and anything is used for effect; characteristically this music owes much to Russian influence, for example, when, with almost amusing naiveté, it strives to improve quality by multiplying the number of instruments in the orchestra. In the same category belongs that most doubtful "beautification" of Bach which Stokowski has been carrying out in Philadelphia by the irreverent but artful addition of basses to the simple instrumentation of the cantor of St. Thomas. In this connection see also Goethe's remark to Eckermann on 14th January, 1827. The author is glad to note that his views are shared by such an eminent expert as Wilhelm Furtwängler (*Gespräche über Musik*, Zürich, 1949).

Note No. 21 (page 68). The science of history:

The idea that the nineteenth century surpassed the eighteenth in historical understanding is now being recognized as a legend, a legend which was only possible on the basis of the nineteenth century view of history. Whoever attributes lack of historical sense to the eighteenth century cannot know Vico, Montesquieu, Herder, Adam Smith, Hume, Voltaire's historical works or Gibbon. Then the study of history was focused on man's intrinsic nature and with the aid of certain values and meta-historic principles one tried to keep out of the morass of factual details (which, it is true, were not gone into too carefully). The nineteenth century, on the other hand, is characterized, first, by the manner in which man, his fate pre-determined, is left to the mercy of the tremendous forces of history and thus crushed; secondly, by the positivist belief that assiduous research of documents would show "what actually happened" and the concomitant delusion that there is such a thing as history without postulates and viewpoints; and thirdly, by so-called "historicism" which reduces everything to historical relativity and is therefore bound to ruin not only the science of history but all other sciences which it influences, by robbing them of all norms of value (which are often based particularly on history).

Note No. 22 (page 68). Jurisprudence:

Here we find the same contrast, both in the eighteenth century's sure sense of value, and in the greater proximity of its jurisprudence to reality and humanity, qualities which differ widely from that "logicistic" formal jurisprudence based on objective positivism towards which the nineteenth century tended. The jurisprudence of the eighteenth century is to that of the nineteenth what the great codes of the former (the Swedish Law Code of 1734, the General Prussian Common Law, and also the Code Napoléon and the General Austrian Civil Law Code) are to the German Civil Law Code, whilst the Swiss can boast that their Civil Code is a true heir of the eighteenth century in its clear conception of justice, its intelligibility and its popular character. By incorporating in the Civil Law Code a great part of the old popular laws, as had the Swedish Civil Code one and a half centuries earlier, Switzerland demonstrated its spiritual kinship with those countries which have successfully checked the rank growth of the professional jurisprudence inspired by Roman Law.

Note No. 23 (page 68). The cult of the "Strong Man":

E. Quinet (*L'esprit nouveau*, Paris, 1875, page 199) said of Mommsen that his Roman History is really nothing but "le Deux-Décembre tranporté dans les cinq siècles de la République romaine." And he repeats what the eighteenth century had already known and what has now become transparently clear: that the real cause of the fall of the Roman Empire was that it was based on naked force. It is not the fall of the Roman Empire that is astounding, but the fact that it did not collapse much earlier—the empire of which Tacitus (*Vita Agricolae,* XXX) says in a memorable passage: "raptores orbis, postquam cuncta vastantibus defuere terrae, et mare scrutantur; si locuples hostis est, avari; si pauper, ambitiosi; quos non oriens, non occidens satiaverit; soli omnium opes atque inopiam pari affectu concupiscunt; auferre, trucidare, rapere, falsis nominibus, imperium; atque ubi solitudinem faciunt, pacem appellant." Cf. Harald Fuchs' study, *Der geistige Widerstand gegen Rom in der antiken Welt,* Berlin, 1938. St. Augustin spoke from experience when he called empires ruled without justice great gangs of robbers (magna latroncitura).

Note No. 24 (page 70). The kinship between the eighteenth and the sixteenth century:
There is indeed an abundance of material to support the theory of the inner relationship between each of these centuries with the preceding one, between the eighteenth and the sixteenth, between the nineteenth and the seventeenth, and perhaps between the twentieth, only starting now, and the eighteenth and the sixteenth. As regards the century of Erasmus, Rabelais, Montaigne, of the well-beloved Queen of Navarre, of "Merry Old England," of Sebastian Franck, Fischart and the Humanists, we would only quote the following from the essays of Montaigne (livre III, ch. 13) in his old-fashioned French: "Si avons-nous beau monter sur des échasses, car, sur des échasses, encore faut-il marcher de nos jambes. Et sur le plus haut trône du monde, nous ne sommes assis que sur notre cul." We confidently leave the reader to draw his conclusions and to decide where lies wisdom and where folly—in the foregoing or in the following example of the nineteenth century cult of the colossal: "Forward without pause, is the battle-cry of the present, and he would indeed not fit the times who would barter the pleasure of unending change which is synonymous with progress, for the mess of pottage of a seemingly quietist past" (Karl Lamprecht, *Deutsche Geschichte der jüngsten Vergangenheit und Gegenwart,* volume 1, Berlin, 1912, page 260). As regards the kinship between the seventeenth and the nineteenth century which we have stressed repeatedly, the very informative book by Karl Joël, *Wandlungen der Weltanschauung,* Tübingen, 1928-34, should also be consulted, though with some caution.
A good example of the difficulties that this theory is likely to present is provided by the reformers of the sixteenth century, particularly Luther and Calvin, the former seeming to fit rather into the fifteenth and the latter more into the seventeenth century; it remains true, of course, that Lutheran orthodoxy and Calvinist puritanism did not really flourish until the seventeenth century when they meet their Catholic counterpart, the fierce theocracy of the Counter-Reformation. On the other hand, a man like Scarron, who similar to Lichtenberg in the eighteenth century, triumphed over his sick body by sheer joie de vivre, is so completely outside his time that one can hardly believe him to be a contemporary of Corneille and Racine (who dared to laugh over Scarron's parody of Vergil only in secret). The intellectual development in seventeenth century England would also require separate treatment. Although the country produced in Hobbes a particularly challenging representative of that century and through the Puritan revolution took a worthy part in the intellectual and spiritual development of the Continent, yet in men like Locke and others the spirit of the eighteenth century stirred at a noticeably early date.

We mentioned that Racine only secretly dared to enjoy Scarron's travesty of Vergil. This absence of all sense of humor in that stilted period of the baroque—the " 'hispanicized' century" (Jacob Burckhardt)—finds particularly amusing expression also in the fact that Racine's attempts at comedy (1688) fell completely flat; "les personnes de goût eurent peur *de n'avoir pas ri dans les règles*" (according to Anatole France, *Le gènie latin,* Paris, 1917, page 176). It need hardly be stressed that in this gloomy century there took place not only the Thirty Years War (which is reflected even on Swiss soil in the violent risings around Jenatsch in the Grisons), but also unheard of colonial crimes, a flourishing negro slave trade, witches' trials, the punishment of running the gauntlet, bloody persecutions and cruelties under Peter the Great, and at the same time the butchering of millions in China. It is on the other hand worth while to remember that not only Hobbes but also Descartes, Pascal and Spinoza paid some tribute to the brutal spirit of the century. A description of how the sun of humanity and reason broke once more through the clouds at the end of the seventeenth century, and this time with great and lasting strength, may be found in P. Hazard's excellent book, *La crise de la conscience européenne,* 1680-1715, Paris, 1936.

Note No. 25 (page 71). The "German Century":

It cannot in truth be gainsaid that there exists a certain kinship between the spirit of the nineteenth century, as we have described it, and the German national spirit, with its predilection for excess, its tendency to go to extremes everywhere, to depart from the human mean, its dogged insistence on taking everything tragically, its tense "on guard" attitude towards everything life brings, its aimless dynamic energy, and the readiness to annihilate one's own personality, symptoms which no observer can overlook and which are traceable through a thousand years of German history. It is typical that there is hardly another country in the world with such an extremist literature, e.g., Stirner, Spengler, Ernst Jünger or lesser writers of the most diverse kind. A contemporary Italian observer (B. Guiliano, *Latinità e Germanesimo,* Bologna, 1940) is quite right in saying that Nietzsche cannot be imagined as an Italian (page 130) and he is also right when he declares: "Mentre il nostro sentimento iniziale è il respetto d'una legge che ci parla dall' alto, il sentimento iniziale della mentalità tedesca è piuttosto quello dell' impeto di un' energia da esprimere, par crearsi oltre ogni commandamento superiore la legge della vita" (page 14), or: "La nostra mentalità latina quando sbaglia serba ancora sempre una sua capacità di eludere i suoi stessi errori e di evitarne le conseguenze ultime" (page 132). An Italian Nietzsche would at least have had that playful operatic manner of a D'Annunzio whom no one can take really seriously. We also cannot help feeling that if constant "bad temper" is such a characteristic feature of the intellectual life of the nineteenth century (which is, as we have seen, still with us), we should blame not only Queen Victoria, who was "not amused" by witticisms uttered at her table, but also and in particular the German influence. Edgar Quinet (*L'esprit nouveau,* Paris, 1875, page 322) obviously had Germany in mind when he wrote: "La mauvaise humeur devenue dogme philosophique. Des arts de mauvaise humeur, une littérature de mauvaise humeur." And finally, even if the results had not proved it, it would nevertheless be plain that the famous "Realpolitik" is only a particular expression of the German love for the phantastic and unreal. (Cf. Richard Mueller-Freienfels, *Psychologie des deutschen Menschen und seiner Kultur,* 2nd edition, Munich, 1930, page 158.)

If one has observed the growing influence of all those intellectual opiates with which the Orient, Russia and Asia have repeatedly seduced Europe and upset its intellectual balance, from Plato to Dostoyevsky and to Buddhism, one cannot deny that an "easternization" of Europe and a displacement of mediterranean moderation and the Graeco-Latin heritage which are the essence of what we call "Western," took place during the nineteenth century. There can be no doubt that unlimited despotism, Caesaro-Papism and collectivism are also part of these Asiatic imports. In this connection the excellent book by Henri Massis, *Défense de l'Occident* (Paris, 1927), whose only weakness is to have overlooked China's exceptional and important position, should be consulted. Confucianism is very closely related to the best traditions of the Occident and it is no coincidence that the eighteenth century was strongly attracted by it.

CHAPTER II

POLITICAL SYSTEMS AND ECONOMIC SYSTEMS

> You are granting the state too much power. It should not demand what it cannot compel. But the gifts of love and the gifts of the spirit cannot be exacted by force. These the state had better leave untouched or else we take its law and post it on the pillory! By God! he knows not the measure of his sin who would make the state the arbiter of morals. The state has become hell because men wanted to make it their heaven. The state is but the rough shell around the kernel of life and nothing more. It is the wall around the garden of human fruits and flowers. But what avails a wall around the garden if the soil is parched? Rain from the heavens is the only answer here.
>
> —Hölderlin, *Hyperion.*

Democracy, Liberalism and the Collectivist State

In discussions regarding the political and economic shape of the future one repeatedly has the comforting experience of being able to narrow down differences of opinion without much effort to an area where reasoned thought can achieve clarity. Every discussion presupposes unanimity regarding fundamental values and ends, and also the willingness of everyone honestly to submit to the ineluctable reason of an argument or the convincing force of empirical proof. As soon as these conditions are no longer fulfilled, genuine discussion becomes impossible, and what takes its place already contains the elements of civil war. But even before that the discussion may degenerate into a heated battle of opinions unless we succeed in basing it on fundamental convictions universally held.

If we may then assume that the fundamentals as well as our entire moral code are axiomatic, and further that there are clearly defined political and economic systems which the great majority are unanimous in rejecting, and further still that there are also certain basic aims of economic and political reform which enjoy an equally general recognition, we may hope to be of some use when attempting to elucidate points where lack of clarity seems to be the only remaining cause of divergent views, where incompatible goals are being pursued or courses advocated which endanger ultimate and generally desired ends.

What we have to clarify first of all is the meaning of those concepts around which discussion revolves today: democracy, liberalism and what we are going to call the principle of the collectivist state. The urgent need for a delimitation and precise, even if only temporary, definition, arises from the careless and

83

faulty manner in which these concepts are generally being employed in everyday discussion. Here it will be most expedient to consider the sociological structure of the collectivist form of government from all angles and thence attempt a correct description of the other forms of government.

From a historical point of view the modern collectivist form of government bears a marked resemblance to those city regimes of antiquity (e.g., Corinth and Megara) which are known as *tyrannis* and which we find again in some of the city republics of the Italian Renaissance. In both cases we witness the brutal usurpation of sovereignty by a minority which rises from the masses, using them as stepping stones by cajolery and threats; this minority is led by a "charismatic leader" (Max Weber) and, in contrast to genuine "dictatorship" (in the sense of ancient Roman law), it considers its rule not as a temporary mandate which, after the national emergency has passed, is to be handed back to the lawful authorities ("mandatory" or "commissioned" dictatorship), but as a normal and permanent form of political organization, which is subject to no control. The widespread use of the term dictatorship to describe the collectivist state of our time is therefore incorrect and likely to lead to wrong conclusions. Every well-integrated state contains in normal, and even more so in abnormal, times a hierarchic-authoritarian element whose mere intensification does not yet produce the collectivist state. Kemal Ataturk, for instance, the creator of modern Turkey, was certainly a dictator in the sense that as the head of the state he ruled practically unopposed, but it would be wrong to place him in the ranks of the collectivist usurpators; his historical function rather approached that of a Roman "dictator" as closely as possible—in contrast to the genuine tyrants, Sulla or Cæsar, who significantly called themselves "dictatores perpetui" —so that after his death the reins of state could without break in continuity pass into the hands of his moderate successor. There is, then, in the Turkey of today no hierarchic and exclusive elite of rulers which recklessly identifies itself with the state and holds a monopoly in arms. Nor do we find there that nervous self-confirmation and drive for ever new mass stimulants in order to prevent the dangerous backsliding into stable everyday life and the equilibrium of normal and continuous social forms, which are the greatest menace to the collectivist state. Where these and some other factors are lacking we may certainly speak of a dictatorship— in the case not only of Turkey, but also of Portugal—but not of a collectivist political system.

While the collectivist state is thus clearly distinguished—as much as its predecessors in ancient times and in the Italian Renaissance— from dictatorship and mere despotism, it is yet incorrect to associate it with the concept of a pre-eminently hierarchic, aristocratic and authoritarian rule and to contrast it with democracy. Wherever this happens, we are faced with a particularly confusing fallacy. Since modern democracy has been won in a heated and passionate battle against arbitrariness and oppression, it is very understandable that the concept kindles associations in us which do not entirely coincide with the true nature of democracy and its inherent possibilities. There is no one who is not deeply moved on reading Abraham Lincoln's famous speech on the battlefield of Gettysburg, that speech which concludes with the words "the government of the people by the people for the people," and is a worthy successor to the speech Pericles gave more than two thousand years before in honor of the Athenians killed in battle. But is it really blasphemy when Oscar Wilde parodies Lincoln's famous phrase as "the bludgeoning of the people by the people for the people"? It is certainly blasphemous toward the venerable Lincoln—but is it also as regards the concept and the dangers of pure democracy? Benjamin Constant, Tocqueville, John Stuart Mill, Alexander Hamilton, Madison, Calhoun, Lecky, and many others who cannot be charged with reactionary views, have pointed out that democracy —and democracy more than any other political system—can lead to the worst forms of despotism and intolerance if bounds are not set to it by other principles and institutions, and it is this limitation in all its aspects that we must call the liberal content of a political structure. There is hardly any need to draw attention to the germs of modern totalitarianism latent in Rousseau or even more in the radical theorists and practitioners of Jacobinism, in order to furnish convincing proof that the collectivist state has its roots in the soil of unlimited democracy when that is not sufficiently balanced and diluted by "nonpolitical spheres," "corps intermédiaires" (Montesquieu), liberalism, federalism, self-administration and aristocratism. It is in fact an important characteristic of the collectivist state, both of the old and the new variety, that it always rises on the waves of a broad mass movement—"cuncta plebes novarum rerum studio Catilinae incepta probabat" (Sallust, *Bellum Catilinae,* 37)—and can only maintain itself on that foundation. It can, therefore, quite justifiably be asserted that the collectivist state is precisely that form of sovereignty in which the *Revolt of the Masses* (Ortega y Gasset) against the cultural and social elite expresses itself. Its antithesis is not democracy which is merely one of many possible vehicles of public authority, but rather the liberal principle which erects a bar against the power of the state—always liable to exceed its limits whatever its form—a bar consisting of non-political spheres, of tolerance and civil liberties; and this principle is, therefore, compatible with democratic as well as non-democratic political systems. This is what we usually have in mind when we picture democracy as the antithesis of the collectivist state, but we know

now of what dangerous obfuscation we are guilty in doing so. There is no denying it: the collectivist state is rooted in the masses (to which professors can belong as well as workers) and it can only exist under conditions which, sociologically speaking, we term spiritual collectivization, that is, conditions of society for which precisely the extreme democratic development is an excellent preparation but which is the direct opposite of the liberal as well as the conservative-aristocratic ideal.

It would hardly seem necessary to examine what constitutes the actual difference between the collectivist state and the pure despotism of, say, a Louis XIV. It seems that their common denominator is the lack of freedom, but the lack of freedom of those times—and we shall certainly not whitewash it—was probably not only less comprehensive, but primarily of a different kind. The sociological and intellectual climate must have been different and what we have just said about the mass character of the collectivist state will help to explain this significant difference. We must, however, add yet another fact, namely, that the collectivist state is distinguished from a genuine democracy, where government is based on free elections, as well as from all forms of monarchical absolutism because it lacks legitimacy and therefore those deep roots in tradition on which even the most indolent and incompetent of monarchs can generally rely. That is why the collectivist state seeks to make good its legally doubtful origin and the absence of the population's tacit and habitual assent by all the means of deliberate persuasion and propaganda calculated to appeal to the strongest motives. What it has to fear above all, is the humdrum everyday life, the quietest customary form of existence, the bourgeois conventionality, and, therefore, its foremost aim must be a dynamism which does not allow the population to recover its breath but dangles before its eyes ever new colossal goals of the future—more and more comprehensive five and ten year plans, whose completion is constantly postponed, and so forth. One cannot imagine that the collectivist state will one day be satiated and will with Faust call out to the fleeting moment: "Linger with me, thou that art so bright!" It is, rather, like a spinning top which can only be kept in balance by rapid gyration. This urge for continuous movement, which is peculiar to the collectivist state, is the primary element, while the choice of aims seems secondary and is made in terms of their dynamic value. Hence its characteristic pragmatism: the interchangeability of principles and programs, and what one might call the autonomy of the means or the fetishistic attitude towards means. This creates a difficulty which baffles all sociologists, namely, to distinguish the real essence of the collectivist state from what are merely facades or means; there is no other way than to see in it the maintenance of the power of the state itself, in the mere "libido dominandi" (Sallust, *Bellum Catilinae*, 2), and to link this absence of a positive program with the general dissolution of values and disintegration of standards.

Political Structure and Economic Structure

Let us now return to our comforting assumption that regarding the ultimate ends of society, we may presuppose essential unanimity. However, we are probably right in saying that agreement on fundamental political aims is far greater than on economic and social programs for the future. Only a few wish to tamper with the liberal-democratic structure of the political system, but many think that they are therefore free to re-fashion the economic system. If they find that a radical transformation of the economic system entails substantial changes in the political constitution, then they believe at least that in the final analysis only what one might term administrative changes are involved, leaving the liberal-democratic core of the constitution intact. To put it bluntly: many people believe that it is no longer possible to resist the trend of the times towards economic collectivism, socialism, the planned economy or whatever one wants to call it, and if that trend necessitates changes in the constitution these can be carried through without any serious risk of copying patterns which have been condemned. It would be false piety—thus one might interpret the thoughts of these people—to maintain a political structure which developed in the age of the stage coach; it should be adapted to the age of the high powered electro-locomotive.

It needs to be said, and said plainly, that people who think along these lines are victims of a calamitous self-deception. There always exists a definite, more or less fixed relationship between a political and an economic system which makes it impossible to combine just any political system with just any economic system, and vice versa. Society is always and in all aspects a whole—politically, economically and culturally—and one would indeed have to believe in miracles if one would expect socialism to be an exception. That is precisely the spiritual tragedy of socialism, which anyone could experience who was its adherent at one time or other and which does not cease to torment every intelligent and upright socialist: the tragedy of a movement which suffers from an incurable contradiction, wanting to complete man's liberation—initiated by liberalism and democratism—by radical means, it is forced to turn the state into a Leviathan. Socialism can be nothing but destructive of freedom in the widest sense of the word. It wants to crown the work of emancipation, yet can result in nothing but the most abject subjugation of the individual. Experience and reflection confirm the

truth of these remarks in so overwhelming a manner that for an
honest socialist of whatever shade there should be no other choice
than either frankly to take upon himself all the political and
cultural consequences of his economic ideals, or to seek other paths
of economic and social reform. The reasons for this have only
recently been demonstrated so frequently and thoroughly that we
can deal with them here in a few brief sentences.

Socialism—it must be agreed—means that the "autonomy of
the economic will," with which we are going to deal later on, is
suspended and replaced by the order from above. Since decisions
regarding the use of the economy's productive forces are no longer
made through the market but in the office of a government agency,
they become politicalized. It is this politicalization of the entire
economic process which provides an almost complete definition of
every kind of socialism and quasi-socialism (statism), and one can
hardly claim any understanding of the great questions of our time
if one does not persistently and at all times keep this in mind.
Everything which heretofore belonged to the "economic" sphere of
private enterprise and private law, is now transformed into something "political"; the market becomes a government agency; every
purchase becomes a state transaction; private law becomes public
law; "being served" in store is replaced by "being dealt with" by
civil servants; the price mechanism is controlled by decrees; competition becomes the struggle for influence and power in the state,
for party offices and government jobs; the supply of raw materials
becomes a question of political spheres of influence; property
becomes a concept of state sovereignty; business decisions are turned
into governmental acts sanctioned by penal law; foreign currency
transactions become capital offences. Henceforward the population
has to use its productive capacities in a manner deemed suitable
by the group dominating the state. Does anyone seriously believe
that not only the election of this group but also the millions of
individual decisions which it has to make every day can be based on
democratic principles and that the sphere of individual liberty can
still be safeguarded? It should be clear at once that the process of
public voting cannot be extended to questions regarding the production of blotting paper and gramophone records, but whether
such, and millions of other goods, and how many of them, should
be manufactured is precisely the decision which has to be made
anew every moment because it is the essence of collectivist economic
planning.

To bring about such a decision all the time in an even imperfectly democratic manner is impossible. This follows also from
another reflection. Everyone knows that a democracy can function
properly only if in all the essential questions of communal life there
exists practical unanimity: *in necessariis unitas*. Even majority

decisions remain unsatisfactory here, because it is hard to see why the rule of 51 per cent. of the voters over 49 per cent. should be much more reputable than that of 49 per cent. over 51 per cent., and even the possibility characterizing every genuine democracy, that the majority decision of today can be replaced by the opposite decision of the majority tomorrow, must, in view of the almost irrevocable character of far-reaching decisions, remain often enough nothing but theory. In such cases, therefore, we can hardly say that it is the "will of the people," the "volonté générale," that decides. How far even the model democracies are removed from this ideal is proved by the mere fact that the financial maintenance of the state always requires more or less irksome compulsion and that taxes are everywhere a form of private expense which affords least pleasure; this would not be the case if the national budget rested on genuinely unanimous acceptance. An ideal democracy therefore presupposes that the people are in almost complete agreement on questions of government. However unattainable this ideal may appear, the problem as such must be clearly discerned and the nearer a country approaches the solution, the better for its democracy. Three essential conditions must be fulfilled in order to come closer to such a solution: first, a certain minimum of national community spirit and uniformity in thinking and feeling (a uniformity which is probably the ultimate secret of English democracy); second, the greatest possible decentralization of government (federalism in Switzerland and in the United States, English local government); and third, and this is perhaps the most important point, a limitation of government interference to those tasks where a maximum of unity can be expected and whose extent coincides with the legitimate sphere of governmental functions, legitimate because they are inherent in the concept of the state. This last observation brings us to the crux of the matter. Unity can only be expected, even in the most favorable circumstances, when national problems of a most general and elementary nature are under discussion. But how would it be possible to effect even a tolerable agreement on all those questions of detail which are the essence of economic processes and which affect individual interests most directly and acutely? The decisions which the state would have to make here are always decisions in favor of this and to the detriment of that group. How can a satisfactory democratic compromise be achieved here? Such decisions can only be made in an authoritarian way; ultimately and essentially they will always be arbitrary and too often they will be made under the pressure of an interested minority.

To this we have to add yet another and even decisive reason. The non-socialist market economy is a process which is made up of innumerable voluntary economic actions of individuals. The market regulates these actions and gives all participants directives for the adjustment of production to the wants of the consumers. Obedience to these directives of the market is rewarded, disobedience is punished in the most extreme case with bankruptcy (that is, compulsory withdrawal from the ranks of the entrepreneurs responsible for the production process) and by destruction of the economic basis of existence. Now socialism means (if it is to mean anything at all), that the democratic ruler "Market" is replaced by the autocratic ruler "State," a further example of how socialism "politicalizes" the economy. It is in keeping with this politicalization that the new ruler of the economy, the state, enforces respect by means which are in accordance with its political nature: orders sanctioned by criminal law. To express it in the starkest manner possible, which will only be found incomprehensible by those not schooled in fundamental thinking: if formerly the bailiff had the final word, it is now the executioner. It should really be no longer open to doubt that socialism goes hand in hand with a thoroughly authoritarian system of government. Whether a state begins with anti-tyrannic socialism or with anti-socialist tyranny, logical development will always see to it that both states finally reach the same point: a perfect tyranny and a collectivism which permeates all spheres of social life. In the long run economic dictatorship can as little exclude political and intellectual control as, conversely, political and intellectual dictatorship can exclude economic control. It is hardly forgivable naiveté to believe that a state can be all powerful in the economic sphere without also being autocratic in the political and intellectual domain and vice versa. "If there are Governments armed with economic power, if in a word we are to have Industrial Tyrannies, then the last stage of man will be worse than the first" (Oscar Wilde). Thus the saying of Hölderlin of a hundred years ago would then come true: what turned the state into hell was precisely that men wanted to make it their heaven. It therefore makes no sense to reject collectivism politically if one does not at the same time propose a decidedly non-socialist solution of the problems of economic and social reform. If we are not in earnest with this relentless logic, we have vainly gone through a unique and costly historical object lesson.

Now it is possible to raise a very serious objection here. Does not the present-day war economy (1940), where even in democratic countries governmental powers are increased so tremendously, prove that socialist centralization and control of the economy are possible without harming the democratic core of the political structure? Do we not see how entire nations all around us willingly put the paramount interests of the community first? In order properly to understand this process which everyone has experienced personally, we must interpolate here a reflection of fundamental significance, which is likely to deepen our understanding of the biology of society and state.

Philosophers of all ages are agreed that man's relationship to the community has always been two-sided. Two souls dwell in his breast, of which the one is gregarious while the other would be alone. There exists an "antagonism between the anti-social and social instincts of man" (Kant), which keeps society at a constant polar tension, the tension between the desire for social unity (integration) and the opposing desire for individual segregation (differentiation). Man is neither an ant nor a raving beast; he has chosen the more difficult path of twofoldedness which is full of tension, the path of "unsociable sociability" (Kant), and only thereby has culture been made possible. It is a clear and unalterable fact of which one must not lose sight in all topical discussions of political, economic or constitutional questions: man seeks the golden mean in his contact with society, not too much, but also not too little, and this normal degree of integration—the feeling of "belonging," the desire to fulfil the social duties of sacrifice and devotion, temperate patriotism, the natural subjection to the elementary duties of community life, the feeling of being at one with the others, of being part of the great whole and having a place therein—is precisely what neither the individual nor the aggregate of society can miss for any length of time without becoming "socially sick." But since we happen to be as we are, we have, on the other hand, no intention of letting ourselves be walled in alive by society as were the unhappy victims of Tamerlane. We are willing to give unto Cæsar what is Cæsar's on the condition that we can keep the rest for God, our family, our neighbors and ourselves, for otherwise we would become "socially sick" in the opposite sense. While in the previous case of "insufficient integration" we suffered from social malnutrition, so now in the case of "hyper-integration" we suffer from social overfeeding, and we can bear the one as little as the other, and this is also true of society as a whole. "La multitude qui ne se réduit pas à l'unité est confusion; l'unité qui ne dépend pas de la multitude est tyrannie" (Pascal).

Social malnutrition is the typical disease of a society which is disintegrating into isolated individuals; where there is no longer that warmth which solidarity generates, where the feeling that with our rights as well as with our duties we occupy a definite place in society, in other words, the feeling of being embedded in the small and in the large community vanishes more and more. Society appears dissolved into a mass of individuals adrift, whose relationship to each other becomes increasingly mechanical and anonymous, based on the market, competition, the division of labor, technology and the law: precisely the pattern that has developed everywhere in the course of the last century. In all countries, in some less, in others more, society has been ground into a mass of individuals, who have never been so closely herded together and so dependent on each other and yet at the same time they are more rootless, more isolated and more like grains of sand than ever before. Whatever one wants to call it—spiritual collectivization, atomization or social disintegration—it is always the same pathological process, viewed from different sides. All the misery, all the problems of our time have their ultimate roots here, and all the new blueprints of our social architects are worthless if they do not take this ultimate and greatest infirmity of our time as their starting point. The individual driven into isolation and suffering from social malnutrition feels forlorn and there exists even a theory, meriting serious attention, which attributes suicide, as a mass phenomenon of our civilization, to the individual "losing his place" ("désencadrement") in society. In their yearning for social integration men finally grasp at everything that is offered to them, and here they may easily and understandably suffer the same fate as the frogs in the fable who asked for a king and got a crane.

Now to turn to the other extreme, namely, hyper-integration: this phenomenon appears, like a fever in the human body, in an entirely normal and beneficient manner when a sudden emergency, an earthquake, for instance, or a vast fire, summons all the defensive forces of society. Instantly the temperature of society leaps up, and entirely of our own accord we sacrifice our privacy in order to be one with society and to lend a hand where we are needed. We subject ourselves without reflection and argument to the most far reaching control from above, and think it perfectly in order for martial law to be declared in an area visited by an earthquake. The same holds good on a larger scale in the case of war. It, too, leads immediately to "feverish" degrees of integration, and then it is possible not only for civil liberties which safeguard the individual's privacy to be extensively suspended, but also for socialist measures to be carried out, measures which represent nothing but the economic side of hyper-integration. All this is completely natural and is no cause for alarm. But it is something entirely different to retain socialism as a permanent peace-time institution; for this would mean that social hyper-integration which socialism presupposes, would be accepted as the normal, permanent state of affairs. This, however, is an altogether gigantic task, because it runs counter to man's very nature, and it can only be performed to a certain degree and for limited periods by artificially keeping the population in that abnormal feverish state which is caused by earthquakes or wars. While for the normal degree of social integration the positive feelings of unpretentious patriotism and a genial liking for one's neighbors suffice, it seems that this is not enough for the spastic degree of integration which the collectivist state requires. In order to achieve that social molecular density which is a prerequisite of collectivism, it is apparently always necessary to incite negative feelings, that is feelings directed against someone or against something, and when no real targets of hate or sources of fear are present they have to be invented. If, then, socialism is to be made the normal, permanent state, it presupposes a political system which manages to maintain the necessary hyper-integration of society by these artificial means, even without war, earthquakes or floods.

Yet perhaps there is ·some way of jumping into the water without getting wet. Instead of transferring the direction of the economy to the state, could one not confidently entrust it to the professional and business associations, made up of non-political experts, the trusts, co-operatives, labor unions and production groups, in short is it not possible to make use of the magic formula of "corporativism"? It seems indeed as if this idea presents a last refuge for many people who are too clever to indulge in any illusions regarding the political consequences of collectivism, and yet believe collectivism to be ineluctable, who resort to it out of perplexity, out of fatalism, or out of a secret desire which clothes itself in the sacerdotal garb of the philosophy of history. We fear that we have to be so impolite as to term this a very unfortunate idea, however difficult we may find it to be discourteous in this particular case. It is the pet idea of all those whose speech is neither yea nor nay, who would like to express freely their aversion to "liberalism" and "individualism" without acknowledging collectivism as the logical consequence, who are looking for a third way, without much understanding of the details of economic life and the biology of society, and who then adopt the formula of the guild state which appeals more to the emotions than to the mind—unhappily without paying the least attention to the plainly discouraging experiences which were made with economic "self-administration" under the Weimar Republic and finally with the veritable farce of the guild state in Austria. And lastly, in the case of some people this idea of a guild constitution is nothing but economic obscurantism.

The professional and business associations offer promising possibilities and, properly integrated into the entity of state and economy, they produce much that is good; however, one cannot render them a worse service than to assign them functions which are bound to corrupt them as well as the whole body politic. For, either the final decision rests with the state after all, and then there is no change in the political outcome of collectivism except that now the all-powerful state creates for itself outer bastions in the form of corporative organizations which serve to carry its will deep into the

private economy; or—and this is the only possibility we are concerned with here—final decisions in the planned economy really
rest with the corporative organizations and then we have something
which corresponds to what mob rule represents in criminal law. If
the regulation of the economic process is no longer left to the
market, it becomes dependent on conscious political decisions which
cannot be delegated to authorities alien to the state without dissolv-
ing it. Genuine corporativism in the democratic state, then, means
that the state renounces great portions of its sovereignty in favor of
economic groups. The "capitalist" market economy has often been
reproached with "anarchy of the productive process"—a very unjust
reproach as everyone familiar with economics realizes. But what
we have described just now would lead to real and grave economic
anarchy. Suppose a secret anarchist society should announce a competition for the best solution to the problem: how can the cohesion
of the state be dissolved in the safest and most unobtrusive manner
—then this answer: "genuine (democratic) corporativism" would
deserve the first prize. Seriously speaking there should really
be no difference of opinion regarding the fact that once we decide
on the course of collectivism the helm should rest only in the
hands of the state and one can only hope that its agencies can
muster the greatest possible independence, expert knowledge and
resolution in guiding the ship, and the utmost lack of consideration
for the whisperings of group interests and lobbyists. Let us adapt
a sentence from the Bible: "Justice raises a people, but pluralism
(that is, the splitting up of the state into spheres of influence for
group interests) is a people's undoing." The anarchy of pluralism,
as all examples teach us, can never be more than a brief interlude.

A grave error is being committed by to-day's professional
organizations in that they are unable to make a clear distinction
between the legitimate and the illegitimate tasks of the professional
associations, and jumble together things which should be kept
strictly apart. The great danger of such efforts lies in the fact that
through the positive and legitimate parts of their program they
tend to attract well meaning people intent on the public weal,
whom they then turn into representatives and tools of the most
negative and destructive ideas. In order not to be confused we
must realize that whenever we speak of "profession," or "vocation,"
or "occupation" we may mean one of two quite different things.
First of all, we mean that men apply themselves to the production
of goods or the rendering of services with devotion, specialized
ability and joyful pride in creation and work, and that they share
the professional interests which result from their similar position
in life and the same technical working processes, without in the
least impairing public interests (aspect A). Secondly, however, we
mean that these specialized producers within the market economy

are at the same time sellers of their products and abilities, and that for reasons which we will explain later they have interests which by their very nature conflict with those of the public and which can only be assimilated by means of competition (aspect B). The doctor is not only the helpful friend at the sick bed (aspect A), but at the same time the man who later on sends us his bill and who has an interest (in his case curbed by a high standard of professional ethics), in making his bills as many and as high as possible (aspect B), and by the same token, we must not forget, in spite of all our esteem for the peasantry and all our interest in the technical questions of agriculture (aspect A), that the farmer, as the soberly calculating seller of his products, has an interest in the highest possible tariffs and subsidies and the lowest possible import quotas (aspect B). It is nothing but romantic obfuscation of the facts not to keep these two aspects apart and to allow the positive feelings created by aspect A, benefit pure group interests by keeping silent about aspect B. Nothing is more desirable than to aid the professional interests in the first sense (A) by raising professional pride and self-confidence and to further it by mutual aid within each occupation (professional training, welfare funds, &c.), and as long as these occupational associations remain within this "A sphere" they deserve our benevolent support. But it is, on the other hand, equally undesirable for them to trespass into the domain characterized by aspect B. In the sense of "B" the professions serve indeed no useful purpose in the integration of man in an orderly political life—they are a disintegrative, not a constructive element.

We must, therefore, adhere to our view: socialism as a permanent peace time institution is an economic system which we can only obtain at the price of the corresponding political system. The political and the economic structure of collectivism are merely two aspects of one and the same thing; they both are the ultimate result and the most radical manifestation of that spiritual collectivization, agglomeration, mechanization, atomization and proletarization which have become the curse of the Western world. If we want to escape this curse, we must, after first ridding ourselves of the inevitable wartime socialism, travel new roads in economic policy which are completely opposed to socialism of any kind. The nature of these new roads will be discussed in detail later on. There remains one thing to be emphasized here, namely, that the correlation between economic and political systems also holds good for the market economy. The market economy as an economic system which depends on the confidence and the enterprise of the individual and on his readiness to save and to take risks, cannot be maintained without certain protective measures and legal principles which offer security and protection to the individual not only in the face of the encroachments of other individuals, but also against the arbitrary interference of the state, and which add up to what we call the constitutional state. The much reviled and frequently misunderstood "human and civil rights" (and we once more want to draw attention to their Christiano-Germanic origin), contain precisely that which, for instance, the old Ottoman Turkey notoriously lacked for developing a flourishing economy: the inviolability of certain laws and rules for the protection of persons and property—the basis of that confidence without which private enterprise cannot continue for long and without which even the peasant dare no longer sow his wheat. The development of the last hundred and fifty years has led us to adopt many dangerous courses and has brought much misery over the world which is crying out for restitution, but we would scarcely want to be responsible for sacrificing lightheartedly its truly greatest achievement: the conquest of arbitrary might through right.

PART ONE—NOTES TO CHAPTER II

Note No. 1 (page 84). The new and unexpected—an essential element in the collectivist state:

On this the chapter concerning "die charismatische Herrschaft" in Max Weber's *Wirtschaft und Gesellschaft,* Grundriss der Sozialoekonomie, III, Tübingen, 1921, page 140 ff., is the primary source of reference. Note also the following remarkable passage from the classic work *De l'esprit de conquête et de l'usurpation,* which Benjamin Constant published immediately after the battle of Leipzig in 1813: "Un usurpateur est exposé à toutes les comparaisons que suggèrent les regrets, les jalousies ou les espérances; il est obligé de justifier son élévation: il a contracté l'engagement tacite d'attacher de grands résultats à une si grande fortune; il doit craindre de tromper l'attente du public, qu'il a si puissamment éveillée. L'inaction la plus raisonnable, la mieux motivée, lui devient un danger. Il faut donner aux Français tous les trois mois, disait un homme qui s'entend bien, quelque chose de nouveau: il a tenu sa parole" (II, 2). On the other hand a statesman like Salazar could not have expressed the non-collectivist character of his regime better than by saying (from Henri Massis, *Les idées restent,* Lyons, 1941, page 20 ff.): "Pour moi je n'ai qu'un but. Ce que je me propose, c'est de faire vivre le Portugal habituellement."

Note No. 2 (page 85). The anti-liberal tendency of pure democracy:

Machiavelli was, according to G. Ritter (*Machtstaat und Utopie,* Munich, 1940, page 87), perhaps the first to recognize clearly that the demon of power is not only to be found in despotic rulers but also in the people and can easily be released by any demagogue, a fact which neither the mediaeval theories of tyranny nor Erasmus seem to have realized. After the French Revolution it is Benjamin Constant in particular who discovers the tyrannical possibilities inherent in democracy and concludes from this "qu'il faut tracer un domaine des libertés et des droits personnels dont le limites soient infranchissables et au souverain et à la nation, et à la loi même" (E. Faguet,

Politiques et moralistes du dix-neuvième siècle, 1ère série, 16e éd., Paris, page 220). Apart from Tocqueville's well known works, whose main theme is precisely this inherent danger of democracy, and those of John Stuart Mill (particularly his essay *On Liberty*), we find the same idea discussed by the American writer John C. Calhoun in *A Disquisition on Government,* 1849, and in *Democracy and Liberty,* 1896, by the English writer, Lecky. It speaks once more for the wisdom of the fathers of the American Constitution that they clearly foresaw the danger of democratic tyranny by the majority and were guided by this consideration in writing the Constitution. It is impossible to understand the American Constitution with its complicated system of "checks and balances" unless one knows that its originators feared the tyranny of a democratic majority quite as much as that of an absolutist monarch from which they had just freed themselves. Theirs is an excellent example of how, with some intelligence, one can avoid jumping from the frying pan into the fire. It is well known how much the Swiss constitution has been influenced by the American, particularly in this respect. To the extent to which one departs in the United States from the spirit of the Constitution, though not from the letter, and reduces the liberal and federal counter-balances, the danger of a totalitarian development within the democracy grows, and this applies also elsewhere.

Once it is realized that neither the state, with its natural tendency towards despotism, nor the masses as such can be expected to produce anything but a tyrannical government, it becomes clear that other supports for freedom have to be found, anti-collectivist counter-balances which neither the state nor the masses can supply. Only those can be the guardians of freedom who really love it: the elite which, with instinctive authority, leads society and all genuine communities below, above and outside the state, the "corps inter-médiaires" (Montesquieu). In this respect, where we find the liberal principle differing so sharply from the democratic, it seems related to the aristocratic, but only if we interpret the concept of genuine aristocracy correctly. "Tout groupement organisé d'une manière durable dans la nation, possédant une pensée commune, des traditions, une direction, une vie propre, est un fait historique qui s'est créé un droit. Il tend au maintien de lui-même et à la sauvegarde de ce droit; il est élément aristocratique et élément libéral, libéral parce qu'il est aristocratique, aristocratique au point de devenir libéral. . . . Un système libéral qui prétend être pratique est forcé d'être aristocratique pour ne pas être illusoire, comme le système aristocratique le plus étroit est forcé d'être libéral pour ne pas tendre simplement à la guerre civile" (E. Faguet, op. cit., page 228 f.). It is typical that both J. de Maistre, the apostle of pure despotism, and Rousseau, the apostle of pure democracy, rejected the aristocratic as well as the liberal principle.

Note No. 3 (page 87). The collectivist state has no program:
This gives us an opportunity to demonstrate how the collectivist state is the last step in that moral and intellectual dissolution of which we have frequently spoken in this book, particularly in the introduction, i.e., that process which has resulted from the general development of Western civilization and can be traced in all countries, though some have more reserves with which to combat it than others. It is here that two phenomena in the history of thought, nihilism (Nietzsche) and pragmatism (William James) become of political moment. Concerning the connection with philosophical pragmatism, see W. Y. Elliot's article in "Political Science Quarterly," volume XLI, 1926, page 161 ff.

Note No. 4 (page 88). The totalitarian character of socialism:
I first dealt with this problem in my article "Sozialismus und politische

D

Diktator," "Neue Züricher Zeitung," 18th and 19th January, 1937; subsequently I received welcome support from Walter Lippmann, *The Good Society*, Boston, 1937, and F. A. von Hayek, *Freedom and the Economic System*, Chicago, 1939, who, later on summarized and perfected these views in his well known book *The Road to Serfdom* (London, 1944, and Chicago, 1945). (Cf. also my study, *Zur Theorie des Kollectivismus*, "*Kyklos*" (Berne), 1949). The following passage should also be remembered in this connection: "The probability of the people in power being individuals who would dislike the possession and exercise of power is on a level with the probability that an extremely tender-hearted person would get the job of whipping master on a slave plantation" (Frank H. Knight in his review of Lippmann's book, "Journal of Political Economy," December, 1939, page 869). See also Elie Halévy, *L'ère des tyrannies*, Paris, 1938; William E. Rappard, *L'individu et l'état dans l'évolution constitutionelle de la Suisse*, Zürich, and Gaetano Mosca, *The Ruling Class* (the American translation of his standard work, *Elementi di Scienza Politica*), New York, 1939, pages 271-328. No one should pronounce a final opinion on this problem without having read this classic chapter of the great Italian sociologist on the political character of collectivism.

Note No. 5 (page 90). The executioner has the last word in the socialist state:

This macabre characterization which many, who lack the proper understanding of the issues involved, choose to ridicule, we find already in the second section of Jacob Burckhardt's *The Age of Constantine the Great*, London, 1939. To those who are still not convinced we point out that the economic control exercised by mercantilism led to the execution of great numbers of offenders. In the important book by the Swedish economic historian E. Heckscher, *Mercantilism*, London, 1935, we find the following concerning French mercantilism during the seventeenth and eighteenth centuries: "It is estimated that the economic measures taken in this connection cost the lives of some 16,000 people, partly through executions and partly through armed affrays, without reckoning the unknown but certainly much larger number of people who were sent to the galleys or punished in other ways. On one occasion in Valence, 77 were sentenced to be hanged, 58 were to be broken upon the wheel, 631 were sent to the galleys, one was set free and none were pardoned. But even this vigorous action did not help to attain the desired end. Printed calicoes spread more and more widely among all classes of the population, in France as everywhere else" (page 173).

Note No. 6 (page 92). Suicide statistics as an indication of insufficient integration:

The theory of "deséncadrement" as the cause of suicide in our time (at least as a mass phenomenon), was developed mainly by the French sociologist, M. Halbwachs (*Les causes du suicide*). It is supported by the decline in the suicide rate during times of war, which we know are periods of hyperintegration.

Note No. 7 (page 95). Occupation cannot serve as a means of national integration:

The English sociologist Ernest Barker (*National Character and the Factors in its Formation*, 3rd edition, London, 1939, page 276), says the following concerning this question: "The nation is not to be discredited because there is much false nationalism abroad. I have sometimes thought that there are three sovereigns which dispute our allegiance. One is blood—

or the idea of a nation as a group of kinsfolk, united by an intimate consanguinity within their gates, but divided from the stranger without by an impassable barrier of difference. That is false nationalism. Another is contiguity—the sweet ties of neighbourliness, strengthened by old and common tradition, which unite the racial blend that inhabits a given territory, and which make it a nation of the spirit—which is reality, and not a nation of the body—which is a simulacrum. That is true nationalism. A third is occupation—the bond of a common profession, which unites its members by the daily and homely ties of common work and interest. This may be, and tends to be, though it need not be, a principle which we may call by the name of anti-nationalism." This idea would obviously have gained in precision if our distinction between the A sphere and the B sphere in the occupational field had been applied.

CHAPTER III

THE SPLENDOR AND MISERY OF CAPITALISM

Ce n'est pas ce qui écrase qui gêne; ce n'est pas une oppression qui révolte, c'est une humiliation. Les Français de 1789 étaient exaspérés contre les nobles parce qu'ils étaient *presque* les égaux des nobles; c'est la différence légère qui se mesure, et c'est ce qui se mesure qui compte. La bourgeoisie du XVIIIe siècle était riche, *presque* en passe de tous les emplois, *presque* aussi puissante que la noblesse. C'est ce "presque" qui l'irritait, et la proximité du but qui l'aiguillonnait; c'est le dernier pas à faire qui échauffe toutes les impatiences.

—EMILE FAGUET, *Politiques et Moralistes du 19e siècle* (1899).

The Nature and Historical Achievement of "Capitalism"

UNDER the influence of Marxist propaganda we have become accustomed to calling the economic system which during the last hundred years has spread across the realm of European-American civilization and thence across the whole world, "capitalism." For a multiplicity of reasons this is an unfortunate habit, and much can be said against such sweeping concepts, nevertheless every attempt to abandon it seems doomed to failure. Even if it were more likely to succeed we could not ignore the demand for a handy and comprehensible expression which conveniently and with a precision adequate for our purpose characterizes everything that, in a historically peculiar manner constitutes the common property of the economic and social development of the Occident during the past century. In this sense and without renouncing any of our very serious mental reservations and misgivings, we shall for the time being continue to use this hackneyed expression, which is so often a temptation to indulge in cheap demagogy. But what exactly are we concerned with here?

Instead of replying to this question with some definition from the text books on economics, we shall, in our own fashion, seek that fundamental lucidity and try to get away from those nebulous generalities which we all find so wearying. However, in order to reach this goal, we must have the courage to be simple and must temporarily shelve all those questions of detail which in the absence of such fundamental clarity we would in any case not be able to solve for lack of orientation.

If, when looking back on the development of our economic system, we wish to obtain a true picture in which the economic questions appear in the right perspective, it is the first and most urgent requirement that we should separate the essential from the unessential, the permanent from the temporary. Our meaning may perhaps be made clearer by a comparison taken from the political sphere with which we concerned ourselves in the preceding chapter.

Not only our traditional economic system, but also the political system of the Western world, namely democracy, is today exposed to criticism from every side, criticism which in both cases is justified where it is directed against abuse and degeneration, i.e., against a development whose existence only a hopelessly myopic person can deny. But here we must distinguish very clearly whether this criticism is aimed at the essence or merely at the changing and multiple forms of democracy, a distinction which is only too often not made. We have become far too accustomed to looking upon parliamentarism, universal suffrage and all those other forms which Western democracy has developed in the course of the nineteenth century, and even the degeneration to which they have fallen victim, as the essence of democracy.

Nevertheless we should have no trouble in agreeing that we are dealing here not with the essence of democracy but merely with forms which are historically conditioned and changeable. In many countries experience has shown that these forms can even falsify the real nature of democracy, and, if we do not bethink ourselves of the difference between form and substance in time, they may gravely imperil democracy itself. In the last resort it is one fundamental question that alone matters: does political authority emanate from the people or from another quarter, are they its ultimate point of reference or is something else? Always and everywhere the basic question is: how is the will of the state formed? and to that there are two and only two basic answers: autonomy or heteronomy, autonomous authority or extraneous authority. If we free the concept of democracy from all the verbiage entangling it and from all historical weeds, there remains as the core the autonomy of the nation (or its subordinate organizations). Around this core one can talk for ever, one can treat it with cheap irony, one can look at it as an ideal difficult to achieve, or, if one insists on being original, as an objectionable goal, but at heart we always know exactly what represents democracy and what does not, and what we are to think of its various manifestations. It would be difficult to label this core as absurd, laughable or inconsistent with human nature; considered in the light of reason and unperverted by all kinds of snobbery it would rather seem to be the most natural and appropriate. Pressed hard enough every right thinking man must side with Abraham Lincoln when he says: "No man is good enough to govern another man without that other's consent."

Everything, however, that has accumulated around this kernel of democracy in the shape of institutions and customs, is hardly more than the political mechanism which changes according to place and time. One cannot render a worse service to democracy than to identify it with the complicated and corrupt parlor game of a democracy degenerated into pluralism. We know today that not only a parliamentary, but even a "direct," a presidential, a directorial, yes, even a dictatorial democracy is possible, always assuming that the link between the people and the will of the state is not severed and that whoever wields power must render account to the people, is subject to its control and can, consequently, be removed from office. We admit, though, that critical border-line cases may arise here. It is evident that chemically pure democracy is as unpalatable as chemically pure water, and that in order to suit our taste admixtures of all kinds (hierarchical leadership, federalist regionalism, private spheres free from the interference of the state, heteronomous balancing factors, traditionalism, "privileges," &c.) are necessary as exemplified by Swiss and American democracy (with the constitutional "checks and balances" mentioned above).

This political comparison can now be of great service to us in trying to settle the confusion arising from the dispute over the nature of "capitalism" because it is very similar to the dispute over democracy. In the same way as democracy is one of two possible answers to the fundamental question "how is the will of the state formed?" that which constitutes the core of our economic system is one of two possible answers to the fundamental problem of economics. The question "how are the productive forces of a society to be used, and who is to make the decision?" is the fundamental problem of any economy, however organized, whether it is the economy of the Pharaohs, of the Greek polis, the economy of Robinson Crusoe, the Sioux Indians, or of modern industrial nations, and always and everywhere some kind of solution must be found. The structure of the economic system is determined by this answer, and here, too, there are in the last resort only two answers: autonomy or heteronomy. The character, manner and quantity of production is determined either by those who are primarily affected by it, that is, by those whose needs are met by this production, or it is determined by other agencies. In other words, the "economic will" either is formed by the democracy of consumers, or by the strength of an autocratic order. There is no third way here.

The autonomy of the economic will is a matter of course in the case of the self-sufficient, barterless economy of the smallest social group where production and consumption are united in the same individual. The peasant or farmer, as far as he is self-sufficient, is economically autonomous unless he is a slave, serf, colonus, &c., of the state itself and thus ceases to be a peasant in the true and noble sense of the word. But the autonomy of the economic will becomes a real problem in the case of the highly differentiated economy with its division of labor as we have it today. There is, however, a solution to this problem, too, but only one: an economic system that is based on the market, price mechanism, private ownership of the tools of production, and competition. It is competition, and only competition which furnishes the totality of the consumers (who are, of course, identical with the sum total of the specialized producers) with that decisive influence on the nature, manner and quantity of production which is exercised by the self-sufficient peasant in the undifferentiated economy on what he produces for his own consumption. If an economic system based on the division of labor is directed by the market and by competition, the productive forces of the people are channelled so as to meet the demands of the consumers. The production program of the national economy (with the exception of the government's administration of the public finances), is therefore drafted by those who cannot fairly be deprived of this right, namely, the consumers. The process of the market economy is, so to speak, a "plébiscite de tous les jours," where every monetary unit spent by the consumer represents a ballot, and where the producers are endeavoring by their advertising to give "election publicity" to an infinite number of parties (i.e., goods). This democracy of consumers has the drawback of a very unequal distribution of ballots—which could, however, be extensively corrected—but it also has the great advantage of a perfect proportional system: there is no nullifying of the minorities' will by the majority, and every ballot carries its full weight. The result is a market democracy, which in its silent precision surpasses the most perfect political democracy.

This is the "planned economy" of the pure market system. What socialist planned economy entails we know already: it means nothing else than that the democracy of the consumers is eliminated and replaced by the command from above. The decision as to what use is to be made of the economy's productive forces is transferred from the market to the office of a government agency; as we saw, it becomes "politicalized," and it takes an uncommon degree of unintelligence or demagogy to maintain that we are dealing here with a harmless, merely "administrative" task, which touches the core of the political system as little as, for instance, the supervision of public hygiene, which we can safely leave to experts. The truth is that here political as well as economic democracy come to an end; and among other things this is apparent from the fact that in all present day socialist states we see the consumer treated as a burdensome fellow who has to accept whatever the state-run or controlled production happens to produce at the moment.

At this point we do not want to engage in a dispute as to how far the democratic character of this "sovereignty of the consumer" falls short of the ideal. Suffice it to say that competition, and competition alone, can solve the task of directing production based on the division of labor in a manner which corresponds to the autonomous system of production existing on the self-sufficient farm of a free and independent peasant. There is no other solution, and there can be none. The self-sufficiency of the free individual (in the undifferentiated economy) and competition (in the differentiated economy) therefore correspond exactly to each other: together both secure, in the economic sphere, that autonomy of which, in the field of politics, democracy is the counterpart. To this serfdom, monopoly and collectivism (planned economy in the narrower and true sense) are diametrically opposed. They force a foreign will on the economy, falsify the consumers' plebiscite, and result in economic despotism. All these are simple truths with which we cannot tamper. We should call them to mind again and again in order to avoid going astray in our reasoning.

It would be very fascinating to continue this comparison between the economic democracy of the competitive system and political democracy. The parallels are indeed surprisingly striking. For instance, each is a highly sensitive artifice which needs constant attention and supervision and can only exist under certain conditions; further, each is unpalatable in an absolutely pure state; and it is probable that neither can stand excessive use and that, if covering too large an area, both are liable to result in dangerous mechanization. Today we have perhaps occasion to reflect whether the expansion of the "economic democracy of competition" over the entire globe in an era of world economy has not led to a certain straining of this principle, to an over-complication which cannot continue for any length of time, and which has, in course of time, produced a far more dangerous reaction in the form of autarky and the "Grossraum" economy. Finally we must strongly emphasize that economic autonomy, as guaranteed by the self-sufficiency of the undifferentiated economy or by competition, and political democracy are mutually complementary in the manner and for the reasons explained above.

The detailed nature of the mechanism of the market economy directed by price and competition can hardly be described here if the reader is to be spared an entire course in economics. However, we may expect his sense of responsibility to restrain him from pronouncing final judgment on our economic system, or even from considering himself to be called upon to heal the sick economy before acquiring the necessary knowledge of its anatomy and physiology. Not everyone is capable of that, but we believe that in what we have said so far we have given clear expression to the decisive point, and also to that which must be obvious to even those without expert knowledge. We make this demand also because nothing can be further from us than the desire, in thus describing the essence of the market economy, to whitewash its historical embodiment, "capitalism"; rather, we shall have ample opportunity duly to criticize its undeniable weaknesses and malformations and to follow up this criticism with extensive demands for reform.

It is in keeping with the anti-materialist tenor of this book that we have characterized the essence of the modern market economy by its outstanding non-materialist achievement, which can best be appreciated if we keep in mind the economic despotism which we would exchange for it if we were to adopt a socialist economic system. Coupled with this there is another non-materialist achievement, vying in importance with the one already mentioned: the political neutralization of the economy, resulting from a pure market system, in contrast to the politicalization of the economy growing greater with every increase of government control over the economy and finally, in the socialist state, devouring everything.

A pure market system means that economic success can only be obtained by rendering an equivalent economic service to the consumer, and that at the same time, failure to do so is relentlessly punished by losses and finally by bankruptcy, which means expulsion from the ranks of those responsible for production (entrepreneurs). Income without equivalent performance and unpunished default (burdening someone else with the loss) are both prevented in this pure market system, which, as we shall show later, has been disastrously falsified by historical "capitalism." In order to achieve these ends, this economic system makes use of a double arrangement, first of all, the above mentioned system of competition and, secondly, the coupling of responsibility and risk (profit and loss chance). This coupling principle, according to which those who guide the productive process enjoy the profits of success and personally bear the full weight of failure, and those who take the chances of profit and loss guide productive processes, is one of the most important, even if increasingly adulterated principles of our economic system, and it would be difficult to prove that it is unnatural and does not fulfil its purpose.

At the same time we can now understand the true implications of the often criticized and morally condemned idea of profit, in which many people see nothing but a mask for anti-social self-seeking, greed and unfair practices. But in reality the role of profit in the pure market economy consists in providing a reliable and irreplaceable yardstick for establishing whether an enterprise is going to be a successful part of the national economic structure or not. Under the rule of profit the entrepreneur who adapts himself, receives from the market an acknowledgement to that effect in form of a bonus, but the entrepreneur who does not fit in is penalized by the market. As a rule the reward is as high as the penalty is harsh, but it is precisely this that leads to an especially effective selection of the managers of the productive process. Since the fear of loss is probably always greater than the striving for gain, we may say that in the last resort our economic system is regulated by fear of bankruptcy. The socialist state would have to create an equivalent for all this: in the place of profit it would have to put another yardstick of success and another system of selection of the managers of production, in the place of bankruptcy it would have to put another penalty for failure. It is, however, very doubtful whether such an equivalent can be found. Up to now, at any rate, it has not been discovered.

The meaning of all this is that in the pure market economy it is not the state and not the individual's political power that determines the process of the economy as a whole or one's success in private business ventures, but the market to which one has to render appropriate services. Economic performance is the decisive factor, not the influence one is able to exert on the state and in political life. The economy ceases to be a political forum, and it is the consumer whom the producer has to flatter, not the cabinet officer; it is the market to which he has to pay attention, not Congress.

The full significance of this non-materialist achievement of the pure market economy, which is, to neutralize the economy politically, may become even clearer to us if we recall its effect on international trade. We are faced with the following immensely important fact: in an excessively populated world in which economic needs and the technique of production—which is dependent on markets being as large as possible—call for world-wide economic expansion and interdependence, the co-existence of giant, medium and small countries, of strong and weak states, of rich and poor regions would in itself lead to a permanent war of all against all for the greatest possible extension of "living space," as long as political possession (sovereignty, "imperium") decisively determines economic utilization ("dominium") or even, as in the socialist state, completely coincides with it. The chief point, however, is that it was the liberal character of the old international economy (which favored the pure market system) which resulted in the highest possible neutralization of national borders, political rule over regions rich in raw materials, and citizenship problems of the individual. There remained sufficient reasons for international conflict, but at least this particular poison of the unequal distribution of raw materials, of differing productive capacity and population density in the various countries, and of the possible antagonism between the political "haves" and "have-nots" had been eliminated almost completely by the liberal order in the heyday of much-maligned capitalism. Thus, and only thus, was it possible at all that small countries like Switzerland could, within the most narrow and barren confines, reach a state of flourishing prosperity. In the same way as the international political order guaranteed their political co-existence, the liberal world economy guaranteed the economic co-existence of big and small countries on a footing of complete equality which precluded the possibility of the exploitation of weak states by politically powerful nations. But what we have now been experiencing for some time, is a development in the opposite direction, the increasing politicalization of both domestic and foreign economic relations. Since the road to prosperity leads increasingly via political power, the impulse is for economic group interests within the country to struggle for domination of the state, and in the field of foreign policy for the nations to struggle among themselves for mastery over the entire globe. Pluralism (the rule of group interests) within the state, imperialism in the world, those are the sad results of the politicalization of the economy into which we lapse the more as we increasingly abandon the principles of the market economy. In both cases we obtain only a short breathing-space whenever an undisputed victor emerges from the fray.

In the pure market economy, in which the economic sphere is on principle separated from the political sphere, the demand for political rule over regions rich in raw materials in order to safeguard the supply of raw materials smacks of the paradoxical, since selling and buying of raw materials takes place in the sphere of private enterprise and under the rule of private law. The fact that a certain state holds political sway over areas in which raw materials are produced does not, in this case, mean that it "owns" the output of raw materials. While it enjoys political sovereignty over these regions ("imperium") and therefore exercises those public and administrative functions (administration of justice, police, taxation, &c.), which are within its province, the owners are private individuals or companies in which citizens of any other state can acquire stock.

"Imperium" and "dominium" are indeed two fundamentally different things—but only in a liberal world ruled by a market economy. In a liberal world economy national frontiers are of no essential economic importance; the world market is more or less a unit where equal opportunities for selling and buying exist for everyone, regardless of national boundaries or citizenship. There can really be no problems of raw material, colonies or so-called "living space." These questions arise only when socialists abandon the principles of the market system and a non-liberal economic policy tends to emphasize increasingly the economic importance of political frontiers and thereby the size of the politically dominated area. If the fact that the individual nations exercise political control over areas of the globe which are unequal in size, is coupled with the erection of economic barriers, so that in the end one cannot even become a boot-black without the requisite passport, this must finally—in view of the highly differentiated character of our modern economy and the varying population density in each region—lead to a situation from which there are only two ways out. Either we will have to be prepared for the nations unleashing—with the truly pre-historic ferocity of the struggle for pastures and salt-pans—a terrible perpetual war for political domination of the entire globe; or, the barriers erected by short-sighted egoism will have to be torn down again. It can only be the one or the other: an unending scuffle for the greatest possible expansion of the closed territories, or return to the ridiculed principles of a liberal world economy with tolerable tariffs, most favored nation clauses, the policy of the open door, an international currency system, and without "Grossraum" politics. These are in truth the only alternatives, and now we would ask you to reflect which course is the more Utopian. We shall discuss what conclusions are to be drawn from this for action in the economic sphere in a later section dealing with the question of an international new order.

Freedom, immunity of the economic life from political infection, clean principles and peace—these are the non-materialist achievements of the pure market economy. However defiled and adulterated it may appear to us in the form of historical capitalism, it would nevertheless be unforgivably shortsighted if we were to deny that even this "tainted" market economy has brought us nearer to those ideals than any other economic system before or since. What even this very imperfect capitalism, which is crying out for radical reform, has done for the liberation of man, we would best learn if we could question as witnesses the shadows of past centuries groaning under the yoke of feudal and absolutist oppression or the subjects of socialist countries. That even the latter cannot answer us, is surely the most striking proof of the true state of their economic system and its non-materialist achievements.

Moreover we must add that this economic system of market economy has, aside from its non-materialist spiritual achievements, performed material feats to deny which would be fatuous. It would also be wrong to make machine technology and the division of labor solely responsible for this enormous material achievement, namely, the increase of total production and of the welfare of the masses—of which one can gain a rough estimate by noting that the real wages of the English worker have increased fourfold between 1800 and 1900. Of course, from a historical point of view, these two factors are the main cause of the increase in productivity, but again only very coarse materialist thinking can ignore two things:

firstly, machine technology and the division of labor could not have been developed if capitalism had not created the economic, psychological and political conditions for it, and secondly, all socialist experiments, in which particularly the use of machines and division of labor are pushed to extremes, show that very disappointing results are obtained if one is satisfied with harvesting these technical and organizational fruits of the market economy, while doing away with its non-materialist motivating forces, namely, freedom, private property, competition and the market. Montesquieu in his *Esprit des Lois* has already insisted upon it: "les terres sont cultivées en raison, non de leur fertilité naturelle, mais de la liberté dont jouissent les habitants dans les échanges," and there is a proverb which says that the hand of the owner turns sand into gold.

However, the great advance in mass welfare during the last hundred years must not make us forget that it is not as great as one could have expected in view of the extraordinary increase in productivity. In fact, there exists a certain disparity which calls for an explanation: the disparity between "progress and poverty," which is a constant matter of concern particularly to socialists of all denominations, leading them to the conclusion that the cause must be sought in constructional faults of the economic system. Again and again one hears it said that in our economic system "economic doctrine" ruins what "technology" has conquered, and it cannot surprise us that it is especially engineers who tend to hold such views and who look down upon economists with something of the contempt which militarists have for diplomats. This is not the place to investigate the many misunderstandings which lie at the root of this opinion held by the socialists and by many engineers, but a few pointers would seem necessary.

We begin by drawing attention to the fact which should be obvious, especially to the engineer, namely, that we can as little expect 100 per cent. efficiency from the best organized national economy as from the most perfect motor. The indignation of the engineer regarding the loss ratio of our economic system therefore resembles the incredulous surprise of the layman in technical matters when he hears for the first time that even our most perfect heat engines utilize hardly more than 50 per cent. of the fuel-generated energy. It is obvious that we have to take into account this percentage of purely technical loss which the engineer knows to be inevitable, if we hear astounding (incidentally, often also exaggerated) figures regarding the efficiency of the modern machine as compared with manual labor, figures which seem to promise us a paradise on earth. But there are many additional factors.

If we take a machine particularly impressive by virtue of its output as well as its complicatedness, an automatic bottle manufacturing machine, which one can hardly accuse of destroying a formerly idyllic handicraft, we have a case which could make us very optimistic. Here is an automatic machine which replaces tubercular proletarian glass blowers and which manufactures products of cheapness and utility, nor do we have to mourn the demise of quality of workmanship. We are therefore all the more tempted to give ourselves wholeheartedly over to the impression that machines, employed everywhere and fully utilized, can multiply human happiness along with total output.

But this impression is misleading. First of all, the example of the bottle machine cannot be generalized, either in the technical or in the human sense. It is by no means the rule that a machine increases productivity to such an extent as in this case, and it is even less the rule that its human and social effects should leave us undisturbed. For this reason alone we have to lower our expectations, and what the machines can do to increase the material welfare of the community is decreased by further liabilities, some of which are extremely important, liabilities which can, with good will, be partially diminished but never wholly eliminated. They are:

(1) expenditure for the manufacture of the machines themselves (machine tools, &c.), an expenditure which consists not only in immense amounts of work and raw material, but also in "capital," that is, in a renunciation of the enjoyment of goods in the present, in favor of a more or less distant future (this sets limits to the use of machines known to every economist and independent of the particular type of economic system);

(2) stoppages in the production of organic and inorganic raw materials (agriculture, forestry, fishing and mining), which form the basis of the total output, but offer only small opportunities of further increase by mechanical devices and must sooner or later be influenced by the law of decreasing returns;

(3) inevitable fluctuations in the utilization of a productive apparatus whose capacity must be able to meet the highest demands (e.g., in the use of electric power), so that in the same way as a certain percentage of a city's housing accommodation must remain vacant if the housing market is to have a "margin," there must always be a certain ratio of unused productive capacity in the entire national economy;

(4) the losses arising from all bad investments which are always loudly lamented, a substantial part of which, however, is nothing but the price for progress and adaptation that has to be paid in experiments of all kinds, a price the socialist state, too, would willy-nilly have to be prepared to pay and without which the development of the last hundred years

would not have been possible at all—without which many
of the readers of this book would not even exist;

(5) the tremendous increase in the cost of education and schooling required for the training of all the experts whom our
modern economic life demands, a vast capital expense
which devours a great part of today's national income and
which must be set off against the technical achievements of
the machine age;

(6) the costs of satisfying the new need for recreation and
amusement which arose only with the monotony of the
machine age;

(7) the increased costs of transportation, distribution and advertising, accompanying the development of industrial production, of big cities and of world trade;

(8) the costs of a government apparatus which is becoming
increasingly complicated and comprehensive as industries
and cities continue to grow, and also correspondingly more
expensive as it requires greater numbers of civil servants;

(9) the deterioration in quality which has been in many cases
the undeniable consequence of the replacement of manual
labor by the machine;

(10) devastations by war which have increased so vastly in the
machine age.

All these drawbacks would also appear in a socialist state which
took over capitalist technology and management, apart from
those which would be experienced in addition in that case.
They hardly suffice, however, to explain the disparity between
the promises of technology and the actual fulfilment during the
last hundred years. This disparity—the gap between the welfare
of the masses and the increase in technical productivity—can likewise not be explained by the theory that the masses have been
deprived of their due share in the progress of productivity and
that this share has been put into the pockets of a few rich men.
We tend to be subject to a kind of optical illusion when looking
at the conspicuous consumption of luxuries by the rich which
makes us forget how small the number of rich people is in comparison with the rest of the population, and what little difference,
therefore, the total amount of their more-than-average-expenditure
makes, when measured against the total consumption of the bulk of
the population. This illusion is refuted by a simple piece of arith-
metic which shows us how insignificant the rise in the average
income of the masses would be if an equal distribution were to be
effected—even on the far too favorable assumption that the sum
total would not diminish under such violent treatment.

We shall probably come nearer to solving the riddle if we

consider what many people seem to forget in this as well as in other connections: i.e., the tremendous increase in population, which took place concurrently. We can actually not only explain the discrepancy in question but also obtain an idea of the vast material achievement of capitalism if we remember that a considerable part of the technical and organizational advance in production has apparently had to serve the one purpose of enabling a greater number of men to exist on this earth, instead of contributing to a greater increase in mass welfare. It thus appears as if the disappointments which capitalism has brought in a purely material sense must to a great extent be explained by saying that this economic system had to divide its immense prosperity creating power in order to fulfil two tasks: to improve the economic lot of the average man, and to provide means of existence for gigantic floods of newcomers.

It is therefore difficult to reject the assumption that in the populous industrialized countries the necessity to choose between "increase in population" and "increase in mass welfare" did not arise only yesterday, and this choice is of even greater importance today. However, it also follows from this that we cannot today simply make short shrift of machines, division of labor, world economy and industry and return to manual production and autarky, since the increase in productivity, which was only made possible by developments in mechanics and organization, has in the meantime been absorbed by the immense increase in population. We cannot simply reverse economic and social development by one or two hundred years without jeopardizing the existence of millions of people, and thereby our social order itself. We must well keep in mind that this hard and sober fact sets limits to our programs of reform; at the same time it should also make us look with discomfort at too fast a reproduction rate and produce a feeling of relief at any diminution.

Of course, we must also warn against the superstition that the existence of the masses is now absolutely dependent on leaving our present overwrought mechanical industrial and urban civilization completely undisturbed. On the contrary: our life—and this is strikingly demonstrated by many experiences made in the war— would be far more natural, healthy and happy if certain technical and organizational developments could be reversed, and this despite the present size of the population. Every cut and dried judgment is misplaced here: the uncritical glorification—which today is hardly taken seriously anywhere—of our technical and industrial civilization, as well as its equally uncritical condemnation on principle. What we need is rather an exact appraisal and investigation of individual factors and the careful weighing of the pros and cons. This applies to the particular problem of machine technology and modern industrialism as well as to the more general one of capitalism as a whole. For the purpose of such an appraisal we now turn to the many and blatant defects and aberrations of capitalism which from the very beginning created the counter-current of socialism and which in our days have led to a veritable mass rebellion against the traditional economic and social system, and this for reasons for which we have great understanding, much as we reject their destructive consequences.

The Liabilities

The basis of our economic system—freedom, private property, division of labor, market and competition—must be affirmed as staunchly as the superstructure which has overgrown it so luxuriantly (as well as the form which historical "capitalism" assumed in the course of the nineteenth century, for reasons to be detailed later) must be condemned. Precisely because one wants to preserve this basis—and its maintenance has become the crucial problem of our civilization—one can hardly be vigorous enough in criticizing all the aberrations, falsifications and distortions which the historical development has brought. Thus the issue in question is the sharp and resolute distinction between the essentials of our economic system and the exchangeable accessories, and only on the strength of such a distinction is it possible to bring about a wise and practicable reform.

Not only democracy, but also the economic system corresponding to it has developed during the last hundred years along certain lines, which might just as well have been different without in any way affecting the essence of the market economy, and which do, in fact, vary considerably from country to country and epoch to epoch. German "capitalism" has always been different from the English, American or French edition, and they all, in turn, vary significantly—and not always to their advantage—from Swiss "capitalism." In the same way the English "capitalism" of 1930 looks entirely different from that of 1910, 1880 or 1850.

The highly differentiated market and competitive system happens to have been organized in this historically conditioned manner, but it could just as well have been arranged in a different way. Today we know only too well that in decisive respects it would have been better if other paths had been taken and extremes thereby avoided. And now we find here the same faulty judgment demonstrated as in the case of democracy: the preponderant tendency to confuse the variable super-structure with the foundation, the appendage with the essence. We have become far too accustomed to look upon all those familiar forms of "capitalism" —monopolies, mammoth industries, stock companies, holding companies, mass production, proletariat, &c.—as the only possible manner in which a non-collectivist and, at the same time, highly differentiated economic system can be organized. On the contrary, however, we should at last seriously ask ourselves whether these outer forms—in which the economy has paid its tribute to the "cult of the colossal" and thus to the spirit of the nineteenth century—do not present an increasingly serious danger to the content. If we no longer like the nineteenth century architecture of a building, nobody draws the conclusion that we should now start to build adobe huts or giant tenements; rather, we adhere firmly to the essentials of construction, i.e., foundation, materials and function. It is, however, true that precisely those people are the best confederates of the revolutionaries who cannot conceive "capitalism" in any other form than the one which history has given it—a very misshapen one unfortunately—and who cling to it with all their might. Both parties agree in equating form and content and, therefore, agree in their conclusion: either this way or not at all. Both are ignorant of a third way, and reformers are equally abhorrent to both. An obtuse conservatism which does not possess enough imagination to think of new forms, nor sufficient intelligence to realize the necessity of these new forms, is bound to breed an equally obtuse radicalism. Their relationship resembles that of the photographic negative and positive of a hopelessly under-exposed snapshot.

Both liberalism and capitalism have for one and a half centuries been weighed down by calamitous aberrations, whose mere possibility today amazes us, and nothing has brought these two so near to the verge of complete doom as the dogmatic belief that this historical and misshapen form was the only possible one, and that in the future, too, no other would be conceivable. If these dogmatic liberals were right, then the essence of political and economic liberalism would indeed be in a very bad way and that is exactly why they are the anti-liberal's most desirable star witnesses. Yes, dogmatic liberalism leads straight to the conclusion that the economic and social system of the Western world is lost beyond redemption—*sit ut est aut non sit*. Since we are just about agreed, in full possession of the facts and basing our opinion on wellnigh irrefutable reasoning, that this economic system should not be as it is—*ut est*—it follows: *non sit,* it should disappear. It is therefore completely logical that it is precisely the most dogmatic liberals who are today most easily overwhelmed by weak pessimism, and from there to capitulation it is often only one step; the psychology of apostasy is a murky and strange story. If the doctrinaires were right. . . . But, thank heavens, they are entirely wrong, like everyone who does not know how to differentiate and to distinguish between essentials and non-essentials.

Let us first of all keep in mind that capitalism has developed in a historical era which, with a few exceptions—Switzerland being the main representative—has unfortunately been decisive for the development of the Western world and has in every respect distorted it so disastrously: it is the feudal-absolutist era where the principle of force and exploitation predominated. Only if one surveys the miserable ages of brute force and the degradation of man through feudalism and absolutism, can one fully conceive what men owe to the liberal-capitalist age for their liberation and relief, and nothing is more characteristic of the progress due to an even very imperfect system of capitalism than the new feeling of dignity, self-esteem, justice and freedom which today has made men so sensitive. Without looking back into history, they are far from satisfied with what has been achieved and demand all the more violently what is still owing to them, as did the French bourgeoisie of 1789 of which Emile Faguet—following Tocqueville's example —speaks in the motto of this chapter. But that capitalism is still owing them so much, is mainly due to that disastrous heritage which it took over from feudalism and absolutism.

This feudal-absolutist heritage finds its most striking expression in the immense accretions of capital and economic positions of power which endow capitalism with that plutocratic trait which clings to it in our imagination and has given it a false start from the very beginning. It is not true that the existing differences in the distribution of income and capital are purely a matter of economic performance and could not be altered without disturbing the laws of the market, and it is therefore also incorrect to ascribe these differences to the mechanism of the market economy as such. Under the rule of an unadulterated market economy and with non-economic conditions at the start being equal, differences in the distribution of income and capital can hardly assume gross dispro-portions, and in the absence of that most people feel them to be just. Violent contrasts between rich and poor, between power and impotence, are rather due to extra-economic ("sociological") posi-tions of power, which bestow economically unjustifiable privileges and which are either vestiges of feudalism or absolutism or were obtained later by unfair means, outside the competition of the market, by establishing monopolies. In both cases the provoking disparity in the distribution of income, capital and power is the calamitous heritage with which feudalism and ruthless and cunning exploiters have saddled us.

Feudal land holdings with whose hardly edifying history we are today tolerably familiar; profits from the slave trade which still flourished even in the eighteenth century and helped, especially in England, to found many a fortune; war and speculative profits of the most questionable kind, pirates' and soldiers' booty, monopoly concessions granted in the age of absolutism, plantation dividends, railroad subsidies: these and many others are the unclean sources of many great fortunes, which then became the basis of the subsequent development. Many of them have vanished today, while others—particularly those founded on feudal mining properties—stubbornly extend into our time like the well-preserved strongholds of robber-barons, though, unlike them, without any claim to protection as ancient monuments. Others, aided by analogous conditions, continue to reappear under our very eyes whenever state and society are weak and short-sighted enough to permit such conditions.

These feudalist remains in the capitalist system are not only responsible for differences in income, capital and power which are alien to the pure market economy—whose guiding principle is efficiency—and burden it with an unjust odium under which property won by honest work and faithful service also has to suffer; it is also at least as important that thereby capitalism, while still in its infancy was turned into wrong paths in so far as accretions of capital resulted which allowed a corresponding agglomeration of enterprises and factories, and thus paved the way to mammoth industries, to "corporate capitalism," to giant enterprises and monopolism. At the same time this partly explains why Switzerland, where, thanks to history, the capitalist system does not suffer from the feudal infection, has not followed the development into mammoth capitalism, but has rather become a country not only with a balanced distribution of income and capital, but also with predominantly small and medium-size enterprises.

The abnormal agglomeration of capital was admittedly only one of the requisites of this lamentable development. The other was the aggregation of proletarian labor. But where did the first industrial proletariat come from? There can be no doubt about the answer. The same power principle which enriched some and gave them a privileged position, dispossessed others and laid the foundation for that uprooted class of the population which is dependent on the constant utilization of its productive power, that class which we call the proletariat and which we have already characterized in the introduction to this book. This was the foundation from which everything else was to follow, thanks to the subsequent rise in the reproduction rate of the proletariat.

This process becomes particularly clear when we study the economic history of Germany and England. In Germany it was the peasants of the feudalist eastern provinces who, dispossessed in the wake of their "liberation" and reduced to rural proletarians, rushed into the factories; in England it was the almost complete elimination of the peasantry in favor of the feudal landowners—mainly in the seventeenth and eighteenth centuries—which provided the reservoir for filling the terrible slums of the first English industrial districts. In both cases proletarization, industrial misery and exploitation are the logical consequence of the destruction of the peasantry, and historically inviolable proof of the cardinal maxim of sociology that a healthy peasantry is the elementary foundation of a sound society. A proof *e contrario* for this thesis is again Switzerland, where, because of the absence of feudalism, a proletariat of disquieting size could not arise. And if, lastly, we turn to the United States, we find that there, too, the development of big business has profited from the feudal pressure in Europe, from where men, turned into rural proletarians, preferred to emigrate and become freer industrial proletarians. As long, however, as America still had reserves of land which could be freely settled, American industrial labor could bargain for material conditions which, in spite of the continuing feudal pressure in Europe, for a long time prevented the rise of an industrial proletariat in the European sense and therefore also of a socialist mass movement appropriate to that class. Since, however, the safety valve provided by free land ceased to function at about the turn of the century, conditions there have, in spite of immigration bars, become more and more similar to those in Europe.

We must at all times keep in mind these dark sources of the historical form of the market economy and of capitalism so decisive for everything that follows, always remembering the old truth that the ultimate source of all the pathological degenerations of a society must invariably be sought in the forcible separation of the people from the soil and the feudal appropriation of the latter. "Latifundia perdidere Romam" is an experience which may serve us as a guide throughout economic and social history, in as much as it seems to admit of no exception. Wherever capitalism was conceived and developed with the socially poisonous taint of feudalism, it has been perverted in a manner which we only understand fully today. The degenerate form of the market economy—modern industrial and financial capitalism with its all powerful accumulation of capital and power, its proletarian masses, its centralization, the elephantiasis of its big cities and industrial areas—is not at all the form in which such an economic system is bound to develop according to its own allegedly ineluctable laws. It is anything but the creature of the often quoted historical destiny, of which fools prate so much, or of the powers of technology to which we have to surrender ourselves unconditionally and which, like any oriental despot, will prescribe our thoughts and actions. It is the creation of history, as formed by men who could also have acted otherwise, it is the work of a pre-liberal, feudalist society and finally, in its later course, the work of badly advised legislators and lawyers.

Our economic world has in the main assumed its present shape

because certain legal forms and institutions have been created—
the stock company, the corporation, patent law, bankruptcy law,
the law relating to trusts, and many others—and because legislation,
the administration of justice and custom have evolved these forms
and institutions in a way which today we can often describe as
nothing but harmful to the community and to the economic system
itself. We must, first of all, become accustomed to the idea that a
healthy economic life is quite conceivable without holding companies, without monopolies protected by law, without patents which
prevent competition, yes, if necessary, even without stock companies and corporations as standard forms of industrial enterprises.
It should also no longer be deemed a heresy to envisage an economic
system in which state subsidies, legal protection, the administration
of justice, state authority and economic policing are quite differently
oriented than is the case today in so many countries—for the small
and against the big, for fairness and competition, and against
exploitation and monopolies, for equalizing justice, and against
privileges, for the easing effects of decentralization, and against
frustrating concentration.

It remains to be seen where these thoughts will in each case
finally lead us. At this moment and at this point we are concerned
with the method of radical thinking itself, the lack of prejudice in
the thorough investigation of problems, the willingness to retrace
our steps into the history of a development that is more than a
hundred years old until we reach the point where we took the
wrong turning, and then to continue forward again on the right
path. All this must be done, however, without for a single moment
forgetting the essential foundation of our economic system, which
it is our purpose to protect and fortify by realizing and correcting
the errors of the past.

The mistakes which have been made in putting economic policies
into effect have their roots, as always, in theoretical errors. The
nature of these errors—errors committed by historical liberalism,
which is to fundamental and true liberalism what historical
capitalism is to the pure market economy—has already become
clear to us earlier in this book, when we were dealing with the
errors of rationalism and liberalism (First Part, Chapter I). As we
saw there, it was a catastrophic mistake to consider the market
system as something autonomous, something based on itself, as a
natural condition outside the political sphere requiring no defense
or support and to overlook the importance of an ethical, legal
and institutional framework corresponding to the principles of
the market system.

Not less deplorable and disastrous, however, was the blindness
and even the smugness with which one gave free rein to an industrial development, which, with sovereign disdain for the vital

instincts of man and for his most elementary spiritual needs, has, thanks to the forms of life and work in the industrial giant cities, reduced the existence of the masses to something completely unnatural. The market, division of labor, commercialization, competition, economic rationalism—they all have, among other things, this in common: there is an optimum in their use, after which their harmfulness increasingly exceeds their utility. Excess and indiscriminate use lead to an artificiality of life which man is by nature not fitted to withstand for any length of time. There are, therefore, limits to capitalism from the very start which one must observe if one does not want to make psychological demands on the people to which they are not equal in the long run, so that they finally answer with a revolt of the masses—the revolt of the excessively domesticated creature. Like pure democracy, undiluted capitalism is intolerable, and among other things this is apparent from the deep dissatisfaction which the commercialization of arts, sciences, education, or the press rouses in us. Today we have achieved the realization, to a great extent unknown to previous generations, that men cannot bear, without excessive harm to themselves and to society, the constant mental, nervous and moral tension which is forced upon them by an economic system dominated by supply and demand, market and technology, nor can they withstand the insecurity and instability of the living conditions which such a system entails. The sum total of the material goods at our disposal may increase through this process, and the often cited living standard may reach those heights which intoxicate a naive social philosophy, but at the same time this leads to a rapid diminution of the sum of that immeasurable and inexpressible simple happiness which men feel in doing satisfying work and leading purposeful lives.

Man's nature, therefore, sets definite limits to the rule of the market principle and in the same way as democracy must permit spheres free from the interference of the state, if it is not to degenerate into the worst kind of despotism, the market system, too, must allow spheres free from the influence of the market, if it is not to become intolerable: there must be the sphere of community life and altruistic devotion, the sphere of self-sufficiency, the sphere of small and simple living conditions, the sphere of the state and of planned economy. In the 1850's there were still leaders of public opinion—for example in Germany the admirable W. H. Riehl with his book *Die bürgerliche Gesellschaft* —who clearly expressed such thoughts without being ridiculed as visionaries, but later more and more of such voices fell silent and capitalism's actual development in most countries is an exact reflection of the ensuing blindness. It goes without saying, that in this respect the socialists were not a whit better than the liberals, for

otherwise they could not have called for an economic order which
is bound to increase man's mental and moral tension to the utmost
degree.

The lack of insight on the part of historical liberalism was
especially great and the actual capitalist development which it
sponsored particularly deplorable since even the living, working
and housing conditions which were determined by industry, competition and division of labor could, with good will and reasonable
intelligence, have been fashioned from the start in a more humane
and natural, and less mechanical and proletarian manner. Infatuated
as one was with everything colossal and tightly centralized, one
paid little attention to a more rational organization of industrial
production; without loss, perhaps even with a gain in productivity
one could have kept down the size of factories and enterprises,
could have preserved and developed old and tested forms of work
while inventing new ones, could have increased the number of
independent businesses and of medium and small-sized factories,
could have maintained a healthy middle class and endowed the
entire economic life with more stability and soundness. That this
would have been possible is proved not only by calm consideration
and investigation of all the measures that could have been undertaken or could have been omitted; but also by the many promising
germs of development which were blindly exterminated; and even
more convincing is the experience of some more favored and
enlightened countries, demonstrable until this day, for we must
always bear in mind that everything good that has been realized
somewhere in the world is a sure index of what could at least have
been achieved elsewhere, too, if one had kept one's eyes open.
Thus it is once more the example of Switzerland which shows that
"capitalism" can most certainly mean something else than vast
Bochums, New Yorks, Manchesters or Pittsburghs, and that there
is no such thing as rigid laws of "capitalism" which proletarize the
middle classes in town and country and concentrate money and
power in fewer and fewer hands, which pitilessly destroy all simple
and natural relationships and are bound to mechanize the economic
and productive process beyond redemption. If, on the other hand,
the development in some of the larger countries has taken such a
much more unfavorable course, one should, before accusing the
economic system as such, take the trouble of investigating the
various reasons. Only then will we have gained a clear picture
and will we be able to assess the full share of blame due to circumstances working from without, historically "incidental" and non-
economic, but above all political: wars, revolutions, inflations and
deflations, domestic and foreign politics, economic policies. Who
can in fairness overlook the fact that it was the World War,
inflation and world politics which so disastrously decimated the

German middle class, for example; devasted the world market and plunged capitalism into the worst crisis of its history?

That is by no means to say that one may entrust oneself carelessly and blindly to the mechanism of the competitive system and its laws. On the contrary: after historical liberalism had already sinned by ignoring the importance of the non-economic conditions that influence the market economy, as well as its anthropological limits and premises, it committed—steeped in rationalist doctrinairism—another error by not paying sufficient attention to the imperfections and defects of even the pure and unadulterated market system. This error—committed in the sphere of economics itself—prevented the realization that the competitive principle is by no means applicable in all fields of production without leading to grave difficulties, further, that there are certain markets which function only more or less imperfectly, that we meet abuses of competition everywhere which must be regulated by the state. Since one failed to realize this, it was only natural that one barred the way to a rational system of governmental intervention and, lacking proper signposts, tended to flounder about in the field of economic policy. This led to further grave mistakes and faulty developments of capitalism in many countries. The different problems involved here and the conclusions we have to draw from them for a timely program of economic reform will concern us in the following section of this book.

And now we are also in a position to give a calm and balanced opinion regarding that defect of capitalism which has perhaps discredited it most of all and which makes it in our day appear so damnable to the superficial observer: its tendency to pass through crises and periods of unemployment, and its inadequate utilization of the productive potentialities. It is a wide field that we are entering and to do complete justice to the question would mean to treat of one of the most difficult chapters of economics in the most detailed manner. But this at least we can say in a few words: we must admit that the equilibrium of the over-capitalized market economy has become unstable for reasons on which the crisis experts are more or less agreed today. Smaller and partial disturbances are in general easily and smoothly overcome by the regulating mechanism of the market; and a flexible competitive system can adapt itself with surprising speed and resiliency to most of the changes in economic "data" (production methods, international trade routes, population figures, consumers' habits, &c.). But from time to time there occur those grave and total disturbances of the equilibrium, which we call crises. Everything suggests that their main causes, as far as they are to be sought within the mechanism of the market economy, that is in as far as they are "endogenous," lie in the imperfections of the money and credit system and of the allocation of capital. For the following reasons, however, too much weight must not be attached to this concession to the critics of the market economy: —

(1) Up to a certain degree, economic depressions are the price that has to be paid for a boom and for the acceleration of economic progress, yes, even for higher productivity which we owe, after all, to a very far-reaching division of labor. The sensitivity of the economic system regarding disturbances of its equilibrium grows with every forward step in the division of labor, but along with it the productivity of the total economy grows as well. If we want to avoid disturbances of the equilibrium altogether we have to return to Robinson Crusoe and his meagre standard of life; if, however, we do not want to do this we have to put up with the greater degree of instability of our economic system. That is the great dilemma in which we find ourselves and in which we have to weigh carefully each consideration against the other. The number of possible decisions has, however, been appreciably narrowed down since the increase in productivity, which we owe to the growing division of labor and the resulting productive techniques, has, as we saw, begun to be used up by the tremendous increase in world population. If—to vary the famous words of the Communist Manifesto (1847)—"it was capitalism that first proved what human activity can achieve," if "it has accomplished greater miracles than the Egyptian pyramids, the Roman aquaeducts and Gothic cathedrals, and has carried out far vaster expeditions than *Völkerwanderungen* and crusades," then it is the spasmodic outbreak of an effervescent and frequently blind spirit of enterprise financed by periodical expansions of credit, that has rendered capitalism capable of these achievements. If, for example, we should have postponed the expansion of the modern railroads until the necessary means had been gotten together without a temporary inflationary acceleration of the economic process accompanied by grave disturbances of the equilibrium, a railroad trip might possibly be just as much a sensation to us today as it was for our grandfathers seventy years ago. What is true of the railroads also applies to all other technical and organizational progress of the last hundred years: its rapid expansion was always coupled with a boom which was inevitably followed by the reaction—the hang-over called depression. The boom is that period in which for the purpose of accelerated economic development all the reserves of the national economy are mobilized; it is, so to speak, a periodical "several year plan" in which for the past hundred years the idea of amassing investments which is at the bottom of the "several year plans" of the collectivist countries today, has been anticipated—only, as with everything spontaneous in contrast to what is consciously organized and advertized, one made less ado about it. Whether such an acceleration of the

economic development is always a blessing is admittedly a different question, and we no longer need to tell the reader how skeptical we ourselves are regarding this point.   But that is not what is at issue here, since all we want to do is to show that one cannot have the one without the other, and that the boom and slump cycle is not quite as senseless as it is often portrayed—especially by those who praise economic progress to high heavens.   But here we have to warn against the dangerous illusion of believing that a socialist economy would find itself in a fundamentally different position and would not experience like difficulties regarding its equilibrium.

(2) In spite of all the more or less disappointing cures which have been tried for the last hundred years, the task of improving our economic system in such a way that the disturbances of the equilibrium are reduced to an unavoidable and tolerable degree, must not be considered insoluble, especially not in view of the insight and experience gained during the last ten years.   Failing such a solution, we are at least able to indicate the ways along which the national economy can be made so resilient and shock-proof that it can bear even grave disturbances of its equilibrium without serious social harm and without general panic.

(3) No intelligent person can deny that the excessively great disturbances to which the economic life of most countries has for decades been exposed, and which finally culminated in the "great depression" (1929-1933), owe their gravity and extent primarily to exterior shocks which have plagued the world since 1914.   It is indeed a miracle that our economic system has not completely collapsed under them, and we have a right to ask whether a different economic system would have shown similar powers of resistance. We should not, therefore, make our economic system the scape-goat for political sins.

(4) Finally, we have to consider that our economic system, during the same period and to a still growing degree, has been distorted almost beyond recognition by reckless interventions and perversions of the most varied kind, and has thus become pro-gressively less able to function, less elastic and less adjustable.   It lost its adaptability and flexibility precisely during a time when these characteristics had never been more necessary, since the conditions for a viable economy had been changing more rapidly and more thoroughly than perhaps ever before.   However, in a process of disastrous interaction the consequences of this discrepancy between the necessity and the ability to adapt oneself, have, in their turn, led to certain measures and insensate interventions which only served to enlarge the rift.   To find a way out of this vicious circle is one of the most important, and at the same time one of the most difficult, of the many gigantic tasks with which our generation is faced.   It is so difficult that not a few have given it up in despair,

but it is after all one on whose satisfactory solution depends the fate of our Western civilization. It would be easier if so many private interests did not have a stake in the present state of affairs which they defend to the last with dangerous stubbornness. One of the most effective defensive weapons in this struggle is to obscure the real position with slogans and ideologies and thereby create the impression that the fight against the adulteration of the competitive system and against the private interests tied up with it, arose from an ideology which has become suspect today. As against this we have to state that it is now simply a question of whether we have the will and the intelligence to re-establish the meaning of our economic constitution, and this means in the first place that the issue is the fight for or against monopolies, for or against the efficiency principle, and for or against the improvement of economic competition serving the good of the community and consistent with our economic system. We shall now proceed to investigate more thoroughly the various aspects of this conflict between self-interest and public interest, of this struggle between the many economic group interests.

The Conflict of Interests in the Economy

Qui autem parti civium consulunt partem neglegunt, rem perniciosissimam in civitatem inducunt, seditionem atque discordiam.

(Whoever favors some of the citizens and neglects the others, introduces the most ruinous evil into the community: division and strife.)

—CICERO, De officiis, I, 25.

It is an elementary maxim of sociology that men, in order to satisfy their needs, can establish mutual relations of a threefold kind: first, the ethically negative relationship of force and cunning (the "medium of politics," according to Franz Oppenheimer); secondly, the ethically positive relationship of altruism; and thirdly, the contractual relationship of parties exchanging market commodities, who reach an agreement as soon as each one believes that he is going to profit by it. Obviously, only in the first and in the last case is there any point in talking of a possible conflict of interests. However, while it goes without saying that in the first instance the interests of the robber and his victim clash irreconcilably, it appears as if in the last case the mysterious institution of the market and the division of labor has actually transformed the original conflict of interests inherent in every "do-as-you-are-done-by" transaction, into a harmony of interests. The historical liberalism of the nineteenth century was, in fact, considerably deceived by this appearance and engendered that optimistic doctrine of the harmony of economic interests which has caused so much mischief, not least because its untenability has finally led us to overlook the partial truth it contains.

In economic life there exists a particularly impressive instance of an obvious harmony of interests between contractual parties, namely, life insurance. We can observe how the life insurance companies endeavor with an almost maternal solicitude to further our most important interest, our health, by publishing health rules or even by offering free operations; but before we allow ourselves to be overwhelmed by this solicitude, we become aware that this, our vital interest, constitutes at the same time one of the most important business interests of the insurance companies. We can, however, hardly overlook that this represents an exceptional case arising from the nature of the contract and not from a peculiarity of the economic system, and that it would take exactly the same form in a socialist state. Life insurance companies can, after all, count on that farmer's being an exception who, suffering a fatal accident as a young man, told my father, who was his doctor, in what were almost his last words, that his greatest comfort was to have put one over on the insurance company. As regards fire insurance there exists by no means always such an identity of interest in the avoidance of damage; the insured person must even be prevented by law from attempting to bring it about intentionally, and even in the case of life insurance the size of the premium causes a very serious conflict which can only be settled by genuine competition among the insurance companies.

We must, in fact, put aside all irrelevant illusions and face the truth that in a society based on the division of labor there exists a natural conflict of interests between the individual producer and the totality of the consumers, a conflict expressed in the fact that every producer has an interest, diametrically opposed to the interest of the consumer, that the prevailing exchange conditions should be as favorable as possible for him and as unfavorable as possible for the consumer. This, however, merely means that it is in the interest of any given producer that the product produced by him should be in as short supply as possible, and it is the interest of the consumers, on the other hand, that the product should be in the greatest possible abundance. In their own interest all will desire a maximum supply of all goods, excepting that one product in whose manufacture any one of them has happened to specialize and on the most profitable sale of which his livelihood depends.

This far from edifying fact is necessarily tied up with the division of labor, and we must take cognizance of it with equanimity in order to discover the true core of the interest conflicts pervading the economy. These conflicts become particularly noticeable when changes occur in supply and demand which alter the exchange relationship. When, for instance, the consumers decide to spend less on alcohol and more on books or travel, we are hardly entitled to act counter to this readjustment in the interest of the distillers concerned, since it is a laudable change in consumer habits and conducive to the general welfare which it is actually the duty of the individual and the community to further. On the other hand, the distillers have a very obvious interest in putting a stop to this shift in consumption. However, if we were to support them in this and recognize their interest as legitimate, we would be defending private interests against public interests and overlooking the elementary principle that we produce in order to consume, and do not consume in order to produce. The same would be true if we were to oppose a change in market conditions caused by the opening up of cheaper sources of supply. This cheapening can come about in two ways which in their nature and effect are fundamentally the same: firstly, by technical or organizational progress, and secondly, by foreign trade. To destroy the possibility of cheap supplies by measures of any kind, be it by the destruction of machines, be it by opposing new ways in distribution, be it by erecting tariff barriers, is undoubtedly in the interest of the industries concerned, but then it would be just as much in the interest of doctors to suppress effective and cheap medicines, and in the interest of contemporary writers to prevent the publication of translations of foreign authors or of cheap editions of the classics.

We are faced with an even more glaring case if, in a more or less veiled manner embellished with economic pseudo-theories and ideologies, an attempt is made, in the interest of the selfish producer, to sabotage not only a beginning improvement in supply, but to bring about a real deterioration by reducing the supply of goods, or at least by presenting such a deterioration as being in the interests of the national economy. If someone smashes every window in a district, we certainly do not wish to assume that he has been induced to do this by the glass industry, but that he has acted in the latter's interest is just as indisputable as that he has grossly violated the public interest. This includes also the well-known case of the destruction of stock piles in order to maintain or increase prices, of the intentional limitation of a product through monopolies, and finally, the fact that in certain circumstances a country's farmers can have an interest in a mediocre harvest. In the early nineteenth century the toast "Here's to a wet harvest and a bloody war," is said to have been especially popular among English farmers, and in a small town of the state of Alabama one could, fifteen years ago, still see a strange monument which the cotton planters had erected to the boll weevil in gratitude for its effective limitation of the cotton crop.

There can be no doubt that it is to the obvious interest of every individual producing for the market that his own product should be in short supply, so that he should have more favorable conditions of exchange, and that he is equally interested in all measures which tend to maintain or even aggravate this shortage. But since the whole purpose of human economy is the alleviation of want, we are faced here with an irreconcilable conflict between public and private interest. Even clever advertising which seeks to gain the consumer's goodwill by flattery, cannot make the least difference here, in fact the untruthfulness inherent in it despite all protestations to the contrary throws a particularly revealing light on the demoralizing character of the conflict of interests. That the interest of every individual in his capacity of producer should be such constitutes a perversity which would appear absurd in any self-sufficient economy. It is, in fact, the product of an economy based on a division of labor which, therefore, suffers from a latent and constant disharmony between the interests of the individual producers and those of the community. We shall hardly be saying too much if we call this disharmony one of the greatest dangers and gravest infirmities of our civilization and if we state that the crudest mistakes and injustices in economic policy and the greatest aberrations of the market economy must be ascribed to this murderous germ which hardens the heart and stupefies the mind.

Now we are also in a position to define more accurately truth and error in the liberal theory of the automatic harmony of interests. The truth is—and this truth is terribly important—that (as far as the selfish appetite of the interests concerned is not curbed by a higher standard of business ethics, by a nobler tradition or simply by the law of indolence, and a highly developed professional code does not prevent, as is still the case with doctors, an all too keen pursuit of commercial advantages) it is the indispensable function of competition within the market economy to adjust opposing interests by insisting on equal value of service and counter-service and by forcing the producers to pursue their own advantage only by way of furthering the interests of the community. It is not merely the division of labor as such nor is it the market alone which leads to a concurrence of interests, but a special arrangement which men must consciously arrive at and must take great pains to maintain, namely, competition. It is necessary not only that this competition really exists, but that it be fair, honest and unadulterated, and neither the one nor the other is a necessary consequence of the division of labor and the market economy. As a community we must strive for the one as well as for the other with serious intent whilst everyone in his individual capacity of producer is most strongly interested in forcing things into exactly the opposite direction and in avoiding—secure in his position of monopoly and privileges of all kinds granted by the state—the highly irksome economic and moral discipline of competition.

It is the incomprehensible and tragic error of historical liberalism to have overlooked this. It was convinced that the market

mechanism and the division of labor would naturally and automatically impel solidarity and honorable conduct, and under the
spell of that false philosophy which led it to believe that the market
economy was either sociologically autonomous, or even morally
reformatory, it was deluded enough to think that, in order to cause
any particular group to act in the interest of the community, all
that was needed was intellectual enlightenment, a scientific appeal
to reason.   This is certainly indispensable but the decisive factor
is still the effective appeal to conscience and a certain minimum of
readiness to renounce or subordinate one's interests to those of the
community—traits with which the normal human being is still
equipped, all contrary evidence notwithstanding.   If, for example,
Jean-Baptiste Say in his liberal utopia "Olbie, ou Essai surdes moyens
de réformer les mœurs d'une nation" (1800), in all seriousness
recommends as the basis of a moral education "un bon traité
d'économie politique," we can tell from the ironic smile which
such a proposal evokes today, what distance separates us from this
strange naiveté.

If we are to go by what pays, we must, unfortunately, admit that
each individual industry looks very well after its own interests,
by obtaining protective tariffs or subsidies for itself and by establishing trusts; the labor unions by insisting on wages which are
higher than those justified by the prevailing state of the market, thus
injuring the public interest, including that of other workers; the
tooth paste manufacturer by persuading the consumer through
indefatigable advertising that without his product life is a failure;
even a whole nation may further its own interests by abusing its
political power for the exploitation of another.   Of course there
are limits to the relentless promotion of selfish interests and once
these bounds are overstepped it is the transgressor himself who
suffers.   Public opinion may not be provoked too brazenly and
no one is interested in letting the "elbow contest" assume proportions where it becomes a war of all against all.   But if one tells the
various group interests nothing else than that loyal observance of
the rules of the competitive price mechanism is in the interest of
all and if no strong moral forces are at the same time working to
curb their appetites, one must not be surprised by the disappointing results.   Honesty is undoubtedly the best kind of ethics, but
unfortunately it is doubtful whether, within certain limits, it is
always the best policy.   One would have to shut one's eyes to the
world and to history in order not to see that individuals, classes
and nations have always enjoyed an easy conscience and untroubled
prosperity while indulging in cheating, in selling the other fellow
short, in exploitation, yes, even spoliation.   This they do, not
burdening themselves with the thought that after them would come
the deluge which sooner or later would destroy such a society

without distinguishing between the just and the unjust. One cannot expect that in our day a dispassionate calculation of profit and loss will prevent people from indulging in such conduct.

After having recognized the fundamental error of the old liberal theory of harmony, we also realize that such unjustified optimism was bound to have a calamitous effect. First of all, this shallow philosophy has weakened every aspect of liberalism, for, by renouncing any strict moral appeal it has deprived itself of a higher dignity and of that attraction which is inherent in every movement which makes demands on men instead of mere promises and appeals to their self-interest or their sober reason. What is worse, however, is that this kind of liberalism tends to lull us into a feeling of safety and finally weakens our resistance against the attacks of the vested interests.

We can gauge how strong this resistance—of an intellectual and especially moral kind—must be if we ask ourselves what is needed in order to make competition and the fair observance of its rules win out against the immense pressure of all the vested interests. Owing to the division of labor every individual is, as a producer, interested in the most favorable exchange rate for the goods he produces, whereas the interest everyone has as a consumer—that is, as a representative of the community—in the reverse exchange relations and in the highest possible service of the manufacturer, is distributed over innumerable goods which one can only buy if one has previously, as producer of a single article, gained an income by making a maximum profit. Hence it follows that the economic judgment of every individual is more strongly determined by his position as a producer than as a consumer, and that, therefore, the concentrated pressure of producer interests has usually no trouble in overcoming the dispersed interests of the consumers. Although the interests of all in their capacity as consumers are larger and of a higher rank than the interest of each individual producer, they are often easily defeated because they are distributed over a far greater number of persons. For the same reason it is also so easy to falsify the facts by all kinds of pseudo-economic theories and partisan ideologies, so that in the end only a few recognize how absurd it is for all producers to obtain special privileges for themselves while total production declines. "L'intérêt parle toutes sortes de langues et joue toutes sortes de personnages, même celui de désintéressé" (La Rochefoucauld). It is sufficiently known that among the many languages of which the representatives of these interests are past masters, the venerable phrases of patriotism occupy a foremost place. Thus, for instance, they persist in nourishing the popular belief that in the field of international economic affairs the interests of the individual national economies are as uniformly arrayed against each other as two hostile armies. In truth, however,

E

the lines of interest run quite differently, namely, right across the individual national economy, in which the interests of the native producers who favor protective tariffs are opposed to the collective interests of the consumers as well as of all the other producers.

But, unfortunately, our economic system and the entire non-collectivist political and social system supporting it, can in the long run only be maintained if the conflict of interests—so far as it is not kept within reasonable bounds by highly developed business ethics—is balanced by a system of perpetually effective and honest competition. An economic system where each group entrenches itself more and more in a monopolist stronghold, abusing the power of the state for its special purposes, where prices and wages lose their mobility except in an upward direction, where no one wants to adhere to the reliable rules of the market any more, and where consequently nobody knows any longer whether tomorrow a new whim of the legislation will not upset all calculations, an economic system in which everyone wants to live exclusively at the expense of the community and in which the state's budget finally comes to devour half of the national income: a system of this kind is not only bound to become unprofitable and thus bound to intensify the scramble for the reduced total profit, but it will moreover in the end suffer a complete breakdown. This is usually called the crisis of capitalism and is used as an occasion for new and revolutionary interventions which complete the ruin and corruption and finally present us with the inexorable choice of either returning to a reasonable and ethical market system or of plunging into the collectivist adventure.

If, in blind despair, we choose the latter, we have not even the excuse that we did not know what was in store for us. And least of all should we expect to find there at last a harmony of interests. On the contrary, there they conflict even more violently than ever before, laboriously and for an uncertain period curbed by the authority of the state, within which the struggle for power and influence fluctuates by means of bribery, intrigues and executions. It is obvious that a question of ethics cannot be solved mechanically by a change of organization, and if society, the state, legislation, the courts and politics have so far been unable to make the competitive system work, why should we believe that they will be able to cope with the infinitely more difficult tasks of a collectivist system? A good indication of how the powerful group interests would profit by a planned economy is the eagerness with which in many countries they advocate a so-called "controlled economy."

The more the economy and the state become plaything and prey of the vested interests and the more elasticity and working capacity of the economic system are thereby impaired, the greater the temptation to seek a remedy in currency manipulation. Following the line of least resistance by keeping clear of the highly tiresome and thankless problems of group egoism and the rigidity of the price and cost structure, one takes refuge in monetary reforms which promise instantaneous salvation from all evils without directly impinging on highly sensitive interests, a solution with "business as usual," so to speak. This seems the most promising method of uniting all the conflicting interests in one's support and of gaining a following where everyone hopes to gain without anyone's getting hurt. This, then, is the heaven of all the unworldly utopians who do not realize what it is all about, this is the fourth dimension where all contradictions are resolved. As the lever of prices and wages becomes more rusty and the resistance to constantly renewed demands on the nation's treasury weakens, devaluation of the currency, foreign exchange control and inflation become welcome loopholes, especially if they are recommended by outstanding economists. The exceptional and completely disproportionate popularity which monetary cure-alls enjoy today all over the world is a direct result of the rigidity and decomposition of our economic system brought about by the stifling growth of special interests. It should, however, be clear that even in the most favorable instance these are only temporary and dangerous palliatives which in the end make matters worse and are unsuitable as habitual remedies. For, whatever one does with the currency, the fundamental problems posed by the economic system itself and the unruly special interests must be solved if economy and currency are not both to fall victim to complete chaos.

We already know that we are not dealing here with the economic system alone. On the one hand it is clear to us that we can only defend our civilization with a well-arranged non-collectivist economy; on the other hand, we have convinced ourselves (in the second chapter) that the struggle among the group interests—the "pressure groups," to use the drastic American expression—leads to the disintegration of the state. By organizing themselves into powerful asociations, the various groups divide political life up in terms of specific economic interests, and political power becomes the price which incites everyone to take part in the struggle. The extent of this alarming development is as clear to us as is the hardly comprehensible error of those who believe in all seriousness that they will be able to base a new and better state, i.e., the corporate state, on these group interests. We also have to add that the unification of the various interests in well organized groups makes matters even worse by producing a "pluralism of the second degree," namely, the creation of an "associational" bureaucracy which, pursuing its special tasks, does not only lend extra momentum to the conflict among the interests but also fights for the interests of its particular group with an intransigence which many of those whom it represents would rather see modified. Since, in addition, this bureaucracy has a professional interest in propagating the interests of others in a manner which constantly proves the need for its services, it tends only too often to persuade its clients to make demands which may be well suited to collective action, but which by no means necessarily correspond to the real and considered interests of these clients. This unwholesome development has probably reached its highest degree in the United States where the spokesmen of special interests—the "lobbyists"— who are entrusted with constantly belaboring the members of Congress in Washington, are among the highest paid specialists. The often very short sighted policy of the labor unions in many countries—especially conspicuous during the last phase of the French Third Republic, but hardly less so during the most recent history of the United States—must also be viewed as "pluralism of the second degree."

But the method which alone holds promise of a remedy is equally obvious to us and since the real and basic origin of the evil is the division of labor, pushed to extremes and interlocking everything in the most complicated manner, our first thought will be to return to a simpler stage by increasing the sector of self-sufficiency and strengthening local relations between producer and customer (handicrafts, &c.) as much as possible. Before judging our fellow men too harshly we should consider that the division of labor has possibly been developed too far, so that the strain on frail human morality has become excessive. We must not forget that the growing anonymity of all social and economic relations has removed those whom we are bound to treat with fairness to an increasingly remote distance. This explains how someone who is punctiliously honest in dealing with people he knows may have no scruples in procuring advantages for himself at the cost of an abstract community of consumers and receiving a subsidy from the state which has to be borne by the shadowy totality of the tax payers. If all these individuals go further and join a gigantic association with paid executive secretaries, the collective ethics of this association tend, in accordance with the laws of mass psychology, to fall even beneath the rather lax ethical standards of the individual. If we find that the professional executives of the associations also have to make a living and cannot therefore afford to be more scrupulous than the members of their association, that in fact they are even forced to talk them out of any scruples they may have, we must not be surprised at the results. Instead of wringing our hands in despair over the wickedness of the human race, we would do better to bemoan a sociological order which of necessity promotes man's less noble traits. Let us also remember that if the bare existence of men is, by virtue of an all-pervasive division of labor and the market economy, made dependent on the continuous sale of a single product or a single service, a cloud of insecurity hovers over them which is bound to make them cold hearted and nervous. The well known dictum that business is no joking matter succinctly expresses this sociological fact, which is further exemplified by the conduct of the farmer who is very much concerned with looking after his interests in the market but very generous with his produce at home and likes nothing more than for his guests to enjoy his food. Likewise, the author who drives his publisher to despair with his demands for royalties, will by no means fetter his wit or count the words in his letters to his friends. Let us then, at least to some extent, return to the old easy-going spirit by assigning less importance to money matters, which is possible by increasing the sector of simple economic relations (self-sufficiency and local selling and buying) at the expense of the sector of anonymous competition, and we shall have taken the first step towards reconstruction. We are convinced that cultivation of the local sphere in this sense will do wonders.

Of course, this measure alone will not suffice because the possibilities of expanding the sector of simple economic relations is, as matters stand today, rigidly limited. But what is to be done about the large market sector? It would be pleasant if we could base our hopes on a sufficiently high standard of business ethics which would cause everyone to strive persistently for optimum efficiency; and it should certainly be our goal to see to it that every producer of goods or services conducts himself as does a respectable doctor who, as yet untainted by commercialism, gives of his best and relies, even without the pressure of competition, on his social good sense when it comes to making out the bill. Until such time, however, we will have to resign ourselves to the fact that in the majority of cases only the re-establishment of unadulterated and honest competition can put an end to the exploitation of all by all rampant today. But in order to achieve this and to maintain competition against all opposition, an urgent appeal to the insight and goodwill of all concerned is once more necessary. It is necessary also in order to keep competition itself untainted because it cannot function unless it is based on certain definite ethical norms: general honesty and loyalty in business, adherence to the rules of the game, making excellence of workmanship a point of honor, and a certain professional pride which deems it humiliating to defraud, to bribe or to misuse political power for one's own selfish purposes. It should in fact be the rule that everyone who does not adhere to the strict code of business ethics, who violates the rules of competition, indulges in monopolistic manipulations, asks the state for economic assistance without urgent reason, and everyone whose advertising sails too close to the wind and whose economic demands are too exaggerated, should be socially ostracized as violating the dictates of decency, and in worse cases as a cheat, as a fraudulent bankrupt, as someone engaging in a "dishonest" profession. If he is rich, this fact should make him all the more suspect. Here again we must take refuge in the "terror regime of decency." Only then may we look upon the problem of the demoralizing conflict of interests, which overshadows everything else, as solved, and we trust man enough to believe that then even today's most ruthless protagonist of group interests will feel better than under present conditions.

We must here address a particularly urgent appeal to the rich, reminding them of the duties imposed on them by their privileged position. While we may fully appreciate the difficulties of the small man, the shopkeeper, the artisan and the peasant whom the struggle for their bare existence makes narrow-minded in the defense of their special interests, we must be adamant in demanding that he who has no real difficulty in making a living uses to the full the unique opportunity offered by his economic independence and that he should have the insight, as well as the will, to look further than the narrow sphere of his own interests and consider the whole picture of existence cooly, with an open mind and uninfluenced by the jargon of his particular interest group. *Richesse oblige.* We must reach the point where a rich man is ashamed to promote economic policies which coincide with his special interests, and where, if he does it, he is not only suspect to others but above all to himself. It should be possible to discuss with leaders of the optical industry the dangerous corruptions of patent usage, and with leading persons in the electric industry the questionable value to the general public of holding companies, without the feeling that one is talking to prejudiced persons who are only able to see things from one angle, and whether or not this is possible should in future become the touchstone of whether we are dealing with a member of the true elite or with a hidebound bourgeois.

We may expect general acceptance of such a program especially since to ascribe the view to us that there are no special interests in need of protection, would be to miss our point completely. On the contrary, we consider it a grave mistake of historical liberalism to have denied that in certain cases the promotion of a special interest may at the same time greatly benefit the community in general. We shall elaborate this theme which we have already anticipated to a considerable extent in the final part of this book.

The End of Capitalism?

Influenced by a few suspiciously agitated writers, many people have during the last years become convinced that capitalism is irrevocably doomed. Those who founder helplessly in the chaos of the present cling to this view which has the additional advantage of giving them the appearance of prophets conversant with the plans of Providence, and enables them to look down with a mixture of pity and ill disguised irritation on those who are still groping for the light. A we-are-all-at-the-end-of-our-wits atmosphere is created and offered as proof of this view. It certainly is not easy to resist this atmosphere, but the longer one reflects on the theory of the inevitable "end of capitalism," the more one is surprised that serious people can be satisfied with this half-baked mixture of error and truth without insisting on greater clarity. What exactly is meant by "capitalism"? The historical form in which it has evolved up to our time with all its perversions, which in the long run are indeed intolerable, or the principle of a market economy as such? The attitude we adopt depends entirely on whether the first or the second is meant, and we must add that it is a harmless pastime to call that form of market economy which the future may bring and which may possibly largely coincide with our ideal, the opposite of "capitalism." We shall certainly not begrudge the prophets of the end of capitalism the pleasure of having been right in this respect.

But does anyone ask for our opinion at all? This brings us to another point about which we are never told the whole truth. Is the end of capitalism, however defined, a consummation devoutly to be wished, a goal for which we should work, and is one merely encouraging people a little by vaguely telling them that the wind is blowing in that direction anyway? Or is it a mere prophecy, an assessment of future chances and an evaluation of all the forces and counter-forces, including the will of men themselves? Or, finally, is it that the "end of capitalism" is a pre-determined process whose course we can deduce according to the rules of the philosophy of history, a process which does not offer any alternative to those who deem it disastrous?

If the first interpretation is meant, our answer must depend on what is understood by "capitalism" and what economic order is to replace it. We need not elaborate here what the answer will be in each case. If, however, we should be advised to adopt an economic system which we believe to be disastrous, namely, collectivism, then the fact that the wind is already blowing that way will only—if we want to maintain our self-respect—redouble our resistance. As to the second interpretation, we have to admit that prophecy is outside our field of competence and that we leave it to the astrologers. If, however, the third interpretation is to be discussed, it will suffice to say that it is a final manifestation of the social determinism of the nineteenth century—with Marx as its spiritual ancestor. And on this issue there is surely nothing more to be said.

We shall now turn our back on these sterile discussions and

decide on the more fertile method of calmly and judiciously analysing the most important changes in the structure of our economic system by attempting to interpret those that have occurred up to date and assessing the probability of others occurring in the future. Of course, we are forced to be very brief here though the subject, strictly speaking, deserves very comprehensive study.

Let us begin with one of the most important changes during the last fifty years, namely, the growing importance of large enterprises, giant industries and monopolies of every kind—a development which cannot be denied. However, before drawing far-reaching conclusions from this, regarding the future of our economic system and the chances of a program of reform opposed to this development, two points have to be strongly emphasized. The first concerns the actual extent of the development and we must warn against over-estimating it. It is by no means true that an indiscriminate concentration of production, capital, incomes and economic power has taken place in all spheres. It is well known that it is not only agriculture that has in most countries successfully resisted this development, but also a considerable part of all other occupations, and even in countries like Germany and the United States, where concentration and proletarization have advanced farthest, it would be wrong to assume that large-scale industry dominates the scene. Regarding England, the continuous increase of small property holders has recently even been represented as a particularly typical phenomenon of that country's development, and as for Switzerland, it is superfluous to go into details once more. However, these observations are only intended to correct exaggerated notions. What has happened is bad enough, but it is not quite as bad as the prophets of doom represent it, and above all, it is not so bad that we should let our hands fall in hopeless despair.

The less so as—and this brings us to the second and even more important point—there are most certainly no overwhelming forces arrayed behind that concentration which has actually taken place, forces against which we would be powerless. It is usual in this connection to point particularly to technical development which, it is asserted, manifestly leads to ever larger industrial and commercial aggregates. In rebuttal we offer four arguments:

First of all, even if we are interpreting this development correctly, we are not the helpless slaves of technology, but as before —if only we wish to be—captains of our fate. Secondly, the argument is incorrect because it can be proved convincingly and in detail that the concentration of plants as well as of enterprises comprising several plants, has, on the average, considerably exceeded the size required by technological considerations. Thirdly, the argument is wrong because even in the past, assuming good will and efficient leadership, technical development could have been steered in a direction which would have decreased the preponderance of large enterprises, and this will certainly be possible in the future, once the engineers are entrusted with the task of social technology. Even the socially blind development of technology has already initiated revolutions which, as proved by electricity and the internal combustion engine, have increased the viability of the smaller enterprises. Since technology does not develop according to the immutable laws of physics, but according to the problems with which it is confronted, and since these problems have so far chiefly been posed by big industry itself, there is no reason why technology should not solve the task of social engineering, which serves to further the technical progress of small and medium enterprises, with the same success with which it has solved the problems of the sound film and of television. But it is first of all necessary that these new tasks and also the social philosophy on which they are based, should vividly and clearly be put before the engineering students at the technical colleges, and we believe that we have before us a very fertile field of co-operation between the social sciences and the science of engineering.

But, fourthly, this argument of technological inevitability is also misleading because it depends entirely on extra-technical factors whether a certain technological process which, for example, favors mass production, is in actual fact really superior from the economic point of view or not. It is obvious that if mass production—at least in the case of consumption goods—influences the character and quality of a product, a mass demand for such mass products must exist in the first place, so that mass production presupposes mass consumption. Fortunately, however, even the most venturesome advertising schemes—which, incidentally, the legislator is free to prohibit—are often not able to inspire such mass consumption and to destroy more dignified consumer habits. Moreover, the superiority of technology applied to large scale enterprises becomes questionable if the machinery for mass production is always inadequately used in times of depression, thus rendering a large enterprise more vulnerable to crises than a small one. And again, this superiority is most sensitive to psychological and organizational factors. The most rational organization of large enterprises and the most complicated machines can be of but little use if the human element is not properly taken into account: it is this factor, after all, which decides whether the organization of a factory will function smoothly or not, and, further, if and when the preponderance of large industries is likely to upset the balance of society itself. If we keep this in mind it may be quite possible that a technology and a plant organization which promises the most economical production calculated on the basis of the visible costs, may in the end prove to be the most expensive for the nation as a whole.

Having dealt with this argument of technological inevitability, we now turn to two further arguments which are closely related and which are based on the assumption that capitalism, world trade and liberalism can only really thrive in a dynamic atmosphere promising everlasting possibilities of expansion and that, for cogent reasons, these possibilities of expansion are now beginning to decrease. The first of these two arguments deals with the exhaustion of opportunities for spatial expansion and for this reason we shall call it the geographical argument, while the other is based on the universally noticeable slowing down of the reproduction rate and we shall therefore call it the demographic argument. According to the first argument the reservoir of square miles which can still be opened up on this earth is almost drained and according to the second argument we are near the end of the increase in the reproduction rate; both seek to prove that the vitality of our economic system is bound to diminish more and more rapidly. But if that be the case, then, the argument runs, the fate of the market economy as an economic system would also be sealed, because, like the collectivist mass state, this system, too, can only live dynamically.

We should know that basically there is very little to be said for these arguments however convincing they may sound. As interesting varieties of that logical error which the American philosopher Whitehead termed the "fallacy of misplaced concreteness," they confuse square miles and men with buying power, the only factor which matters in the expansion of markets. The possibilities of marketing all over the world depend solely on the possibilities of a universal expansion of production and there is no reason why in certain circumstances extensive market expansion should not be replaced by intensive expansion—that is to say for a given area and number of people. Because buying power is in actual fact exercised by individuals, the sum total of the demand is erroneously—and herein lies the "fallacy of misplaced concreteness"—thought to depend on the number of persons. One confuses people with francs, pounds and dollars. Admittedly there exist certain inelastic needs where total demand depends more or less on the number of people, but in all other cases demand is, quite independent of the number of people, an expression of buying power and that in turn is dependent on production, in other words on the success with which one satisfies the needs of others. The number of Christmas trees which can be sold is on the whole determined by the number of families, but value and number of gifts which are placed beneath them vary from family to family according to the income of its head, at least in the case of those gifts which, like gramophone records, do not usually depend on the size of the family. If, then, the increase in population ceases, the production of goods with a very inelastic demand (for instance Christmas trees, baby carriages and oatmeal), cannot expect further expansion, but is there any sense in envisaging a saturation point for all imaginable goods? Would a hundredfold increase of to-day's production suffice to lift the mass income to that level which in the higher income brackets is today looked upon as necessary in order to live? The geographical argument has hardly more in its favor. While in the previous case people were confused with money, square miles are now taken for francs and dollars, a new "fallacy of misplaced concreteness" which is responsible for all the misuse which the term "space" has to suffer today. Of course, the size of the market is not dependent on the number of square miles, but on the volume of purchasing power, and this again on successful (that is, economically appropriate) production. This then destroys the assumption that capitalist world trade is only possible if its operating area is constantly expanding. Its volume is not determined by space nor by the existence of unexplored islands in the Pacific Ocean, but by the level of the total world purchasing power and this again depends on world production being balanced, so that the individual producers produce for their mutual unlimited needs and not haphazardly without meeting each other's demands.

Our remarks should, of course, not be taken as denying that the impending end of spatial and demographic opportunities for expansion will bring about changes of very great and diverse importance in the structure of our economy. For this and for other reasons it must be expected that the impetuous dynamism of economic development will give way to a more measured pace, and also that forces are at work which may lead to a reduction of exaggerated industrialization and internationalization. However, we have to deny most emphatically that the system of the market economy is dependent on such dynamism and that as soon as this abates it would be forced to make room for a collectivist economic system. Notwithstanding all the problems of adaptation, which we do not want to discuss here, it is, on the contrary, very probable that our economic system will in the long run merely gain by such a slowing down. We can, therefore, only regret that the tremendous destruction of the present World War will force us for many years to continue relying on capitalism's proven dynamic powers which will be needed in their full strength for the task of rebuilding the devastated cities, industries, ports, railroads and ships. During that period the entire discussion about the problem of the possibilities of capitalism's economic expansion will remain purely academic.

This brings us to the question which is in everyone's mind today, of how the present war will affect the fate of our economic system.

Here, too, we shall make no prophecies, but merely elucidate difficult problems in order to gain a basis for a reasoned and balanced opinion. Returning to the thoughts we have just elaborated, we shall begin by stating that, in contrast to widespread views, we may in certain circumstances and with certain qualifications count on there not being a long period of world-wide unemployment and depression after this war, but rather an extraordinary impetus to production. We are not only borne out in this by the experiences which occurred, after shorter or longer periods of reconversion and demobilization difficulties immediately after the end of hostilities, in the past, but we are also supported by certain considerations which make such an outcome probable. The first of these we introduced earlier when we mentioned the vast needs of reconstruction which are bound to follow in the wake of this war. Whether and how quickly this will develop into a post-war boom admittedly depends to a very large degree on the success with which the exceedingly difficult immediate post-war stage and the conversion of war production to peace-time production will be passed—and here we must of course be cautious enough to take into account the at present completely unforeseeable possibilities of upheavals. But once this dangerous phase is weathered, the experience of the world in the 'twenties should teach us to curb the all too unbridled and tempestuous course of a reconstruction boom in order to avoid a new recession. Our cautious prognosis is the more likely to come true the more we see to it that rational measures—as, for instance, the well-known method of compulsory saving in war-time which Keynes recommends—keep war-time inflation and the subsequent deflationary rebound in as narrow limits as possible.

Then there is another consideration for which we shall have to go a little further afield. We should start by saying that the final sources of the utter disorganization of international economic life and of the grave functional disturbances of the market system are to be sought in the great physical and spiritual shocks which the advance of economic and political collectivism has caused in the world. The collectivist principle represents such an exceedingly radical invasion of our traditional world of values, emotions and concepts, and the political practice of the collectivist world has had such a startling and upsetting effect, that the spiritual reflexes on which the functioning of the market system depends, have failed to an increasing extent. All the more or less brilliant explanations of the economic crisis of the past decade, which seek its causes in the purely economic domain, have thus missed the essential point: the destruction of the spiritual and political fundaments of our economic system.

It is plain what this means in terms of the present situation:

should we succeed in mastering the collectivist invasion after the end of the war, the situation will be so much more clear-cut and free of strain that it will make recovery of a hardly imaginable extent possible. The tenacious paralysis would find release and new life would pulse through every vein. The body economic would regain its natural reflexes and its old elasticity and would not require experimenting with new-fangled medicines. A loosening of the spasm can, however, only be expected if it is clearly understood that the struggle of our time between the collectivist and the non-collectivist principle is being waged as between two irreconcilables and must be carried through to the end as such. But this means that the non-collectivist world must not make any concessions to collectivism which go beyond the most urgent necessities of the war economy and that it must purge itself of all inclinations to flirt with the collectivist idea. This is certainly not asking too much, as it can easily be shown that we need not be too frightened by the spectre of economic chaos and paralyzing depression after the war, if only the divorce between the collectivist and the non-collectivist way is made decisive and final.

The aforesaid answers that unjustified fatalism which, if we resignedly surrendered ourselves to it would have such a stifling effect that it would indeed justify a pessimistic prognosis. In this way we want to correct the view that the economic consequences of the war will in any case be such as to leave us no choice than to succumb supinely to economic and political collectivism, thereby depriving the present hour of world decision of its deeper meaning. Such a view is certainly false. It can be demonstrated that this fatalist idea is to some extent based on simple errors of logic which have only to be corrected—and that it is here not a matter of optimism or pessimism. That is particularly true of the financial effects of the war of which many have a downright apocalyptic vision, with inflation, devaluation and other acts of despair as the *ultima ratio*. However, to warn against an exaggerated estimate of the general burden of debt with which this war will end everywhere, is by no means a sign of financial irresponsibility.

It must also curb the fatalism based on the view that one cannot reduce state control and interventions once more to tolerable dimensions after the proportions they have assumed during the war. It is unhappily only too certain that a thousand interested parties will fight such a reduction tooth and nail, and it is just as certain that they will paint the probable consequences for the entire economy in the darkest colors. This is all the more reason for us to point out that the transitional difficulties of a return to the forms of a free economy tend to be enormously overrated. Certain experiences after the last war—the surprisingly smooth de-control of housing in Germany or of foreign exchange regulations in Austria—

rather prove that cures of this kind are much less fearful than the resisting patients would make us believe.

If there is no room for fatalism then everything depends on whether men understand that the present is a critical hour in the history of the world, and that they act to show whether they desire a development towards collectivism and economic Caesarism or not. This brings us back to the crux of the whole dispute. This desire, or its absence, is by no means a question of the free and independent decision of the individual: it depends on the social climate, in which the opinions and the will of the people at the helm have developed. However, the factors which determine this climate can be described more accurately, and thence it is only one step to influencing them. And that is what we are aiming at in all our efforts, not at preaching, lamenting and arguing.

The essential point is this: it is probable that men will fatalistically allow themselves to be carried by the current of collectivism as long as they see no other positive goal, firm and tangible, before them; in other words, as long as they know of no counter-program to collectivism over which they can really wax enthusiastic. It is indisputable that weighty considerations draw us in the direction of collectivism, and what is still lacking today are the proper counter-arguments of an inspiring alternative program which will release new energies. We would grossly deceive ourselves if we believed that the watchword of a mere return to the point of departure, viz., historical capitalism with all its attributes, could become the battle-cry which will bring us victory over collectivism. Such a restoration is by no means what we aim at, nor could we reconcile it with our conscience. It is not really possible to ignore the fact that the collapse of the liberal-capitalist world order was to no little extent also caused by its own deficiencies, misdirected developments and perversions. Just as little is it disputable that the final causes of the breakdown lie deep in the human, intellectual, moral and political sphere and can in the final analysis be reduced to the by now sufficiently well-known formula of the "spiritual collectivization" of our society and the resulting "revolt of the masses." A decisive part in this development has been played precisely by those economic and social factors of which the liberal age is by no means innocent and for whose treatment we must have a free hand without being dogmatically tied to the economic program of historical liberalism.

PART ONE—NOTES TO CHAPTER III

The observations made in this chapter are based on a system of economic theories which it was impossible to develop in detail in the text. We, therefore, expect that readers will either be fair enough to ask themselves whether more could have been said within the space available, and informed enough to fill in the necessary details themselves. In so far as the latter is not the case, the author sees himself forced to refer to some of his other publications in the field, especially *Die Lehre von der Wirtschaft* (5th edition, Erlenbach-Zürich, 1943), and *Crises and Cycles* (London, W. Hodge, 1936). The latter publisher subsequently brought out another book by the author on behalf of the Rockefeller Foundation, entitled *International Economic Disintegration,* which will give the reader further information on important points. Finally the author refers the reader to his books, *Civitas Humana* (London, W. Hodge, 1948) and *Internationale Ordnung*.

Note No. 1 (page 100). The fundamental problems of every economic system:

Regarding this question consult particularly Walter Eucken, *The Foundations of Economics,* London, 1950. Cf. also my *Lehre von der Wirtschaft,* chapters 1 and 2.

Note No. 2 (page 103). Advertising as a disturbing factor:

It must be strongly emphasized that advertising on its present scale represents one of the gravest problems of the economic structure, the more so since those who have an interest in it naturally know how best to advertise themselves and exert tremendous power over the press. It therefore belongs to those subjects which are not usually criticized and analyzed as bluntly and with as much forthrightness as they deserve. This is especially true where advertising is no longer even kept within bounds by a vestige of tradition and good taste. It is undeniable that the "sovereignty of the consumer" which we mentioned is seriously impaired by the suggestions which advertising puts out in an attempt to replace his true needs by imaginary ones. At the same time advertising becomes a dangerous instrument of monopoly ("monopoly of opinion") and of big business. Since, moreover, nobody has a commercial interest in propagating rest and leisure by advertising, it takes its due share of responsibility for the sterile excitability of our time, for its "empty activity." Here we are faced with particularly important but nonetheless soluble tasks of reform. The best book on this problem is A. S. J. Baster's *Advertising Reconsidered,* London, 1935.

Note No. 3 (page 103). The automatic mechanism of the market economy:
Cf. my book *Die Lehre von der Wirtschaft.*

Note No. 4 (page 105). Producers' economy and consumers' economy:

It is, incidentally, a widespread misconception to imagine that our economic system is organized solely for "profit," where profitableness determines the character of production, while the collectivist economic system is a genuine "consumers' economy" in which production is geared to the needs of the population. On the contrary, it is undeniable that, as long as competition safeguards the principle of optimum efficiency our present economic order is nothing but a consumers' economy, since the accurate and incorruptible scales of the market decide what is profitable. Can an economic system in which, when its principles are scrupulously adhered to, the demands of the consumer spur the producer to highest performances to satisfy these demands, be called anything but a consumers' economy? The difference between the communist consumers' economy—which exists, by the way, only as an ideal and in practice breaks down only too miserably—and our own is that the motivating forces and the organization for meeting demands differ, and quite definitely in our favor. If then one wants to brand our economic system as a profit economy, it is only logical and fair to call the communist system a bureaucratic economy.

Note No. 5 (page 110). Curtailments in the production of raw materials:

The over-production of raw materials during the last decades often tempts superficial observers to overlook that it is for the greater part based on the rape of irreplaceable natural reserves and that the consequences are already making themselves felt in many instances and in an alarming manner. The most tragic example is the increasing deterioration of the soil in wide agricultural areas—especially overseas (thus in the so-called "dust bowl" of the United States, the scene of the well-known novel by John Steinbeck, *Grapes of Wrath*), but also in Europe (e.g., the "steppefication" of Germany!). We also point to the annihilation campaigns against the forests on all continents and against the whales of the ocean. Cf. E. Pfeiffer, *The Earth's Fall*, London, 1947; I. Bowman and others, *Limits of Land Settlement*, New York, 1937; G. V. Jacks and R. O. Whyte, *The Rape of the Earth, a World Survey of Soil Erosion*, London, 1939; F. Osborn, *Our Plundered Planet*, London, 1948; G. O'Brien, *The Phantom of Plenty*, Dublin, 1948. Regarding Europe, we point to the inevitable consequences of the excessive use of artificial manure and to the progressively more serious problem of every country's water supply, caused by the enormous water consumption of industries and big cities.

Note No. 6 (page 112). The population problem:

A more detailed presentation will be found in my *Lehre von der Wirtschaft*, pp. 80-94.

Note No. 7 (page 115). The after effects of feudalism and absolutism:

It might be very fruitful to gauge the influence exerted by the more or less vigorous feudal-absolutist remnants on the development of capitalism, by looking at the present day economic structure of various countries. It will then be found that owing to the diversity of this influence, there exist widely differing national types of capitalism, a circumstance which provides us at the same time with an index of the possibilities of reform. Regarding Germany, for instance, we find among other things a very strange and disturbing absence of instinctive opposition to monopolies which pervades the entire history of German capitalism and has led to an early and comprehensive monopolist organization of industry (usually in the form of cartels). Even during the social-democratic regime—always inclining towards organization and concentration—this attitude persisted, and there can in fact be no doubt that it is an expression of the national character in the economic sphere, and, as we know, that character was shaped by feudalism and absolutism. Almost the same reasons which explain why Germany had a Reformation but no Revolution like England or France, also explain why its attitude towards any kind of monopoly has always been strangely weak and therefore proved to be so susceptible to every form of monopolist ideology. There has always been—perhaps with the exception of Prussia's liberal period from 1818-1879—a certain reverence for monopolies in Germany, and a cartel was, as it were, next in rank to Court and Church. The feudal aroma of the cartels has always been unmistakable, especially in heavy industry whose leaders have always felt attracted to the landed aristocracy, both socially and as regards their economic policies. Monopolies were institutions of which to speak disrespectfully, or even to call by this gross name, was considered very unrefined and as plebeian as the public use of a tooth pick. (Cf. Wilhelm Röpke, *German Commercial Policy*, London, 1934, and the author's other book, *The Solution of the German Problem*, New York, 1947.) It is an exceedingly interesting question which has not yet received sufficient attention why monopolies have developed just as vigorously in the United States, though here there has always been a passionate and traditional hostility towards them. We may surmise that the reasons are twofold: (1) the stormy development of the country's prosperity which, as long as it lasted, absorbed all energies and seemed to offer a chance to everyone, and (2) the weaknesses of the American democracy which have permitted the political influence of vested interests to flourish unchecked. However, in contrast to Germany, there has always been a strong section of public opinion in the United States passionately repudiating monopolies and today, the era of opening up the country having been concluded, it has assumed such proportions that this question ranks high on the list of national problems.

Note No. 8 (page 116). Proletarization:

The industrial proletariat is merely the particularly conspicuous and best known expression of a far more general process of "proletarization." The latter term applies, as we have already mentioned in the introduction, whenever big business, concentration of capital and a predominant market economy (at the cost of self-sufficiency) have resulted in a large part of the population's becoming dependent, urbanized receivers of indirect incomes (wages and salaries), members of the industrial-commercial hierarchy, and wherever that economic and social collectivization has set in to which we have to return again and again. It is also characteristic of such a proletarized world that it can no longer think in anything but terms of money and income. Cf. G. Briefs, *The Proletariat*, New York, 1937; G. K. Chesterton, *The Outline of Sanity;* Hilaire Belloc, *An Essay on the Restoration of Property*, London, 1936; L. Romier, *Explication de notre temps*, Paris, 1925, and the author's *Civitas Humana*, London, 1948.

Note No. 9 (page 118). The blindness of historical liberalism:

The economic history of the last hundred and fifty years abounds with examples of the blindness of the liberals towards the fact that the market requires a firm legal framework and is by no means sociologically autonomous. We merely mention that as early as 1772 the English Government revoked highly important market policing laws (against "regrating, forestalling and engrossing"), with the vigorous support of Adam Smith himself. An even far more radical liberal (J. R. M'Culloch) was later responsible for the abolition in 1824 of further anti-monopoly laws (Combination Acts against conspiracy). (Cf. W. H. Hutt, *Pressure Groups and Laissez-Faire*, "South African Journal of Economics," March, 1938.)

Note No. 10 (page 120). Thwarted possibilities of development:

I cannot refrain from quoting here a passage from the book, first published in 1851, by W. H. Riehl, *Die bürgerliche Gesellschaft* (6th edition, Stuttgart, 1866, page 360): "We find proof of how even the mere appearance of a family life can protect the factory worker from the proletarian outlook, among the Westphalian foundry workers who, being the most sought after men in their strenuous occupation, travel to the Rhineland in order to labor there in the smelting plants; they are distinguished both by their industry and their high moral character. . . . Their families stay at home in West-phalia on the small fraction of a farm with which the father has been paid off. The husband thus practically sees his wife and children only once a year. And yet from this one yearly visit he takes back with him to the life of the factory the sense of family life and the sterling qualities of the West-phalian burghers and peasants; the whole year through his consciousness of these keep him upright and efficient." Until recently similar conditions obtained in the Turkish coal mines of Zonguldak, but here, too, a blind spirit of progress declared them outmoded without reflecting whether they did not offer possibilities for new forms of industrial organization likely to prevent proletarization. The attitude towards domestic industries was similar. Cf. also the description of former working conditions in Franz Schnabel's *Deutsche Geschichteim neunzehnten Jahrhundert,* 3rd volume, Freiburg, 1934, page 288 f. At the same time as Riehl the like-minded Frédéric Le Play published his documentary report *Les ouvriers européens* (Paris, 1855), the conclusions of which led him to write his famous and still topical book *La réforme sociale* (first published in Paris, 1864). Both books are a veritable mine for the social historian who wishes to inform himself as to how much was still sound at that time.

Note No. 11 *(page* 121). *Economic crises:*
    The author's own views can be found in his above mentioned book, *Crises and Cycles* (London, W. Hodge, 1936). Cf. also Gottfried Haberler, *Prosperity and Depression,* 3rd edition, Geneva, 1941.

Note No. 12 *(page* 123). *Economic crises and the socialist state:*
    It is an illusion entirely at odds with reality that socialism promises a paradise of economic stability. Economic disharmonies of every kind will even become chronic under socialism and they will be further distinguished from the acute and temporary crises in the capitalist system by the additional fact that the socialist government will suppress their immediate economic manifestations by every means in its power and will shift them from the economic apparatus to the periphery, i.e., it will burden the consumers with them. In other words, the primary tumor will, now, so to speak, produce metastases in the most distant parts of the social organism: there is an end to bankruptcy, and if some inventiveness is employed in the disposal of incon-venient masses of men, all visible unemployment also vanishes; we are saved the sight of open abscesses, but by means of a therapy which drives the germs of the disease into the arteries and into the most distant parts of the social organism. The suppression of the superficial symptoms of economic disharmonies does not mean, therefore, that one has removed the dis-harmonies themselves. It rather means that the mechanism which indicates the location of the trouble has been destroyed, a timely and correct diagnosis has become impossible and the powers of recovery inherent and active in our economic system have been paralysed. The economic machine continues to "work" in some fashion, but the population, robbed of its elementary rights and freedoms, has to bear in a multitude of ways the consequences of the neglected and aggravated disturbance of the equilibrium. There will always be something new in the way of unpleasant surprises without one being able to foretell what shape they will assume in each case: "several-year-plans" in endless procession, purges, and then war—the *ultima ratio.* The socialist state

is obliged to use practically any and every means in order to avoid reverses. and crises, because its entire prestige is at stake once it has assumed responsibility for the proper functioning of the economy. Every economic crisis becomes—since every aspect of the economy has been politicalized—a crisis of the socialist state itself. Cf. Wilhelm Röpke, *Socialism, Planning and the Business Cycle*, "The Journal of Political Economy" (Chicago), June, 1936; Wilhelm Röpke, *Totalitarian "Prosperity": Where Does It End?* "Harper's Magazine" (New York), July, 1949. See also the author's study, *Zur Theorie des Kollektivismus*, "Kyklos," 1949, and the literature mentioned there.

Note No. 13 (page 124). The conflict of interests in the economy:

I am reserving a more thorough analysis of this subject, which is so important but very much neglected by economists, for a special treatise. Cf. Philip H. Wicksteed, *The Common Sense of Political Economy*, revised edition, London, 1933, volume 1, pp. 349-357, and my *Lehre von der Wirtschaft*, pp. 96-104.

Note No. 14 (page 124). The errors of the liberal theory of the automatic harmony of interests:

Consult the admirable essay by Walter Sulzbach, *Liberalismus*, "Archiv für Sozialwissenschaft," volume 59, 1928, pp. 382-395, in this connection. The conclusions applying to the special sphere of international harmony are easily drawn. The doctrine—which has been made especially popular by Norman Angell's well-known book, *The Great Illusion*—of the harmonizing and pacifying effect of close international economic relations as such, is perfectly right in stressing the solidarity of international interests within a liberal world economy, but it contains the same error as the harmonic theory of economic relationships within the state: if the nations are not in any case of a peaceful and chivalrous disposition, they will now as then by means of economic and political machinations try to gain all kinds of special advantages at the cost of other nations, thus undermining the liberal world economy itself. "Free trade, good will and peace among nations" Cobden had proclaimed as the motto of the English Free Trade Movement, but "good will and peace among nations" are the premises not the result of a liberal world economy. Naturally the same holds good here as in the national economy: it is to one's own interest to be ruthless within reason.

Note No. 15 (page 132). Group egoism in the United States:

Group egoism in the United States has always been particularly unbridled and has hardly been surpassed even by its German counterpart which reared its head especially after the end of the First World War. It is typical that precisely under the "New Deal" with its unprecedented subsidies, it has assumed downright dangerous proportions. Once more it has been demonstrated that state aid is by no means supplied where the need is greatest, but where the greatest political pressure can be brought to bear so that the weak even have to contribute towards the support of the strong. The pinnacle of this development was probably the Silver Purchase Act of 1934, a law which, under the pressure of the silver interests, obligated the American Government to buy up silver at exceedingly high subsidy rates until the silver reserves had reached a quarter of the gold reserves. That is to say, the silver interests forced the government, by means of domestic political blackmail, futilely to squander more than a billion dollars, almost to double the price of silver, to burden the silver market with completely abnormal and in the long run untenable conditions, and finally to destroy the monetary system of the countries with a silver currency (especially China)—and all this for the sake of an industry which employs a total of eight thousand workers—that is, as much as the American watch-making industry. The world supply of silver in 1939 can be estimated at 403 million ounces, the consumption, however, at hardly 100 million ounces. The American government, due to the rule of the interest groups in Congress, was forced to buy up the difference, and only now (1941) that it seems to have less urgent need of the votes of the silver interests, can it envisage a cessation of the silver purchases. In order to form a just opinion of the pluralism of the labor unions and the farmers, one must bear in mind such shameless cases of the exploitation of the state.

Note No. 16 (page 136). Structural alterations in our economic system:

For a more detailed description the reader is referred to the author's book's *International Economic Disintegration* and *Internationale Ordnung*.

PART TWO

ACTION

Chapter I

ABERRATIONS AND BLIND ALLEYS

Sanabilibus aegrotamus malis ipsaque nos in rectum genitos natura, si emendari velimus, iuvat.

(The ills from which we suffer are not incurable and to us, who are born to do right, nature herself extends her help if only we want to be cured.)
—SENECA, *De ira,* II, 13.

Loose Thinking

EVERYDAY experience constantly proves that many people, especially on questions regarding the life of the community, tend to think in very vague terms which easily make them miss that crucial nuance which sharply divides truth from error. One continually discovers in conversation that the agreement one had believed to be established, is deceptive, as soon as one's partner draws conclusions which show unmistakably that he has not understood the point at issue. After emphatically agreeing with the criticisms of liberalism and capitalism and after seeing himself confirmed in some of his pet opinions, he thinks it a matter of course that now steps should be taken which we know to be harmful and which will, in the final resort, only make matters worse. Most people's ability to exercise intellectual discrimination is not subtle enough and their imaginative powers are not sufficiently developed for them to be able to think of other methods than those which can ultimately only serve to support economic and political collectivism. Monopolies are an evil? Then the state should take them over, or establish an official Monopoly Department. We have concerned ourselves too little with social problems up to now? Then let the state organize the workers and make them all members of a national pension system. The old spirit of peasant life and craftsmanship is on the wane? Then one should rally the peasants and craftsmen and make them attend training courses in professional pride and love of tradition. International economic relations have become anarchic? Then it is about time that an international planned economy was introduced. It is unnecessary to continue this painful game of questions and answers.

The rough-and-ready character of everyday thinking is particularly apparent in the fact that people assume that they have to decide between two alternatives only and see no other possibility of choice. Their thoughts move according to the simple formula of "either—or," beyond which they are unable to see and therefore they cannot perceive the possibilities outside these alternatives:

> . . . Like on a barren heath an animal
> Led in a circle by an evil ghost,
> While all around it all is pleasant green.

151

They think that one can only choose between revolution and reaction; between fascism and communism; between inflation and deflation; between the stability of domestic prices and the stability of foreign exchange; between the decay of the family and continued population increases; between degenerated democracy and authoritarian despotism; between nationalism and internationalism; between a devitalized civilization and barbarian savagery; between lasciviousness and asceticism; between rationalism divorced from reality and irrationalism destructive of all culture; between disorder and organization; between a romantic hostility towards progress and an absurd over-estimation of technology and economics; between weak pacifism and arrogant militarism; between individualism and collectivism; between the mushroom growth of cities and dull rusticity; between being either hammer or anvil; between the imperialism of the one side and that of the other; and, similarly, in the end between historical capitalism and liberalism at one end of the scale and socialism at the other end. "La loi de double frénésie," as Henri Bergson called it.

We can take it for granted that by now most people have decided against one of the two possibilities, i.e., against capitalism (putting it roughly, against the principle of laissez-faire), not the least reason being that there are still some of its exponents who follow the same formula of "either—or" and do not tire of emphasizing that there is no other choice than that between capitalism and socialism. We, therefore, need not fear that one will again choose the false path of historical capitalism, and so we can now conclude our indictment of it; understandably enough, we are rather inclined to protect it against exaggerated attacks and foolish insults with the chivalry due to the vanquished.

On the other hand, the great majority today would by no means openly come out for a particularly pronounced form of socialism. The profound influence of propaganda and contemporary examples notwithstanding, most people are still restrained by a certain timidity, since the criticism levelled at socialism for a century has not remained completely without effect nor have the powers of resistance of healthy instincts ceased to function. In the Western countries it is still only a minority—though an especially active and fanatical one—which adheres to the extreme Russian example or even openly adopts the word "communism," and one hears very little today of the "expropriation of the expropriators," the "socialization of the means of production," and similar slogans of civil strife. Although today the term "socialism" has lost much of its old flavor and has almost acquired citizen rights, one is still not merely careful in its application but also endeavors to invest it with a more harmless content; one embellishes it with modifying adjectives of every kind by speaking of "Christian," "national," "confederate," "liberal" socialism; one is soothed by terms such as "planned economy," "controlled economy," and others, and the contents of the programs correspond to the more harmless sound of the words.

There can be no doubt that wide circles find it very irksome that the only alternative should be between capitalism and socialism and serious efforts are being made to avoid it and find something new. However, loose thinking habits are also in evidence here, in that all too often one still chooses a program which—at times only by a hand's breadth—leads past the right "Third Way" into the wilderness and finally ends in collectivism.

In view of these experiences, which everyone will confirm, we are forced to begin this section, which is devoted to action, with a few negative words in order to furnish the right path with various guide posts which will show us the points where we must take care not to go astray.

Socialism

Concerning undisguised socialism only a few words are needed in order to characterize its harmful effects on society, especially since it has long ceased to be a utopia giving room to every whim of the imagination. Now that it has become reality it is just as little permissible to think of socialism as a paradise as to stamp it an absurdity. Socialism is not a utopia, but a tragedy—that is the point at issue today. But just as we judged capitalism primarily by its non-materialist and not by its materialist performance, we should also beware of basing our judgment of socialism primarily on the probability of its failure in material affairs. We have found Nietzsche's suspicion that socialism is "tyranny brought to a zenith" (*Will to Power,* 125) confirmed, and started to prove it earlier in this book. This statement tends to touch the present day advocates of socialism in their most sensitive spot and embarrasses them more than the former purely economic critique; however, up to now no serious attempt at refutation has come to our knowledge nor can we well imagine how it could effectively be made. These circumstances have led some socialists to revise their concepts and to think up forms of socialism which they believe safe from this fundamental criticism. That there is no justification for their belief, we shall show later on.

It should further be said here that socialism—helped by the uprooted proletarian existence of large numbers of the working class and made palatable for them by just as rootless intellectuals, who will have to bear the responsibility for this—is less concerned with the interests of these masses than with the interests of these intellectuals, who may indeed see their desire for an abundant choice of positions of power fulfilled by the socialist state. Thus it is not the industrial proletariat which is the breeding ground for socialism but the academic and intellectual proletariat and therefore it is here that the danger for society is greatest and a remedy most urgently required. Of course, we would bitterly wrong many intellectuals and would ourselves become guilty of a psychology which we have often repudiated if we were to deem motives of naked self-interest an adequate explanation here. Faith, devotion and a passionate sense of justice are the decisive forces here too, but that they have chosen socialism as their object can alone be explained in terms of the proletarian collectivization of society in general and of the intellectual proletariat in particular. This will also supply the explanation of the striking fact that the artistic world supplies a considerable number of the adherents of socialism, although they should certainly know that art and literature have to vegetate in a thoroughly murderous climate in the collectivist state, and would do well to reflect how a man like Cézanne, who was enabled by his father's money to paint for thirty years to his heart's content without a financial care in the world, would have fared under a socialist regime. The world of today is full of artists, writers and scholars who do not know the first thing about economic and sociological matters, yet wielding the authority acquired in a quite different field, they set themselves up as judges of our economic system and passionately subscribe to this or that fashionable form of socialism. We could quote a list of many illustrious names here (Romain Rolland, Bernard Shaw, and others). Not all had, like André Gide, the opportunity to correct their opinion by experiencing communist reality and still fewer his honesty to confess his error publicly.

But whatever the origins of socialism may be, it is obvious that it will exacerbate the arch evil of our time, namely, spiritual collectivization and proletarization, to a hitherto unknown degree and will thus completely correspond to political collectivism, which is the despotic mass state. We need say nothing more regarding this. What we have to stress, however, is that socialism of this kind, which completely mechanizes and disintegrates society, will prove to be a rape of society's intangible and organic forces and reserves, precisely because it brings to a conclusion a process which began before it and which made its development possible. Merely in order to keep going, the socialist state will grasp at every and any means and will impiously smother the wellsprings of our society: tradition, the treasure of solid principles from the stability of the currency to the inviolability of person and property, continuity, small communities, law and peace. Without thinking of the more distant future, it lives from hand to mouth, glad to be able to prolong its existence for another year and without knowing the humble feeling of being embedded as an infinitesimal period of time between an immeasurable past and an equally infinite future. The forests are cut down and with the humus the peasants and craftsmen vanish too. Extreme insecurity and instability spread in all walks of life. Is it not true that in our glorious age of planning things have already come to such a pass that it is hardly possible to make plans for more than a week ahead? Socialism is, indeed, the reign of arbitrariness.

In all other respects, too, everything threatens to become far worse than under the worst form of "capitalism." To be sure, the position of the workers in a giant industrial plant today is very unsatisfactory, but will their dependence not become downright intolerable when they are confronted with only a single employer, the all powerful socialist state? One need only listen to the inveterate socialist talking with deepest contempt of the peasant and the "petit bourgeois" and with the greatest enthusiasm of technology, large-scale enterprises and everything bombastic, in order to recognize the super-Americanism which threatens us from that quarter. As shown by the collectivization of agriculture in Russia, an invasion of large-scale production methods must even be expected into fields where, in our economic system, small enterprise has successfully maintained itself—an expectation which is all the more justified since the collectivist state has a strong political interest in the agglomeration of tamed and dependent masses, easily fanaticized and supervised.

One need hardly inquire into the nature of the fair distribution of commodities in the socialist state. Undoubtedly the masses will be flattered as they have never been flattered before in history, and be fed with equalitarian phrases to which emphasis is lent by the persecution of the old social elite. Just as certainly a leaden atmosphere of grey proletarian uniformity will pervade the whole country, leaving hardly a glimmer of brilliance and color; we shall then have uniform dusk in which "all cats look grey." However, in our experience nothing justifies our expecting a miracle: that, for instance, the new elite dominating the state might ascetically renounce the opportunities of privilege afforded by their all powerful position. Aside from that it must be remembered that social justice does not only involve the equal distribution of income and property, but above all the equal distribution of power. After all, socialists do not solely and not even primarily, intend to abolish private ownership of the means of production in order to do away with unearned incomes but in order to eliminate the power derived from such property. But where is there a greater concentration of such power than in the socialist state? Whether one calls the beneficiaries of this power "owners" or not, does not alter the fact that that is what they are as regards their crucial function. That is why one can say that the head of a collectivist state is the largest owner known in history, because in the only sense in which one can possess something so gigantic, the whole country is his "own." His position would not in the least be altered if in accordance with civil law the property were formally made over to him. But there is one thing that he will miss, what in our society even the smallest peasant enjoys, thanks to our social and legal order: the sanctions of the constitutional state which guarantee the safety of his property and assure him that the tree he planted on the land which he inherited from his ancestors, will give shade to his great-grandchildren. Conversely, it is true that wherever socialist developments have removed these sanctions, private property has lost most of its legal content. When the point has been reached where political "unreliability" can lead to the confiscation of one's property, the position of the owner rapidly approaches that of a mere socialist functionary of the state; as everything else in a state drifting towards socialism, property has been "politicalized" and thereby divested of all meaning and dignity.

Although we have placed these spiritual dangers of socialism in the foreground, we can as little ignore its disappointing material achievements as we can, conversely, ignore the obvious superiority which capitalism displays also in this respect. Since, however, considerable preference—which we think unjustified—has been given in the extensive literature up to date to the danger of socialism's failing in material production, and since this contention is by no means essential to our argument, we are surely entitled to refrain from further elaborations. However, it seems necessary to us to correct a widespread misunderstanding which has gained a footing as the result of present day experiences. Many people believe that the critics of socialism can be impressed by the fact that in socialist countries one works as much as elsewhere, that huge buildings are being erected and that the wheels of industry turn no more slowly than under capitalism, and as further evidence one usually points to the rising figures of the national income which those countries report. For many reasons, which space forbids us to detail here, these optical impressions as well as the statistical figures are deluding. We would have to ask for an accurate investigation of the vast unproductive costs of the socialist bureaucracy (of the "waste of planning"), further we would want to know with what increased—and often hidden—output of labor this production is bought, and lastly to what extent foreign capitalist countries have voluntarily or involuntarily contributed to it. We would also be interested to know the extent of the stock of machines, experience and education, taken over from the pre-socialist era, with which the socialist state entered on its rule and for a long time was able to cover up its own deficit. But all this is not even decisive. Rather, the point at issue is not the production of objects in a technical-physical sense, but "production" in the economic sense, i.e., adapted in its various components to the needs of the population. It would be uncharitable to ask for more precise information regarding this point in the socialist state.

All these damning arguments have, as we said, caused the more farsighted among socialist theorists of our time to re-orient themselves and to work out new forms of socialism which will stand up to such present-day criticism of socialism as has become irrefutable. The interest in such theoretical constructions is very small if for no other reason than that they are really nothing but the ingenious products of painstaking cogitation behind dusty desks which are ideally suited for academic discussion, but hardly for practical execution, and which in part are only intended to serve the purposes of subtle propaganda. Mental edifices which are so complicated that one has to take the greatest pains—often unsuccessfully—to understand them at all, condemn themselves. If in addition these socialist theorists—we find them today primarily in the Anglo-Saxon countries—do not even pay the slightest attention to the sociological premises of their programs, we are really entitled to pass them by and go on to the next point on the agenda. But we will extend ourselves sufficiently to point out that their theoretical conceptions alone are highly questionable.

Society—a Machine

Socialism is given a special, but for our time characteristic, note by the still influential techno-scientific rationalism of which a writer like the late H. G. Wells was an exponent and which his countryman, Aldous Huxley, has depicted in his utopian novel, *Brave New World,* with justified ruthlessness in all its gruesome consequences. Here we have another opportunity for observing how the spirit of the nineteenth century rises from its beginnings to a paroxysm which could only lead to absurdities. Marx had called his socialism "scientific" to give it that prestige which the nineteenth century valued above everything else, but science, as he and his contemporaries understood it, was still primarily philosophy and sociology, in short the humanities, though in the confused sense with which Hegel and Comte had endowed them. But today "science" has acquired the Anglo-Saxon and French meaning of the exact sciences which comprise mathematics and the natural sciences, as contrasted to the humanities which can not aspire to such dignity and are therefore not considered as quite acceptable. If we now hear that to organize society in a socialist fashion and with a planned economy, is to shape it scientifically, that means: vitamins, microscopes, logarithms, slide rules, atomic fission, psychoanalysis, physiology, mathematical statistics, hormones. Just as formerly, in an unenlightened age, man followed his taste in what he ate, but now in conscientious boredom eats according to vitamin and calory charts, social life also is at last to be arranged by the planning hand of the scientist and made the object of strictly scientific rationalism. It is a domineering and blindly arrogant form of science which confronts us here with intimidating gestures; clothed in the sacerdotal robe of the white laboratory coat, it looks at us through gleaming spectacles in a concerned and penetrating manner or perhaps with the somewhat synthetic and false solicitude of the posters of the pharmaceutical industry aiming at the layman.

In this conception of the world men occupy a rank not higher than that of the dogs on which the Russian physiologist Pavlov carried out his famous experiments with the "conditioned reflexes," and the social question now becomes a kind of bacillus which only has to be discovered by employing the "exact" methods of mathematical statistics—the method of "multiple correlation," of the elasticity coefficients of demand and supply and so forth, and then, at a scientific world congress—the more participants, the better—the appropriate panacea is found. Men are categorized and directed in every situation and in every stage of their development by means of checks and counter-checks according to highly elaborated testing procedures; the predictability of their opinions is thoroughly investigated in order to deduce from it forecasts of their future conduct, and finally "scientific" methods are worked out for forming and shaping man according to an image which in turn is prescribed by "science." Thus there arises in the eyes of these reformers what one of them (Karl Mannheim) in all innocence called the "modern social technique," i.e., "the more and more conscious handling, directing and interrelating of human instincts, of the modes of thought and reaction in modern mass society; whereby society transforms itself into a kind of machine."

What such a "machine society" looks like in its final stage one may read in Aldous Huxley's *Brave New World*. It is the civilized hell of a society rationalized to the last degree, in which only one fact has been overlooked—man himself with his perennial traits as he was created in God's own image. Such a "scientific" planning of society is indeed on a level with "scientific" courtship, "scientific" family life, a "scientific" religious service, a "scientific" Christmas celebration, or a "scientific" village fair. The proposal, made in all seriousness, that in such a society the "un-planned," the spontaneous and the irrational would of course in accordance with the plan be assigned their scientifically appropriate place, is not much better than the old undergraduate joke of ordering freshmen at a meeting of the student association to burst into laughter at a given point. Goethe's saying that everything wise has already been thought of, may be adapted to apply to everything foolish. Here, too, it is hardly possible to invent anything new.

The most intelligent among those "social engineers" who demand the complete "functionalization" of man—the sociologist Karl Mannheim, mentioned above, is one of them—have at least this advantage over the others that they clearly recognize the process of our society's spiritual collectivization. It seems all the more incomprehensible that they cannot draw any other conclusion from this than to push the process of collectivization to a truly horrible extreme by "scientific" social planning, that is, by total collectivism, measuring the different modern forms of collectivism with completely unequal standards so that one cannot help thinking that in the collectivism condemned by them they only object to the roles not being filled to their satisfaction. This would indeed be incomprehensible if one did not bear in mind that these collectivists accept spiritual collectivization as something ordained and unalterable. That collectivization itself should be done away with, does not occur to them at all, which only proves that they have already been so completely submerged in the process of collectivization that they are no longer able to look beyond it.

Compatible and Incompatible Economic Policy

If we now leave the sufficiently discredited field of pure collectivism and turn to the many intermediary forms of economic policy which can neither be termed liberalism nor collectivism, we are faced with a problem which is far from easy. While we repudiate the former as well as the latter it is nevertheless clear that in this intermediate sphere—of interventionism or statism—there must be a dividing line separating legitimate from illegitimate interventions, final boundaries to overstep which would in the end lead to collectivism. But precisely in this respect ideas are still very confused.

This confusion may be attributed to the mental picture in which the various possibilities of economic systems are arranged along a straight line, at one end non-intervention and laissez-faire, and at the other the complete interventionism of the collectivist system. Any increase in intervention appears, therefore, in an approach to the totality principle of collectivism, as a gradual concession: seen from the laissez-faire end it is a betrayal, viewed from the other end it is a half-measure. This highly unsatisfactory situation is not improved by branding the totalitarian principle an exaggeration of things which are in themselves right, and by preaching moderation. It is, of course, quite right that here, as everywhere else, quantity makes a difference and that at a certain point quantity turns into quality; it is indeed very important to stress this in order to make clear that an interventionist economic policy has its Rubicon. One cannot continually intervene without finally reaching a point where the highly developed nervous system of the market economy refuses to function. The powers of the market economy must, then, either be restored by a lessening of intervention or must be completely replaced by collectivism. This crisis was reached in Germany in 1935 and in France at the end of the Popular Front Government; in the former case it was overcome by a step forward, in the latter by a backward turn, whilst in the United States the battle seems still (1941) to be waged with changing fortunes.

In accentuating this we feel the urgent need to overcome the mere criterion of quantity, and to seek the dividing line in the quality of intervention itself. Here we find that a differentiation between two groups of state intervention is of foremost importance, for which we have suggested the terms "compatible" and "incompatible" interventions: i.e., those that are in harmony with an economic structure based on the market, and those which are not. Interventions which do not interfere with the price mechanism and with the automatism of the market derived from it are compatible, they let themselves be absorbed as new "data"; interventions which paralyse the price mechanism and therefore force us to replace it by a planned (collectivist) order, we call incompatible. Let us quote a significant example: the reconstruction of the external equilibrium of a nation's economy by means of currency devaluation is a weighty intervention which has to be carefully considered and should only be applied in the gravest emergency; however, it does not paralyse the price mechanism but only represents a possibly very disturbing and harmful new condition ("datum"). Basically it is not an indigestible foreign body in our economic structure however much one must advise against it for other very serious reasons; it is, in fact, a compatible intervention. In contrast to this, exchange control is doubtlessly an incompatible intervention as it makes it impossible for the market to retain its balance by means of the automatic play of supply and demand, and therefore forces the state to adjust the trade balance, which heretofore took place automatically, by official order. Exchange control is, therefore, similar to all other forms of a ceiling price economy. A further example is afforded by a comparison between fundamentally compatible protective tariffs on the one hand, and the incompatible quota and clearing policy on the other. Whilst tariffs represent nothing but a (possibly intolerable) burden on prices which is assimilated by the trade in the same way as, for example, obstacles in freight traffic, which force up shipping costs, are assimilated, but otherwise leave it unfettered and do not interfere with the regulating influence of the price mechanism, the regulation of foreign trade by means of quotas and clearing agreements means that the state suspends the automatism of the market and has to replace it by definite governmental control. If one wants to gain a clear understanding of the difference by an extreme example, it is only necessary to compare the completely compatible character of regulations concerning store closing-time ordinances and the observance of the sabbath with a prohibition of investments.

The incompatible character of an intervention is revealed when, by paralysing the price mechanism, it creates a situation which immediately calls for further and even greater intervention, transferring the regulating function so far carried out by the market to a government agency. If the government introduces rent ceilings, the divergence between supply and demand in the housing market grows ever greater as rents remain below the level which is necessary to promote construction and lessen demand. Consequently, the state is forced to go further and ration housing, and as at the same time building activity collapses under these conditions, it must finally take over housing construction under its own management. . In addition, this tends to lead to a "freezing" of the housing situation—everyone clinging to the home which he was lucky enough to get hold of, without making any adjustments if his family should decrease—and to a progressive diminution of mobility. This should teach us that the price mechanism is an essential part of the mechanism of our whole economic system and that one cannot do away with it without in the end being forced down a path leading to pure collectivism.

If, then, one decides to permit incompatible intervention, the result is an unending dynamic chain of cause and effect and everything begins to go downhill. The state has joined battle with all the forces of the market which must be fought to the finish. More and more extensive measures become necessary in order to counter the constantly recurring reactions of the market, reactions which at first become all the more violent the deeper and more extensive the interference is. At length the state can consider the battle half-way won for an indefinite period when it has reached the *ultima ratio* of all incompatible interventions and of all forms of collectivism, i.e., capital punishment. For this reason it is, we repeat, not a macabre joke, but the terrible truth, when we say that in the market economy the sheriff has the last word—and in the collectivist state the executioner. The motto of incompatible interventionism is always: *aut Cæsar aut nihil,* as the most recent history of foreign exchange control has demonstrated most convincingly.

We also have here an opportunity to give a precise definition of a term which today is used in a somewhat indiscriminate and confusing manner. We mean the magic term "planned economy" ("planning"). There is no doubt that it owes most of its present

F

day popularity to the circumstance that it is being more and more used in a sense which in the end embraces every imaginable economic activity of the state. But as today everyone demands some kind of economic action from the state, the generous use of the term "planned economy" is excellently suited for promoting such activities and for persuading the masses that the world is moving towards planned economy. The term lends itself to this very well as it is difficult to imagine any economic action which is not based on some sort of "plan," i.e., one which has no definite goal. The introduction of tariffs, too, is based on preconceived notions as to what constitutes a desirable production structure for a particular country, but it would be absurd to maintain that a tariff policy is synonymous with planned economy. The same applies to railroad and highway construction, and public works of all kinds which today enjoy popularity as a means of combating unemployment, can also not be described as planned economy. Most cities have fortunately been built according to some sort of plan, and currency and finance policies in the various countries have more and more assumed the character of regulating measures geared to the economic process as a whole.

If all this is to be called planned economy, the term completely loses its meaning. Then we would have had a planned economy since the dawn of history, since economic life has always been subject to certain regulations and collective influences, and capitalism itself would, of course, also be a pure planned economy, as the legal and institutional frame of this economic system has been created after systematic deliberations which included a preconceived idea of the competitive economy as a whole. Capitalism was consciously "planned" as an economic system which could manage without a "planned economy." We conclude from this that if the term "planned economy" is to retain any meaning, it cannot be applied to every kind of economic policy based on a "plan," as there is no economic policy to which this would not apply, including the liberal policy whose plan it is not to "plan." It is therefore not a plan as such which characterizes the planned economy, but a particular method of planning, i.e., that which is opposed to the methods of the market economy. For, while the latter is based on the complicated interplay of spontaneous decisions made by all the parties connected with the market, it is the essence of the planned economy to replace this mechanism by official orders and to transfer the decision of how the production capacity of the national economy is to be used, from the market to the government.

It is evident, then, that the term "planned economy" is misleading and should be replaced by another which would better characterize the contrast between it and the market economy. It would perhaps be appropriate to speak of a "bureaucrat economy" or a "command economy." But as long as we retain the old term, we should no longer permit its vague use and should ask that it be reserved for defining an economic policy which substitutes the government's orders for the mechanism of the free market. Such an economic policy of planning makes use, however, as we shall soon see, of incompatible intervention, and conversely we can describe this form of intervention as typical of a planned economy. We further differentiate between a single (incompatible) measure of the planned economy type and a completely planned economic system, the latter being the case when the whole economic process (or at least one or more of its decisive parts, such as the price mechanism and the investment of capital) is removed from the control of the market and directed by the government. Such a totally planned economic system is at the same time identical with what we call collectivism or socialism. We have seen clearly that occasional measures of the planned economy type (incompatible interventions) always tend towards a completely planned economic system. We therefore have every reason for locking this group of economic measures into the poison cupboard of our economic pharmacy. We conclude our observations with the clear-cut statement that we—indignant at such an attempt to dupe us—refuse to be presented with the choice between laissez-faire and planned economy as the only alternatives. There are not two, but three possibilities, namely: laissez-faire, compatible state intervention and incompatible state intervention (planned economy). We think that it is now without further explanations understood why we prefer the second possibility—compatible intervention—if and when the functioning of the market necessitates economic adjustment.

Social Welfare

Nothing is more dangerous than the vague feeling of no longer knowing where to turn, and the almost irresistible urge to permit empty and high-sounding phrases—which look like a radical new beginning but in reality present no solution—to conjure up a way out. Some suggest planning, others devaluation of currency, "stamp money," or the corporate state. Others again suggest comprehensive social services for the masses, "social welfare," as the benevolent expression goes nowadays.

Almost every word in this book written so far bears out the fact that we are even more radical than most in thinking social injustice to be one of society's gravest defects, a defect which has destroyed civilization again and again since it began thousands of years ago, and that we are prepared to advocate equally radical action. However, the problem of widely divergent differences in income which is sapping the lifeblood of a nation and the question of establishing a minimum of social justice, are not what is to be discussed here nor the community spirit which makes men act for each other, a spirit on which our entire future depends. Rather, we must resolutely resist any demagogic attempt to present the situation as being a simple choice between two possibilities: the social Darwinism of laissez-faire which would let every one engage in the struggle for existence by himself, making the best of the highly unequal opportunities of today, and would leave everything to automatic selection—"the survival of the fittest"—on the one hand; and an all-embracing public welfare system which aims at protecting each individual from the cradle to the grave against the vicissitudes of life as far as possible by means of retirement pensions and a blanket insurance against all untoward incidents. We are most decidedly of the opinion that here, too, there is a Third Way which alone can lead to a satisfactory solution. This view, however, obliges us to declare social mass welfare and assistance to be the aberration which in truth it is.

If one wishes to follow an extreme policy of social assistance (social eudaemonism), it is first of all necessary that one should point out the truism that in social matters one cannot overstep certain limits without destroying the secret spring of a healthy society, i.e., the sense of responsibility. The more the state takes care of us, the less shall we feel called upon to take care of ourselves and our family, and the less we feel inclined to do so, the less we can expect help from others whose natural duty it would be to assist us when in need, the members of our family, our neighbors, our friends, or our colleagues. We have at last found in the state a secular God whom, like the lilies in the field, we may burden with all our cares, and at the same time all true charity which can only thrive on spontaneity and readiness to help, but is already beginning to be despised, will die out. Since the state, however, represents nothing but the whole community, its assistance funds are limited by the possibilities of taxing its citizens, possibilities which, as we have demonstrated above, are already being exploited to the full because all the producers demand assistance—thus illustrating the famous definition of the state by the French economist, Fr. Bastiat: "The state is the great fiction by which everybody wants to enrich himself at the expense of everybody." Thus in both cases the candle is being burned at each end: whilst the efforts of the individual are on the decline, his demands on a treasury which can only be filled by all doing their utmost, are growing. To rephrase Abraham Lincoln's well-known observation: one can help some of the people all the time, one can help all the people some of the time, but one cannot help all the people all the time.

But more is involved than merely the financial limits of a social welfare policy. The health of society itself is at stake if we continue along the path of mechanized social welfare which completes the disease symptoms of a collectivist society. It cannot be gainsaid that today large numbers of the people are looking forward to the realization of the ideal of everyone receiving an old age pension and in the face of the insecurity and isolation in which the individual finds himself as a result of proletarization and collectivization, one will have to have some sympathy for this. But it takes more to understand why those who should be more far-sighted support these popular demands instead of realizing that it is our task to pull up the evil by the roots and at last energetically oppose collectivization itself as the soil in which the idea of universal pensions thrives. We constantly encounter the same error: all the problems and dangers threatening us can finally be reduced to the process of collectivization, but instead of realizing that it is necessary to lessen collectivization, one sees no other way out than to apply solutions which are really nothing but a logical continuation of the mistakes. What applies to collectivism and totalitarianism in general is true of mechanized social welfare in particular. In as far as an overall pension scheme is a genuine form of insurance, i.e., in so far as it is based on the responsibility of the individual, it is difficult to see what more the state can do than to further it by propaganda and organization and finally compulsory social insurance. But the more the state goes beyond this and uses taxes to supplement the scheme, the more we perceive how the center of life, welfare and community spirit is shifted from the natural and obvious mutual aid association of the family and other genuine communal units, to the state. Everyone should be aware that to treat this as a basic principle instead of as an exception, which may in certain circumstances be unavoidable, will have quite unpredictable consequences. Concurrently with our endeavors to relieve the masses of having to think and to occupy their leisure and, whilst they are losing their basic freedoms—yes, even the desire for such freedoms—we lull them with many of the amenities of civilization, only to degrade man finally to a completely domesticated creature, to a tail-wagging pet. The spurious "freedom from want" kills all the genuine freedom. We can call this the "ideal of comfortable stable feeding" and thereby describe what the Ancients expressed by the words "panem et circenses." At any rate, paying taxes, sticking stamps and standing in line waiting for rubber stamp wielding bureaucrats, are not the activities which first come to our mind when we try to envisage a healthy solution of the social problem.

Full Employment

After having had several opportunities to draw attention to the dangerous by-paths which at first seem hardly suspicious but finally end in the broad road to collectivism, we must deal with one which is particularly deceiving, especially because we see so many wise people whom we would like to trust taking it. We are speaking of the dangers in which a too venturesome business cycle policy can involve us.

Referring to observations which we have made earlier, we point out once more that, especially concerning the question of the successful control of crises and mass unemployment, a deep despondency and lack of confidence in more cautious measures has gained ground everywhere, whilst at the same time the desire for such control has, understandably enough, become more urgent, and undisguised collectivist experimenting with the business cycle has not failed to make an impression. We need not repeat what can be said against this in general but point out that extremely difficult and hotly debated questions are involved which cannot be gone into here. We must rather confine ourselves to a few remarks, sufficient for a preliminary orientation, with the sole intention of shedding some light on the dangers which are threatening a sound economic and social system particularly in the form of new anti-crisis programs.

It is probable that nothing has more contributed to the despondency mentioned above and to the preference given to collectivist business cycle experiments, than the experiences gained during the past decade in the United States. No one has been able to avoid feeling utterly downcast about the on the whole hardly successful battle which the richest and most powerful country in the world has been waging in order to re-establish its economic equilibrium, and many have concluded that deep in the entrails of the capitalist system there is a mysterious worm destroying it. However, we believe that, as a rule, these experiences are being quite wrongly interpreted.

Everyone who a decade ago was convinced that the economic recovery of the world depended in the first place on a policy of credit expansion carried out by the big creditor nations, was relieved when in the spring of 1933 the new Roosevelt Administration seemed determined to carry out such a policy. Immediately before the new President assumed office deflation in the United States had reached such proportions that there was no alternative but to adopt a vigorous and bold policy of expanding domestic purchasing power. But everything was subsequently spoiled because Roosevelt—for reasons which must partly be attributed to the perplexity of his economic experts, partly to domestic conditions, and partly to the necessity of at the same time carrying out a radical reform of the structure of American capitalism—involved his business cycle policy in an almost disastrous state of confusion and under the spell of this confusion pulled levers which upset the whole mechanism of recovery—one may well say up to the present day (1941). Misled by the doctrine that economic recovery should be initiated by an increase in prices (instead of by an increase in demand) and by the primitive idea of "under-valuing" the dollar to meet the price of the pound sterling which had been devaluated in 1931, the American Government began to devaluate the dollar, a course which circumstances had by no means called for. Whilst this policy turned the London World Economic Conference of 1933, a last rally to save the world economy, into a miserable failure whose effects are also still felt today, the United States managed, thanks to devaluation —and not even without difficulties—to effect a domestic and speculative increase in prices. As soon as prices suffered a recession, the tendencies towards planned economy and monopolies which had been present for some time received such an impetus that now that chain of laws and subsidies of all kinds (the New Deal) set in, which largely destroyed the essential element of the recovery mechanism: the elasticity of the economic system as well as business confidence and readiness to invest. At the same time unskilled hands meddled with the complicated and sensitive price-cost-structure of the American economy by reviving the popular economic theory of the purchasing power of wages and the introduction of wage and labor regulations in the National Industrial Recovery Act, accompanied by price controls of all kinds. Small wonder that the New Deal was not a roaring success in view of such a concentrated attack on the reaction mechanism of the national economy and on the groups (producers, consumers, savers and investors) on whom the economic process, and on whose favorable psychological state, recovery depends.

It would be unfair not to appreciate the extremely difficult position in which Roosevelt found himself at that time, or the energy and skill which he demonstrated in many ways. The main fault, as we have observed, rested with his economic advisers and the domestic party constellation for which he had to make allowances. Above all we must not forget that circumstances forced a twofold, contradictory task on him: besides having to put business on its feet again, he was at the same time obliged radically to reform the capitalist structure of the country. Anyone who, in the 'twenties, travelled in the United States during the years of prosperity must have recognized that this uncurbed form of capitalism with its speculative frenzy, its all-embracing commercialism, its dominant monopolies and its yet practically unsolved social and agrarian problems, could not be maintained for long and was in need of a thorough reform. The collapse of prosperity, which was, at the same time, a collapse of the system itself, however, made the reform of the structure as unpostponable as bringing about normal business conditions again. This posed a very serious dilemma, since structural reform at this moment, when it was important to revive business confidence, demanded measures which to some extent were bound to run counter to the interests of these very business men, as, for example, the necessary drive against the huge private monopolies of the public utilities. All this must be appreciated, and yet one can hardly believe that a compromise could not have been found which would to some extent have harmonized structural reform with the business cycle policy. For this purpose a different business cycle policy would first of all have been necessary, including a firm outline of the principles which were to be respected in all circumstances. One of these principles should have been the inviolability of the currency, but this was the first to be sacrificed in a particularly ostentatious and happy-go-lucky manner.

The argument that at that time the Roosevelt administration had no other choice but to devaluate the dollar does not hold water. In 1933 the United States was one of the few countries in the world which, in contrast to most others, could have afforded a domestic expansion policy of gigantic dimensions (possibly including huge subsidies to the needy farmers) without requiring devaluation or exchange control in order to avoid a crisis of the balance of payments. There the crisis was not characterized, as in Germany and England, by an "external drain" (outflow of gold and non-renewal of foreign credits), and with the backing of the huge gold and foreign exchange reserves one could boldly have faced all possible dangers of this kind—including that of a gigantic bearish speculation against the dollar. The American Government, however, by starting with a devaluation anticipated the threats which it might have had to meet if the domestic expansion policy had outgrown all bounds, thus acting like a man who, before going sailing, first jumps into the water in order to anticipate the danger of getting wet in case the boat should capsize. It could quite easily have tested the actual extent of the much quoted over-valuation of the dollar, and if in the course of American expansion a gold outflow had taken place, it would not have harmed the United States and would have been a blessing for the rest of the world, burdened with deflation; at the same time it would have resulted in an upswing of prices and the business cycle outside the United States and thus helped to re-establish the international equilibrium. This appears all the more so as there seems to have been no reason why the United States could not have followed as successfully as, e.g., Australia, a policy combining credit expansion and a lowering of price (reduction of prices and wages). This would have been sound policy.

In 1933 the Roosevelt Administration could have laid the basis for a steady recovery and earned the gratitude of the whole world if it had inaugurated a policy of effective expansion at home (by an extensive program of public investment, farming and unemployment subsidies, special incentives for new private investments, scaling down of taxation of enterprises and production, and other well considered measures), combined with a policy of giving some margin to the price and cost structure and of resolute adherence to the gold standard (even at the cost of suffering a considerable outflow of gold), and if by such a mixture of boldness and an appeal for confidence it had caused the spark struck by the state to reach private industry. Instead of that an effective expansion policy was introduced much too late and with too much hesitancy, and an attempt was made to set the recovery mechanism going by currency experiments which could only create a short-term speculative boom, by artificial wage and price boosts and by production regulations; to put it figuratively, one used fuel of the wrong type which was bound to lead to the carbonization of the engine—and in addition to that one threw handfuls of sand into the bearings. This conjured up the danger that the New Deal would in the end merely result in a huge national debt and an economy which through planning and monopolies had become lethargic and almost impossible to operate.

In fact it turned out that the original calculation that the Government's boost of purchasing power would set off the private investment drive that was due, was wrong. Every time the Government's injections were withheld it appeared that there was no private initiative which could take the place of public initiative. The motor would not start and one found that the fly-wheel had all the time been set in motion by the starter and not by the motor. Every time the public's purchasing power was increased, it was as if the American Government stepped on the starter in order to start the revolutions of the fly-wheel of economic activity, always with the fresh hope that the motor would start this time. But experience up to date (1940) indicates that the motor itself is out of order. It can hardly surprise us if an unmistakably anti-capitalist atmosphere is created, if private investment is discouraged both actually and psychologically by wage increases, by giving a free hand to monopolies harmful to the public interest and by other developments. The normal reaction mechanism fails to function and in the end the critical point is reached where one must decide whether one should subject what is left of the market economy after all these interventions to collectivist control or whether by reducing control and freeing business life one can rehabilitate the normal reaction mechanism.

Of course, the supporters of a collectivist economic policy in the United States also realized that the motor had failed. But the attitude which they adopted towards it was absolutely typical. Some of them put the blame on the stubborn "capitalists" who had sabotaged the efforts of the government by an "investment strike," and thus they associated themselves with those who attributed the

Russian famine of 1932-33 to sabotage on the part of the "liquidated" peasants who should have patiently allowed themselves to
be deprived of all their possessions. Others invented a new theory
for this occasion—the theory of the "mature economy"—according
to which the United States had reached such a degree of wealth
and economic maturity that there were not enough opportunities for
private investment and a continuous boosting of public purchasing
power was necessary. Up to the present day one has carefully
evaded the highly inconvenient question of how private investments
would be stimulated if one would not follow a business cycle policy
aimed at prosperity, to justify which policy this theory of the
"mature economy" has been invented.

We have dealt with the economic developments in the United
States so extensively not in order to indulge in belated recrimina-
tions, but in order to correct certain opinions which are threatening to gain a considerable influence on the future economic policies
of all countries, and to show at the same time that the American
economic situation, which is of decisive importance for the world,
could be saved today, as it could have been saved then, if only it
were correctly analysed. And as regards the United States of
today, we have the encouraging impression that a certain change
of heart has taken place and that in influential circles opinions
have gained ground which are akin to our own. It would, therefore, appear as if our words should be addressed less to the leading
men in the United States than to quite different people who are
still flirting with the idea of a semi- or quarter-socialist business
cycle policy.

These people are under the spell of a business cycle mentality
which has gained ground everywhere partly under the influence
of fashionable economic theories, partly as a result of the experiences
of the last world wide depression. It is the mentality which
advocates "full employment at any price."

In common with many other catchwords of our time, the term
"full employment" has a dangerous quality that it is calculated to
disarm all criticism from the start. Everyone advocates full employment in a reasonable sense, because no one considers involuntary
mass unemployment for more than a short period as anything but
a national disaster. And if in addition it is understood that in
practice there can never be and never has been absolute full employment, that there is always a certain normal quantity of unemployment whose decrease (due to "over-employment" and manpower
shortage) is as pathological as its increase, and lastly, that this
state is quite tolerable from a human and social point of view,
perfect agreement obtains. Differences of opinion, therefore, do
not arise concerning the goal but merely the means and conditions
by which this goal is to be reached.

We hold the view (for which we have given reasons above), that the problem of the economic equilibrium can be solved within the limits set to us if we wish to preserve the essence of our economic system. In contrast to this, the school of "full employment at any price"—of the "business cycle engineers" as we shall call them—is determined to take over permanent direction of the economic process in a manner which endangers the core of our economic system—without, we believe, really and permanently achieving its aims. By means of a complicated "business cycle mechanism" the factors of the economic process—total income, wages, savings and the volume of investments—are to be continually balanced against each other within the economy so that the equation is resolved regardless of what has caused the disturbance in each case (be it a shift in demand, wage and price relations, changes in technology, disturbances in international trade, or bad speculations and misguided investments); regardless also of whether this policy forces one to adopt planned interventions of all kinds (investment prohibitions, official price and wage regulations, official demand and supply control) or to close the economic frontiers (particularly by exchange control, a measure viewed with alarming unconcern). Let us illustrate this more drastically: one can either convey fishes which have been stranded, back into their element, or one can pump the water level so high that all fishes, wherever they may have got to are reached by the water. The last procedure is what the school of "full employment at any price" envisages; whatever the individual conditions may be, however high the wage level, whatever the cause of unemployment, whether structural or due to a slump, whatever the stage of the business cycle, whether deepest depression or unsupportable boom—purchasing power must always be pumped up to a level ensuring "full employment." For this continuous pumping a type of machinery has to be used which gained considerable notoriety during the last depression: the silent mechanism of the "cheap-money-policy" which was employed particularly in England, and if the worst comes to the worst, the combination of public investments and public indebtedness incurred in order to alleviate the crisis, and all their consequences in the various forms of autarky and planning. According to this view a boom has to be maintained under all circumstances and the crisis is simply an accident which only a backward economic theory can associate with the alleged dangers of an exaggerated boom.

Such a doctrine is bound to be popular. After the world has for many years—and indeed far too inactively—put up with a devastating depression, people will only be too eager to make every and any sacrifice in order to forestall the repetition of such a tragedy even on a smaller scale. And, if, to make matters worse, even leading economists (particularly the late J. M. Keynes) come and tell us in rather incomprehensible books that what we have to sacrifice for the sake of economic stabilization is not, as was taught formerly, the inflationary boom but only this moth-eaten doctrine of the alleged dangers of the boom—then we must not be surprised that they are applauded. The whole question of economic equilibrium and mass unemployment is seen as a mere problem of continuously prolonging the boom by means of the business cycle mechanism and thus, in an exceedingly dangerous manner, attention is diverted from the deeper causes upsetting the equilibrium, any knowledge of which is felt to be highly inconvenient. But the school of "full employment at any price" can also adopt economic nationalism in a manner particularly attractive to the masses, by giving the appearance that in the past it had only been the lack of the nation's autonomy and the necessity of having to consider foreign market conditions which, under the regime of the gold standard, could force a particular country to put a stop to its business boom. If the thermostat of the gold standard or of any other international currency system prevents us from reaching and maintaining the business cycle at the desired temperature, one should do away with the thermostat and replace it by a system of exchange control or of a paper currency which can be devaluated at any time—thus one could interpret the doctrine of the business cycle mechanism and full employment.

We have said that such a control of the economic process jeopardizes the essence of our economic system without in the end really and permanently attaining the desired stabilization. That indeed is the concise formula to which we can reduce our criticism. A continued policy of increasing and prolonging the boom finally reaches a point where the recession can only be delayed by means which do away with the market system and lead to collectivism. It is decisive here that the boom develops forces inimical to the equilibrium (whose nature is described by the theory of crises) which grow in strength the longer one forestalls the natural recession.

To sum up, a policy of "full employment at any price" has the following results: every attempt to maintain the flagging boom at maximum revolutions produces certain reactions in our economic system, each of which must now be suppressed. However, as long as the causes of the disturbed equilibrium continue to exist and are even strengthened, every suppressed reaction is replaced by a new, intensified reaction, which then evokes even more stringent measures of suppression. A policy of full employment will therefore lead to the piecemeal scrapping of our economic system: the external reactions will be cut short by controlling foreign exchange (mere continued devaluation very soon proves to be inadequate) and blocking foreign trade, and finally, whether one wants to or not, one will end with wage, price, capital and investment control and for this purpose will have to adopt the necessary political stage properties of collectivism. But the longer this road is followed, the more, as the example of the United States shows, the market economy's ability to function is paralysed until the well-known critical point is reached where the collectivist sphere can no longer be increased without the private sector being simultaneously rendered incapable of further reactions, so that one either has to collectivize it as well, or reconvert the collective sphere into a private one. The question of what things will be like under a *collectivist* control of economic developments—which replaces the organic market mechanism—need no longer concern us here since we assume agreement on the fact that a business cycle policy which threatens to lead us towards collectivism is thus already adequately characterized.

All this certainly does not mean that we are advising against a well-considered and sober control of the business cycle, and especially the author, who as early as 1931 had asked for a positive business cycle policy and had met with much opposition, particularly from subsequent adherents of the full employment school, finds such an idea quite foreign to his thinking. But here, too, he is of the opinion that one should not stagger from one extreme to the other and counsels moderation and observance of the limits. Regarding business cycle policies there is also, apart from the alternative between laissez-faire and collectivism (including involuntary collectivism) a Third Way. In order to realize this clearly it should be borne in mind that the problem of economic stabilization is seen in a completely false perspective if it is viewed as a mere problem of business cycle policy. Rather, it is basically a problem of the total economic and social structure, which in turn must be seen against the background of the general crisis of civilisation. The great structural problems of our time must be solved, whatever business cycle policy we may be following, but if, and as long as, they are not solved, the structural disturbances also cannot be settled permanently however highly contrived the policy of the business cycle may be. There is even the grave danger that the boldness of such a policy will only serve to accelerate the general process of structural disintegration. Over and above all the problems of the mere market mechanism there are problems of a higher order which are more important than anything else, and they must be solved whatever our plan of action in the restricted field of the market mechanism may be. It is obvious that particularly for a small country like Switzerland which is so very dependent on unimpeded and maximum trade relations with foreign countries, the possibilities of an autonomous regulation of the business cycle are extremely limited.

PART TWO—NOTES TO CHAPTER I

Note No. 1 (page 153). Critique of socialism:

Since the publication of this book, the author made some further studies on the theory of collectivism which are to be found in his books *Civitas Humana, Internationale Ordnung,* and *Die Krise des Kollektivismus.* His most recent contribution to the subject in his article *Zur Theorie des Kollektivismus,* "Kyklos" (Bern), 1949, where he also referred to some of the most recent publications on this vast problem. Generally, he wants to emphasize the importance of the following books: F. A. v. Hayek, *Collectivist Economic Planning,* London, 1935; Walter Lippmann, *The Good Society,* Boston, 1937; J. Jewkes, *Ordeal by Planning,* London, 1948. As for the well-known book by Joseph A. Schumpeter, *Capitalism, Socialism and Democracy,* New York, 1942, he confesses that he found it as an apology of socialism even less convincing than as a criticism of "capitalism" (cf. his revue of this book in "Erasmus," Speculum Scientiarum, International Bulletin of Contemporary Scholarship (Amsterdam-Brussels), 1947, 1). In particular, Schumpeter does not give an answer to our arguments proving the incompatability of socialism and liberal democracy, and at the end of his book he even conveys the impression that he is prepared to accept them.

Note No. 2 (page 155). Socialism exhausts the economy:

A well known French philosopher (whose main occupation is farming) expresses this vividly in the following words: "Chaque essai novateur représente un coup de fouet qui communique à l'organisme collectif une vigueur factice au prix de la consomption d'une réserve vitale. On dilapide les plus obscures, les plus profondes resources du corps social (je pense à des choses aussi diverses que la stabilité monétaire, la continuité et la saine spécialisation professionnelles, l'insertion de l'individu dans les vieux cadres locaux, familiaux et religieux), au profit d'une réussite éphémère, d'une euphorie d'agonisant. Le salut de l'heure présente a pour rançon la dégradation de l'avenir. Que sait-on aujourd'hui . . . de la vraie politique, de cette sagesse patiente et silencieuse qui regarde, qui crée des réserves? Le stigmate essentiel du socialisme (et quelle nation n'est pas aujourd'hui plus au moins infestée du virus socialiste?) réside là; il méconnaît, il détruit les réserves, les lentes réserves dormantes, la patience conservatrice des organes profonds. Là où sont les puits de la vie—les puits de la tradition, de l'autorité, de l'expérience où s'abreuve obscurément la caravane sociale—il voit des parasites et des obstacles. Il confond réserve et inutilité" (Gustave Thibon, *Diagnostics,* Paris, 1942, p. 23). Montesquieu means the same when he says: "Quand les sauvages de la Louisiane veulent avoir du fruit, ils coupent l'arbre au pied, et cueillent le fruit. Voilà le gouvernement despotique" (*De l'esprit des lois,* V, 13). Cf. also the very impressive paragraphs in H. Taine's *Les origines de la France contemporaine,* Le régime moderne, I, page 153 f. and page 180 ff.

Note No. 3 (page 157). Hybrid forms of socialism:

The theoretical constructions which we mentioned in the text are intended to take the wind out of the critics' sails by proposing to retain the essential institutions of capitalism—market, competition, price mechanism, free choice of occupation and consumption—and only to abolish the private ownership of the means of production ("market socialism"). This suggestion appears to us as brilliant as that of playing bridge with oneself. In all seriousness: either one gives business the power of disposal which the market presupposes, and then it exercises the functions of ownership—or one really deprives it of property and all its functions, and then the power of disposal which the market necessitates is abolished. Competitive economy can be planned centrally as little as a game of cards. A discussion of these ideas of a "market socialism" could possibly be considered if there were never any changes at all in economic life. Cf. F. A. Hayek, *Individualism and Economic Order*, London, 1949, pp. 181-208.

Note No. 4 (page 158). "Social technique":

The quotation in the text is taken from Karl Mannheim's article *Zur Diagnose unserer Zeit* ("Mass und Wert," September/October issue, 1937). His views are presented more elaborately in the book characteristically entitled *Man and Society in the Age of Reconstruction* (London, 1940). The common spiritual ancestor of all collectivist social engineers was probably Edward Bellamy, the American author of the futuristic socialist novel, *Looking Backward* (1888), whilst the idea of social "scientific" organization itself dates as far back as Saint Simon.

Note No. 5 (page 166). Crisis theories and policies:

The difficult subject has been further analyzed by the author in *Civitas Humana* (English edition, London, 1948, pp. 196-223) where also further references will be found. The whole discussion centers around the doctrines of the late Lord Keynes (*The General Theory of Employment, Interest, and Money*, London, 1936). While their influence has been enormous, criticism —partly on the lines indicated in the text—has recently become more noticeable (besides Haberler's *Prosperity and Depression*, see: Henry C. Simons, *Economic Policy for a Free Society*, Chicago, 1948; *Keynes' Contributions to Economics*, Four views by R. F. Harrod, Alvin H. Hansen, G. Haberler, J. A. Schumpeter, "Review of Economic Statistics," November, 1946; L. A. Hahn, *The Economics of Illusion*, New York, 1949; J. Rueff, *The Fallacies of Lord Keynes' General Theory*, "Quarterly Journal of Economics," May, 1947; Hans Gestrich, *Kredit und Sparen*, Jena, 1944; L. H. Dupriez, *Des Mouvements Economiques Généraux*, Louvain, 1947; Luigi Federici, *La Teoria della Piena Occupazione*, Bologna, 1949). From among the author's own works the following might be mentioned: W. Röpke, *Crises and Cycles*; W. Röpke, *Praktische Konjunkturpolitik, Die Arbeit der Brauns-Kommission*, Weltwirtschaftliches Archiv, October, 1931; W. Röpke, *Trends in German Business Cycle Policy*, "Economic Journal," September, 1933; W. Röpke, *Die sekundäre Krise und ihre Ueberwindung*, Economic Essays in Honour of Gustav Cassel, London, 1933; W. Röpke, *Vollbeschäftigung*, "Economist" (Dutch), 1938, Nos. 7-8; W. Röpke, *Streifzüge durch die neuere konjunkturtheoretische Literatur*, "Zeitschrift für schweizerische Statistik und Volkswirtschaft," 1940, issue No. 1. For more details on the question of the American New Deal, consult: A. S. J. Baster, *The Twilight of American Capitalism*, London, 1937; W. Röpke, *Die Nationalökonomie des "New Deal,"* "Zeitschrift für Nationalökonomie" (Vienna), 1934, Volume V, issue 5, and W. Röpke, *Crises and Cycles*.

Note No. 6 (page 169). Monopolistic interference with the American business cycle:

During the past years, i.e., up to the last war, it seems to have been of decisive importance that the exorbitant wages which the building laborers and the not less exorbitant prices which the building material industry seem to have succeeded in securing for themselves in the United States, have throttled building activity and thereby paralysed one of the most important factors of the business cycle. To set things right here is surely better than evolving elaborate business cycle theories.

Chapter II

BASIC QUESTIONS OF REFORM

"Le gouvernement en dehors de sa sphère ne doit avoir aucun pouvoir; dans sa sphère, il ne saurait en avoir trop."
—Benjamin Constant.

The Route—"The Third Way"

Let us glance back once more at the road of collectivism which we are under no circumstances prepared to take and do not even want to approach along the deceptive by-paths which we have just mentioned. Its details are sufficiently known: abolition of freedom and of the sphere of private personality, extreme mechanization, rigid hierarchies and proletarization, the kneading of society into a dough-like lump, unrelieved dependency of each on the dominant group with its arbitrary and changing plans and programs where man in his uniqueness and dignity means nothing, power and the bureaucratic machine everything. Human dignity, freedom and justice have completely vanished there and, to round off the picture, even material productivity leaves much to be desired.

But we also know that this is not an entirely new and revolutionary state of affairs which has succeeded an idyllic non-collectivist existence. What we are facing is rather the last stage of a long pre-collectivist development which smoothed the way for total collectivism: the increasing mechanization and proletarization, the agglomeration and centralization, the growing dominance of the bureaucratic machinery over men, monopolization, the destruction of independent livelihoods, of modes of living and working which satisfy men, the disruption of the community by ruthless group interests of all kinds and the dissolution of natural ties (the family, the neighborhood, professional solidarity, and others). Of course, important differences of degree become apparent between the various countries, differences which show at the same time how far a particular country has remained sound and healthy.

Now it cannot well be denied that this process of the progressive hardening of the arteries which finally ends in the apoplexy of collectivism, has taken place in the era of a world order which—rightly or wrongly—is called liberal. The apologists of this world order cannot offer the excuse that this development must solely be attributed to the fact that economic liberty, one of the points on the liberal program, has not been realized with sufficient seriousness and radicalism. Our previous investigation of the perversions and malformations of capitalism has already shown us that this excuse is not adequate. The exclusive emphasis placed on economic liberty as a postulate—which is certainly important, but by no means sufficient and in any case necessitates further elaboration—tends to divert attention from other equally weighty matters. That becomes quite clear when we realize that laissez-faire and economic liberty are by no means antipodal to collectivism, that they are, rather, quite compatible with many shortcomings of the pre-collectivist stage. A return to domestic and foreign economic liberty would very likely lead to the disappearance of many—we even believe, of most—monopolies, and in other respects, too, there might be a turn for the better, but in some respects also for the worse. Above all: would the remaining aspects of the disease of our time be altered to any great extent? For example, would a country now without peasants and craftsmen be able to get them back by returning to a system of comprehensive economic freedom? Would the proletariat vanish? Would society acquire a stable economic and social equilibrium? Would it become, in a very elementary sense, a just society? Would it invest work and life of the individual once more with meaning and dignity? But if a return to economic freedom is insufficient to achieve all this, can we really advocate it with a good conscience? And how can we expect men to warm to this postulate? Where is the vitality necessary for carrying out such a revision of our economic policy?

This once more places before us—in a new perspective—the problem which has accompanied us throughout this book and whose solution, we hope, is gradually taking more definite shape: the problem of an anti-collectivist alternative program which meets the real situation and the justified desires of men. We saw again and again that the fight against collectivism only holds promise of tangible success if we succeed in revitalizing the liberal principle in such a manner that satisfactory solutions will be found for all the now obvious defects, the breakdowns and deficiencies of historical liberalism and capitalism, without interfering with the structure of the market economy's competitive system and our whole economic system's ability to function. The non-collectivist world will only be able to deal with the dangers of collectivism successfully when it knows how to deal in its own way with the problems of the proletariat, large scale industrialism, monopolism, the multitudinous forms of exploitation and the mechanizing effects of capitalist mass civilization.

Economic freedom as an essential form of personal liberty and as a premise of everything that follows belongs undeniably to the total picture of a society which is diametrically opposed to collectivism. While this social order is necessarily based on economic freedom, other factors are also essential. In order to recognize the true antithesis of a collectivist society we must look far beyond economic freedom. We shall find it in a society in which the greatest possible number of people leads a life based on private property and a self-chosen occupation, a life that gives them inward and, as much as possible, outward independence, which enables them to be really free and to consider economic liberty as a matter of course. It is at the same time a form of society whose arbiters are not the proletarians—with or without white collars—not the vassals of a new industrial feudalism and retainers of the state, but men who, thanks to their way of working and living, depend on no one but themselves and do not allow the affairs of the world to touch them; these are to be found among the best types of peasants, artisans, small traders, small and medium-sized businessmen in commerce and industry, members of the free professions and trusty officials and servants of the community. They set the tone not because they are a minority which has usurped power, but because their number will be so great that they will determine the character of society. Whatever one may think of it, no one will dispute that only such a society and not one which is herded together in large cities, giant enterprises, tenements, mass associations, trusts and monopolies of all kinds, represents the true antithesis of collectivism. The conditions enumerated here have already taken us half or three quarters of the way along the road to collectivism—in spite of all the remnants of economic freedom— and it will not take long to cover the rest of the way. The misery of "capitalism," we must point out to the socialists, is not due to some men owning capital, but rather to others not owning any, and thus being proletarians. Sufficient millenia have passed into recorded history for us to have learned in a most convincing manner that whenever the lamp of freedom, of the enquiring mind and of humanity has illuminated the darkness, it was in times when a sufficient number of people had a modicum of private property and were therefore in a position to shake off their economic dependence on the state or the feudal lord. It rests with us whether one of the most magnificent of these periods, which started with the rise of the cities in the Middle Ages and reached its peak in the liberation of the peasants, is now again to come to a close.

These remarks are intended to show once more the kind of measures with which the defense and re-establishment of economic liberty and the accompanying battle against selfish vested interests must be conducted in order to fulfil our counter-program of the "Third Way"; they are also intended to show the more important aspects of this program, the character of the philosophy behind it, and with which of the more or less clearly felt grievances of the under-privileged we concern ourselves. Economic liberty and competition are self-evident postulates where the arch evils of collectivism and monopolism are involved, but they are only part of a many-sided and comprehensive general program. This program lays down the firm frame which will give the necessary support to the freedom of the market. Decentralization, promotion of smaller production and settlement units and of the sociologically healthy forms of life and work (after the model of the peasant and the artisan), legislation preventing the formation of monopolies and financial concentration (company law, patent law, bankruptcy law, anti-trust laws, &c.), strictest supervision of the market to safeguard fair play, development of new, non-proletarian forms of industry, reduction of all dimensions and conditions to the human mean ("à la taille de l'homme," as the Swiss poet Ramuz put it so well); elimination of over-complicated methods of organization, specialization and division of labor, promotion of a wide distribution of property wherever possible and by all possible means, sensible limitation of state intervention according to the rules of, and in keeping with, the market economy (compatible state interventions instead of incompatible interference à la planned economy), while care is exercised to reserve a sphere for the actual planned economy—these are some of the main points which we would mention, though for the time being only in the form of headings open to misunderstanding. We add, however, that perhaps the Swiss reader is the least likely to misunderstand these since he has the example of his own country before his eyes, a country whose economic and social structure corresponds in decisive respects largely to our program. How much still remains to be done in that country, too, in order to make the imperfect more perfect and the diseased healthy again, we need not go into here. All the more should we stress, however, that the fundaments are still sound that what has become subject to disease and disintegration seems relatively easy to cure, compared with the gravely pathological state of the big industrial nations. It therefore seems advisable to us to recommend not only, as is frequently done today, the political but also the economic and social constitution of Switzerland as a model for the rehabilitation of the world after this war. Switzerland, in any case, refutes by its mere existence every cynical doubt regarding the possibility of realizing our program.

Our program is to be one in which everything is balanced. It must therefore appeal more than any other to the willingness of the reader to follow our thoughts with sympathy and understanding and not to pick out this or that point for premature praise or criticism. However, in the case of some readers we have to reckon with the possibility of being misunderstood as siding with trends which are foreign to us. All endeavors would be in vain if we were

to be misunderstood on one decisive point: the necessity of competition. That is why we shall add a few words on this subject.

However unsatisfactory and even misleading a program of
reform seems to us which has to offer nothing but the postulate of
economic freedom, we nevertheless hope that we have left no doubt
that economic freedom—to be more exact, competition—is indeed
the *conditio sine qua non* of any recovery of our sick society. How
to maintain the freedom of the market and of competition happens
to have become the crucial problem of the non-collectivist world,
and if we fail to solve it everything else will be pointless. But—
and that is the other side of the problem—we are bound to fail in
this task if we devote ourselves solely to this problem and neglect
everything else or push it aside with gentle sarcasm. However
radical our thoughts and demands should be concerning the questions so far discussed, we must be on our guard not to transcend
the limits set to us, if we are really concerned with the essentials
of the economic order of a free society. Such an economic order,
we recall, is the opposite of collectivism, monopoly and—in the
field of agriculture—of peasant serfdom (including serfdom to
the state). In saying this we have—with the exception of the
sphere of agricultural self-sufficiency—defined this constitution as
a competitive economy. But has that term not already become in
our eyes somewhat ambiguous? Is it not often associated with
matters which seem to be at variance with the rest of our program?

To this we have to reply first of all that outside the sphere of self-
sufficiency, we only have the choice between monopoly and collectivism on the one hand and competition on the other. Even if we
did not particularly like competition, we would have no other choice
and would thus be forced to make the best of it. That is precisely
the task of a reform policy, however radical in other respects, which
will prove that this problem is by no means insoluble. There is a
world of difference between the competitive principle and the frequently perverted form of competition as it is practised today. One
must further note that the economic order of a free society presupposes competition only in as far as that economy is a market
economy dependent on the division of labor. Competition, therefore, is only one of the pillars on which such an order rests, while
the other is self-sufficiency. We are, therefore, free to modify the
competitive character of the economy in full harmony with the
principles of our economic order, by enlarging the sphere of marketless self-sufficiency, and we should make full use of this freedom
within the limits which have been set to us for reasons already
discussed. This is a new and important point illustrating the
inestimable importance of sustenance farming and the "rurification"
of the industrial proletariat. Here we should add that in the
domain of handicrafts and of the small tradesmen—of "local trade"

as we called it—competition lacks that often inhuman anonymity and brutality which we find, for instance, in the international stock exchanges; competition within a small, controllable circle, can perhaps be compared to the democracy of rural communities and communal self-government.

We must further note that it is merely a matter of making competition outside the sphere of self-sufficiency the paramount but not the exclusive principle; chemical purity is as little aimed at here as in the case of democracy. Thus it is naturally understood that, in accordance with well thought out tenets, a considerable section of the economic sphere is reserved for the economic activities of the public authorities. Planning also has very definite and positive tasks particularly in the realm of regional development. But we shall have to remain quite firm and make no compromises as far as monopolies and "monopoloids" are concerned. Wherever they are unavoidable (as, for example, in the important sphere of the so-called utilities, e.g., communications and electricity, but also in many fields of raw material production), we should adopt the attitude that if a monopoly must be permitted, it should only be in the hands of public authorities and is quite insupportable as a private monopoly. Fanaticism must be as far from us as that sloppy lack of principles to which the world has succumbed in the past twenty years.

Finally, we must stress most emphatically that we have no intention to demand more from competition than it can give. It is a means of establishing order and exercising control in the narrow sphere of a market economy based on the division of labor, but not a principle on which a whole society can be built. From the sociological and moral point of view it is even dangerous because it tends more to dissolve than to unite. If competition is not to have the effect of a social explosive and is at the same time not to degenerate, its premise will be a correspondingly sound political and moral framework. There should be a strong state, aloof from the hungry hordes of vested interests, a high standard of business ethics, an undegenerated community of people ready to co-operate with each other, who have a natural attachment to, and a firm place in society.

Those who have already agreed with us in our defense of competition, may perhaps find it somewhat wearisome that we cannot yet decide to leave this extremely important subject. As, however, there is a possibility that there are a few readers who are not yet fully convinced and cannot yet overcome their mental resistance against the principle of competition, we will go further by strongly emphasizing two points. In the first place we once more feel called upon to deal with an idea which many may have been pondering without expressing it: that competition is most uncomfortable and wearing, whereas we long for the peace of a secure position in the market, where we do not have to fear every day that the better and cheaper services of another may perturb us, and we hope to enjoy this peace the more tranquilly the more successful we are in finding a nicer word for the crude term "monopoly." That is quite human and excusable as long as one keeps this feeling within certain bounds. Our sympathy even extends so far that we would like to see competition shaped and controlled in such a manner that it loses all traces of its cut-throat and nerve-racking character. In saying this we must stress with even more emphasis that the efforts which the competitive principle demands from us will never become unnecessary, particularly not if we decide to choose collectivism. All those who today groan under competition and would employ any means to protect their position in the market against inconvenient competitors, cannot be shown convincingly enough that the collectivist state would be a much harder task-master than competition. Collectivism knows perfectly well that its success will be all the greater, the more it succeeds in insuring that discipline and effort with which the competitive system burdens the producers, and under collectivism there will be fewer chances than before of clinging in unmanly fashion to comfortable nests. If competition has chastized us with whips, the collectivist state will chastize us with scorpions (1 Kings, 12, 11). Indeed, in economic life we can never do without that pitiless, yet beneficent discipline, if we do not want to make the acquaintance of that anarchy which we know only too well from the recent history of great countries. However, there are only two kinds of such discipline, i.e., that of competition, or that of the state as task-master. Between these two lies our choice. To speak against competition and to evade the problem of monopolist and interventionist industrial feudalism with all the only too familiar phrases, simply means taking the side of collectivism.

The above also answers the objection that, if one rejects unadulterated competition, one need not necessarily accept collectivism, since there exists, after all, what we are impolite enough to call, monopolism. Monopolist-interventionist capitalism can only exist as a relatively short intermediate phase, just as in the political field the distortion of democracy through the anarchy of group interests (pluralism) can never be permanent. We want to print this sentence in italics and impress it again and again on all who openly or secretly flirt with the monopoly principle: *our economic system and everything else that we defend in it against collectivism, can in the long run only be maintained as a competitive system which continually ensures discipline, hard work, decency, harmony, balance and a just relation between performance and payment.* We cannot honestly and effectively defend what is so near to our hearts if, instead of employing the same strong words against monopoly and subsidy capitalism as we do against collectivism, we agree to weak compromises and a dishonest play on words, and we can hardly blame people if in the end they come to the conclusion: then let us rather have collectivism.

Competition which encourages producers to compete with each other in terms of performance, also assigns a function within the market economy to the principle of ownership—which we believe to be of such outstanding importance—a function which safeguards it against attacks, in contrast to monopolies which make honest defense of property so difficult. Here again there is no problem in the sphere of straight-forward self-sufficiency, and it is only the differentiation of society through the division of labor that creates difficulties. In a non-feudal society the property of a peasant who produces primarily for his own needs and with the help of his family, is as much a matter of course—if we may use a comparison already employed by Cicero—as is the legal right I have to my theater seat. Just as it would be unfair and, at the same time, senseless, if I would claim such a right for several seats simultaneously as I can only use one seat at a time, so right and function of peasant property in a non-feudal society are based on the fact that the maximum size of the property corresponds automatically on the one hand to the ability of tilling the soil, and on the other to the needs of the peasant family. Thus no sensible person regards the peasant's property as a problem which conflicts with our sense of justice and that is also one of the reasons why even the socialists have never evinced much liking in their programs for artificially turning it into such a problem. And we may be sure that in this case a provocative concentration of property will never take place.

A completely different picture is presented by the highly differentiated industrial society where we can as little as in feudal society expect a natural self-limitation of property and its exact adjustment to its function. Just as feudalism, it would open the doors to limitless enrichment and exploitation, if it were not for the institution of competition which forces the owner of the means of production to constantly justify himself by corresponding performance and which makes the income from such performance functional profits and excludes functionless enrichment. It is competition and competition alone which presses the owners of the means of production into the often inconvenient role of social functionaries and trustees of the means of production available in the national economy. Since those who perform this role badly have to cede their property to others, petrification as well as agglomeration of property are prevented. There are indeed very few great fortunes which have been created solely by superior competitive performance within the frame of a strict market economy, and there are even fewer which can be conserved within this frame. These few fortunes, however, firstly represent no really serious social problem and secondly they lack the provocative character peculiar to the illegitimate fortunes. The cause of property is strong and hardly refutable under the rule of competition, but weak under the rule of monopoly. Here again competition is analogous to self-sufficiency so that competitive property corresponds to self-sufficient property. On the other side, monopolist property and feudal property are parallel cases, and we have therefore spoken of modern industrial feudalism in a very definite sense. But in the same way as feudalism was in all countries sooner or later tamed by monarchical absolutism, monopolism, too, will have to expect to be displaced by centralizing collectivism, unless it surrenders in good time to competition. Monopolistic, interventionist and industrial feudalism must decide whether it wants to be replaced by competition or by collectivism. In the long run it will hardly have any other choice.

The Tools of Economic Policy

After having decided on the general direction reform should follow and having outlined what we mean by the program of the "Third Way," we must now make a few general observations concerning the various methods which should be chosen in order to reach this goal. First and foremost, we must make the distinction between compatible and incompatible intervention with which we are already familiar. After what we have said above, there is no need to state once more that we have very sound reasons for preferring the compatible to the incompatible interventions in all circumstances. If we wish to avoid the down hill path to collectivism it will always be in our interest to realize our economic aims by attempting changes in the framework of the economic system, but not by interfering with the actual mechanism of the market economy itself which is characterized by the price mechanism and by competition. Such a procedure requires foresight, thought and an intimate knowledge of the economic mechanism, but if we try hard enough we shall always find that there is scarcely any problem in the economic sphere which does not offer some opportunity for compatible adjustment.

In saying this, we really only paraphrase what one of the fathers of political economy, Léon Walras, the famous head of the so-called Lausanne School expressed in the following words in his *Etudes d'économie sociale* (1896):

"I bow down before the holy name of liberty and declare that it would be contrary to all order, if the state, interfering in my private affairs, began to weigh, select and apportion my food, my clothing and my accommodation, and to watch and control my inclinations and thoughts. . . . But I should like to be told whether the name of authority is less lofty and whether it is more in keeping with order, when individuals take the function of the state upon themselves. . . . In the first case we have despotism and in the second, anarchy. The one must be avoided as much as the other and for this purpose a line must be drawn between the individual's sphere of initiative and action, i.e., liberty, and the state's sphere of initiative and action, i.e., authority. We can establish this line by simply distinguishing between two things. There is an order of the integrated whole (*ordre d'ensemble ou d'unité*) and the order of varied detail (*ordre de détail ou de variété*). The former causes all the musicians in a concert to play in time, the latter sees to it that they all play different parts. If the various parts as well as the measure were to be subjected to the order of the integrated whole, an unbearable consonance would result with all harmony destroyed. But if, conversely, the measure together with the different parts is subjected to the order of varied detail, a horrible discordance is the result and harmony is destroyed again. If we apply this differentiation to the problem of the social order we can see at once the line of demarcation between the field of liberty and that of authority. Man is a moral being i.e., a being that fulfils its destiny in freedom. It is therefore completely against the order of detail if the state interferes in every action by which the individual achieves and maintains the position appropriate to it in society, because thereby it would suppress the moral personality of each individual. On the other hand, man is a moral being only within society, i.e., within the natural environment in which human destiny is fulfilled. It is therefore entirely opposed to the order of the integrated whole if the individual assumes the function of the state in any action which concerns the delineation, maintenance and improvement of the social frame, because thereby the moral personality of man is again suppressed through the destruction of the elements absolutely necessary to it. Freedom of the individual as regards his position, authority of the state as regards the conditions—that is the formula according to which we can distinguish and adjust to each other the spheres of rights and duties of the individual and of the state."

If one wants to express the matter even more clearly—and perhaps in a more felicitous way, in some respects, one might take advantage of the well-known simile of traffic control. As long as traffic control is confined to laying down and enforcing traffic regulations, backed by the whole force and incorruptibility of the state—by licensing vehicles and drivers, marking traffic routes, controlling traffic itself and giving instructions for the proper conduct on the road—it fulfils an absolutely necessary task whilst every individual is still quite at liberty to decide whether and where and how he is going to drive. This control of traffic—which is all the more necessary the more complex and intensive the traffic becomes —represents our compatible interventions and the official determination of conditions, of which Walras spoke. However, it would be an entirely incompatible intervention and thus akin to planned economy if the traffic police would, absurdly enough, attempt to determine the "position" (Walras) of each individual on the road and to direct every move as an officer directs a column on the march. Incompatible interventionism, planning and collectivism mean in fact nothing but the transfer of military principles to economic life.

It is a permanent task of economic policy to lay down and enforce the norms and standards of economic life. There must always be certain laws and institutions which form the framework in which the economic process takes place. The major part of the reform which we have to accomplish is to change, extend and strengthen this permanent framework in accordance with the program of the "Third Way." In addition, there is another no less important task. Within the legal and institutional permanent framework the economic process will always produce certain frictions which are temporary by nature, changes which will bring hardship to certain groups, states of emergency and difficulties of adjustment. This is where special dynamic problems arise concerning which we shall always have to ask ourselves two questions: firstly, whether or not economic policy should interfere and, secondly, what is the best method to be adopted.

The nature of the problem becomes clear when we recall that extremely important conflict of interests in the economy with which we dealt above. Whenever certain changes in economic life demand a re-grouping of production, a grave dilemma arises because this re-grouping is as much in the interest of the community as it brings loss and hardship for the producers involved. Faced with this problem, historical liberalism, following its dogmatic program of laissez-faire, tended to pass over the frictions and adjustment difficulties in the economy with a grand gesture, and to refer the threatened economic sector to the relentless but finally universally beneficial economic laws. It was certainly right in saying that a declining economic sector could only in exceptional circumstances demand to be saved by the rest of the community. An economic policy which strives to conserve such a sector in spite of the shift in demand or changes in technology, in accordance with the inverted principle of Mephistopheles "everything that exists is worthy not to perish," would in the long run, and if applied generally, be quite intolerable and bound to ruin any national economy. However, the dogmatic refusal of state aid in any form

and the feeding of the afflicted with hopes of the balancing tendency
of the market economy, have contributed to the pendulum's swing-
ing to the other extreme, i.e., from laissez-faire to intervention for
preservation (or "obstructive" intervention, i.e., obstructing the
natural process of development). The old form of liberalism was
bound to evoke all the more anger because in theory the laissez-
faire principle was supposed to apply to everybody, but in practice
powerful groups had always been able to look after their own
interests, whilst the weak were only too often the losers. These
weaker members of society who were helpless in face of a misfortune which they could not master and who naturally enough
clung to their position, in addition had to let themselves be branded
reactionary ignoramuses and egoists. Again and again this has
been the fate of the craftsmen, the wine growers, the small tradesmen, the unemployed and similar groups, and many are still in
this situation today. We do not intend to defend all the desperate
attempts of these groups, but if liberalism only permitted the choice
between laissez-faire and reactionary intervention for preservation
(which is in fact the principle of the "wild life reserve" in economic
life), was it surprising that those affected by misfortune chose the
latter and put liberalism on a par with an unconstructive and cruel
dogmatism, a dogmatism which, when it came to the problem, did
not even know how to apply the same yardstick?

Here, as everywhere else the solution of the problem is to be
found in a "third" direction: neither in laissez-faire nor in intervention for preservation (obstructive intervention) but in intervention
for adjustment (constructive intervention). Instead of counteracting
the tendency to establish a new balance by subsidies, &c., as would
intervention for preservation, adjustment intervention accelerates
and facilitates the attainment of such a balance in order to avoid
losses and hardship, or at least reduce them to a minimum. The
ultimate aim of adjustment interventionism is the same as of the
laissez-faire principle, but now it is to be reached with the support
of all those not affected adversely by the change, and, therefore,
with the good will of all; everyone will look hopefully forward to
the new balanced situation and not bitterly backward to the vanishing old conditions and the forces destroying them. Instead of the
production branch which is forced to make a change being left to
find new ways by itself, as was usual under the old form of
liberalism, adjustment intervention will actively promote this process
by constructive reorganization plans, credits, re-training courses
and publicity campaigns. It neither wants to dam the natural
course of development by the concrete walls of intervention for
preservation—which will in the end give way in any case—nor does
it wish to turn it into the wild falls of laissez-faire. Here, too, a
third method will be adopted: the flow will be controlled and

channelled, whilst its course will be shortened as much as possible. The pendulum which previously swung wildly from one extreme of laissez-faire to the other of obstructive intervention, will come to rest in a reasonable, central position of constructive adjustment intervention.

Let us illustrate all this by an example: if the evidence that a permanent crisis is afflicting the wine growers of a country—partly owing to a reduction in alcohol consumption, and partly owing to foreign competition—becomes irrefutable, this resulted in the past only too often in a most unfortunate state of affairs. On the one hand, the wine growers led a stubborn fight of ever growing bitterness against misery and debt, determined to defend their economic position to the last by steadily increasing wine tariffs, by subsidies, lost credits, compulsory admixture of alcohol, reduced taxes on wine and an increased taxation of competing beverages, by government purchases and all the other weapons from the only too well-known arsenal of this type of economic policy. But, on the other hand, the other producers, the consumers and the liberal theorists also formed a front and pointed out to the wine growers that their special interests were not those of the community and that it was up to them to adapt themselves to the new situation. In practice this controversy usually ended in a half-hearted compromise which consisted in putting always new and always inadequate bandages on the wounds of the clamoring wine growers, allowing the crisis to drag on painfully and to poison the political atmosphere. The struggle came out into the open whenever it appeared that the high and ever-increasing tariff rates made it impossible to conclude advantageous trade agreements, so that the export industries of the country became those most directly affected. However, since the crisis in one economic branch—which we have at random illustrated by the wine growing industry—was accompanied by many other crises in the country's economy, the general effect was bound to be disastrous both economically and in the field of politics and public finance, and we do no more than repeat what we said earlier, if we place a large part of the responsibility for the present state of the world on just this total effect of intervention for preservation.

Adjustment intervention, however, would consist in the representatives of the community getting together with the wine growers and giving them an exact and unbiased picture of the general situation so that both parties could then draw up a plan for the reorganization of the wine growing industry, for which the state would make available its specialists and its financial assistance. An exact market survey would be made by the Office of Statistics (which would thus become a permanent testing ground for economic diagnostics) and in this way a rough estimate would be obtained concerning the extent by which the wine industry should be reduced.

Thereupon all vineyards would be classified in such a manner that, first of all, those most favorably situated would be eliminated as not requiring any help, and those most unfavorably situated as not fit for further wine production. For this latter category a switch to other forms of production would have to be arranged with the competent counsel of all experts; the wine growers affected by this would receive free advice and re-training opportunities and would have to be helped with all available means over the first difficult years of conversion. Finally, as regards the vineyards of average success, they could be relieved by increasing the consumption of grapes through the creation of an efficient marketing organization, a change-over to more suitable types of wine, and, if necessary, by effective publicity—such as, for instance, free equipment of all soda-stands with hand grape squeezers on the pattern developed by the California orange growers.

The methods outlined here must not, of course, be taken as practical suggestions open to cheap criticism. They are merely intended to illuminate, by presenting a hypothetical case, the principle which forms the basis of the idea of adjustment intervention. The facts are, after all, ever-recurring: the crisis of one branch of industry means the slow movement of capital, labor and land towards a more profitable use. It would be unreasonable and in the long run unfeasible to try to stop them or to lure them away from this path by creating artificial market conditions and doling out economic charity; but it is also both unreasonable and harsh to leave those afflicted by the crisis to their fate on this trek through the desert, except for the ones who are strong enough to get along without our help, even though they have an interest in convincing us of the contrary. This must at the same time be the principle of any rational unemployment policy.

If we turn to other functions of economic action, it seems as though compatible intervention is too weak a tool to deal with more radical tasks, and particularly the tasks of a distribution policy whose aim is a more equitable distribution of income and property. This impression, is however, completely fallacious: we find rather that also in this field—so important in the big industrial countries—compatible intervention is not only applicable, but that here as everywhere else, it should be given definite preference over cruder methods. We cannot here go into the difficult details of such a compatible distribution policy. But let us note that it is certainly in accordance with the market economy, if the state with the means of compulsion at its disposal (especially taxation) carries out a readjustment of income levels in order to effect a more equitable distribution, and it is equally entitled to grant subsidies out of tax revenue for, say, workmen's housing or for piping water to mountain villages. Indeed, it is true to say that today a great part of the public finance policy consists in such a fiscal redistribution, supplemented by private charity. Although certain limits may not be exceeded in the use of these measures, unless the productive process itself is to be partially paralysed—limits which today (1949) have been reached in socialist countries like Great Britain and Sweden—it is clear that these are not measures which touch the core of the market economy itself, i.e., the price mechanism and competition.

It must also be understood that it is by no means contrary to a compatible economic policy, i.e., one that respects our economic constitution, if the state itself manages individual enterprises or even whole branches of production and now appears on the market in the capacity of producer or merchant. The same is true of public work projects which the state inaugurates in order to bridge or overcome a depression. One must, therefore, not fall victim to the widely current misconception of looking upon the nationalization (or communalization) of individual enterprises as a genuine collectivist measure; on the contrary, public enterprises are completely in harmony with the basic laws of the market economy as long as the state as enterpreneur respects them and as long as it is not a case of general nationalization which completely eliminates the market economy. Thus we need not fear to raise the question whether in certain cases the transfer of enterprises to the state is not an urgent dictate of a rational economic policy. We have already seen that this question might be answered with an emphatic "yes" in those cases where for technical and organizational reasons monopoly is inevitable, but inadmissible in private hands. As we know, we are here concerned with that group which is growing more and more important, the so-called utilities (railroads, postal communications, municipal transportation, gas, water, electricity, radio). That there is a strong presumption for these enterprises belonging to the state and its subordinate units, may today be called a generally acknowledged fact, but we must certainly consider whether this principle should not also be extended to some monopolies of raw material production. At any rate, such measures could be kept within the framework of a compatible economic policy and need not put us on the road to collectivism. There exists, therefore, no basic objection to the proposal of counter-acting the dominance of individual industrial monopolies by letting the state appear as a competitor with its own enterprises, except for the one objection that every not absolutely necessary extension of the state's activities is an evil, not least in the interest of the state itself.

It is also extremely important to realize that its monetary policy offers the state far reaching possibilities for a compatible economic policy, and demands constant vigilance and supervision. Particularly in this field, far-sighted liberals have at a very early date

yielded to the necessity of intervention and have subscribed to a
view expressed by the English statesman, Lord Overstone, in 1840,
in the following words which are worth remembering even today:
"For the purpose of drawing up enlightened and beneficial laws
it is necessary to differentiate between those cases where the principle of unimpeded competition is applicable, and those where
exclusive privileges, accompanied by undivided responsibility, are
necessary for the public weal. Such last-named cases exist, although
they may be relatively restricted in number. And wherever they
occur, they are by no means insignificant or unimportant. The
power to create money belongs to this category as much as the
royal prerogative to mint coins." That the principle of laissez-faire
is not applicable to the coining of money, is indeed obvious if one
realizes that it is senseless to speak of "money production" in the
same way as of the production of goods. For here it is not a
question of producing as much money as possible and as cheaply as
possible with the help of competition, but rather of strictly regulating its amount and its speed of circulation so that neither too much
of it (inflation) nor too little (deflation) can cause harm. This
control can only be carried out by the governmental authorities
responsible for it and this all the more so since the problems and
difficulties of monetary control have, through the immense
expansion of deposit money (checks and remittances), grown to
such an extent that we cannot yet boast of having really mastered
them. Nonetheless we have to admit that a compatible economic
policy cannot do all the work. There exists a sector which must
be strictly defined, where genuine planning must take place. The
sphere of this planned economy is primarily determined by the
tasks which of late have been summarized by the term "regional
planning" (in England: Town and Country Planning). Regional
planning is based on the observation, confirmed by sad experience,
that the highly important task of developing the soil and the
natural reserves of a country in a manner consistent with the
interests of the present as well as of future generations cannot be
left to the control of the market alone.

Political and Moral Prerequisites

Of course, the more we burden the state with various tasks, the
more insistent becomes the question: how about the state itself?
Are we not perhaps committing the frequent mistake of turning
the state into an ideal which does not correspond to sober reality?
Quis custodiet ipsos custodes? Who is to guard the guardians?

It would indeed be very unrealistic if we were to call for an
economic policy which presupposed such a moral and intellectual
perfection of the organs of the state that in practice it could never

be attained. In this respect, too, one should not overburden human beings but should rather confront them with simple and straight-forward tasks and keep temptations away from them. For this very reason it is advisable to base economic policy on definite rules and fixed principles and to restrict the sphere of arbitrary action as much as possible. The economic system must, so to speak, be an unbreak-able toy—"fool-proof" is the telling English expression. In that consists the insurpassable strength of the market economy and, vice versa, the great danger of collectivism. For this same reason we should beware of artificial monetary systems and give preference to a quasi-automatic system such as the gold standard. It is easy to criticize the gold standard and to draft—on paper—a more perfect monetary system. Nevertheless, we adhere to the gold standard because it is distinguished particularly by the fact that it preserves the stability of the currency, as one of the most precious possessions of the national economy, against the inevitable imper-fections of conscious governmental manipulations. We must further realize quite clearly that an economic policy which makes interven-tion for preservation (through protective tariffs and subsidies of all kinds) its rule, must, according to unalterable sociological laws, lead to open or disguised corruption and generate a poison which in the end will spell ruin for the nation. Ordinary interventionism and pluralism (i.e., the disruption of the state by group interests), are in fact, as everyone should know, very close relatives.

By renouncing this interventionism and the ruthless exploitation of the state by the mob of vested interests, we can create the pre-requisites for a trust-worthy state and a clean public life. But on the other hand, this same renunciation presupposes a really strong state, a government with the courage to govern. A strong state is by no means one that meddles in everything and tries to monopolize all functions. On the contrary, not busyness but independence from group interests and the inflexible will to exercise its authority and preserve its dignity as a representative of the community, mark the really strong state, whereas the state that acts as a maid of all work, finally degenerates into a miserable weakling and falls victim to the vested interests. A market economy and our economic program presuppose the following type of state: a state which knows exactly where to draw the line between what does and what does not concern it, which prevails in the sphere assigned to it with the whole force of its authority, but refrains from all interference outside this sphere—an energetic umpire whose task it is neither to take part in the game nor to prescribe their move-ments to the players, who is, rather, completely impartial and incorruptible and sees to it that the rules of the game and of sports-manship are strictly observed. That is the state without which a genuine and real market economy cannot exist. Benjamin Constant envisaged it when he wrote the words which form the motto of this chapter: "Le gouvernement en dehors de sa sphère ne doit avoir aucun pouvoir; dans sa sphère, il ne saurait en avoir trop."

Of course it is not sufficient just to demand such a state. One must rather develop the structure of the state in such a fashion that it meets our demands as far as possible. This poses a problem whose extent and importance can hardly be exaggerated. To deal with it properly would require a book of its own so that here, too, we are forced to restrict ourselves to a few pointers and hints. We have to start with the negative observation—not unfamiliar to us— that there is no more disastrous way to obstruct the desired development than by erecting one of the types of the corporate state, so much discussed today, to make the vested interests themselves the masters of the state and thereby assign them a legitimate place in its structure. It is our plain duty not to solidify and legalize the political influence of the vested interests, but reduce it. The means to be employed for this end require careful and expert investigation which we do not feel competent to make here. But this much is certain, if the authority of the state is to be strengthened it is absolutely necessary that it should be headed by a qualified civil service small in numbers but equipped with the highest standard of professional ethics and a pronounced *esprit de corps*. At this point, too, the difficult questions of political constitutions, administration and party rules should be discussed.

It must always be remembered that nowhere in the political sphere is the authority of the state expressed as directly as in the administration of justice. Nowhere else are integrity and impartiality of the civil service usually of such a high quality as among judges. And, therefore, confidence is nowhere as great as here, nor the readiness to accept the decision made as final. And lastly, we find nowhere else such reluctance to influence decisions illegitimately. Indeed, the law courts of a country are the last citadel of the authority of the state and of trust in the state, and no state is completely lost where this citadel is still intact. This leads us to urge more insistently than has ever been done before that the law courts should be made organs of national economic policy and that they should be given jurisdiction over matters which up to now have been left to the administrative agencies. How such a judicially directed economic policy is likely to work in practice can best be learned from the example of the American anti-trust legislation (since the Sherman Act of 2nd July, 1890) according to which the highest courts of the land decide in civil or criminal proceedings whether an act of a monopolistic nature, prohibited by the law and listed as an offense, has been committed. Such an economic policy presupposes, of course, that the law schools afford more opportunities to future judges to acquire a knowledge of the principles

G

of our economic order than has so far been the case—to the great disadvantage, alas, of the highly important commercial law practice.

But where shall we find the people who desire this kind of state? To which group should we turn in order to form a vanguard for carrying out our program? We have asked this question already in the introduction of this book and replied to it there: we do not appeal to any single group and its special interests at all, because it seems to us to have been the great mistake of the past to appeal to the "interest" of people, rather than to what is common to them all, i.e., reason and an elementary sense of decency, justice, order, community spirit, chivalry and a conciliatory disposition. Man is a being with many facets—*ni ange, ni bête,* to quote Pascal's famous words—and everything depends on the side of his nature to which we appeal, to the better or to the worse, to that which makes him vicious like a chained cur or to that which makes him friendly and peaceable. If the author may be permitted to close with a personal anecdote, he must confess that he will always remember a small event in his life which took place more than twenty years ago in the main railroad station in Hamburg. About to consign his baggage, he saw the official behind the counter trying to persuade an American negro to take out baggage insurance, hoping thereby to earn the commission paid by the insurance company. Unfairly exploiting the fact that the negro was unfamiliar both with the language and local customs, the official was trying to tell him that such an insurance was practically a necessity, when suddenly his colleague interfered and, flushed with anger, shouted at him in front of the public: "Don't you see he is a foreigner who can't understand you? You ought to be ashamed to take advantage of him." The other was shame-facedly silent, and the incident was closed. Whenever we are asked who are the people to whom we address ourselves, we cannot help thinking of that honest railroad official in Hamburg, and we believe that there is something in most men which one need only arouse and encourage in order to make them the brethren and comrades of our friend.

PART TWO—NOTES TO CHAPTER II

Note No. 1 *(page* 178*). The "Third Way":*

The program which we call by this name has an intellectual history which goes back to the beginning of the nineteenth century and some of its elements—though nothing more—can be found already in the works of Sismondi, Proudhon, Mazzini and Riehl. Names such as Kropotkin (*Fields, Factories, and Workshops,* 1899) or Le Play (*La réforme sociale en*

France, Paris, 1864) hold important places in this history. So do Southey, Thoreau, Ruskin and Geddes. Among contemporary writers significant affinities can be found in G. K. Chesterton's *An Outline of Sanity,* in Hilaire Belloc's *An Essay on the Restoration of Property,* London, 1936; Lewis Mumford's trilogy (*Technics and Civilization,* 1934; *The Culture of Cities,* 1938; *The Condition of Man,* 1944), R. Borsodi's works (*This Ugly Civilization,* 2nd ed., New York, 1933; *Education and Living,* New York, 1948), and several others. Today many efforts are being made in various countries to clarify and define our program in detail. (Cf. Wilhelm Röpke, *Grundfragen rationeller Wirtschaftspolitik,* "Zeitschrift für schweizerische Statistik und Volkswirtschaft," 77th year, No. 1, 1941). I proposed the term "Third Way" in my book *Die Lehre von der Wirtschaft* (Vienna, 1937, now 5th ed., Erlenbach-Zürich, 1949) and others took it up, as for example recently in the American tract: *The City of Man. A Declaration on World Democracy* (by Alvin Johnson, G. A. Borgese, Thomas Mann and others, New York, 1941). In the economic policy of several countries various beginnings have also been made, for example in Belgium (*L' expérience Van Zeeland en Belgique,* by *** Lausanne, 1940), in Sweden (Marquis W. Childs, *Sweden: The Middle Way,* New Haven, 1936) and in Australia (William R. Maclaurin, *Economic Planning in Australia,* 1929-1936, London, 1937). Important clarifications in the realm of the history of society and thought may be expected from an as yet unpublished book by Alexander Rüstow (University of Istanbul). A short time ago I heard that Franz Oppenheimer used the term "Third Way" for his program of reform which is in some respects related to ours, and in some others quite different (Franz Oppenheimer: *Weder So noch So: Der Dritte Weg,* Potsdam, 1933). It always seemed ridiculous to me to consider this term eligible for a "patent" in the scientific sense, and to make it the object of a priority dispute. Anyone who has realized the truth: *tertium datur,* is bound to think of it. The conception of the "third" plays, by the way, an almost mystical role already in de Bonald's works.

Since the first appearance of this book (1942), the subject of a reformist economic and social policy has been further developed on lines not too dissimilar from what I call the "Third Way." Among these I mention: Frank D. Graham, *Social Goals and Economic Institutes,* Princeton, 1942; J. M. Clark, *Alternative to Serfdom,* New York, 1948; C. Bresciani-Turroni, *Economic Policy for the Thinking Man,* London, 1950; Luigi Einaudi, *La Terza Via fra i Secoli XVIII e XIX,* "Rivista di Storia Economica," June, 1942 (study by the actual President of the Italian Republic on the first Swiss edition of the present book); Walter Eucken, *Die Wettbewerbsordnung und ihre Verwirklichung,* "Ordo," Jahrbuch für die Ordnung von Wirtschaft und Gesellschaft, vol. II, Godesberg, 1949; Alexander Rüstow, *Zwischen Kapitalismus und Kommunismus, ibidem;* A. P. Lerner, *The Economics of Control,* New York, 1944; J. E. Meade, *Planning and the Price Mechanism,* London, 1948; A. Müller-Armack, *Wirtschaftslenkung und Marktwirtschaft,* Hamburg, 1947; Gustave Thibon, *Retour au Réel,* Lyon, 1943; W. H. Hutt, *Plan for Reconstruction,* London, 1943; Henry C. Simons, *Economic Policy for a Free Society,* Chicago, 1948; Frank H. Knight, *Freedom and Reform,* New York, 1947; Jacques Rueff, *L'ordre social,* Paris, 1948; Jacques Rueff, *Epître aux Dirigistes,* Paris, 1949. In a wider sense, also books like Louis Bromfield's *Pleasant Valley,* Aldous Huxley's *Science, Liberty, and Peace,* and le Comte du Nouy's *Human Destiny* belong to this group. Since 1942 I tried to refine and develop my own ideas on the subject in the following publications: *Civitas Humana; Internationale Ordnung; Klein- und Mittelbetrieb in der Volkswirtschaft,* "Ordo," Jahrbuch für die Ordnung von Wirtschaft und

Gesellschaft, vol. I, Godesberg, 1948, pp. 155-174; *Die Krise des Kollektivismus*, Erlenbach-Zürich, 1947; *Das Kulturideal des Liberalismus*, Frankfurt/Main, 1947; *Die Ordnung der Wirtschaft*, Frankfurt/Main, 1948; *Die natüraliche Ordnung*, "Kyklos," (Bern), vol. II, 1948, pp. 211-232.

Note No. 2 (page 182). Industrial feudalism:

Cf. particularly the book, mentioned above, by an Assistant Attorney General of the United States, Thurman W. Arnold: *The Bottlenecks of Business*, New York, 1940. To this we add the following outspoken passage from the English "Economist" of 15th June, 1940: ". . . the set of notions that sees its ideal of an economic system in an orderly organization of industries, each ruled feudally from above by the business firms already established in it, linked in associations and confederations and, at the top, meeting on terms of sovereign equality such other Estates of the Realm as the Bank of England and the Government. Each British industry, faithful to the prescription, has spent the past decade in delimiting its fief, in organizing its baronial courts, in securing and entrenching its holdings and in administering the legal powers of self-government conferred on it by a tolerant State. This is the order of ideas that has transformed the trade association from a body of doubtful legality, a conspiracy in restraint of trade, into a favoured instrumentality of the State, until membership in such a body has become as necessary to the businessman who wishes to be successful as an old school tie has been to the ambitious Conservative politician. It is the order of ideas that led to the Import Duties Act being drafted in such a way as to put a premium on self-seeking monopolies and a discount on the public interest; that turned 'high profits and low turnover' into the dominant slogan of British business; that raised the level of British costs to the highest in the world. It is a set of ideas that is admirable for obtaining security, 'orderly development' and remunerative profits for those already established in the industry—at the cost of an irreducible body of general unemployment. It is emphatically not a set of ideas that can be expected to yield the maximum of production, or to give the country wealth in peace and strength in war." We have quoted this passage at length, because it gives an excellent picture of the development which can be observed in England and in other countries, but nowhere as clearly as in the one time citadel of liberalism and free trade. Cf. also: Ben W. Lewis, *Price and Production Control in British Industry*, Chicago, 1937.

Note No. 3 (page 187). Adjustment intervention versus intervention for preservation:

Adjustment intervention is the same as what Alexander Rüstow (*Deutschland und die Weltkrise*, "Verhandlungen des Vereins für Sozialpolitik in Dresden 1932," Munich, 1932, page 62 ff.) called "liberal interventionism." This extremely important subject has recently been treated extensively by Allan G. B. Fisher, *The Clash of Progress and Security*, London, 1935; Allan G. B. Fisher, *Economic Progress and Social Security*, London, 1945; W. H. Hutt, *op. cit.*; Carl Major Wright, *Economic Adaptation to a Changing World Market*, Copenhagen, 1939; N. F. Hall, *Enquête préliminaire sur les mesures d'ordre national et international visant à relever le niveau d'existence*, Société des Nations, Comité Economique, Geneva, 1938. The problem has already been clearly stated by Philip H. Wicksteed in his book, first published in 1910, *The Common Sense of Political Economy*, where he says (in the revised edition of 1933, volume 1, page 357): "To mitigate the penalties of failure, without weakening the incitements to success, and to effect an insurance against the disasters incident to advance, without weakening the forces of advance themselves, is the problem which civilization has not yet solved."

Note No. 4 (page 189). Distribution policy:
On this difficult subject cf. Wilhelm Röpke, *Die Lehre von der Wirtschaft*, 5th ed., Erlenbach-Zürich, 1949, pp. 227-259.

Note No. 5 (page 190). Levers provided by monetary policy:
The best description of the basic problems involved here will be found in the small book by Friedrich Lutz, *Das Grundproblem der Geldverfassung*, Stuttgart, 1936.

Note No. 6 (page 192). Problems of political structure:
The literature on this subject is by no means extensive, but we recommend: Walter Lippmann, *The Good Society*, Boston, 1937; Walter Eucken, *Staatliche Strukturwandlungen und die Krisis des Kapitalismus*, Weltwirtschaftliches Archiv, October, 1932; and Alexander Rüstow's books, *op. cit.* I repeat that subsequently I have dealt with this subject extensively in my *Civitas Humana*. Whilst stressing the outstanding importance of the civil service one must, of course, not overlook the problems it presents. They are due to modern officialdom having grown up together with the modern centralized state, thus being at one and the same time indicative of the disintegration of the old social units and of spiritual collectivization. These problems can be exemplified most palpably by the position of any village policeman: if he succeeds in enforcing the full authority of the state in the village he will remain outside the village community with all the resultant consequences which in the long run he will find intolerable; but if he wants to be part of the community, he is forced to make continual compromises. The moral of this would seem to be that all centralism is indeed a necessary evil and can only be defended as such. Cf.: F. Le Play, *La réforme sociale en France*, 2nd edition, Paris, 1866, II, pp. 406-440; Odilon Barot, *De la centralization et de ses effets*, Paris, 1861; Max Weber, *Wirtschaft und Gesellschaft*, Grundriss der Sozialökonomik, III, Tübingen, 1921; G. Mosca, *The Ruling Class*, New York, 1939, page 83 ff.

Chapter III

AVENUES OF APPROACH AND EXAMPLES

Natura tamen infirmitatis humanae tardiora sunt remedia quam mala; et ut corpora lente augescunt, cito extinguuntur, sic ingenia studiaque oppresseris facilius quam revocaberis.

(Due to the natural frailty of humankind remedies are slower to take effect than disease, and just as the body grows imperceptibly but declines rapidly, it is likewise easier to stifle talent and competition than to recall them to life.)

—Tacitus, *Agricolae Vita,* III.

Once again we must raise our voice to combat the deeply embedded belief that there are magic cures for the recovery of our sick world, a patent medicine which we only need to swallow in order to be suffused at once by a feeling of radiant health, or an Archimedean Point from where society and the economy can be set right at one pull—the belief that a transformation is possible from one day to the other if only we can be persuaded to follow this or that euphonious program. It is the common belief of all those who expect salvation from the "grand solution," from intricate organizations, from international conferences, from committees and central councils, from all kinds of economic "blueprints," from planning offices, from scientific bodies and from decisive surgical operations in the economic life, basing their hopes on all kinds of new constructions—with a trust that would touch us in its innocence if it were not so exceedingly dangerous.

The practical value of all programs and proposals based on such a belief is next to nil, but the damage they cause is immense, even if they only remain on paper, because they divert the attention of men from essential and urgent—although inconspicuous—tasks and raise hopes whose non-fulfilment leads to the lethargy of despair. Therefore, we must not tire of warning most urgently against all patent solutions and doctrines of salvation and we must insist that there exist no miracle cures and no Archimedean Point, no lever which we merely have to pull in order to put everything right again. All this we must leave to ambitious quacks, of whom there is no lack whether they act in good faith or bad. The modest role which befits us is that of the honest physician who tells the sufferer from chronic gastritis that it is senseless to add new bottles to his already well assorted collection of medicines, and that he can only expect recovery from a change in his habits, supported by proven household remedies and medicines, together with air, movement, mental equilibrium and moderation in all things. However clear the general picture of the disease may appear to him, the physician will nevertheless openly admit to himself that he is by no means sure which combination of medicaments and remedial conditions will procure the best results. Any gesture reminiscent of the Dalai Lama must be as alien to us as to such a physician—though it may disappoint our readers. What we counsel is this: less boosting of prescriptions and less hatching of projects, more care in the diagnosis and more circumspect modesty in therapy; and we ourselves shall follow this advice most closely.

We must, therefore, become familiar with the idea that our program of action must be multifarious and elastic and that a long period of reconditioning has to be passed before the pathological state of our society can take a turn for the better, according to the words of Tacitus which are the motto of this chapter. Basing our action on what exists at present, we must carefully probe at many points in order to find out the weak places in the economic and social structure and see to it that they are reinforced, but all this at the same time with a radical spirit which keeps the great general aim of a free, just, de-collectivized, de-centralized and de-proletarized society before our eyes and encourages us to undertake, where necessary, even incisive operations. In order that this over-all aim should be fixed firmly and clearly in our minds, we must come to as detailed an understanding as possible concerning basic questions and the general system of co-ordinates into which every detail has to be fitted. Only when this has been done, can we go ahead, with the advantage, however, of having guidance and standards for every individual question. First of all, we must know the goal of all our various reforms, the general state of society which we envisage and for what extra-economic reasons we aim at it; then, with a little reflection and good will regarding the concrete details we can hardly miss arriving at the relatively best solutions. Then, and only then, may we expect that all will co-operate in the common task with real civic pride and will feel inspired and interested as people who are responsible for the whole. Otherwise we shall have nothing but thrashing of phrases and the quarrels of group interests. This is why it is so highly important to point out over and over again, how deeply and widely everything is interrelated, a task to which the foregoing part of this book was devoted.

It will therefore be understood why we hesitate to answer the question, perhaps already being asked impatiently, what immediate and detailed action should be taken, and why we realize in all modesty that we can often offer no more than hints and examples for discussion. To work out a detailed plan of action, surpasses the strength and experience of one man even under the most favorable conditions; this is therefore the point where it becomes necessary to appeal for co-operation to all those who have similar aims and think along the same lines. We thus cannot do better than simply ask everyone to work for the common task, and in the meantime to demonstrate independently what conclusions are to be drawn from our program of the "Third Way." We exercise this restraint with a clear conscience since, as long as we do not know the permanent political shape which Europe will assume, there can be no question of a long term economic policy; we must, rather, live from hand to mouth. Until that time nothing more can be expected from practical economic policies than wise and flexible adaptation to the needs of the moment. By making a virtue of necessity we can in the meantime reflect quietly what is to be done permanently, after real peace has returned and it has become possible to think and act on a long term basis.

There is also a special reason why it is advisable that on this occasion, where it is a matter of basic principles, we should severely limit the elaboration of a detailed program. Though we are certainly of the opinion that science is by all means competent, after having diagnosed the disease of our society, to draw the logical conclusions for the therapy, yet the scientist who recommends political and economic measures is bound by certain limits which he cannot overstep without entering the field of subjective, and therefore debatable, opinions. We have every right to claim that the principles of our program are both scientific and objective in character, as, after all, it does not consist of a subjective and arbitrary list of miscellaneous wishes but has naturally evolved from the problems confronting us and from the experiences common to all of us; therefore, all those who have the necessary intelligence, knowledge and good will will agree on it after some discussion. However, the more we progress from matters of principle to those of detail, the greater becomes the degree of subjectivity and, therefore, the greater the number of points on which agreement can no longer be presupposed. The more we go into detail, the more, too, grows the danger of the basic outline becoming blurred by too many and —worse—even hotly debated details, but the important thing at this stage of the discussion is precisely the basic outline. We shall certainly not get anywhere if we kill each fundamental thesis with more or less justified qualifications and modifications in every case, thus permitting the essentials to be perpetually watered down. The outcome of such a procedure has been experienced *ad nauseam* by a world which for decades has been confused and disoriented.

With these reservations, justifications and explanations in mind we shall now proceed to go a little further in the presentation of our program of action, beyond the hints and allusions made so far, and to attempt to render them more precise by discussing individual points. Whatever subject we consider first, our reflections always begin with the basic point at issue. Everything leads us back to the ultimate dilemma from which we want at last to free ourselves. We know that the economic and social system of all the highly developed countries has become untenable in its present form and that peace and our civilization depend on a thorough reform. In the good old days such a conviction would have implied no real inconveniences, and some believe that they can still afford this comfortable ease today: one would simply have become a socialist and intoxicated oneself with all kinds of phrases such as "socialization," "planning," and "economic democracy." But in the meantime it should have become plain to even the blindest that this is the wrong path which can lead to no good, and which not only leaves the essential questions unsolved but makes them even more acute. Socialism, collectivism and their political and cultural appendages are, after all, only the last consequence of our yesterday; they are the last convulsions of the nineteenth century and only in them do we reach the lowest point of a century-old development along the wrong road; these are the hopeless final stages towards which we drift unless we act. Thus all these schemes are still entirely on this side of the new and positive conception of society, and therefore nothing is more ridiculous than the revolutionary pose of the collectivist. The new path is precisely the one that will lead us out of the dilemma of "capitalism" and collectivism. It consists of the economic humanism of the "Third Way," of which we spoke in the last chapter.

Peasants and Peasant Agriculture

What does this mean, in practical terms? It means in the first place a return to economically balanced forms of life and production which are natural and satisfying to men. By saying this we do not want to commit the opposite mistake of deprecating the city, trade and industry, or the bourgeoisie: it means first and foremost that we should again become conscious of the economic, social and communal foundation of the primary organic production process, i.e., agriculture. Of course, not agriculture *per se,* but a form of agriculture with a very special economic and sociological structure, i.e., one carried on by a free peasantry. It is not so much the production of food and organic raw materials as such which interests us here, as that particular form of production which we call peasant production, for it alone possesses the inestimable sociological importance which we have made the basis of our argument and we have it alone in mind when we speak of agriculture as the last mighty refuge in the face of the collectivization, mechanization and urbanization of our time and lament its decline as the "flight from the land." Although anyone who has a financial interest in the non-peasant forms of agriculture will be very interested in persuading us that such a differentiation is purely artificial, we nevertheless insist on considering all forms of feudal, capitalist or collectivist large-scale agriculture a calamitous aberration and a destruction of that wellspring of society which peasantry and peasant agriculture represent. "Wheat factories," "pig breeding grounds," collective farms, incorporated plantations with colored or white wage slaves, appear to us from this point of view not only as uninteresting, not only as the mere transfer of the pattern of large-scale industrial enterprises to basic organic production, but as something far worse: as the annihilation of the peasantry which is the very corner stone of every healthy social structure, and as a refusal to oppose spiritual collectivization even where such strong and natural forces would aid us. Whoever looks upon agriculture as an industry like any other, whilst in reality, in the form of peasant agriculture, it is far more than this and becomes a comprehensive way of life, cannot logically look upon the flight from the land with other eyes than, say, upon the "flight from the textile factories," and whoever restricts his thinking to the rational and technical field of the agricultural engineer and concentrates on artificial fertilizer, tractors and maximum yield, is bound to pass blindly by the sociological problem posed here: the maintenance and confirmation of the peasantry and of peasant agriculture with the whole of its subtle economic, social and spiritual structure, so difficult to describe to one not acquainted with it. Not agriculture *per se* is the backbone of a healthy nation but peasant agriculture alone, whilst the non-peasant form can even become the source of pernicious diseases.

It is an essential characteristic of peasant agriculture that the size of each farm does not exceed the working capacity of one family together with those who have become members of it and a few additional and often temporary agricultural laborers; as a rule it is the property of the farmer, thus embodying tradition and the succession of generations; it is embedded in the social organization of the family and the kinship group, of the village, of the co-operative peasant associations and the occupational and neighborly community to which every thought of competition is alien; and lastly, following the cycle of nature and its laws, it is a mixed holding and embraces both cattle raising and tillage in various combinations. By saying this we have also shown that the peasant holding is the scene of life and work, of production and consumption, that it provides shelter and working quarters, brings men and nature together, affords satisfying and purposeful activity and immediate enjoyment of its fruits, promotes in an ideal manner the independent development of personality and at the same time the warmth of human fellowship, and thereby counter-balances the industrial and urban aspects of our civilization with tradition and conservatism, economic independence and self-sufficiency, many-sided activity and development, proximity to nature, moderation and tranquility, a natural and full existence near the scources of life, and a humble integration into the chain of birth and death.

A peasant who is unburdened by debt and has an adequate holding is the freest and most independent man among us; neither food problems nor the threat of unemployment need worry him and the subjection to the moods of nature which he exchanges for that of the market and the business cycle, usually ennobles a man instead of embittering him. His life, from whatever angle we view it, is the most satisfying, the richest and the most complete in terms of human needs. The fact that the peasant freeholder tends to stick to his holding and his calling in spite of the most adverse conditions and if necessary accepts the hardest possible working conditions which, materially speaking, push him far below the existence level of an industrial laborer, proves that he really agrees with our estimate of the peasantry. Another very important point to complete our picture is that the peasant economy demonstrates that a type of family is possible which gives each member a productive function and thus becomes a community for life, solving all problems of education and age groups in a natural manner; so very different from today's average family which has been degraded to a mere consumption co-operative, devoid of all other meaning.

We may, in fact, sum up by saying that the peasant world together with other small sectors of society, represents today a last great island that has not yet been reached by the flood of collectivization, the last great sphere of human life and work which possesses inner stability and value in a vital sense. It is a priceless blessing wherever this reserve still exists, as in the greater part of continental Europe, and it is a great misfortune for a country if, as in England, it has been destroyed to such an extent that even its loss is no longer realized. As Oliver Goldsmith said in his *Deserted Village* (1769):

> "But a bold peasantry, their country's pride,
> When once destroyed, can never be supplied."

If, therefore, we want our sick society to recover, our predominant and foremost endeavor must be to maintain and, if necessary, augment this reserve.

It is of course true that even in the eighteenth century, there existed besides a most impressive and genuine regard for peasant life, a false and superficial enthusiasm for the peasantry, which in the saccharine conception of opera and ballet peasants simply served as a further diversion for a blasé court society and nobility, but in no way seriously concerned itself with the real peasantry. The circle of shepherds and shepherdesses around Marie-Antoinette at Trianon was oblivious of the miserable state of French agriculture and the sorry plight of the half-starved peasants oppressed by feudalism; they would have been shocked had they been told that stable manure is the soul of agriculture. If we want to beware of such arcadian lyricism and treat this subject realistically, we must first of all define more accurately what really constitutes a sound peasantry and then fearlessly denounce its degenerated forms.

Such soundness we shall find neither in those regions where feudalism has just been overcome (like in Russia) or extends almost into the present (like in Hungary, Poland, Spain, Southern Italy, and large areas of Eastern Germany), nor in areas where rural over-population and the continued subdivision of property have created (like in Bulgaria and Yugoslavia) a type of proletarized and narrow minded dwarf peasant. In addition, the complete subjection of the country to peasant agriculture brings with it the danger that the rural districts cannot afford an intellectual elite with the necessary leisure. The picture of the healthy peasant which we envisage has nothing in common with the oppressed and ignorant beast of burden which thousands of years of exploitation and suppression by the feudal lord or parsimonious nature have created. It is rather the picture of the Swiss, North-West German, Scandinavian, Dutch, Belgian and French peasant who is proud to call himself "Bauer," "Boer" or "paysan." This European peasant is also by no means identical with the English tenant-farmer (who, after the complete victory of feudalism over the English yeomanry, has taken the place of the former peasant) and just as little with the average North American farmer who represents the colonial type of the landlord as speculative businessman. And finally, the more a collectivist economic and social system demotes him to the position of a state-serf, to a cog in the machinery of a planned economy, to an owner whose property title is politically dependent on good conduct and arbitrary laws, the more he ceases to be a peasant in a sense worthy of this name; and here it is useful to recall that it was exactly this precarious state of ownership which was Rousseau's ideal.

We see, then, that many conditions have to be fulfilled in order to create and maintain a genuine and healthy peasantry, and we need not be surprised that in the midst of our modern world which is so alien and in many respects even hostile to him, the peasant is exposed to many dangers and forces of decay, and that even in the countries favoring the development of the peasantry all is not well. If, on the other hand, one considers that peasant agri-culture must maintain itself against so many threats—feudalism, socialism, capitalism, mechanization, and last, but not least, nature which has to be mastered anew every day—one is forced to admire its tremendous vitality and to draw comfort and hope from it. But that, of course, does not settle the problem: we are, rather, faced with the sober question of what can be done in order to preserve peasant agriculture, to strengthen it and to revive it where it has been destroyed. With this question we enter the wide and disputed field of rational agrarian policies and must therefore restrict ourselves to some essential remarks for the purpose of orientation.

The primary question here is this: Is it true, as both pessimists and the vested interests maintain, that the peasant agriculture of industrial countries is based on such weak foundations that it can only be preserved by a continuous policy of protection and subsidies —somewhat along the lines of a national park? If this widespread view which is often dogmatically presented as self-evident, were really correct, we would indeed be faced by an exceedingly serious situation. Admittedly, agriculture is that part of the national economic system to which the principles of a free market economy could always be applied only with broad reservations, the peculiar conditions obtaining here having always confronted economic policy with special problems which could not be left to solve themselves. Especially in this sector, then, a particularly high degree of far-sighted, protective, directive, regulating and balancing intervention is not only defensible, but even mandatory. It is also certain that the national importance of a viable peasant agriculture can under certain circumstances justify the community's shouldering certain temporary or even permanent burdens, always supposing that they are justly distributed. But such a policy of peasant protection— only this is under consideration here, not the general protection of agriculture—has, in the nature of things, certain limits, which cannot be overstepped without seriously imperilling the economic and social equilibrium of the nation nor, possibly, without damage to agriculture itself. These limits are rather narrow and in most industrial countries they have already before this war been exceeded to a considerable extent.

It is, then, all the more important that the pessimistic and defeatist doctrine, which fundamentally amounts at the same time to a disparagement of peasant agriculture, seems to be unfounded. For the agriculture of the industrial countries there does, in fact, exist an optimum structure, which makes it possible to carry out successfully an agrarian policy which tends to preserve and strengthen peasant agriculture with a minimum of economic nationalism, protectionism, subsidies and collectivism, and by an exceedingly fortunate concurrence of circumstances this optimum structure is that of a highly developed peasant agriculture devoted to specialized production. These circumstances are the following:

(1) It is precisely in specialized agricultural products (dairy products, eggs, meat, fruit and vegetables) as opposed to staple products (especially grain), that the small holder's farm of the European type naturally excels; and it could still be considerably improved by bettering agrarian techniques and training the peasants accordingly.

(2) This type of production for which the peasant farm possesses a natural superiority over large-scale enterprises, happens to be at the same time naturally located in the European industrial countries, that is, near the centers of consumption (i.e., within what is called "Thünen's inner circle"). That means in the industrial countries the specialized production of the small-holder enjoys a natural competitive advantage not only because this kind of farm is particularly suited for this type of production, but also because it is favorably situated from a transportation point of view, especially when low feeding stuff tariffs enable it to take advantage of the position which the more distant zones of world agriculture enjoy in the field of staple production. It is well known that the peasant agriculture of free trading Denmark has become the model for this form of agrarian structure; without any form of agrarian protection it has not only maintained its peasant agriculture but even developed it to admirably high standards and thereby contradicted the pessimistic opinions of the opponents of free trade in a most impressive manner. Denmark's example also corrects another mistaken notion which might arise from the term "specialized peasant production": the idea that such a form of farming is bound to lead to a one-sided development of cattle raising and a wastage of arable land. The opposite is true. Intensive agriculture will always be diversified and will be based on a combination of cattle raising and crop farming, thereby maintaining the biological balance. Such a system not only completes the organic cycle of farming but also achieves the economic and social advantage of the farm's greatest possible self-sufficiency. In fact, contrary to widely current ideas, Denmark's arable area has been trebled between 1871 and 1912, whilst the number of heads of cattle has only been doubled; during the same period the agricultural population increased by a quarter, and all this took place without any protective tariffs and subsidies, though on the basis of an extremely high standard of peasant culture and an exemplary organization of agricultural co-operatives. Denmark's example should be of particular importance to a country like Switzerland where a certain one-sided development—dairy farming—has taken place in preference to tillage, a fact which is being rightly lamented and could lead to the erroneous conclusion that these two branches of production are mutually exclusive within the peasant agrarian structure, rather than what they really are, namely, complementary.

(3) It is the above named type of agricultural produce ("protective food") which meets the physiological and habitual needs of the urban and industrial population, who require strong nerves rather than muscles.

(4) Specialized agricultural production, if it is to be carried out rationally, requires an agrarian technique which maintains the

fertility of the soil, a factor of particular importance today when even in Europe erosion is more and more endangering this fertility.

(5) Because it also includes a large variety of farm produce, it can distribute production and marketing risks efficiently, can maintain the equilibrium of the biological process, convert the peasant into an adaptable agriculturalist with a many sided occupational training, and permit the farm to develop a high degree of self-sufficiency which makes it "crisis-proof" because it becomes independent of the fluctuations not only of the sellers' but also of the buyers' market.

(6) This ability of a farm (not overburdened by debt) to resist economic crises which is founded on the distribution of risks and self-sufficiency, is further increased by the fact that costs in the form of money wages do not play any appreciable role because of the peculiar labor structure of a peasant farm. The power to resist crises can also be heightened by revitalizing peasant industry and crafts. This extremely important work has been performed in Switzerland by Dr. Ernst Laur's excellent "Heimatwerk" organization, the venerable "Okonomische und Gemeinnützige Gesellschaft des Kantons Bern," founded in the eighteenth century, or the "Hemsloejd" in Sweden; but they have done it quietly and without the fanfare of the "great programs." Quite apart from the cultural education which these organizations provide, they not only extend the field of peasant self-sufficiency to include handicrafts, but open up additional sources of income by making use particularly of compulsory leisure periods in the winter. This marks an important step towards the solution of the, in every respect difficult and peculiar, problem of the mountain peasant who deserves our particular sympathy in the hard struggle he leads to make a meagre living. At this point, however, we must not forget that the peasant economy's ability to resist crises more successfully only applies to the small holding unburdened by debt. All the more serious is the problem presented by the notoriously heavy indebtedness of wide regions of European and even of overseas agriculture, an indebtedness caused by the over-capitalization of agricultural real estate values in the past, so that in this respect agriculture rests on a capital structure which can in the long run hardly be maintained. How to solve this special problem and how to prevent a recurrence of this process, we lack the space to discuss here.

(7) Especially in the case of specialized agricultural produce we can count on great reserves of demand which have not yet been tapped but would, in conjunction with the production stoppages which may be expected from the well-nigh universal exhaustion of the soil, avert the danger of a new agricultural over-production crisis. We want to recall that the income as well as the price elasticity of the demand for these products is, in contrast to that

for the staple products, remarkably high, so that an increase in that part of the consumers' income which can be used for buying food or a lowering of the prices of specialized agricultural products leads to a more than proportional increase in demand. How great the elasticity of demand is, i.e., how far the demand for the specialized produce containing protein, fats, vitamins and minerals can be expected to expand if mass incomes increase or prices diminish, has been demonstrated by the experience of all the industrial countries after the last great economic crisis. This demonstration would have been even more striking if the increase in mass income (with a simultaneous increase in employment and wages) had been accompanied by a lowering of agricultural prices. It can be stated as a fact that these demand reserves have only recently been recognized in their full extent, and the famous investigation of the nutritional state of the world carried out by the Economic Department of the League of Nations has greatly contributed to this. This investigation has opened the eyes of many people regarding the great gap between the actual demand for food and what, physiologically speaking, it could and should be throughout the world, and the tremendous amounts which would be necessary in order to eliminate the existing malnutrition of a great part of the earth's population. This potential demand could be released by the following methods: (a) lowering the retail price of specialized foodstuffs, which, by a corresponding decrease in production and marketing costs, would enable us to reach that stage which has already been attained by leading farms and in whole countries like Denmark. This reduction of costs presupposes a more rational form of peasant production, a decrease in feedingstuff tariffs, a high development of agricultural production and marketing co-operatives, as well as the greatest possible cut in trading profits which have been unduly increased in many countries by the unrational organization of the food trade and quasi-monopolist associations of all kinds. If, for example, we learn from the investigations of the Department of Agriculture that in the United States the trading profits for such important foods as milk, meat and fruit amount to 300 per cent. and that the share of the farmer in every dollar spent by the American consumer for foodstuffs has dropped from 53c. in 1920 to 41c. in 1939, or even that the tobacco planters, confronted by the impenetrable monopoly of the big tobacco companies, in some years receive less for their entire crop than the net profit of all the companies put together, one obtains an idea of the big task that has to be done here. (b) An increase in the purchasing power of the urban and industrial consumers, as regards their total income as well as the part available for buying food. High total incomes presuppose a minimum of unemployment and high wages, and also the availability of a great part of the consumers' income for food presupposes low prices of the non-agricultural goods and services. Since nothing promotes both requirements as much as the reasonable and positive integration of the national economy into the world economic order, guaranteeing a flourishing export industry, a low price level and a price mechanism as free as possible from monopolist influences, we find that it is precisely peasant agriculture which should have a strong interest in counteracting autarkic tendencies. A national economy impoverished by an autarkic policy offers no market for the high grade specialized products of peasant agriculture. The resulting decline in the sales volume might even force the distressed farmers to ask for subsidies from a population which, lacking purchasing power, can in any case hardly afford more than minimum quantities of butter, cheese, milk, eggs and meat; however, it should be clear that this would be a policy of burning the candle at both ends, and a well-advised peasantry should take exactly the opposite road and cut through the vicious circle by combatting all autarkic tendencies. From this it also follows that the peasantry is as interested in preventing the formation of monopolies of any kind as the urban industrial consumers. (c) A purposeful policy of nutritional hygiene which makes it its task to bring about a desirable change in consumers habits by instruction, education of young women in home economics, people's restaurants, price reductions and other measures.

(8) By rousing this latent demand for high grade foods ("protective foods" in contrast to staple foods), the "collateral" demand for agricultural staples (grain, potatoes, root crops, &c.), is necessarily also increased since specialized production is, after all, largely a process of refining staple products and changing quantity into quality. Thus, in order to produce a certain number of calories, the production of quality foods, counting all the stages from the staple product up to the final commodity ready for the market, requires a relatively large area. As we saw, these additional staple products are most rationally produced partly on European peasant farms, partly in the border zones of the world agricultural area; the European peasant economy itself will thus assume a useful place in the international division of labor in agriculture and the danger of international over-production which tends to threaten every national agriculture will be averted.

(9) Another extremely important point is that it is chiefly specialized production which, thanks to the intensity of the labor required, its family character and the moderate area it needs for operation, is able to tie a maximum number of people to the land and thereby maintain the beneficial influence of farming and country life.

(10) It would be wrong to imagine that such an agrarian

structure in the industrial countries would endanger food supplies in war-time. It should be remembered that the most important staple products—particularly wheat and sugar—are highly suitable for long-term storage, so that war-time stock piles can be carefully accumulated. On the other hand, the livestock of the peasant farmer presents an extremely important war-time reserve which has the advantage of not having to be stored, whilst the agrarian methods of specialized peasant production promote the fertility of the soil to a high degree which in itself is a valuable asset in times of war.

We have now enumerated the most important conditions and considerations which make a rational peasant agriculture, adapted to existing conditions, and well-integrated into the world economy, appear as that form of agriculture which not only can be successfully preserved but even presents the optimum agrarian structure of the industrial countries. Indeed, if peasant agriculture did not exist it would have to be invented. It is this form of agriculture towards whose maintenance and strengthening the efforts of all those must be bent who consider a strong, populous and socially sound agriculture as the highest aim of a far-sighted policy. Since, however, it is at the same time the optimum agrarian structure and in line with natural development, it can—and this is the important conclusion with which we confront the defeatists and pessimists in agrarian matters—be maintained and furthered by a minimum of state interference and, if both sides show sufficient good will, it can change the unholy and poisonous conflict of interests between town and country, from which the pure protectionist agrarian policy has suffered so much, into friendly co-operation.

This conclusion seems to us all the more convincing when we use the agrarian policy which so many European industrial countries have favored as a comparison and reveal its basic error. It consisted in making grain production the pivot of agrarian protection, and thereby inaugurated an agrarian policy which not only hindered each country from producing whatever it was most suited, but also put peasant production at a relative disadvantage, not to mention the repercussions which the industrial population had to suffer. The long list of sins of this policy of stimulating grain production (which has at the same time led to a good deal of exhaustion of the soil), makes depressing reading: (1) It has further increased the world over-production of grain by making possible the production of an additional amount at increased costs; (2) it has thereby decreased the international total, marketable at profitable prices, and (3) has considerably contributed to the circulatory disturbances of the world economy, lowering the income of the industrial and urban masses by increasing unemployment and lowering wages;

(4) the latter fact has, in conjunction with the relative increase in grain prices, compressed that part of the total income likely to demand specialized products, and has thus put this highly important branch of agriculture into a difficult position; (5) this crisis in specialized agricultural production has in turn led to ever more comprehensive and incisive protective measures; and finally, (6) the policy of primary grain protection has raised the production costs of specialized production by increasing the prices of supplementary feedingstuffs and has thus contributed also from the production angle to the difficulties of this branch of agriculture. Briefly, these campaigns to increase grain production acted as an explosive in the world economy, they have driven a deep wedge between the interests of town and country, they have lowered the state of nutrition and, above all, they have in the long run proved to be bad agrarian policy because they have led to a dangerous over-intensification of cultivation and to a relative weakening of precisely that form of agriculture which, in the industrial countries, is made imperative by practically every factor—location of industries in the world, nutritional science, cultural aims and population policies.

At this point we must warn against a disastrous tendency to confuse an increase in self-sufficiency resulting from peasant agriculture with an expansion in land cultivation carried out by the non-agricultural classes, with the goal of national autarky in food-stuffs. These are, indeed, two things which should be kept strictly apart, even by reserving the clumsy expression for the second. To use them indiscriminately is an error of logic of the type which is called "conceptual realism": individual self-sufficiency is the self-sufficiency of an actual and tangible economic unit, viz., the family, and therefore a genuine, thorough and remedial alteration in the economic and social structure of the country; autarky, how-ever, is only the forcible limitation of the otherwise unchanged functions of the market to the area within the historically con-ditioned national frontiers, it is "self-sufficiency" in an abstract sense, for it is based on no concrete economic unit, as in the case of genuine (individual) self-sufficiency, at least not as long as we do not live in a communist state in which the nation itself becomes the concrete economic unit.

We are faced here with a simple question of logical distinction. A policy of "self-sufficiency" is designed to make the concrete unit of the family more independent of the market as such, whereas it is the aim of "autarky" to make the national market independent of the foreign markets. The first case represents a real and funda-mental alteration of the economic cellular structure (limitation of the market sector in favor of the marketless sector of self-sufficiency); the second case, however, represents only the replace-ment of one (the foreign) market by another (the home) market, a substitution which has primarily only political significance and can be defended only on that basis. In the first case the family is emancipated from its dependence on the market, in the second case the national sector of the market severs its ties with the international market. Therefore, the first emancipation neutralizes the price mechanism and the law of costs and takes place without resorting to economic means of compulsion (tariffs, quotas, import embargo, foreign exchange control), which would fit the totalitarian collective state and also presuppose its structure if they are to be carried through effectively. We insist on this distinction just as much because we advocate more self-sufficiency as because we reject autarky. We should be compromising what is so near to our heart, namely, the economic and social structural change inherent in "self-sufficiency," most seriously if we were to confuse it with "autarky," and speak in the language of the advocates of an extreme economic nationalism.

We, too, consider it both desirable and likely that the international division of labor should and will be modified in the agrarian sector, but this is only desirable and rational in so far as it takes place as a natural consequence of changes in the internal economic structure (by enlarging the sphere of self-sufficiency and perfecting the economic equilibrium of the peasant farms) and not as the result of economic compulsion (i.e., trade barriers).

We shall endanger all our efforts if we are not quite clear on this point and become entangled with economic nationalism which we should not touch with a ten-foot pole. It is very necessary that we should protect ourselves against being misunderstood in this respect and being used for goals which are completely foreign to us. The structural changes not only in agriculture but, beyond that, in the whole national economy, which we have at heart, will lead to an agricultural recovery of such an extent that it will allow agriculture to abandon almost entirely the crutches of protection and subsidies. We should get accustomed to the thought that a positive "peasant and agrarian policy" can be something quite different from such a system of protection and subsidies. To this observation we link an appeal to all experts on this subject to view the problem from this angle and to devote the sum total of their experience and ingenuity to its solution, being convinced that an agriculture which has to be maintained like a natural reservation and is dependent on the economic charity of the state and the consumers, is unsound and can bring no satisfaction whatever to the good agriculturalist who has his job at heart. The time has really come to devote all one's energies to the task of changing this unsound state of affairs, by determining what type of agriculture is best suited to industrial countries, and developing a detailed reform program based on these findings. It is a quite wonderful coincidence which can hardly be stressed sufficiently, that, as we have plausibly argued, a mixed farming process, aiming at specialized production, is, in fact, this optimum type. Realizing this, we can disassociate ourselves from all those plans which would revolutionize agriculture by the establishment of collective enterprises which can be characterized as a kind of neo-feudal estate and which would destroy the unique sociological-vital structure of the peasant enterprise. It is precisely the values of such a peasant structure which must always be given pride of place, whereas every kind of "industrialization" of agriculture is diametrically opposed to our efforts. We should indeed be glad that peasant agriculture together with the handicrafts has until now proved such a firm bulwark against industrial mechanization. This does not in any way touch on the feasibility of co-operation between independent peasant holdings. This is indeed a consummation devoutly to be wished.

Artisans and Small Traders

In order to estimate the value of the functions of the artisan and small trader, we would remind the reader once more of the great and supremely important goal, namely, to promote and strengthen all forms of living and working which have not yet succumbed to collectivization and proletarization, wherever they can be found. From this viewpoint, we must now, having dealt with the peasantry, turn our attention to the artisan and the small trader whose occupations are in many ways similar or even interrelated, and who, like the peasants, too, deserve all the well-planned assistance that is possible.

The unintelligent objection that this would simply mean re-hashing the old fashioned middle class policy is not going to deter us. It is true that such a policy has in the past often been discredited by the self-centered and narrow-minded efforts of groups bent on obtaining special privileges and has therefore acquired a somewhat musty smell. Only too often one could not avoid the impression that certain occupational groups were simply to be preserved in moth-proof camphor. A thorough airing is urgently needed here but if one watches these groups more closely one gains the comforting impression that in many instances they are motivated by a new and more hopeful spirit.

The camphorous odor of the old "middle class policy"—and the same applies, as we saw, to the agricultural policy of certain vested interests—was in the final analysis caused by discouragement. The members of the middle classes had lost all confidence in their own strength and ability to take their place alongside the large enterprises, and believed that they had only the choice between complete ruin and artificial conservation. However, naturally choosing the second possibility, they courted the danger of obstructing the general development by their purely negative policy of restraint and rigidity. But, in the meantime, it has become apparent that the small enterprises can hold their own far better in the face of big business than had been believed in the initial period of intoxication with industrial expansion, and they have every right to become self-confident once more. The statistics of industrial countries prove that as a concomitant of the growing differentiation of economic life, the complexity of requirements and the increasing importance of personal services ("tertiary" production, as against the "primary" production of agriculture and the "secondary" production of industry), the number of small independent enterprises has not decreased, but increased. Also, in the light of the most recent technical advances which, thanks to electric motors, internal combustion engines and the improvements in machine tools, are excellently suited to small enterprises and have greatly benefited them, the idea that a large-scale enterprise is *a priori* superior must be thoroughly revised. Whilst in the case of agriculture there was really never any doubt that mechanical development would leave the age-old dominance of the small enterprise untouched and whilst one is now contritely returning to this insight wherever one has sinned against it as in the United States, the artisans and small traders are also stubbornly maintaining their position which is characterized precisely by its difference from industrial production. The "selling factory" which mechanizes trading activities has not yet been invented, and it is not likely that either custom tailoring or hand made furniture will be replaced by the conveyor belt as long as there are people who are able to appreciate the quality of such work.

It is remarkable how deeply the contempt of the peasantry and of the "petit bourgeois," common to both Marxist and feudalist thought, has permeated the thinking of our times and the old "middle class policy" bears indeed some traces of the resentment of a man who at heart believes that his capabilities are not fully appreciated. All this will have to be completely changed and the progressive revaluation which will entail an outward redistribution of social power will become the very index of the recovery of our society. What is needed all along the line is an inward and outward recovery, a re-arrangement and increase of the independent small and medium sized enterprises, a strengthening of their self-confidence and their encouragement by sound economic measures.

What then is the present position of the artisans? This is a subject of which we do not by any means know enough yet, but it is certain at least that the former defeatist attitude is no longer in order. Although in the middle of the last century the astute German sociologist, W. H. Riehl, could describe the craft guilds as the "ruins of the old burgher class" which "are still littering modern middle class society," it is not too much to say that considerable parts of these ruins have in the meantime been restored to a quite habitable state.   It is particularly interesting to note in this connection that conditions vary most markedly from country to country.   In Germany, Austria, Switzerland and in other European countries a sturdy class of craftsmen has survived whilst the United States may as correctly (i.e., with some exaggeration) be called the country without craftsmen, as England the country without peasants.   As always, such international differences are experimental proof that the high level of preservation and adaptation which has been attained in some particular place could, with good will, be reached elsewhere too, and that the problem is by no means one of pure economic accountancy.

The popular argument that industrial mass production is bound to destroy the artisans obscures the truth.   It only applies if the identical product is actually being manufactured more cheaply by industrial mass production than by an individual craftsman.   No nail-smith can hope that his craft will be resurrected because in his field there exists clear price competition for the identical product which will unequivocally be decided in favor of mass production.   But there are many other cases where the industrial product is not only distinguished from the work of the artisan by its cost but also, in a more or less obvious manner, by its inferior quality. In such an instance it is no longer a question of pure price competition but rather of competition between substitutes (as, e.g., between margarine and butter).   The better quality of the artisan's product is in this case not only a matter of taste but also of greater durability.   There is a wide sphere here where the lower cost of manufactured goods is weighed only very loosely against the better taste and greater durability of both materials and workmanship of the handicraft product, in fact, the decision is usually left to thoughtless and ignorant consumption habits.   In so far as this is true, it is not primarily mass production which is throttling craftsmanship but the collectivization of consumption habits which first makes mass production possible.   This collectivization of consumption habits has progressed in varying degrees in different countries, probably farthest in America.   It goes hand in hand with the disappearance of the traditional ways of life and is, therefore, a symptom of the general crisis of society.   To the same extent as this crisis is successfully overcome the artisans, too, will benefit, and it is certain that much can be done here by an intensive education and publicity program which should, if possible, already start in the schools.   The case is quite different where the above mentioned process of weighing the advantages against the disadvantages actually takes place, and the cheaper mass produced commodity is simply preferred owing to lack of money, in spite of the clear, if depressing, knowledge that in the end it is really more expensive. Is there another instance where an organized system of payment by instalments is as necessary and legitimate as here? Should not what applies to the automobile (which may be out of date or be driven to pieces within a year) at least also apply to well-built furniture (which the grand-children will still be able to use); particularly at a time when, as some economists assure us—though prematurely, as we have shown—in such a handicraft-less country as the United States the population no longer knows what to do with the accumulation of savings? These questions well deserve some consideration. They at least give us some inkling of the direction in which our thoughts might profitably travel if we want to aim higher than the old "middle class policy" and achieve the *aurea sectio* between conservation and progress. Anything further that might be said on this extremely important subject will be dealt with when we discuss the general problems and possibilities of a policy of optimum size enterprises.

As we have seen, it is by no means in all cases technical and physical factors which decide the battle between handicrafts and industry, but rather those subjective and imponderable forces which determine demand. This always applies when the products of the craftsman and of industry are different from each other, and it is only due to our shortsightedness and ignorance if we think that the handicraft product and the industrial product are identical. Only too often do we thoughtlessly follow a fashion which favors mass produced commodities, and only slowly do we come to realize that these also have great disadvantages. However, where we know from the beginning that our funds are insufficient to pay for expensive craftsmanship—the custom tailored suit, hand-made furniture—we find that the system of paying by instalments has a very legitimate function, which in turn necessitates that the banks take more interest in the small enterprises than they have done so far. And apart from that, one can argue that in this way the growing wealth of a nation which permits wider and wider sections to give preference to hand-made products will benefit the artisan, provided, of course, that the consumers are properly instructed and informed regarding this subject. In so far as the increase in the nation's wealth is based on growing mechanization and industrialization, the economic situation of the artisan would rather become more secure—always supposing that a sense for quality production has been maintained and promoted among the people—and a counterbalance to the mechanization in the industrial sector would automatically be established. Of course, as so much rests on the appropriate direction and schooling of demand, success will chiefly depend on whether the advertising of the large, rich enterprises can be kept within bounds or be balanced by similar joint advertising campaigns of artisan associations. This particular case proves most convincingly how the dangerous instrument of advertising can become the effective weapon of an economic policy aiming at the good of the community.

All these considerations, however, presuppose that the craftsmen maintain the vitality and proud tradition of their work and do not succumb to a dull and discouraged sloppiness which grants easy victories over sluggish small enterprises to the vigorous large-scale undertaking which is kept on its toes by high capital investments and wage bills. The consumer's preference for craftsmanship must be reciprocated if it is to have permanence, but perhaps it is in many cases a feeling of faintheartedness and of being pushed into the background which paralyses the craftsman and degrades him to a botcher. Professional ethics and pride in one's work do not permit petty cunning and carelessness; they are tender plants which require constant care from all sides, posing psychological problems as complicated as those of pedagogy. An experience of the author may throw some light on this point: he had entrusted a difficult job of shoe repairing to a cobbler in his neighborhood instead of to the repair shop of a big department store and was disappointed when the shoe was returned completely ruined. Without letting this experience discourage him, he told the cobbler that he had preferred to give him the work rather than the department store in order to do his modest bit in encouraging a small craftsman, but that he had expected correspondingly careful work. The cobbler seemed greatly affected and since then has taken great care and is successful in satisfying his customers. Since, however, not all customers would demonstrate such patience there is a lesson here which all artisans should learn. Those consumers who can at all afford it should not shrink from the sacrifice of a few cents in order to carry out an economic policy of their own and support artisans to the best of their ability for the good of the community, but they must find in the artisan himself a willing partner to this scheme, ready to give his best. We should be unwilling to make awards for incompetence and indolence, and that is also why that convenient but shortsighted policy of merely preserving the middle classes which, like the old guild policy, would keep out the draft of competition, must definitely discomfit us. Instead of constantly hatching new plans for restrictive practices and conserving the status quo, we should exert our inventive powers to show the artisans ways of self-help, ways of increasing their efficiency, and assist them by rational means to maintain and widen their sphere of activity. Only such an attitude among craftsmen can assure that inner soundness which makes the preservation and strengthening of their occupations appear to be so exceedingly important from the viewpoint of the general social structure. Thus, we see that what we said regarding the peasantry applies here too.

What is true of artisans is paralleled by the conditions existing among small traders whose occupation is in many cases interrelated with that of the craftsmen. As in the case of handicrafts the sociological significance of the small shops consists in rendering indispensable services and at the same time providing the basis of an independent livelihood for many people. They afford a form of life and work which permits a high degree of self-determination, the enjoyment of purposeful work, the warmth of social contact and a well integrated family life. In these respects, of course, the small trader falls far short of the artisan, let alone the peasant, because he is to all intents and purposes wholly absorbed in the business of selling and easily dispenses with the "objectifying" influence of creation which protects men against the bare struggle of interests. That is why his occupation tends to be so characteristically bereft of the weight of professional tradition and a laboriously acquired education. Beyond doubt, we are here entering a zone in many respects problematical and further characterized by the fact that all kinds of marginal beings tend to settle here— people with indefinable training and professional suitability. It is not a field circumscribed by example and tradition, but a sphere with wide open boundaries and of a somewhat heterogeneous composition in which rootless commercial adventurers exist side by side with the very different type of the solid storekeeper who, similar to the artisan, is supported by traditional and professional honor. For these reasons it is also a sphere of peculiar hazards and conflicts in gaining a livelihood on which one can only express an opinion after very careful consideration. The picture is even more complicated by the fact that conditions vary greatly in the different branches of the retail business, thus requiring different sociological and economic valuations. It is, therefore, impossible to do justice here to the problem of the small trader.

De-Proletarization and Decentralization of Industry

While the lives of peasants, artisans and, to a lesser degree, of small traders constitute the most important sectors of non-proletarian existence and only require to be preserved and furthered, the opposite is true of industry where conditions of life and production are practically calculated to lead to proletarization. Here, then, the strongest and most intelligent efforts are necessary in order to counteract the natural tendency towards proletarization and to find forms of industrial life and organization which will lead to the de-proletarization of workers and employees. Since originally the majority of the people led a well-integrated and non-proletarian

life as peasants and craftsmen, the essentials of an industrial de-proletarization policy will consist in rendering the working and living
conditions of the industrial worker as similar to the positive aspects
of the life of the peasant and artisan as possible. This logically
presupposes that industry is dispersed in the open country and the
small towns, and that regional planning combats its tendency to
concentrate in the big cities.

It seems rather obvious that a start should be made with the
traditional intermediate forms between industry on the one hand
and the peasant and artisan enterprises on the other, and that
it should be pointed out that the *rural trades*—the rural mills, the
small distilleries, the small brick-works, and similar enterprises—as
well as the *rural domestic industries* represent forms of manufacturing organizations which deserve to be closely studied. For our
purpose they vary in value, of course, and in their present state
they are far from ideal but, though today we realize this more and
more, it would be exceedingly short-sighted if, instead of infusing
them with new life, we should praise their disappearance as "progress." Even from the point of view of better nutrition there is
considerable lamenting that the old country mills, where the
peasants had their grain milled for a milling fee, have today almost
totally been displaced by the big commercial mills, and there are
experts who tell us that this is one of the reasons for the deteriorat-
ing quality of bread.

The traditional rural trades are the original form of decentralized
industry, to which modern industries should, as far as possible,
return in order to enable their workers and employees to become
well integrated in their surroundings, and the example of Switzerland, in particular, shows how beneficent such an industrial structure
can be. This all the more if the plant management follows a
clear-sighted policy of facilitating their employees' settlement on
the land. What can be done in this field is shown by the well-
known experiment of the Bally shoe factories (Schoenenwerd,
Switzerland), which deserves special praise: this company assists its
workers and employees in acquiring a house and adequate garden
plots by negotiating the purchase of land for them, advising them
on building and finance matters and affording them financial aid;
over and above this the company sells arable and pasture land at
low prices, pays for the land to be fertilized and ploughed, employs
an agricultural inspector to advise its workers, awakens an interest
in agriculture by instruction, lectures, competitions and exhibitions,
maintains a model training farm, promotes cattle rearing by being
instrumental in the purchase of sound milch cows of a suitably
small breed and in arranging for expert advice, purchases locally
tested seeds and seedlings, and encourages the raising of poultry,
rabbits, &c., which are so very important for this type of semi-

agricultural life. It should be especially stressed here that these are not factory settlements in the sense that the workers do not only work for the firm but are also its tenants, and thus doubly dependent on it. That would be a deterioration rather than an improvement of their condition and their proletarian dependence would be increased. This policy, as demonstrated by the example of the Bally shoe factories, has nothing in common with those patriarchal "welfare institutions" which assume the function of guardians and have therefore always been rightly criticized. On the contrary, this policy is anxious to assist the workers to acquire their own house and land and thus in a decisive way to save them from their proletarian existence. In this connection we would also point out that the decentralization of industry in England which the air attacks have made necessary has had such a good effect on the health of the workers that it has been decided to utilize this experience after the war.

Another question is how far and by what means it is possible to transform the organization of an industrial plant in such a manner that the work will acquire the meaning, self-determination and rhythm which characterize the working life of the artisan. Without sacrificing the output rate of industrial production methods, the de-personalizing and mechanizing effects of the old large-scale industrial enterprise, its massiveness, its minute division of labor and its barrack-like atmosphere, would have to be replaced by forms which are diametrically opposed to the conveyor belt and the Taylor system. We do not consider ourselves competent to give an expert answer to this question and confine ourselves to emphasizing how important the problem is and pointing to the various beginnings that have been made (Hellpach's "Gruppenfabri-kation," Rosenstock's "Werkstattaussiedlung," the "fabrique dis-persée," and others) which prove in this instance too that where there is a will there is a way. Further problems to be solved here are the re-awakening of the worker's professional pride; his personal and occupational interest in the problems of production, which should be more than the mere desire for a large pay check and the shortest possible working hours. Unless he is to remain a pro-letarian in his way of living and in his outlook, it is also necessary that he should receive recognition as a partner in the plant com-munity which values his special knowledge; the industrial nomads whose life is measured by the short periods between pay days should be replaced by a type of worker who has ties not only with the soil but also with the factory and enjoys conditions of employ-ment which promise some security, not perhaps guaranteed by legal titles that are difficult to enforce, but at least by custom and good will, conditions which include the claim to paid vacations, for example. Such a development, which is everywhere showing encouraging signs, will contribute much to the solution of the major problem of de-proletarization. But in addition to developing close relations to the soil and to his place of work, the proletarian must in all circumstances be divested of his chief material characteristic, viz., his unpropertied state, he must be given the chance of attaining that degree of relative independence and security, that awareness of kinship and tradition which only property can give. It is well if he can rent gardening plots cheaply, but it is better if he owns a house and arable ground. More than that, he must also be able to acquire freely disposable funds and become a "small capitalist," possibly by being given the opportunity of acquiring stocks. The perennially discussed idea of letting the workers share in the profits of an enterprise by the distribution of stock to them, meets with the objection, never entirely silenced, that the risk of unemployment is a sufficient burden for the worker without the additional risk of losing his capital. However, one would have to consider whether this objection could not to a great extent be met by creating preferential labor stocks or by labor investment trusts (as in England). At this point we should also remember the beneficial activities of saving banks, mutual building societies, co-operatives and similar institutions.

It must of course be realized that industry cannot be de-centralized and attuned to the working habits of the peasant and artisan if, as compared with large-scale enterprises, this adjustment results in a noticeable decrease in output which upsets all estimates of its profitableness. However, even if certain sacrifices have to be made as regards immediate and measurable profitableness and technical practicability, it must nevertheless be stressed that this sacrifice will be repaid in a wider, social sense and may in the long run even redound to the advantage of the enterprise itself. If we take into consideration all the sociological consequences of proletarization, we are, as we saw above, entitled to the conclusion that in certain circumstances the mechanical organization of industrial plants which permits the cheapest form of production on the basis of measurable costs, may in the end prove to be the most expensive for society as a whole. As has been frequently emphasized in the course of this book, at present even the purely technical and organizational efficiency of large-scale industrial enterprises tends to be greatly over-estimated. This may be aggravated by an optical illusion which frequently traps the uninformed. Mammoth factories and giant enterprises force themselves upon our attention, with advertising doing the rest, whilst a great number of smaller undertakings is less conspicuous. Added to this, the birth of a new big business enterprise or trust is heralded with great publicity, whilst the liquidation of old ones takes place behind the scenes. This gives rise to a somewhat distorted picture of the true importance of, and numerical proportion between, larger and smaller enterprises and we need only glance at the sober tables of statistics to learn that the importance of the smaller enterprises is still far greater and in some countries, indeed, even on the increase (as, e.g., in Sweden, where from 1913 to 1935 the average size of industrial plants decreased from 39 to 28 workers). It is sufficiently well known that Switzerland, more than any other country, has demonstrated not only the viability, but in many fields even the superiority of the smaller enterprise. It must also not be forgotten that the development of large-scale undertakings is often determined by irrational motives: by the desire for commercial prestige, a struggle for power, and finally even by an acquisitive mania which in other men expresses itself more harmlessly in collecting antique china or stamps. Such motives can find expression all the more if the so-called "self-financing" of the concerns increases, permitting them to expand without depending on the capital market and therefore without the regulating function of the interest rates.

The actual tendency for small plants and enterprises to maintain themselves can be vigorously promoted by an appropriate and well-planned policy of optimum sized enterprises, a policy which will counteract the economic and social policy favoring large-scale enterprises which so often wins out today. This task seems so very foreign to most people who still suspect it of being an attack on "progress," that we have hardly begun to examine it for all the possibilities it offers. Apart from solving some of the problems by taxation, it would, for example, be quite feasible to entrust public authorities with the task of making available costly experimental stations, model workshops and testing plants not only, as today, for agriculture but also for small industrial undertakings, thereby reducing that category of costs which is so likely to put the small enterprise at a disadvantage compared with big business. It is also of special importance that appropriate measures are taken to organize credit distribution in such a way as to improve the *supply of capital for small businesses* and remove the defects in the capital distribution process (stock exchanges and banks) still existing in this respect. After all, we are not dealing, as the abstract theorists like to presuppose, with a uniform central catch-basin where the capital of the national economy accumulates and from where the money, regulated by uniform capital interest rates, is distributed, but with a great number of more or less separate individual basins which are represented by the various groups in the credit system. This easily causes economically unjustified discrimination which may decisively influence the industrial structure of the national economy. There can be no doubt that in many countries (particularly in the United States) small industries are the losers as regards their capital requirements. It would be one of the urgent tasks of such an optimum size policy to set this state of affairs right and counteract the dubious effect of banking concentrations, which easily favor large-scale industrial credit, by developing special methods and institutions for the encouragement of credits for small industries. It should be understood that this must not be dubbed a "pro-middle class policy" and burdened with all what has indeed discredited the latter.

New Trends in Social Policy

Tragically enough one of the factors which favor large-scale enterprises, and therefore proletarization to a considerable degree is a particular type of social policy which we shall call "the old-style social policy." Blindly ignoring the fact that the root of the evil is to be found not in material causes but in proletarization, that working class problems are, therefore, in the first place problems of personality, this type of social policy has only too often sought to solve matters by social legislation which necessitated a more and more comprehensive and growing welfare bureaucracy, by a definite pattern of collective bargaining contracts, by an unhampered policy of battling for wage increases and a decrease in working hours—in short, by all those methods which we have learnt to associate with the term social reform—thus trying to remedy the symptoms without even thinking about the cure of the basic ills. This symptomatic treatment has aggravated the disease itself by still further increasing the powers favoring proletarization. As the Popular Front episode in France and the New Deal in the United States have shown such a welfare policy can, in fact, have this paradoxical result since "it talks the worker out of the only saving idea, namely, that the working class is able to reform itself on its own and, therefore, can also improve its conditions without in the process having first to reform the whole world" (W. H. Riehl in 1866). But it particularly tends to apply schematically, experiences it has made in large-scale industrial enterprises to the medium and small enterprises, thereby making their life so hard that they have to abandon the field to big business. The result of such a "progressive" form of social policy is the further proletarization of the country. How, over and above that, it has succeeded in proletarizing and commercializing what was once a free profession which embodied, as hardly any other, the non-commercial professional ideal in the best sense of the word, is shown by the state of the German and British physicians who since the development of the increasingly comprehensive compulsory health insurance system have become supervised health workers handling patients like parts on a conveyor belt.

I think I never realized more clearly how concepts are opposed to each other regarding this problem than when, some years ago, I had a discussion with a leading official of the International Labor Office. I was asked to attend a meeting dealing with the problems of the agricultural laborer, a subject which was then being newly included in the program of the Office, and I made the following points in my conversation with this official: "Your Office is an expression of one of the worst diseases of our society, the name of which is 'proletariat.' You think that you can effectively combat this disease with higher wages, shorter working hours and as comprehensive a social insurance system as possible, and you consider it your task to extend the top results achieved by such a policy in one place to as many other production branches and countries as possible. At the moment you are dealing with agriculture. I do not want to say anything against your efforts, but is it not really time that you conceived your task to be greater, and investigated the question whether forms of agriculture could not be found and developed which would not permit the disease to which your Office owes its existence, i.e., the proletariat, to arise in the first place? And should it not quite generally be your final and highest goal to make yourself superfluous by promoting de-proletarization instead of continuing to move in the old rut? How about taking a greater interest than heretofore in peasant family farms, the support of artisans and small traders, the technical and organizational possibilities of loosening up large-scale enterprises, the diminution of the average size of factories, workers' settlements and similar projects?" "Why, you are a Catholic, are you?" he replied, to which I gave the obvious answer that one did not have to be a Catholic in order to see things this way. At the same time I recalled that dogmatic old-time liberal to whom a friend of mine in Rotterdam was proudly showing a number of workers' allotments and who on seeing these happy people spending their free evenings in their gardens could think of nothing better than the cool remark that this was an irrational form of vegetable production. He could not get it into his head that it was a very rational form of "happiness production" which surely is what matters most. The main issue is that our social reformer as well as the old-fashioned liberal both really belong to the same world, a world which to us today seems very passé. Both are completely blind to the vital and imponderable values, and in spite of their controversies they have this in common that they are unable to think in other terms than in those of money cost and profit.

It is clear, therefore, that we gain a new perspective once we realize that the workers' question is a problem of life as a whole and working and living conditions in general, rather than an economic problem in the narrower sense. It is the problem of the proletariat as such, which cannot, therefore, be solved by means of the old-style welfare policy and may, in fact, as we saw, even be aggravated by it. Of course, as long as we have a proletariat, this form of welfare policy will have a limited function, and in this narrower field of wage regulations, trade unionism, factory inspection and social insurance much intelligent work has been done and doubtlessly still remains to be done. But when viewed in the light of the great and comprehensive task of welfare policy, all these measures appear to us almost like taking an aspirin for a toothache. That task is really to attack the source of the evil and to do away with the proletariat itself—to achieve what the Papal Encyclical *Quadragesima Anno* (1931) has termed the *Redemptio Proletariorum*. True welfare policy is therefore equivalent to a policy of eliminating the proletariat whilst henceforth the old-style welfare policy would have to concern itself only palliatively with the hard core that still remains, and thereby of course greatly loses in importance. This task also deprives welfare services of their former character of something independent, which has always seemed somewhat absurd and an expression of the distorted conditions of our time, and incorporates them in a sensible policy concerning itself with the problems of peasants, artisans and small traders, industrial questions, settlement, housing and distribution schemes.

This also adds a new and more hopeful note to the most difficult and important task facing the welfare services: the reduction of unemployment. This problem is so urgent that the danger of repeating ourselves must not prevent us from discussing it once more.

As we saw above, many tend to approach this question with a sort of economic "Maginot Line Mentality." They believe that it is only necessary to organize some kind of bulwark and to seek protection behind it in order to be automatically secure from all economic disturbances—some sort of one hundred per cent. bombproof monetary system or some sort of planned economy. The results so far obtained in this direction have been highly disappointing. In reality the problem is in the long run presumably insoluble in this manner, even by applying the most rational monetary and credit policy. The problem of economic stability and unemployment is not simply one of business cycles but in the final analysis one arising from the economic and social structure as a whole even if one disregards for the moment the difficulties of a politically completely disjointed world. Today's economic crises must be understood in their gravity and tenaciousness against the background of a world which has been almost completely "proletarized" and has succumbed to economic and social collectivization, a world which has, as a result of this, lost its inner resilience and regulating mechanism and with them the psychological climate of security, continuity, confidence and inner balance it needs. In brief, the

H

economic crises which are getting so uncontrollable belong to a world which has "coagulated" socially and economically and it is therefore no accident that they weigh most heavily on those countries which have gone furthest down the road of proletarization, mechanization, centralization and "coagulation," i.e., England, Germany and the United States. The main cause of this instability is to be found where common sense would look for it first: in the over-complication of the social apparatus, in the excess of concentration and interlocking, in the preponderance of wage earners, in deficient adaptability which is bound to grow worse with increasing concentration and interlocking, and in the fact that adaptation will have to be carried out by way of ever greater units and ever more agencies and that the individual's ability to adapt himself decreases in the same ratio.

We hope we shall not be misunderstood in this: we do not wish to detract from the importance of a sensible business cycle policy which influences the economic mechanism as a whole by regulating the volume of credit and similar measures, but in the first place such a policy is, as we saw, limited to a narrow sphere, and secondly even in the most favorable instance there is always an insoluble remainder of instability which has to be dealt with. This remainder has increased continuously, whilst the ability of the individual to resist these shocks has steadily decreased. The most extreme examples of this tendency are perhaps some American farmers who had become so specialized and so dependent on their current money incomes that when the crisis came they were as near starvation as the industrial worker. At the other, more fortunate end we see the industrial worker in Switzerland who, if necessary can find his lunch in his garden, his supper in the lake, and can earn his potato supply in the fall by helping his brother clear his land.

Let us illustrate our point with another example: a smooth automobile ride depends on two conditions, the smoothness of the road and the quality of the springs. A road can never be so smooth that we can do away with the springs. But the bumpier it is, the better our springs will have to be. Now as regards economic stability, the prospects of a smooth road are worse than ever; we must expect that it will even get bumpier in spite of all the refinements of the business cycle policy. It is logical that we must therefore provide better springs so that our economic and social system will be in a better position to absorb the shocks. It can easily be seen that the program of economic and social reforms which we have sketched here has, apart from other points, also the effect of greatly improving a country's internal resistance to shocks because it combats proletarization, agglomeration and organizational over-complication and thereby the actual causes of the economic upsets while minimizing their consequences for the individual.

Speaking in medical terms, such a program of social reform is, therefore, not a therapy which only deals with local symptoms but one which overhauls the whole constitution and aims at reconditioning, and as it strikes at the root of the social problem it is truly a radical policy. As such it must, as we saw above, aim at a widespread diffusion of property without being afraid of using the appropriate means to effect the smoothing down of sharp differences in property. Its goal must not only be de-proletarization but also what we describe by the rather vague and easily misused term social justice. If one spends some thought on this concept one will finally realize that it essentially rests on a particular concept of social equality, a form which L. Walras in his *Études d'économie sociale* called "égalité des conditions" as opposed to the inevitable "inégalité des positions." In the light of this goal it seems as just to us that the starting conditions should be the same for all competitors ("égalité des conditions," equal opportunity) as that they should be differently rewarded according to their different performances ("inégalité des positions"). This gives us a framework within which we can discuss in detail the manifold measures of this type of social policy which we are, however, reserving for special treatment.

Market Policy (Control of Competition and Restraint of Monopolies)

All partial measures in whatever field they may be taken and however well thought out and necessary they may be, must always be in harmony with, and converge toward the main goal of economic reform: the goal of achieving that complete economic order which seems the most desirable in the light of all the considerations which have been discussed here at length. The center of this economic order will, as we realized, have to be a free market and genuine competition, in which, under fair and equal conditions, the success of the private enterprise will be measured in terms of its service to the consumers ("performance competition"). However, a free market and performance competition do not just occur —as the laissez-faire philosophers of historical liberalism have asserted—because the state remains completely passive; they are by no means the surprisingly positive product of a negative economic policy. They are, rather, extremely fragile artificial products which depend on many other circumstances and presuppose not only a high degree of business ethics but also a state constantly concerned to maintain the freedom of the market and of competition in its legislation, administration, law courts, financial policy and spiritual and moral leadership, by creating the necessary framework of laws and institutions, by laying down the rules for competition and watching over their observance with relentless but just severity. In economic life, too, the saying holds good that liberty without restraint is license, and if we desire a free market the framework of conditions, rules and institutions must be all the stronger and more inflexible. Laissez-faire—yes, but within a framework laid down by a permanent and clear-sighted market police in the widest sense of this word. The freedom of the market in particular necessitates a very watchful and active economic policy which at the same time must also be fully aware of its goal and the resulting limits to its activity, so that it does not transgress the boundaries which characterize a compatible form of interventionism.

As we can only make a selection from the abundance of the problems confronting the market police, we restrict ourselves to one which is more important and obvious than all the others: the problem of monopolies. This problem is so palpably important because the urgent necessity of combatting the monopolies cannot be doubted as their economic and social harmfulness is almost unanimously acknowledged. Wherever monopolies seem unavoidable for technical and economic reasons (particularly in the case of the above-mentioned utilities), the state or the community will have to be satisfied either with exercising a strict supervision over the enterprises run by private monopoly or with changing the private monopoly into a public one. Apart from that, however, it will be a case of fighting the monopolies themselves and reconverting them into part of the competitive market, realizing that they present one of the worst perversions of our economic system and, at the same time, that they can only be effectively combatted by elimination, not by supervision.

Monopolies are in fact a falsification of the market economy, constituting a privilege and at the same time a violation of the principle that higher profits can only be gained through corresponding performance which is determined by the unhampered play of supply and demand (principle of a fair *quid pro quo,* an equivalence of reciprocal services). Not only are monopolies socially intolerable but they also interfere with the economic process and act as a brake on productivity as a whole. An economy infested with monopolies will succumb to a slow process of auto-intoxication of a chronic character, becoming acute in its later stages and bound to destroy the market economy completely and with it the democratic and liberal structure of state and society. The economic system loses its elasticity and adaptability; the rigidity of the market paralyses the numerous balancing factors, thereby aggravating and lengthening the economic crises and retarding recovery. Monopolistic

privileges dull all efforts to give the best possible services and lead
to an economically, socially and politically unbearable agglomeration of economic power, resulting in an increasing concentration
of the control over the whole process of the national economy in
the hands of a few who need render no account, whereby the workings of the economic process are progressively obscured.   This
obscurity becomes the breeding ground for all manner and degrees
of corruption; it becomes more important to them that public
opinion should be misled and that the advantages gained should
be held by any means, than that the consumer's demands should
be satisfied as plentifully and cheaply as possible; instead of the
maxim "large turnover and small profits" we now have the opposite.
"small turn-over and large profits," and eventual possibilities of
increasing sales by decreasing prices remain unutilized because
monopolies may prefer the combination of high prices and little
production; monopolies permit an arbitrary differentiation of prices
to the advantage of one group of buyers and to the disadvantage of
other groups; the price policy of monopolies withholds from the
consumers the better and cheaper possibilities of living provided by
technical progress and mass production and halts the equalizing
mechanism which, if there is free competition, sees to it that the
workers who have become unemployed due to technical and
organizational progress find new work in a short time.

If we identify the "public interest" with that of the consuming
community it is clear that monopoly violates this interest.   It leads
to an allocation of productive forces other than that corresponding
to the preferences of the population with regard to what and how
much of everything wanted shall be produced.   Most arguments
in favor of some organizational and technological advantages of
monopoly (e.g., that it facilitates mass production) miss this point.
Just to give a hint as to what I have in mind: monopolistic concentration of the press may make the newspaper much cheaper,
but what do we read there?   The cheapest of all, indeed, would be
the single paper of the totalitarian state which has no rivals any
more.   We must not assume that monopoly is an obstacle to technological "progress" as such, but it is likely that it favors that sort
of progress which is less wanted on the base of the subjective
valuations of the consumers, and to retard that which is really
wanted.   We all want better and cheaper houses, but here all sorts
of monopoly—not to forget labor monopoly—are in the way condemning millions in the industrial countries to satisfy one of the
most essential wants badly and at excessive costs.

Privileges, exploitation, rigidity of the market, the distortion of
the economic process, the blocking of capital, the concentration of
power, industrial feudalism, the restriction of supply and production, the creation of chronic unemployment, the rise in living costs

and the widening of social differences, lack of economic discipline, the uncontrollable pressure on state and public opinion, the transformation of industry into an exclusive club, which refuses to accept any new members—all these comprise monopolism's list of sins and we are not even sure whether we have completely exhausted it. To avoid any impression of sanctimoniousness we add that, *mutatis mutandis,* the labor unions, too, may develop extremely harmful and dangerous monopolistic powers, particularly when they have succeeded in obtaining the privilege of being the sole representatives of the workers and have received extensive powers from the state. Among others, the well known encroachments committed by the labor union leaders in the United States teach us that this is not an exaggerated assertion.

In order to be able to estimate the chances of successfully combatting monopolies, we must remember that in the great majority of cases it was the state itself which through its legislative, administrative and judicial activities first created conditions favorable to the formation of monopolies. There are in fact not many monopolies in the world which would exist without privileges having been consciously or unconsciously granted by the state, or without some sort of legislative or administrative measure, legal decision or financial policy having been responsible for it, and the fact that hardly any one today properly appreciates this connection makes it all the more dangerous because it makes the actual power which the state can exercise over the monopolies appear much less than it actually is. That the state acted as midwife is quite clear in those cases where a monopoly was expressly granted by a special charter, a procedure which is particularly characteristic of the early history of European monopolies. Even then, however, the grant of monopolies appears to have been a sign of the state's weakness since the state in this way usually tried to free itself from debt, as for example when in Germany Maximilian I granted monopolies to the Fuggers. To similar transactions the Bank of England (1694) and a large number of the big British trading companies owe their existence, and even in our days it was possible for a man like Ivar Kreuger to persuade weak states—among them even the Weimar Republic— to enter upon an infamous agreement granting him the monopoly for the manufacture of matches in return for his taking over the national debt.

It is very useful to recall that in monopolism's early days and right up to the nineteenth century, certain legal rights were established by granting individual privileges which today, due to a most regrettable trend of events, have lost their character of being exceptional and have become a matter of course, so much so that most people have completely forgotten that these rights were originally based on privileges granted by the state and, in spite of their everyday legal aspect, are still that. We are thinking in particular of the legal status of patents and corporations which have proved to be of such importance for the development of modern monopolism. Today we accept both as a matter of course. We, therefore, have to do some thinking and look back into history in order to realize that these are legal institutions which are of very recent origin and were only created after long debate during which the very serious dangers they involve were clearly recognized. As regards patents, there can be no doubt that they are nothing but monopolies expressly granted by the state, with the peculiarity, which accounts for the existence of a patent law, that patents seem justified because they protect intangible property. In order to appreciate fully the effects of the present day patent laws one need only imagine them as abolished in their modern sense and replaced by compulsory licensing, thus leaving the fair compensation of the inventor untouched but depriving big business monopolism of one of its chief supports.

The responsibility which the corporations bear for the development of monopolism is not as plain, and yet it is perhaps the greatest of all. Only, in this case, the relationship is not direct, since the issue of the charter of incorporation does not immediately grant a monopoly as in the case of patents, but creates the conditions necessary for the agglomeration of capital and concentration of manufacturing processes which stamp a great deal of modern industry as more or less monopolist. Although big business and monopolies are not necessarily identical, it is obvious that as an enterprise grows and the number of competitors shrinks correspondingly, the possibility of a monopolist or semi-monopolist control of the market increases, that the market is further and further removed from free and genuine competition, and that the agglomeration of capital and economic power results in a predominance which easily clears the way to monopolies.

This is where the problem of optimum sized plants and the problem of monopolies meet: everything that tends to expand the size of plants or enterprises promotes monopolies, just as anything which counteracts such expansion at the same time promises effectively to counteract monopolies. No one can doubt that corporations not only greatly further the concentration of enterprises but in many cases have alone made it possible. If our economic system can with some justification be called "monopoly capitalism" it is because it has to such a far reaching extent become a system of "corporate capitalism," but this corporate capitalism is the creature of legislation, a product of the work of corporation lawyers and an edifice which rests on the thoughtless multiplication of concessions which the state granted originally only after a most careful consideration of each case and as an exceptional and solemn event.

Today we realize how problematical this legal creation is from every point of view, since the discussion concerning the reform of corporation law seems never ending and has already led to several revisions. Although we are still far from being able to find an answer to all the questions which have arisen, it nevertheless seems as if agreement has been reached on several points. This applies especially to the manner in which the misuse of corporations leads to a particularly questionable interlocking of enterprises, made possible by the establishment of holding companies. It is significant, for example, that in the United States today the battle against monopolies concentrates chiefly on the holding companies whose prohibition would indeed restrict the corporations to that function which alone can justify their dangerous privilege: the raising of capital in cases where large scale production is inevitable. It is also quite obvious that investment trusts and limited liability companies require strict supervision and that the huge capital concentration in the hands of the life insurance companies presents a grave danger unless there is a thorough overhaul of the rules governing investment. In all these respects the experiences of the United States are particularly valuable and lately the reports of the government instituted Temporary National Economic Committee have given us an impressive picture inviting suggestions for reform.

In the case of patents and corporations the state itself has forged and is protecting the legal instruments by which monopolies can be established, but the position is the same where monopolistic power is based on an agreement between independent enterprises (cartel agreements) to which the state is granting legal protection and support by legal sanctions. As it could just as well refuse to extend such protection to a monopoly agreement, and that common sense would regard such a refusal as most natural, we see that here, too, the state is expressly granting monopoly concessions, and of the most dangerous kind to boot. No one, for example, can doubt that the economic development of Germany would have been quite different and much less hampered by monopolies if the German Supreme Court decision of 4th February, 1897, had not created a precedent and legalized cartels, in contrast to the United States where they have been outlawed since the Anti-Trust Law of 1890 (Sherman Act).

But even if the state creates the necessary conditions for the establishment of monopolies by specific or general, conscious or unconscious, direct or indirect concessions, their development is effectively kept in narrow limits as long as they are confined within the national frontiers and have to compete on equal terms with foreign enterprises. This barrier is only removed when the particular monopoly either becomes international or is protected against foreign competition by the state's throttling imports, and here it should be noted that even an international monopoly as a rule presupposes that the particular group of countries exercising each national group is protected by tariffs. From this it follows that in a large number of cases a protectionist trade policy may not be a sufficient, but certainly is a necessary condition for the formation of monopolies. While the protectionist countries, Germany and the United States, have at the same time been foremost in developing industrial monopolism, free trade, although not preventing the (desirable) formation of business pools for the purpose of rationalizing production and reducing costs, effectively prevented such pools from following a monopolist market policy, and not until protective tariffs had provided the necessary conditions in 1932, did English industry in a surprisingly short time and to a really frightening degree assume monopolist forms.

There is no need to explain in great detail that all these monopolies which the state has created present as many possibilities of effective counter-measures as in each case the state actually only needs to take back what it has granted. But this by no means exhausts the possibilities of anti-monopolist measures. Not only can the state put a stop to monopolies by avoiding all action that might promote their formation, it can go further and supplement or replace its passive anti-monopolist policy by an active policy, by attacking the causes of monopolies outside its sphere—for example, certain forms of advertising—by trying to re-establish competition through setting up its own enterprises or by favoring the development of private competitive business, or finally, by prohibiting monopoly agreements and heavily penalizing violations of these prohibitions. That this last mentioned method is quite feasible has been proved by the example of the United States where the Sherman Act of 1890 prohibits all monopolies and all monopoly agreements and even today is still the basis of commercial law in America. If this law has so far proved to be so ineffective it is due to the American government at the same time doing everything to further monopolies indirectly, particularly by increasing tariff rates. Thus the American anti-trust law is an attempt to carry on the battle against monopolies even when no change is made in the economic conditions which favor it. But even a struggle in such difficult circumstances would have brought considerable success if the law had been executed vigorously and interpreted sympathetically by the courts. Both these factors, however, were notoriously lacking until recently, but now that the Sherman Act is really being seriously carried out, remarkable success can be recorded which gives the lie to the dangerous defeatism regarding monopoly policy, and proves that here, too, the state can effectively enforce its authority if it so desires.

Finally, it should be noted that monopolist power can be success-

fully attacked from the side of demand by instructing and informing the consumer. It is particularly the notorious ignorance of the
majority of consumers as regards the goods they buy and their lack
of knowledge about economic budgeting which permit semi-monopolist concentrations and continuous infringements of the principle
of equivalent services in the market for consumption goods. Here
we are faced with a great task which has not yet been sufficiently
recognized and in whose solution housewives' associations, consumers' co-operatives, small traders' organizations, schools and
public bodies should share.

Summarizing our findings, we emphasize that the general
principle should be the destruction of monopolies instead of mere
monopoly control which is politically dangerous and mostly
illusionary. How this is to be done depends on the various causes
of monopolies which must be explored in each case and attacked
accordingly (tariffs, subsidies, privileges, abuse of publicity, patent
laws, company laws, laws and jurisdiction on all sorts of economic
associations, &c.). As a background of such a policy an Anti-trust
law after the American example (without its drawbacks and lack
of enforcement) would be necessary in order to establish the fundamental legal principle of a competitive society. Besides that we
recommend a policy of encouraging competitors (private, co-opera-
tivist, or public) wherever markets have become sticky (e.g., in the
highly important case of the building industries). For the public
utilities we favor governmental (or municipal) monopolies under
strict control of representative democracy. An important help
might be the establishment of a special state board charged with
the thorough investigation of all cases of monopoly and with X-ray-
ing the whole structure of the economy wherever there is something shunning the light. The findings of this board would get
the widest possible publicity, which, in itself, would be an efficient
measure against monopoly. They would also be used by legislation
or jurisdiction as instruments of anti-monopoly policy.

The recommendation to make public utilities governmental
monopolies has not been given by us without a good deal of
reluctance. Any enthusiasm in this respect will be damped by the
well-known experiences which have been made almost everywhere
with public enterprises. In theory, public monopolies might be
geared consciously to the common interest, and in the case of the
state-owned (municipal) public utilities we must cling desperately
to this hope. In practice, however, everything depends on the kind
of government and on the kind of monopoly. The more monopolies are taken over by the state, the more likely it is that the
government will be of the wrong kind.

The case of the public utilities is the only concession we would
be prepared to make to the idea of public monopolies, and even this

we do only grudgingly and with an open mind for the possible disadvantages of this solution. Generally, we do not consider the nationalization of private monopolies, as projected by socialist governments, as an adequate solution of the monopoly problem. On the contrary, nationalization would create the worst possible monopoly, that of the collectivist state, while we have no guarantee that it will be even exploited in the public interest (which would be very hard to define, anyway).

Let us finally stress that we must combat most energetically the defeatest notion that "monopoly has come to stay." The return to a genuinely competitive society is possible if we want the conditions necessary for such a return. One of the most important among these is in our view a simultaneous change of our whole economic and social system in favor of drastic decentralization of cities and industries, of the restoration of some more "natural order," more rural, but less urbanized, mechanized, industrialized, proletarized and commercialized. People will not like to face competition unless they have some firm stand. They must not feel lost in this present dehumanized world. Competition is a necessary social arrangement not a social gospel likely to make us enthusiastic. It is a negative concept which derives its strength from the fact that we like the alternatives, i.e., monopoly and collectivism, even less. It must be supplemented by something which is humanly positive.

An International New Order

We have purposely left the question of an international new order until the end of this book and have at the same time incurred the disadvantage of not being able to devote the space to it that it deserves. Our reason for this is twofold. Firstly, it should by now be plain that the international reform of our economic system must not only correspond in its basic aspects to the reforms carried out in each country, but in fact presupposes such reforms, just as the decay of the international economic order for the past decades can only be understood in terms of the decay of the national market economies. Here too, charity begins at home, and nothing seems to us to illustrate the confusion of our world better than the fact that many recommend the return to a liberal international economic order but favor collectivist tendencies at home without even realizing that they are contradicting themselves. Secondly, however, it is obvious that the instability of the international situation today (1941) imposes on us a certain restraint when discussing international affairs in view of the uncertainty of future developments.

But whatever shape the world of the future will assume, one thing is certain: after this war and for the first time for innumerable ages truly gigantic problems will *have* to be faced and solved by humanity as a whole notwithstanding all the devastation and passions which the war will have left in its wake. Let us explain what is at issue. Ethnology, anthropology and philology seem to be in agreement today on the "monophyletic" origin of man from a primeval horde, closely knit and maintaining peaceful relations by virtue of a common language, descent and surroundings, and thus the progress-drunk picture of history of the past century, with which we have already dealt, is completely reversed. It is becoming more and more likely that originally there really existed a society living in a small and easily surveyable area, closely confined by natural obstacles, a society in which unity, friendliness and peace reigned and whose members, fighting an arduous battle against the forces of nature, had neither cause nor taste for killing each other.

If this hypothesis—which in a strange way recalls the old myths of the "Golden Age" and the "Tower of Babel"—is correct, we can confidently assert that after thousands of years mankind today finds itself for the first time once more in a position which in decisive aspects is similar to the starting point.

After thousands of years of segregation and wandering, mankind has once more reached the borders of a thoroughly familiar world which this time encompasses the whole planet and in which we find practically everywhere men to whom we feel related at least as regards outward living conditions. This earth no longer harbors anything strange that might attract the adventurous and rapacious; it has been divided up and whoever wants to expand his domain can only do so by trespassing on the property of men of his own kind. We have completed the inventory of our planet and know now that there are no empty spaces, no other Mississippi valley, no second Argentine, no new Canada, open to mass settlement, and it is perhaps our good fortune that now, when the earth is fully populated, the truly unique population increase of the last century seems slowly—much too slowly, in truth—to be ebbing. These billions of people who are jostling each other on the earth today are not only conditioned by the increasing uniformity of their civilization, but are, at the same time, dependent on an apparatus of mass supply which spans the whole earth and forces them to co-operate in the economic field whether they want to or not. If we add to this that progress in communications has led to a tremendous shrinking of distances, we can say without exaggeration that the majority of mankind today live in a closer and more active social and economic relationship than did the subjects of any of the great empires of the past. The individual nations have become like cantons that will have to decide how to adjust themselves to this development.

After decades of fumbling a decision will at last have to be made, now that all the inadequate solutions have been tried out and everyone has come to realize the real reason why the world cannot get peace: the intolerable contradiction between those forces and necessities which strive for co-operation on the one hand and international political anarchy on the other, in short, between the necessity for international integration and actual disintegration, between ruthless nationalism and a world-wide development of trade and civilization. This contradiction must indeed be reconciled, but none of us will doubt that it is a task more difficult than any which mankind has ever had to solve. Here, as always, the first step toward a solution consists in our clearly understanding the nature of the problem, soberly estimating the possibilities of a solution and then plainly announcing the conclusions which force themselves upon us, while leaving it to the statesmen to make such use of them as they believe they can answer for before history.

The period between 1814 and 1914 has proved that, with good will all around, the solution of the problem is not impossible. At that time there really existed an international economic order worthy of this name, which fulfilled those conditions which alone give meaning and permanence to international economic integration. This international economy was not merely the aggregate of foreign trade statistics of the various nations but a genuine organic unit in the sense of an interdependent system of international economic relations. As such the international economy was at the same time "multilateral," i.e., able to move freely without being hampered by exchange controls, clearing agreements and quota regulations (bilateralism) and able therefore to transfer import and export transactions from one country to another whenever necessary, and in this way profit from any change in prices ("arbitrage"), thereby bringing about a real price union without which no genuine economic integration is possible, nationally or internationally. The canalization of international economic relations as they have become customary today in the age of clearing agreements, was unknown, but that in turn presupposed that world trade had at its disposal a genuinely international currency system, a condition which, as is known, was met by the gold standard. Thus this world economic order was necessarily not only a market and a price union, but at the same time a payments union. Indeed, the one is not possible without the other and once one has admitted the necessity of an international economic order, one will also have to accept its conditions for better or for worse. But all this presupposed that the individual states' interventions in international trade were restricted to such measures as—being of a compatible kind—might reduce full economic integration but could not disrupt it. These interventions consisted chiefly in import tariffs whilst Great Britain and her crown colonies—supported by the liberal commercial policy of smaller countries—represented the free trade core of the international economic system.

All these conditions, on the fulfilment of which our former and indeed any world economic system depended and depends, themselves presuppose another factor of a higher and extra-economic nature, viz., the existence of the firm political and moral framework of an international order. Economic integration—a network consisting of the division of labor, the mutual exchange of products and the specialization of production, coupled with the precarious dependence which it imposes on the individual worker—cannot extend further than the sphere of political, social and moral integration which guarantees a minimum of law, order, security, and dependable ethics. And conversely, political, social and moral disintegration, the decay of the indispensable extra-economic framework, will sooner or later entail economic disintegration. This constitutes the simplest and most elementary law of economic history, which allows of no exception; and it also explains the dissolution of the modern world economic system.

The grave risks involved in the intricate inter-dependence of individuals can only be borne if a strict legal order and an unwritten but generally recognized code of minimum ethical standards ensure that all members of a society based on the division of labor, feel secure in an atmosphere of mutual confidence and safety. Economic integration—i.e., an extensive form of the division of labor—can only develop to the extent to which the conditions providing a successful legal system and an accompanying ethical code are fulfilled. While within the national economy the community and the state guarantee law and order, an intensification of international trade has always resulted in particular difficulties because the establishment of international order belongs among the exceptional achievements of world history. If, in spite of that, world trade could develop so fabulously during the nineteenth century, we find that it was due to that century really succeeding in establishing an international order which however distant from the ideal state, represents nevertheless an achievement whose extent we can only today recognize in its entirety. What was the nature of this order?

Today we are agreed that the Middle Ages, however much we may find fault with them in other respects, possessed to a very high degree an international order which lost none of its effects because it was essentially of a moral-theological nature and its denominational limitations confined it to Christendom. After this order, on whose basis a remarkable "medieval world economy" was developed, had been disrupted by the evolution of national absolutism, Europe was engulfed by an anarchy in which law, order and security threatened to disappear and in which, as under the "law of the jungle," the weak were completely at the mercy of the strong. The creation of a new international order became imperative, and the entire European history of the last four hundred years may be looked upon as one great struggle for the solution of this gigantic task. Three ways were open, and all three have been tried with varying success. The first is the co-operative method—a firm international organization of states, a "Civitas Maxima" (Christian Wolff)—and this concept engrossed leading European intellectuals again and again, whilst the League of Nations was the first and unfortunately unsuccessful attempt to translate it into practice. The second way is the imperial way, the establishment of a European empire by force, but here again all attempts—from Charles V to Napoleon—have miscarried, fortunately for Europe, and until today it has been England's historical mission always to help avert this misfortune in her own interest. There only remains, then, the "Third Way," which Europe—lately together with the entire civilized world outside of Europe—has successfully followed: the way of that international order which we saw at its peak in the nineteenth century and which we shall proceed to describe now.

It has become customary to call the international order of the nineteenth century a *Pax Britannica* in which the *Pax Romana* of antiquity and the *Pax Christiana* of the medieval Church are supposed to have found their direct successor. It is true that England's predominant position—approximately from the Treaty of Utrecht until the First World War—was an essential pillar of world trade whose decay England should not have regarded with equanimity, if only in the interest of world trade, without helping to procure a modern substitute. But we must not be content with this as yet very crude conception. We must first of all note that hegemony may mean very different things. While it is absolutely correct that the liberal world order can hardly be conceived without the core of British power, trade and finance, it is nevertheless decisive that this core itself was, after all, liberal and thus made possible a liberal world trade, and that is precisely the reason why the world in the last resort tolerated the British Empire. Of course, this core would not have been able to lead without the power and prestige of the British Empire, but this is no valid objection to a liberal world economy and even less is it a justification for an un-liberal world empire, of which we may doubt whether it could even exist. It is at any rate significant that the British Empire became much more open to criticism the moment it renounced, a decade ago, the liberal tradition, and took the path of economic nationalism.

We must further remember that the *Pax Britannica* was only a part of the international order which assured world trade, and perhaps it was not even the most important one. It is a wrong view, derogatory to the non-British world, that in the final analysis only English sea power has kept the globe in order to the degree required by an intensive and multilateral world trade. No, all civilized countries participated in this as long as they looked upon tacit respect for an unwritten international order—a secularized *Pax Christiana*—as a matter of course. A network of long-term treaties spanned the world, based on the universally acknowledged law of nations, the adjustment of tensions between large and small countries—the often misinterpreted "balance of power"—an international monetary system (the gold standard) and a high degree of consensus on the concepts of law and national legal norms. This external order was pervaded by an atmosphere of a certain loyalty and fairness in international relations which made it unchivalrous, dishonorable and inconsiderate to overstep certain limits of national egoism and to disregard obligations and "rules of the game." This secularized *Pax Christiana* was the true basis of world trade at the destruction of which the ideological termites had worked for generations until suddenly the proud and recently refurnished edifice collapsed.

There is no point in decrying this liberal and multilateral world economy unless first of all one understands and appreciates its greatest achievement, for only thus can we recognize how difficult are the problems with which a reconstruction of the world economy confronts us. Not only did it provide that world-embracing apparatus for satisfying the needs of the masses without which our world, notwithstanding all autarkic tendencies, is no longer conceivable, but beyond that—and just because it was a true, i.e., a multilateral, economic world order—it ensured the political neutralization of international economic relations in a manner which has already been described in this book. Only now that this true world economy no longer exists and a number of piecemeal exchange relations have taken its place, can we realize the true extent of that achievement and the urgent necessity again to create an equivalent, if we want to give peace and order back to the world.

But how can the reconstruction of a genuine world economic order be effected? Will the regional or continental blocks, which have been discussed so much recently, play an important role in it? It is impossible to discuss this unless one has previously agreed that these "Grossraüme" look very different according to whether they are open or closed, whether they are of a co-operative or imperial character, whether they are welded together by compulsory bilateral agreements or whether they afford free "multi-laterality." Now, if the "Grossraüme" are closed and imperial and of a compulsorily bilateral character, they cannot be expected to solve the problem of the reconstruction of a genuine world economic order. They would merely perpetuate the war of all against all, since one could not rely on a permanent saturation of such autarkic regions nor on a genuine balance of interests within each area concerned. The dissolution of the world economy into such areas is the expression and the result of international disintegration, it may even be its climax, but it represents by no means a victory over it.

The evolution of economic "Grossraüme" which we have witnessed for the past decade is indeed nothing but a manifestation of that process of bilateralism in the world economy whose last stages are compulsory clearing agreements. Compulsory bilateralism is, however, only another term for the disintegration and decay of the world economic order, which is quite incompatible with such a two-sided compulsory relationship and can only be conceived as multilateral. Only when it is multilateral is the world economic order, just as any national economy, a market, price and payments union, and only then can it also be a production union. However, multilateralism is quite incompatible with any trade policy making use of more than a moderate degree of protective tariffs. A multilateral world economy presupposed that international trade is uncontrolled and that that equality of trading conditions obtains which was formerly guaranteed by the most-favored-nation clause incorporated in commercial treaties, but it also requires that in no case should there be clearing compulsion (a compulsion which is no less detrimental to multilateral world trade, even if several countries are parties to it). The old form of multilateral world trade represented an extremely functional and intricate switchboard where the economic relations between the nations were related to each other in such a manner that the industrial states could obtain their industrial raw materials without the slightest difficulty by re-exporting their products sometimes by way of several other countries, and where the nations producing raw materials could sell their products on a uniform world market, and could pay for their foreign debts and keep their currencies in order without chronic difficulties. If at that time the industrial states had neither a raw material problem nor a foreign exchange problem (in present-day jargon, "a dollar shortage"), the key to that mystery was the multilateral character of world trade, a discovery which, however, many people still seem to ignore. This also gives us an idea of the devastating effects of bilateralism during recent times. It destroyed the switchboard and short-circuited the world economy, and the result was the decay of world trade and all its effects with which we are faced today, its division into individual blocks, its politicalization, the destruction of its market, price and payments union, and, finally, the sudden appearance of a "raw material problem" which began to harass several industrial nations.

If, therefore, we must seek the true solution in exactly the opposite direction, the obvious way is, of course, a return to a liberal and multilateral form of world trade with tolerable tariffs, most-favored-nation clauses, the policy of the open door, the gold standard, and the elimination of closed compulsory blocks (with their machinery of exchange controls and clearing agreements). It is very easy to acquire the reputation of being a realist by declaring such a return to be utopian. No doubt it is that, but saying so will not get us anywhere; rather, a careful study of all the obstacles in the path should be made in order to ascertain under what conditions the essentials of a genuine (i.e., free and multilateral) world economy can be realized. By adopting this procedure, we are trying to solve the problem of reconstructing the world economy by a "Third Way," too, i.e., by an economic and social structure which releases us from the sterile "either—or" of collectivism and laissez-faire and which seems to us the only possible way out, both domestically and internationally. We get a clearer idea of what this "Third Way" looks like in the world economic order if we remember that there are two chief obstacles in the way of the establishment of free and multilateral world trade: the ambitious aims and collectivist methods of present-day domestic economic policies (the decay of the market economy) in every country, and, very closely linked to these, international political anarchy.

The former obstacle can only be overcome by finding a solution for the problems of domestic economic policy which is in keeping with the program of the "Third Way" and which, not being collectivist in domestic affairs, also does not place collectivist shackles on foreign trade. The second obstacle, however, forces us to the conclusion to which all such thoughts must necessarily lead: the necessity for a true world union, whose structure must be genuinely federal, i.e., composed of regional and continental sub-groups. That is the positive content with which we can endow the concept of international blocks. No one is naive enough to believe that such a transformation can be carried out without the leadership of a dominating group of nations. It is our firm conviction, however, that such a group will dominate and lead permanently only if its actions are ruled by the insights which have been traced here, if it arranges the world in accordance with the concepts of liberty and equal rights and the old principle "suum cuique," and if it considers its task as a trusteeship which devolved on it in one of the most critical moments of the history of mankind. The decisive factor will not be outward power, but in the last analysis solely intellectual and moral maturity.

PART TWO—NOTES TO CHAPTER III

Note No. 1 (page 201). Peasantry and peasant agriculture:

The problems discussed in this chapter are more fully dealt with in my book *International Economic Disintegration* (London-New York, 1942, Part IV). There I wrote (pp. 112-113): "The author is fully aware that the word 'peasant,' having clearly disparaging connotations, is no real equivalent to the French word 'paysan' or the German word 'Bauer.' It is clear, however, that the word 'farmer' must be reserved for a special type of agriculturalist who often is not a 'paysan' or 'Bauer.' Other terms which have been suggested to the author by his Anglo-Saxon friends—like 'agricultural freeholder' or 'farmer yeoman'—sound too artificial and laborious. The only possibility left, then, would seem to be to retain the word 'peasant,' and to ask the Anglo-Saxon reader to forget for the moment its pejorative sense until a better term is suggested. That this is not an insolent demand is proved by the fact that good English writers like G. K. Chesterton have used it before in a clearly laudatory sense. It has been shown, therefore, that it can be done. The reader should also be reminded that no less an author than J. Stuart Mill wrote, in his *Principles,* special chapters which bear the title 'Of Peasant Proprietors' (Book II, chap. VI-VII) and which, from beginning to end, are a real panegyric on peasantry in the continental sense. 'The generality of English writers,' he says (*Principles,* ed. by Ashley, London, 1929, p. 256), 'are no better acquainted practically with peasant proprietors, and have almost always the most erroneous ideas of their social condition and mode of life. Yet the old traditions even of England are on the same side with the general opinion of the Continent.' Nor should it be forgotten that William Thornton published in 1848 his *Plea for Peasant Proprietors,* to say nothing of Wordsworth and other poets. So we feel in very good company. It is, of course, not without deep significance that it is so difficult to find an English equivalent of 'paysan' and 'Bauer,' for if the thing itself existed there would be a word for it. The rather disreputable sense of 'peasant' arises surely out of the fate of peasantry under British feudalism, and the Anglo-Saxon settlers transplanted this sense to the United States and the Dominions. It seems that in the United States the word has fallen still more into disrepute by the fact that the reminiscences of old-world feudalism have been freshly supplemented by the new feudalism in the Southern States, which was based on the subjection of people belonging even to another race of a different color. It is more than probable, however, that in the United States there are more real peasants in the very respectable French, Scandinavian, Swiss or German sense than the habit of abhorring the term itself would suggest. It is equally probable that on the average they are quietly prospering, which explains why we hear so little about them. At all events, the whole question is badly in need of a thorough investigation."

It must indeed not be forgotten that agriculture in the overseas settlements—"farmer" agriculture—was in the main developed by peasants who had escaped the feudal oppression of their European homelands and naturally carried with them and perpetuated a conception of the peasant which dated from that time and was not modified by the European liberation of the peasants. Both in an economic as well as in a sociological sense the overseas farming system contains generally only little of the peasant element. The "farmer" system and the "peasant" system are two quite different types of agriculture. Whereas the "old world" type of peasant agriculture has developed historically from the self-sufficient peasant holding with its correspondingly diverse production program and only gradually has begun to produce for the market, the basis of the overseas type of agriculture has from the beginning been a specialized and commercial form of production for the market. How near, however, the peasant system comes to the natural form of agriculture is shown by the fact that overseas agriculture is gradually adopting certain features of peasant farming, partly for reasons of efficiency, partly in order to reduce the risks of a highly specialized and commercialized form of farming. Characteristically enough, it is above all in the United States that more and more experts are now recommending such a development—even including the self-sufficient "subsistence farm." This drive converges with a development which can be observed in the agriculture of the tropical countries. Here a capitalistic large-scale form of agriculture has been developed which we call the plantation system. This system is not only most regrettable from a social point of view, and perhaps for this reason plus the growing emancipation of the colored people cannot be maintained much longer, but is, at the same time, burdened with all the dangers of capitalist overproduction, which has, particularly during the past ten years, become an economic world problem. As in the case of non-tropical agriculture there are three ways of solving this problem: (1) unfettered and free competition and non-interference with economic forces; (2) planned regulation of tropical raw material production; and (3) the reconversion of capitalist and speculative specialization and a return to the mixed farming methods of the peasant. It becomes increasingly clear that the last mentioned solution (the return to peasant methods in overseas raw material production) is the method which—apart from being attractive from the human and social aspect—seems the most suitable for overcoming an era of intolerable speculative-capitalist exploitation. It also seems as if this development is beginning to make its way in a quite natural manner, unless it is throttled, as in the Netherlands East Indies, by state regulations in the interest of the plantation corporations (cf. J. van Gelderen, *The Recent Development of Economic Foreign Policy in the Netherlands East Indies,* London, 1939, page 53 ff.). In favorable contrast to this is the plan of the Belgian Prime Minister, Paul van Zeeland, to carry out a policy of introducing the peasant system in the Belgian Congo (*L'expérience van Zeeland en Belgique,* Lausanne, 1940, page 187). In the cocoa growing districts of the Gold Coast, too, peasant agriculture has proved successful among the natives. This development is a particularly good illustration of the essence of the "Third Way": neither speculative-capitalist large-scale enterprises, nor a mechanically planned economy, but a third method—in this case, peasant agriculture.

It is, as a matter of fact, not only of philological interest but at the same time very revealing in this context that the German world "Bauer" is not derived from "bauen" (to build) at all, but from "Nachbar" (neighbor)—the Dutch word for neighbor is to this day "buur"—and thus expresses the friendly warmth of the village community. (F. Kluge, *Etymologisches Wörterbuch der deutschen Sprache,* 10th edition, Berlin, 1924, page 43.)

Note No. 2 (page 205). The special position of agriculture:

The following points will briefly stress the extent to which agriculture occupies a special place as compared with other branches of production:

(1) It is in every aspect an organic process which is subject to natural forces and has a number of important consequences (limitations of mechanization and division of labor, constant necessity of conserving the soil by means of a complex system of precautions, a tendency of decreasing returns, irregularity and uncertainty of the harvest, the unchangeable rhythm of the seasons or even longer periods necessary for growth, the difficulties of

storage, necessity of mixed farming, a smaller optimum size of the enterprise than in industry).

(2) The socially conditioned forces controlling supply and demand are of a special character in the case of agriculture (little elasticity of supply and demand, and consequently agrarian crises of a special type). For these reasons no parallels can be found in agriculture for such phenomena as unemployment, closing down of plants, advertising, formation of trusts, financing by sale of securities and many others familiar to industry.

(3) Because of its peculiar structure, agriculture has specific problems of agrarian credit, property, leasehold tenure and inheritance which result in the grave problem of agrarian indebtedness.

(4) For various reasons agriculture has to struggle with a particular labor problem which makes it difficult for it to compete with industry in the labor market under the same conditions. This is actually another reason why a family farm is preferable to a large agricultural enterprise.

(5) The sociological peculiarities of agriculture, make it not a business just like any other but a form of living to which one is born. Hence the peasant's conservatism and love for tradition and the possibility of two farmers of widely different ability existing next to each other. A peasant produces primarily to cover his needs and only secondarily to sell a surplus, whereas it would be silly to suppose that Mr. Ford first makes cars for his own family and sells them only as far as some are left over.

All these peculiarities (and there are many more we could mention) explain the recurrence and the particularly stubborn character of agrarian crises and the special place agriculture occupies in the modern capitalist system—leading to the question of how far it fits into this system at all. There can be no doubt that during the past hundred years agriculture has to a greater or lesser degree always been one of the problem children of capitalist development and has called for special economic policies.

Cf. C. v. Dietze, *Landwirtschaft und Weltbewerbsordnung,* "Schmollers Jahrbuch," vol. 66, 1942, pp. 129-157; C. v. Dietze, *Bauernwirtschaft und Kollektiv,* "Schweizerische Zeitschrift für Volkswirtschaft und Statistik," vol. 82, 1946, pp. 230-259; W. Röpke, *International Economic Disintegration,* chap. IX; W. Röpke, *Das Agrarproblem der Vereinigten Staaten,* "Archiv für Sozialwissenschaft," volumes 58 and 59, 1927-1928.

Note No. 3 (page 206). Agriculture in Denmark and in England:

It is well known that Danish agriculture was able to develop in such an exemplary manner under free trade after Denmark had decided to escape the international wheat crisis in the 1870's and 1880's by changing its agricultural system from one-sided wheat production to more intensive cattle raising largely on cheap imported feedingstuffs, instead of following the example of Germany and other countries who decided to adopt an increasingly strict policy of protective tariffs. This energetic and courageous re-adjustment required, of course, spiritual resources which Denmark found among its excellent peasant stock and in the profound intellectual and religious reform movement (people's universities, &c.) which under the leadership of Bishop Grundtvig, followed the defeat of 1864. Denmark's example contradicts the opinion based on the experiences of England, that free trade is bound to ruin agriculture, and that sound agriculture must be paid for by a policy of protection and subsidies. This is a very crude idea which pays no attention to the special and complicated conditions responsible for the decay of English agriculture during the nineteenth century. This decay overcame an agricultural system which had lost its strength, its vitality and its social soundness because it had lost its peasantry. It was not free trade that injured English agriculture and forced it into dubious paths, but the preceding destruction of the agrarian peasant order through feudalism. This is also substantiated by the fact that even when English agriculture was relatively prosperous—as during the time just before the First World War—it continued its extensive trend (by way of turning arable land into pastures) without interruption. "Unfortunately we cannot believe that the establishment of a reliable price-system with good marketing as a basis for the industry would be enough by itself. During the years before the war when agriculture was doing well, land still continued to be laid down to grass because a living could be got that way in place of more active cultivation" (Lord Addison of Stallingborough, *A Policy for British Agriculture,* London, 1939, page 217). Cf. also Sir William E. Cooper, *England's Fatal Land Policy,* London, 1913.

Note No. 4 (page 207). Agricultural methods that ravage the land:

In all quarters suspicion is increasing today that the extravagant ideas concerning the stepping up of agricultural production were due to technical and mechanical conceptions which were most inappropriate for agriculture. Danger signals are appearing which indicate that the most important production factor of agriculture, i.e., the soil, exhibits definite symptoms of exhaustion when too vigorously exploited by mechanical and chemical means. The experience of the United States in this respect has become particularly well known. Especially those semi-arid areas in the Middle West whose initially so successful opening up was only fifteen years ago the bugbear of the older wheat growing districts, have in the meantime deteriorated into the dreaded "dust bowl" where the land, robbed of its humus, has become a sandy desert: this, by the way, is the ghostly symbol of a society tired and atomized by thoughtless mechanization. Everywhere—in India, Africa and Australia, as well as in certain parts of Europe—soil erosion has become a grave problem and there are experts whose pessimism goes so far as to prophesy the most serious consequences for the food supply of the world within a generation if the present tendencies of agricultural production should continue. The often mentioned "steppefication" of Germany (due to the chemical forcing of the soil, thoughtless deforestation, and the consequent lowering of the ground water level, the excessive exploitation of the soil and the over-industrialization of certain areas) also should be mentioned here.

Note No. 5 (page 207). Reserves of demand for agricultural produce:

The League of Nations report mentioned in the foregoing chapter is the "Report on Nutrition." Cf. also F. L. M'Dougall, *Food and Welfare,* Geneva, 1938. We quote here some figures to illustrate the growing importance of the "new" foodstuffs: in 1938 the total value of the world export of fruit was greater than that of wheat and meat, and from 1909-13 to 1934-35 the consumption of fruit in England rose by 89 per cent. (E. W. Tessin, *Welthandel mit Früchten,* Internationale Agrar-Rundschau, March, 1939).

Note No. 6 (page 209). Specialized production requires increased acreage:

In order to illustrate this important fact we quote the estimates of the American expert, O. E. Baker (from "Internationale Konferenz für Agrarwissenschaft," Leipzig, 1934, page 363):
Acreage necessary for the production of the annual food requirements per capita (=1.4 million calories):

Sugar beets	-	-	- 0.28	tomatoes	-	- 1.47
cane sugar	-	-	- 0.34	apples	-	- 2.35
potatoes	-	-	- 0.76	pork and bacon	-	3.10 + 0.1 pasture
corn meal	-	-	- 0.79	milk	-	2.35 + 1.6 pasture
wheat flour	-	-	- 1.45	beef	-	- 11.30 + 2.5 pasture

Note No. 7 (page 210). The sins of the wheat protection policy:

As a rule the wheat protection policies of the European countries were in favor of large estates and detrimental to peasant agriculture. Cf. W. Röpke, *German Commercial Policy*, London, 1934; A. G. Street, *Farming England*, London, 1937; C. T. Schmidt, *The Plough and the Sword: Labor, Land and Property in Fascist Italy*, New York, 1938. From a wider view: W. Röpke, *International Economic Disintegration*, chap. XIII; L. Robbins, *Economic Planning and International Order*, London, 1937, page 134 ff; and the League of Nations monograph, *Considerations on the Present Evolution of Agricultural Protectionism*, Geneva, 1935.

Note No. 8 (page 213). Neo-feudal estates or collective farms:

It does not make much difference whether one calls the communal enterprises, consisting of a large central estate and surrounding peasant holdings, which some agrarian reformers envisage, neo-feudal estates or collective farms. In both cases their structure is in essentials that of the East-German estate which subjects the peasants to a system of allowances in kind and it is immaterial what more or less tempting name we give to this system. As regards the Russian collective farms system one need only recall that it necessitated one of the most cruel mass exterminations in order to overcome the opposition of the peasants to this new order and that subsequently the Russian government saw itself forced to expand constantly individual peasant farming again. It is most characteristic that the peasants on the Russian collective farms as soon as they had been assigned private garden plots proceeded to farm these most intensively while neglecting their work on the collective farm and constantly reducing the latter by illegal means ("Economist," 27th September, 1941). It seems that nothing in the world can serve as a substitute for peasant ownership. And it must further be remembered that the Russian peasant is far less attached to his land than his European counterpart. On the Russian experience and on the fate of the German peasant under the collectivist policy of the Third Reich, see the two studies by Professor v. Dietze, mentioned in Note 2.

Note No. 9 (page 217). Policies encouraging the crafts:

Cf. Fritz Marbach, *Theorie des Mittelstandes*, Berne, 1942; Emil Anderegg, *Schweizerische Gewerbepolitik auf neuer Grundlage*, St. Gall, 1940; W. Röpke, *Die Funktion des Klein- und Mittelbetriebes*, "Handwerk und Kleinhandel in der modernen Volkswirtschaft," St. Gall, 1947, pp. 21-40. A thorough sociological investigation of occupations would have to consider that several professions based on academic training also show traces of the craftsman, for example, the occupation of the apothecary, which, however, due to the development of large-scale pharmaceutical industries and the trade mark system, is unfortunately, but characteristically enough, doomed to a process of decline which one might describe under the heading "From Mortar and Pestle to Drug Store." It is possible that new trends in medicine may bring about a desirable renaissance in this field.

Note No. 10 (page 218). Small traders:

On this comprehensive and much discussed subject consult: Richard

Buechner, *Einzelhandel und Mittelstandspolitik,* Zürich, 1940, and Fritz Marbach's book mentioned above. We would mention that regarding this subject one should refrain from dogmatism of any kind and consider the best possible solution to be a balance of the various forms of enterprise in the retail trade (small traders, consumers' co-operatives, large trading enterprises). One will also have to distinguish between the various branches of retailing and recognize—perhaps with a heavy heart—the particularly problematic character of the grocer.

Note No. 11 *(page 222).* *The optimum size of industrial enterprises:*

As regards the influence which self-financing has on the size of an enterprise, cf. W. Röpke, *Die Theorie der Kapitalbildung,* Tübingen, 1929, page 18 f. In this connection it should also be pointed out that in Japan the small industrial enterprise plays an outstanding role and has proved to be very viable (T. Uyeda, *The Small Industries of Japan,* London, 1938; E. Reubens, *Small-scale industry in Japan,* "Quarterly Journal of Economics," August, 1947). The industrial re-organization of China under Chiang-Kai-Chek in the form of co-operative small enterprises ("Indusco"), also deserves mention here. The whole question was recently thoroughly investigated in the United States by the Temporary National Economic Committee (in particular in the report of the Federal Trade Commission, *Relative Efficiency of Large, Medium-sized and Small Business,* Washington D.C., 1941) which plainly proves the average superiority of the medium-sized and small enterprises.

Nobody who is really informed can deny either the strength of small business in Switzerland or its beneficient effects, but there are some who believe that the case of Switzerland can be dismissed as an exception. That this is not true is proved by the fact that conditions in many other countries (Württemberg, Austria, Italy, Belgium, Holland, or France) are rather similar. On the case of Württemberg, see: Erich Preiser, *Die württembergische Wirtschaft als Vorbild,* Stuttgart, 1937. General references for the question of optimum size: S. R. Dennison, *The Problem of Bigness,* "The Cambridge Journal," November, 1947; A. D. H. Kaplan, *Small Business: Its Place and Problems,* New York, 1948; T. K. Quinn, *I Quit Monster Business,* New York, 1948; K. Gruber, *Die Zusammenhänge zwischen Grösse, Kosten und Rentabilität industrieller Betriebe,* "Zeitschrift für Nationalökonomie," 1948; J. M. Blair, *Does large-scale enterprise result in low costs?* "American Economic Review," May, 1948; Colin Clark, *The Conditions of Economic Progress,* London, 1940; W. Röpke, *Civitas Humana;* W. Röpke, *Klein- und Mittelbetrieb in der Volkswirtschaft,* "Ordo," Jahrbuch für die Ordnung von Wirtschaft und Gesellschaft, vol. I, Godesberg, 1948, pp. 155-174.

On the problem of the geographical decentralization of industries ("dispersal") consult: J.-F. Gravier, *Paris et le désert français,* Paris, 1947; E. T. Peterson, *Cities are abnormal,* Norman, 1946; *La Modernisation de la Vie Rurale,* Association des Maires de France, Paris, 1948; W. Röpke, *Civitas Humana.*

Note No. 12 *(page 223).* *The care of the sick and the problem of the medical profession:*

The economic and social aspect of medicine presents an extremely grave and as yet unsolved problem which can be mentioned here only in passing. But we may at least say that compulsory health insurance of a whole people is no solution but merely one particular aspect of the general disastrous collectivization and proletarization, i.e., part of that river which is carrying its murky waters into the sea of collectivism. We cannot elaborate here what form a true solution might take and the experiences one would have to make use of in working it out. How much easier, healthier and more human all such questions appear under the simple and neighborly conditions of the open country is shown by the recollections of the author whose ancestors were country practitioners as far back as the eighteenth century. Neither his father nor his grandfather nor his great-grandfather knew of anyone whose poverty excluded him from their medical assistance; their services were paid for automatically in the way of neighborly intercourse, perhaps by wood cutting in the fall or by lending a hand in the garden or in the fields. A family doctor, in the sense of a secular confessor, only the landed gentry could afford, but this was a luxury which had the advantage of permitting the medical ancestors of the author the luxury of tending the poor. Human relations were pleasant in every respect in this world until it was gradually permeated by the collectivization which also invaded the open country, a sad process which deserves to be described by some one who knows it from personal experience and observation.

Note No. 13 *(page* 228). *The fundamental error of the laissez-faire principle:*
    The old liberal concept of a state with a "neutral" function in economic affairs is based on the completely erroneous idea that one can "do without" the state in a differentiated social economy. But this idea is not feasible, as in all circumstances the state must provide the legal conditions under which the economic process takes place. Whichever method it adopts in determining these conditions influences the economic order. Thus the state interferes in any case, the question merely being how and where.

Note No. 14 *(page* 228). *The sins of monopolism:*
    In this connection the following should be consulted: Franz Boehm, *Wettbewerb und Monopolkampf,* Berlin, 1933; E. Chamberlin, *The Theory of Monopolistic Competition,* 5th edition, Cambridge, Mass., 1946; W. Lippmann, *The Good Society,* Boston, 1937; Walter Eucken, *Foundations of Economics,* London, 1950; A. Wolfers, *Das Kartellproblem in Lichte der deutschen Kartelliteratur,* "Schriften des Vereins für Sozialpolitik," volume 180/1, Munich, 1931; A. Wolfers, *Uber monopolistische und nicht-monopolistische Wirtschaftsverbände,* "Archiv für Sozialwissenschaft," volume 59, 1927; A. R. Burns, *The Decline of Competition,* New York, 1936; L. Miksch, *Wettbewerb als Aufgabe,* 2nd edition, Godesberg, 1947; A. Rüstow in "Schriften des Vereins für Sozialpolitik," volume 187, Munich, 1932, page 60 ff.; W. Röpke, *Kapitalismus und Konkurrenz-system,* "Zeitschrift für schweizerische Statistik und Volkswirtschaft," 72nd year, No. 3, 1936; T. W. Arnold, *The Bottlenecks of Business,* New York, 1940; also the monographs of the Temporary National Economic Committee, Washington D.C., 1940-41; J. M. Clark, *Alternative to Serfdom,* New York, 1948; E. S. Mason, *Industrial Concentration and the Decline of Competition,* Explorations in Economics . . . in Honor of F. W. Taussig, New York, 1936; Walter Eucken, *Die Wettbewerbsordnung und ihre Verwirklichung,* "Ordo," vol. II, Godesberg, 1949; Henry C. Simons, *Economic Policy for a Free Society,* Chicago, 1948; C. Bresciani-Turroni, *Economic Policy for the Thinking Man,* London, 1950.
    The effects of monopolism can often assume unexpected and complicated forms. For example, it may happen that the abolition of price competition results in the struggle for customers being conducted with the aid of an extravagant and unctuous publicity (as in the American cigarette industry) or through luxurious packaging and make-up, or through all kinds of unnecessary and unwanted services (the "service" of gas stations, &c.). The uncomfortable

sleeping cars of the American Pullman Company should also be mentioned in this connection, and if in the United States automobiles are cheaper and better than houses that is also due to competition existing in the former industry but not in the latter. If Henry Ford had not courageously fought the automobile manufacturers' combine from the beginning, a standard automobile would still cost $5,000 (according to T. W. Arnold, *op. cit.,* p. 121). This gives rise at the same time to the depressing question whether such pioneers could today still win out against the monopoly associations and restrictive economic policies.

Note No. 15 (page 231). Questionableness of the patent system:

In the same measure as the corruption of the patent system and the abuse of patents by the big business monopolies have become more apparent, the discussion of this subject has increased and the will to carry out radical solutions has become stronger. Cf.: L. Walras, *De la propriété intellectuelle,* Etudes d'économie sociale, 2nd edition, Paris, 1936, page 247 ff.; L. Einaudi, *Rileggendo Ferrara—a proposito di critiche recenti alla proprietà letteraria ed industriale,* "Rivista di Storia Economica," 1940, No. 4; A. Plant, *The Economic Theory Concerning Patents for Inventions,* "Economica," February, 1934; T. W. Arnold's above mentioned book, passim; Alfred E. Kahn, *Deficiencies of American Patent Law,* "American Economic Review," September, 1940; W. Hamilton, *Patents and Free Enterprise,* Temporary National Economic Committee, Washington D.C., 1941; Hearings of the Temporary National Economic Committee, part 2-3, 1941 (which, like Arnold's book, offer convincing proof of the impossibility of today's situation); H. G. Fox, *Monopolies and Patents,* Toronto, 1947; *The Patent System,* Symposium of Law and Contemporary Problems, Durham, 1947; G. Gather, *Reform der Patentgesetzgebung,* "Ordo," vol. II, Godesberg, 1949, pp. 270-307. The dilemma of the patent system consists on the one hand of having to protect intangible property (compensating the inventor and encouraging new inventions) but of having, on the other hand, to avoid granting monopolies. The best solution seems to consist in temporary patent protection and in the establishment of a system of compulsory licenses, which would permit everyone to make free use of the invention on payment of a fee. The minimum requirement would be to limit the actual patent to a short term of a few years and then to replace it by compulsory licensing. Those acquainted with the situation know to what degree the modern patent system has developed into a weapon of the big against the small, since the rich can indiscriminately make use of intimidation by threatening patent actions in which the man of limited means cannot afford to become involved. The case of the copyright is essentially different from that of patents as already Henry George (*Progress and Poverty,* Appendix) has clearly demonstrated.

Note No. 16 (page 231). Corporations and holding companies:

Cf. W. Lippmann, *The Good Society;* Norman S. Buchanan, *The Economics of Corporate Enterprise,* New York, 1940; E. Welter, *Erneuerung des Aktienrechts,* Frankfurt a. M., 1929. These books also discuss the more general problems concerning stocks, whose solution must likewise occupy a foremost place in every comprehensive economic reform program. A convincing picture of the sins of the holding companies is drawn by A. S. J. Baster, *The Twilight of American Capitalism,* London, 1937, pages 8-12. That they cannot be justified by the allegedly favorable effects of the financial concentration of enterprises, was recently shown by the comprehensive investigations of the American Temporary National Economic Committee in which striking case material was quoted (*The Relative Efficiency of Large,*

Medium-sized and Small Business, T.N.E.C., No. 13, Washington D.C., 1941). The holding company (in contrast to the purely productive corporation) is the means by which the tremendous concentration of capital in the United States has been effected, and which is rightly felt to be intolerable. The Temporary National Economic Committee has illustrated its importance by the statement that today two hundred of the biggest corporations own 52 per cent. of the entire American corporate capital. The interlocking of enterprises would be hit by the simple provision that no corporation may hold the stocks of another. Likewise, one would have to see to it that investment trusts do not develop into holding companies and do not exert powerful influence on the companies whose stocks they hold (e.g., by the provision that they may only own stocks of an individual corporation or a branch of manufacture up to a certain maximum percentage of their total investments, that its executives may occupy no position in a corporation, that they may only hold stocks without voting rights, &c.). Further interesting reform proposals will be found in Henry C. Simons' *A Positive Program for Laissez-faire,* Chicago, 1934.

Note No. 17 (page 233). American anti-monopoly policy:

The antecedents of the Sherman Act are of interest here. After President Cleveland had called protective tariffs the "mother of trusts" and had thus directed the attention of anti-monopolist public opinion to this point, the Republican Party, in order to save the high protective tariffs from the anti-trust movement, suggested that the trusts should now be combatted without lowering the tariffs. It promised an anti-trust law and on the strength of this promise President Harrison was elected.

Note No. 18 (page 234). Combating monopolies by consumer instruction:

It is a matter of constant surprise to what degree the ignorance of consumers concerning goods and market conditions results in their being over-reached, as a matter of course, regarding prices and quality, and to what extent it is therefore also possible to confuse them by advertising, while the purchaser of capital goods and raw materials tends to be protected against this by his professional and specialized knowledge of the merchandise. Up to a certain point the system of brand names offers a remedy against being sold inferior goods, but in this case the consumer must pay for his ignorance of the merchandise with an increased (monopolistic) price. A satisfactory solution can, therefore, only be expected from measures which remove this ignorance as far as possible. Such measures should consist, for example, in training the consumer—perhaps even in his school period—in testing the quality of merchandise; further, impartial agencies should constantly investigate the market of consumption goods regarding the qualities offered and publish their findings without fear or favor. If authors and publishers must justly submit to relentless criticism of their products we have, by the same token, the right to expect that newspapers and journals exercise constant criticism of the consumption goods offered in stores or boosted by advertising, by means of spot checks, and that they should not shrink from saying that, e.g., the clasp-knives offered in their city can be placed in this or that category, that the knives offered in store X are by no means as stainless as they are made out to be, that the new Y radio does not possess the qualities advertised, that Z toothpaste has a manufacturing value of so and so many cents, &c. In case this seems utopian, the public authorities would have to assume the task of supplying the necessary information. Cf. also the monograph of the Temporary National Economic Committee (No. 10), *Consumer Standards,* Washington D.C., 1941.

Note No. 19 *(page* 237). *Genuine multilateralism essential to an international economic order:*

True multilateralism does not only consist in the adjustment of trade taking place actually between three and more countries (actual multilateralism). There must also exist a guarantee that every bilateral relation can at any time be changed into a multilateral one and vice versa, and that complete freedom obtains regarding the choice of the import and export country according to the change in prices (virtual multilateralism). While actual multilateralism will never amount to more than a fraction of the total world trade, virtual multilateralism must, so to speak, be one hundred per cent., if a permanently effective price arbitrage, a real interdependence of economic relations and genuine economic integration are aimed at. That is true of the world economy as well as of every national economy. Such a genuine multilateralism can therefore never be "arranged," "canalized" and enforced, and this shows how problematic the expression "multilateral clearing" is. Canalized multilateralism always presupposes a central control office which only shares the name with the "central" point of a genuine world economy—which may be said to have formerly been represented by London. For the same reason we cannot draw any parallel between present-day clearing practices and voluntary accounting via a mutual banking house, which is likewise called clearing. The latter represents nothing but a book-keeping operation and does not in the least affect genuine multilateralism, either within the national economy or in the world economy. As in the national sphere, multilateralism in world trade also presupposes a genuine payment union with free convertibility of currencies, i.e., an international currency system untrammelled by foreign exchange controls. Thus in practice we have in the last resort to choose between an international currency system (like the gold standard) and the clearing system, and this choice is equivalent to that between a world economy and no world economy. Cf. W. Röpke, *Internationale Ordnung,* Erlenbach-Zürich, 1945; W. Röpke, *International Economic Disintegration,* chap. III; J. B. Condliffe, *The Reconstruction of World Trade,* New York, 1940, page 282 ff. That bilateralism spells for the smaller countries a particularly serious limitation of their freedom of movement and thus a considerable deterioration of their position, as compared to the free world trade obtaining in the past, is obvious without further explanation. They become economically dependent on their powerful clearing partners (politically they either were already dependent or will become so now), at the same time they are liable to be constantly exploited, and it would indeed be strange if such opportunities were not made use of. Thus an entirely new system of political and economic imperialism would arise from this bilateralism, an imperialism which in its economic power of exploitation could be compared in some respects with that of the Byzantine Empire, in contrast to the so-called "imperialism" of the liberal age which in return for making great capital gains could at least show the real opening up and economic advancement of the colonial areas. To speak indiscriminately of exploitation in the case of that former "imperialism" is rather risky, because, as a rule, the exploited regions were still better off than if they had not been opened up at all. That "imperialism" provided—in part very lucrative—profits, but they were not usually derived from exploitation. In so far as force was really used—and only then can one speak of imperialism—it is a gross distortion of the truth when Marxist and near-Marxist writers make it appear as if this imperialism had been an essential component of the world economy. A worse misinterpretation is indeed hardly possible. That genuine imperialism was not an essential part of the world economy, but rather a foreign body which had been introduced into it by the aggressive policy of the great powers. A "pure" world economy would not only have always been possible, but would have been infinitely superior to that tainted by imperialism. Cf. regarding the problem of imperialism: L. Robbins, *The Economic Causes of War*, London, 1939; E. Staley, *War and the Private Investor*, New York, 1935; W. Röpke, *Internationale Ordnung;* Walter Sulzbach, *National Consciousness*, Washington, 1943.

Note No. 20 (page 238). Medieval world economy:

We know today that in the Middle Ages there already existed a very intensive trade over large areas, so that we are certainly entitled to speak of a medieval world economy which was by no means limited to certain articles of luxury. This system collapsed at the beginning of the modern era and in the age that witnessed the development of the national states and the mercantilist economic policy, it made way for a phase of a less differentiated economy. Like the world economy of antiquity, that of the Middle Ages, too, disintegrated simultaneously with the political system on which it was based. Cf. F. Rörig, *Mittelalterliche Weltwirtschaft*, Jena, 1933; H. Pirenne, *Economic and Social History of Medieval Europe*, New York, 1937.

Note No. 21 (page 239). Pax Britannica and the secularized Pax Christiana:

The personal representative of the *Pax Britannica* in the nineteenth century in its sublimated form and as support of the general secularized *Pax Christiana* was primarily Gladstone. His person and his mission become especially clear to us if we look upon him as the true opponent and counter-type of Bismarck (cf. Erich Eyck's excellent book, *Gladstone,* Erlenbach-Zürich, 1938).

Regarding the system of international law of the secularized *Pax Christiana,* we read in G. Radbruch's *Einführung in die Rechtswissenschaft,* 2nd edition, 1913, page 128: "The legal nature of international law is as little impaired by the absence of legislative powers as by the absence of the powers of administering and enforcing justice, e.g., by the fact that the state whose rights have been violated can only resort to war. For often the legal maxims valid within a state are also not enforceable without this being made a reason for denying their legal character. The guarantee of regular observance which we have recognized as necessary for the concept of a valid code of laws is as much a feature of the law of nations as of that of the individual state. International public opinion, moreover, sees to it that violations of international law are much rarer than those of a country's domestic laws, and further, that such a violation of international law may not openly be acknowledged as such but must be justified before international law by every conceivable sophistry." We leave it to the reader to measure the distance between then and now.

Note No. 22 (page 241). Restless dynamism of the "Grossraüme":

We have explained towards the end of Note No. 19 why one cannot count on a genuine balance of interests within an imperial "Grossraüme." But the idea held by some writers (among them the American author Lawrence Dennis in his book *The Dynamics of War and Revolution*) that the world could be divided into several imperial "Grossraüme" ("Socialist Imperialism," according to Dennis) without an early outbreak of a global struggle for predominance is just as unjustified; the same applies to the assumption that such a "Grossraüm" will one day proclaim that it has been satiated, or to the utopian notion that the Saurians, after securing their territory, will peacefully lie down like lambs next to each other and begin to co-operate. Every empire will rather have the elementary aim to extend its more or less "closed block" economy over the widest possible basis of the politically dominated and economically exploited area and, as F. Fried (*Wende der Weltwirtschaft,* Leipzig, 1939, page 389) so very rightly remarks: "then the territorial possessions of the individual nations assume decisive importance and the dispute over these questions passes progressively from the economic to the political plane." This international scuffle over the feeding-trough caused by the "politicalization" of world trade will never cease until one power attains sole and undisputed world hegemony on a lasting basis. The less so as the historic origin of these economic empires and their socio-logical character would turn them, just like the collectivist national economy from which they stem, into a deficit economy—this time of a continental order—which would always be dependent on an increase in wealth from outside. The greater the empire the greater also its need for further annexations.

Note No. 23 (page 242). The restoration of an international monetary system: For the details, see my book, *Internationale Ordnung.*

INDEX

255